PRAIRIE BOYS AT WAR

Korea: Volume I
June–October 1950

M. M. Helm

D0861255

Library of Congress Control Number: 2014906610
ISBN: 978-0-9960959-0-7

Prairie Boy Books
420 8th Avenue South, Suite 11
Fargo, North Dakota, 58103
mhelm@cableone.net
Orders may be placed at PrairieBoyBooks.com

Interior design and layout: Prairie Boy Books
Cover design: Raul Gomez
Author photo: Joel Hegerle
Cover photo: A halftrack from the 21st AAA accompanies members of the 19th Regiment, 24th Division, advancing in Korea. U.S. Army photo by CPL Warren McDonald. (National Archives SC-381804)

Printed in the United States of America

Contents

Introduction

I'm not sure I believe in destiny, but I distinctly remember the first time I heard the word *Korea*. I was perhaps three or four years old, not quite up to my mother's waist, and I was hanging on her leg in the breeze-way between our house and garage. My oldest brother came home, and they had a hushed conversation about someone who fought in *Korea*. When I asked questions, they changed the subject: *Korea must be important*.

I didn't hear anybody mention Korea again until my movie writing days (1992-2008), when a carpenter working on our house told me about his Marine uncle who fought at the Chosin Reservoir. I was spellbound and have since written a full account for Volume II of the *Prairie Boys* series.

My first bonafide research into the war began in 2005, when writing radio scripts for Dakota Datebook, a daily history-based program airing on Prairie Public Radio. My job was to identify an event or person in North Dakota history for each day of the year and write about it. This was a big challenge, and I looked for every possible angle for identifying good stories.

Over time, I realized combat veterans often have multiple dates to work with, and I soon came across the story of Woodrow Wilson Keeble, who grew up in Waubay, SD, and Wahpeton, ND. Keeble was a WWII veteran who volunteered for the front lines in Korea, and he was decorated three times in 10 days in October 1951. His men put him in for the Medal of Honor, but the paperwork got lost. Twice.

I wrote several Datebooks about Keeble, but unlike other subjects, I could never quite let go. That missing Medal of Honor bothered me, so I started tracking down men who fought beside him and found several from Companies G and H, 19th Infantry Regiment, who remembered him vividly. I also found men who didn't know him, but all shared incredible stories, sometimes while choking back tears. It was the first time I understood the Korean War went far beyond the bounds of a police action or mere conflict (and I make no apologies for calling it a war).

With great patience, these men began teaching me about war, beginning with the difference between a squad (about 10 men) and a division (thousands of men). I slowly reconstructed the battle in which Keeble fought, and at the National Archives I learned it had a name. It was called Operation Nomad, but trying to find more information dealt me my first lesson on the history of that war. Only by digging through faded command reports and studying the hundreds and hundreds of casualties did I come to learn how brutal it was – yet folks back in the States at that time believed Americans were no longer involved in combat operations in Korea, despite many thousands of casualties in the fall of 1951. I was dumbstruck.

Following the successful quest for Keeble's Medal of Honor in 2008, I accepted the position of historian for the 24th Infantry Division Association, which provided me more opportunities to study the war in depth, as well as interview more combat veterans and ex-POWs.

Eventually, I decided to write "a little book" about North Dakotans decorated in Korea, but after some time I broadened the scope to include the entire upper-prairie region. This was at first ambitious and then a bit overwhelming; I had no idea there would be so many compelling stories, and it was difficult to stop researching in order to focus on writing.

The combined volumes of *Prairie Boys at War* will tell the history of the entire war. Although there are some sections that explain troop movements, politics, and the origins of the arms race, this series is mostly about our farm boys, our Boy Scouts, our football players, shortstops, orphans and high school dropouts. It's about Czechs, German Russians, Norwegians, Sioux warriors, Finns and Metiź. They were miners, musicians, deer hunters, grape growers, cowboys, and appointees to our distinguished Military Academies. They were commanders, juvenile delinquents, paratroopers, WWII retreads, prisoners of war, jeep drivers, jet aces and frog men.

All had one thing in common: they were tough young men who came of age during the Great Depression.

Not everyone in these pages was decorated. But every man who received the Medal of Honor, Navy Cross or Distinguished Service Cross is included, and by covering these, I was forced to flesh out battles (like Operation Nomad) that have rarely, if ever, been covered in the existing historiographies – including actions with 100% casualties.

I would like to note I've taken pains to make this book easily understood by nonmilitary folks (like myself). There are many who want to understand what their loved ones endured, and I hope this book may help. A word of caution, however: if a man used profanity, I felt he deserved that right, and very seldom have I tried to soften or censor his words.

Are There Mistakes in These Pages?

Absolutely – depending who you ask. After six years of intense research, I can say beyond a shadow of a doubt that no account of battle exists on which everyone can agree. I have come to liken it to a bus accident in which some walk away, some go to the hospital, and others are killed. Each person – from the sleepy guy in back, to the driver of the other vehicle – will have different versions of what happened. All recollections will be vividly recalled and accurate, but a perfect overall account is impossible to achieve, mostly because those who died have no voice.

My job, as I see it, is to get as close to the original source as possible, so I first try to find the man whose citation belongs in these volumes. If he was killed in action or has since passed, I try to locate his memoirs or letters he sent home from the battlefield. Barring that, I search for family members and/or the men who fought beside them.

Sadly, there are many for whom I can find no information, not even an obituary. For these men, I have done my best by falling back on history books, but even these can lead to dead ends.

It's a quirky testament to prairie culture that while I've had limited success by contacting schools, churches, libraries and chambers of commerce, a call to the local grain elevator often works best for tracking down family members.

Note on Citations for Valor

Combat veterans can tell us some men did not earn their decorations, while hundreds, possibly thousands, of others should have been decorated but weren't, particularly if there was nobody left alive who witnessed their actions.

There were also cases in which high-ranking officers (particularly

General Ned Almond) dipped down on the battlefield to hand out indiscriminate silver stars. Some were deserved; others were not.

Even the recipients, themselves, often disagree with what their citation states. Thus, the reader is cautioned to take each citation with a grain of salt, because there were also rare cases in which men in the rear were decorated, because they could pull strings.

As for our Nation's highest honor, the Medal of Honor, I do note the Marines were far more likely to decorate living recipients than the Army. And, not surprisingly, officers were more likely to be decorated than recruits and regular army doughboys. After reading hundreds and hundreds of citations, I believe several young men in these pages deserved the Medal of Honor, and I have been truthful about these.

Note on Sources

It's no longer the trend to cite sources of information within the body of a chapter, but I have done so for one central reason. When I read a history book and want to know where the information came from, I find it tedious to hold my place while I page through to find the chapter or end notes or, worse, dig for it at the end of the book. I find it less disrupting to find everything on the same page, and I'm betting others do, too. I used the same reasoning when placing photos within the chapters rather than in a separate section of the book.

Acknowledgments

This journey has been long, sometimes emotional, and often difficult, and I need to thank hundreds of people for supporting me along the way. First and foremost are those combat veterans who so generously shared their war experiences, sometimes at great psychological pain to themselves.

Others who helped include historians, military organizations, librarians, newspapers and colleges, as well as families and friends of the men covered in these pages.

Special thanks go to Doug Sterner, who has worked tirelessly to create a database of all decorations and citations awarded in American military history (website *Military Times Hall of Valor*). Without his exhaustive research, the courageous actions of most of the men in this book would remain unknown to all but their families.

I also wish to thank Ted and Hal Barker for their nonstop, though often thankless, efforts to document every Korean War casualty via their website *The Korean War Project,* and to allow others to honor the dead within those pages.

I am also thankful for the give and take I've enjoyed with other researchers and authors including John Durand, Lynnita Brown (website *Korean War Educator*), Addison Terry, William Richardson, Uzal Ent, Sam Holliday, Ralph Hockley, Edward Gray and many others.

I am also grateful to John Durand, Bonnie Helm and Jerry Helm for their assistance with editing and proofreading and to Raul Gomez's patience and generosity was we labored over the cover design.

When all is said and done, however, this project would not exist if it weren't for the patience and uncomplaining support of my husband, Roger Gress. You have kept us afloat during these long, lean, research years, and I am profoundly grateful you've had my back. Thank you.

Part I

★

DELAYING THE ENEMY

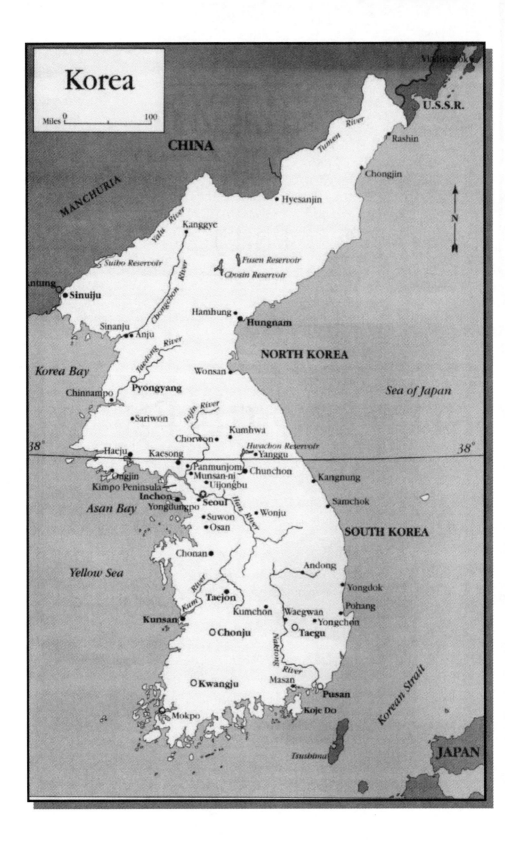

Chapter 1

FIRST AMERICAN HERO

"America's first Korean war hero has begun his third postwar tour of duty in the Far East. Capt. Gordon D. Mohr of Minot, N.D., won the first Silver Star granted an American in Korea for valor during the first few hours of the fighting on June 25, 1950."
Pacific Stars & Stripes, 31 July 1952

"IT WAS THE damnedest thing I have ever been through," Gordon Mohr told reporters as he had his wounds dressed. "The tank was firing like crazy, but we were so close it couldn't hit us."

It was June 25, 1950, the day North Korea invaded South Korea. A subsequent newspaper report reads:

> Mohr was one of 55 American soldiers who swam and paddled across the Han River to escape capture in Seoul Wednesday, only a few jumps ahead of a Russian-made North Korean tank. First Lt. Gordon Mohr of Minot, N. Dak. and Capt. Elmer Lowery of San Diego, Cal., ran in front of the Russian tank for 8 blocks before they could cross the river to safety.[1]

The attack had begun in the predawn darkness, and Mohr, a member of the Korean Military Advisers Group (KMAG), was notified at 6:30 a.m. that Seoul, the capital of South Korea, was about to be overrun. The invasion was unexpected, but it was by no means a surprise – at least not to Mohr or his fellow advisors. Friction between North and South Korea had been plentiful, with frequent border clashes, ever since Korea had become a divided piece of real estate in 1945.

---

[1] *Mason City Globe Gazette.* 28 June 1950.

WOUNDED YANK—Lt. Gordon D. Mohr of Minot, N.D., a military adviser attached to the South Korean forces, talks with newsmen at U.S. Army headquarters in South Korea as he has a shrapnel wound dressed. He was wounded at Yong Dong Po.

Newspapers carried this photo of Mohr after his daring action and escape June 25, 1950. (Courtesy AP)

The Stage is Set

Korea comprises a peninsula about the size of Minnesota that lies at the crux of historic invasion routes between China, Japan, and Indochina. As such, it has been invaded and occupied by others for centuries. Most recently, Japan had carried out a fearsome 50-year occupation that ended when the nearby island nation was defeated in WWII.

To oversee the ouster of the Japanese government from Korea, the Allied victors made a fateful decision to split the responsibility between two superpowers: Franklin Roosevelt's American troops would occupy the portion of Korea south of the 38th Parallel, while Joseph Stalin's Soviet troops would occupy the portion north of the parallel.

When the Cold War developed, Korea became a major testing ground for whether communism would be allowed to spread unchecked and without consequences.

The sequence of events leading up to the Korean War was complex; the short version is that the United States helped set up a democracy headed by Dr. Syngman Rhee, 73, who returned from exile to become the first president of the newly organized Republic of Korea (ROK) in 1948.

Rhee was a feisty and sometimes impetuous leader prone to impulsive moves, and he was eager to reunify Korea with himself as the ultimate leader. This was worrisome, and American officials dragged their feet in response to Rhee's determination to the build up his military forces and arms. Thus, when the war began, South Korean forces were somewhat under-prepared and definitely under-equipped.

Meanwhile, Joseph Stalin fostered a communist regime led by Kim Il Sung – the father of a new North Korean dynasty. Kim had equal intentions of reuniting Korea – but under his communist rule. Stalin approved of Kim's aggressiveness, and he provided the young leader's army with excellent training, cutting-edge weaponry, and new Russian T-34 tanks like the one that chased Gordon Mohr through the streets of Seoul.

The United States and the Soviet Union had since withdrawn the majority of their occupation forces from the peninsula, and conditions were ripe for the fledgling nations to collide. The resulting war would, in effect, be fought by the two superpowers, both of which now had nuclear weapons. But on the face of it, the involvement of the Soviets compared to the Americans appeared quite different. President Truman openly supported South Korea with military support, but Joseph Stalin claimed the Soviets were merely interested bystanders.

It was under these circumstances that Korea became the Cold War's flashpoint for armed aggression, including direct involvement by another emerging superpower: "Red China."

Mohr in the Lead Up to War

Orphaned at age four, Gordon Mohr was adopted and raised by a Michigan farm couple. As an adult, he attended Moody Bible College in Chicago before moving to North Dakota. In 1942, he joined the Army, serving in North Africa and the South Pacific during WWII. He was stationed in Japan with occupation forces until his discharge in 1946, when he moved to Sanish, North Dakota. He later wrote:

> I went back to ranching in North Dakota, near Minot. For several months I pastored a little Northern Baptist church in Sawyer, ND. With an active interest in young people, and as acting basketball coach for Sawyer men's H.S. basketball team, I was able with God's help to build up the church."[2]

Mohr returned to active duty in 1948 and was sent to Korea to join "a small group of personnel who had been given the difficult and often frustrating task of training the fledgling army of the new Republic of South Korea."

Communist cells in South Korea tried several times to oust President Rhee, including one attempt in the southern port city of Yosu in October 1948. South Korea's 14th Regiment was stationed there, as described by Mohr:

> ... when Korea was divided along the 38th Parallel, the northern section came under Communist control. Almost immediately, a school was begun in Pyongyang, the capital of the north. This was a very special school, made up of Communist young men from both North and South Korea. They were given extensive training in the art of infiltration. Their main task was to infiltrate the military apparatus of South Korea so that, at a given signal, they could take over South Korea by military coup.
>
> The day for the takeover was October 18, 1948. But as often happens, there was a mistake in the plans that caused the coup to go haywire. Instead of a nationwide takeover, the revolt broke out in only a few areas.
>
> The center of the revolt was in Yosu, Challo'namdo Province. This happened to be the infantry regiment I was advising. When orders came down from the North, about 2,800 men from the Fourteenth Infantry Regiment, joined by

---

[2] *The Oakland Tribune (UP).* 20 Oct 1948. Mohr, Gordon (LTC AUS Ret) "From Darkness into Light." Circa 1998; "Communist Terror in Peaceful Heaven." Circa 1975. Web: 8 Jul 2010. www.scripturesforamerica.org. Reprinted with kind permission of Ike Mohr.

approximately 1,700 civilians, broke into the armory of the 14th Regiment and after overpowering the guards, made off with about 5,000 M-1 rifles, machine guns, light mortars and ammunition that had recently arrived from the States.

This armed force marched into the neighboring city of Yosu and after dispersing the police force, moved north along the peninsula to the little city of Sun'chon. Sun'chon was an industrial city of about 175,000 population . . . located strategically, with five roads and five railroads, coming into the city like spokes on a wheel. It was the center of the most fertile rice producing area in Korea.

The rebel force attacked the police of Sun'chon and, after a day of bitter fighting, forced their way into the city and laid siege to the police station in the center of town. I had been away at Division Headquarters in the city of Kwan'ju 96 miles to the north when the revolt broke and had raced to Sun'chon with a company of Korean infantry from the 14th Regiment, in an attempt to head the rebels off before they reached Sun'chon. To my utter disgust, the Korean soldiers who accompanied me joined the rebels and left me with 45 frightened policemen who took refuge in the police station.

We were under siege for several hours when a Korean sergeant, under a white flag, asked to speak with me. He told me that if I would come out, I would be given safe conduct along with any police who would surrender. My orders from KMAG Headquarters in Seoul had been quite plain. I was to remain in the area as an observer but was not to become involved in any action.

We were taken to the center of the city, near the Court House – an area about a block long and possibly 100 feet wide, a sort of park area with trees and flower beds. Seventeen policemen had decided to come with me. These were seized and bound as soon as we were out of sight of the police station. I was left to my own, still armed.

On arriving at the courtyard, the bound men were forced to kneel in the street and were executed by being repeatedly stabbed in the chest and abdomen with bamboo spears. While this was going on, a large crowd began to gather in the street. Tensions were running high and fear was evident on every face. From various directions in the city, you could hear screams,

shouts, and the sound of rifle fire. Then the first evidence of
Communist takeover began to show up in the arrival of groups
of civilians under armed guard. These were the families of
police, religious leaders, politicians and school teachers.

It has always been the policy of the Communists to set up
People's Courts in every country they take over. The People's
Court is a peculiar organization made up of a judge, a
prosecuting attorney and the victim. If you are a member of the
"bourgeoisie," you are a candidate for the People's Court. The
"bourgeoisie" of course are property owners and so-called
"enemies of the people." These People's Courts are used for
two purposes. First, to frighten the populace so that they will
not put up a fight and, secondly, to get rid of anyone who
would normally have a stabilizing influence on the community.
These people are brought in by family groups. In the Orient this
means groups of up to forty or more people.

In Sun'chon, they were herded into the courthouse square
at the point of bayonets and were then mowed down by massed
machine gun fire, until at the end of two hours over 265 bodies
of men, women and children were piled beside the square and
the street ran red with Korean blood.

Mohr watched helplessly as the rebels committed atrocities against the
police chief and his wife. At a certain point he tried to step in, but he
was struck down. He awoke in a dark cell with another American,
Lieutenant Stewart Greenbaum. They didn't know it, but martial law
had been declared, and U.S. Army Headquarters had by now reported
they were "reasonably sure" no Americans were involved in the fighting.
No (known) rescue team was on the way. Mohr writes:

> About 10 o'clock in the morning – I believe it was the second
> day – I was taken to the Court House for trial. The Court Room
> was large – about twice the size of a basketball floor – jammed
> with people. When they saw me, they began to scream: "Kill
> him! Kill the Meguk-noam!" (Kill the no-good American!)
>
> I had been frightened many times before, but never like this.
> As I passed through the crowd . . . many of whom had been my
> friends a few days before . . . they spit at me, beat on me with
> their fists and cursed me. One woman scratched down the side
> of my face, leaving five bloody furrows. Only a few days before,

her little boy had been in an accident. I had taken him to the hospital and had paid the bill from my own pocket. I could not understand why she now hated me. It was only after much study that I realized this was one of the methods by which Communism controls people. They become so frightened for their own life, they will do anything to prove that they are friends of the Communists – even if it means a husband turning in his wife, or a mother her children.

I was taken to the front of the room, where there was a raised platform [with] a long, heavy oak table. Behind this table, sat a little Korean man dressed in a high-necked Mao-Tse Tung jacket and a black skull cap. At one end of the table was a heavy oak chair with wide arms.

For several minutes the little man wrote on some papers without looking up. Finally in exasperation I began to speak to him in Korean: "I am an American officer," I said, "I want to be turned loose."

Leaping to his feet, he began to scream at me in Korean: "How can a running dog of the imperialist Wall Street warmongers ask anything of a representative of the people? Sit down!"

I sat down in the big chair, and he [said]: "We are your friends. Everyone knows that you Americans are slaves of the rich men on Wall Street. We do not want to hurt you. All we ask is that you cooperate with us and you will be set free."

"What do you want?" I asked.

"I have here a paper," he said. "It is a list of the crimes you Americans have committed in Korea. Sign it!"

He showed me a list, written on rice straw paper in the ideographic writing of Korea. One of the statements said that we [were attempting] to make Korea one of our states. Before I had a chance to think, I shook my head and was answered by a blow on the side of the head that knocked me to the floor...

In the following days, Mohr was subjected to several forms of torture.

I woke to the sound of thunder in the room. At least I thought it was thunder. Then I realized that somewhere in that room was a loud speaker which was turned up to full volume. Hour after hour, for maybe sixteen to eighteen hours at a time, it would blast out one line of Communist propaganda until I thought I would go out of my mind. There was no hope of sleep [and] no way to escape the voice. In addition to this mental torture, the guards would take turns playing with me. They would hang me from a beam with a rope around my ankles and leave me suspended where my fingertips would barely brush the ground. (After fifteen hours of this, your mind is ready to crack.) Another game was to sit me on a stool, looking into a brilliant light, then beat me any time I moved.

Mohr experienced a conversion that went beyond his religious training.

I still thought I was going to die, but I wasn't afraid to meet my God anymore. During the night, someone came into the cell and threw an old pair of ragged khaki pants across my legs. I managed to crawl into them. Then in the morning, two men came for me. They took me back to the courthouse. My morale was at rock bottom, because I believed my time had come to die.

As we entered the courtroom, I saw a Korean sergeant leaning against the door. He was a man who had been friendly with me. His name was Yu Chang Nam. We called him "Pak Sah" which in Korean means "Professor." He had been a High School teacher in civilian life. A ray of hope stirred in my heart, and as we passed him I cried out, "Pak Sah, for God's sake, help me!" He responded with an oath, hitting me across the mouth with the back of his hand and screaming . . . "You stupid, crazy dog, drop dead from apoplexy!" Cursing and yelling like a madman, he rushed to the front of the room, screaming how he hated all Americans and that Meeguk-noam, pointing at me, worst of all. For ten minutes he raved about what a bad fellow I was. Then pausing dramatically, he said: "I would like to take this Meeguk noam (bad guy) out and kill him." The civilian judge gave his permission and Pak Sah left the room.

In a few minutes he returned with six men armed with rifles. As they took me from the room, Pak Sah whispered to me: "Mohr San, when the rifles fire, drop dead." . . . They took me into the street, and driving off the curious onlookers who wanted to go along and see the fun, they took me down a crooked cobblestone street for several blocks, until we stood before a stone wall on the edge of the mountain.

My memory of those next few minutes are as clear today as they were over twenty-seven years ago. I can recall the sound of the sergeant's voice as he gave the orders for the rifles to be raised. . . . Then I heard Pak Sah give the command "Fire!" and when the rifles went off, I jumped instinctively. But almost instantly I realized they had fired over my head . . . but I fell to the ground and lay there.

Pak Sah came up and leaned over Mohr and whispered he should take shelter with a Southern Presbyterian missionary, Dr. John Crane.

Reporting for *Time* magazine, Carl Mydans described execution squads moving from house to house killing "rightists" as they slept. Others were marched to collection points, where some 500 civilians were executed in the next two to three days. Mydans watched in horror as an equally brutal retaliation was carried out by South Koreans against "leftists" after the rebels were driven out.

Mydans also reported on Mohr and Greenbaum's ten days at the Presbyterian mission, writing:

From one of the doctor's shirts and a few colored rags, the ladies made a 16-star, eleven-stripe U.S. flag and put it up.

Rebels in the surrounding hills decided to kill the group at the mission, but Pak Sah once again saved Mohr's life, shouting, "No, no, not them; they are my friends."

The Invasion: June 25, 1950

At first, Mohr and his fellow advisors suspected the North Korean invasion was just another border clash. But by 8 a.m., the communists were striking in many different sectors at once. They were using Soviet tanks, and when it became apparent their main destination was Seoul, Mohr and his fellow Korean Military Advisors knew it wasn't just a raid.

Mohr is believed to be the first American to be wounded in the Korean War, earning the first of his four Purple Hearts that day:

. . . my jeep was hit by a 122 mm shell that blew off the whole rear end. I was hit 97 times, from my buttocks to my shoulders. But here is the interesting part of this story – a few moments before, I had loaded my vehicle with food, blankets and stores from an evacuated American home. As an afterthought I threw a cot mattress on top of the load and all the shrapnel that hit me was wrapped up in cotton batting.

Several days later, Mohr was also mistakenly strafed by American planes.

They came in from behind, and there was no chance to take cover. My jeep was riddled with 27 fifty-caliber bullets, all four tires were flattened, and shells coming in over either shoulder clipped off the steering wheel just above my hands.

It was for his actions on the first day of the war that Mohr became the first American decorated for gallantry in the Korean War.

Gordon Mohr (U.S. Army)

*In a general order published July 12 by U.S. forces in Korea, and made public in Tokyo Thursday, 1ˢᵗ Lt. **Gordon D. Mohr** of Minot, N.D., was awarded the **Silver Star** for gallantry in action. According to the citation, Lieutenant Mohr, an adviser to one of the South Korean Army units, joined his unit on June 25 when it was under heavy attack by North Korean forces including heavy armor. When enemy armor launched an assault on his unit, Lieutenant Mohr, realizing it was in grave danger of being overrun, secured an antitank gun and using his own vehicle as a prime mover, personally moved the gun to the front without infantry support and fired at the enemy tanks. The officer fired the gun at the assaulting tanks until both his weapon and vehicle were overrun and destroyed. He then escaped on foot and rejoined his unit. (Pacific Stars & Stripes. 20 Jul 1950.)*

Chapter 2

FIRST FATALITIES

*"A man killed in a police action after 3 days smells just like one killed in a real war." * Martin Russ, *The Last Parallel.*

PRIVATE FIRST CLASS Kenneth Shadrick became known as the first American soldier to die in the Korean War when he was killed in action on July 5, 1950. He was not actually the first soldier killed, but his death was the first to be observed by newspaper reporters – and so began his legend.

At least thirty other Americans had already died by then. Two North Dakotans and two Minnesotans were among them, but all four of their deaths were in some way confusing and/or controversial.

Vernon Lindvig & Maurice Olson

It was typhoon season in the vicinity of the Yellow Sea, and troop transports, including ships and planes, struggled against high winds, rough seas, heavy rain and fog. On June 28, three days after the war broke out, three American planes were destroyed in part because of these weather conditions.

First Lieutenant Vernon Lindvig,[3] 26, was one of six airmen killed that day. Vernon and Emogene, his wife of six years, were from Aneta, North Dakota.

Their daughter, Valerie Elliasen, never knew Vernon, but she was told that in his youth her father was a "golden boy – a good athlete, a

---

[3] Korean War Project Remembrance. WWW.Koreanwar.org: 20 Feb 2 2010. Also author interview with Valerie Elliasen, Feb 2010.

basketball star, good student, a happy, kind young man who was the only blond in his family."

Lindvig was stationed at Yokato Air Base in Japan serving as a radar observer on an F-82G Twin Mustang attached to the 35th Fighter-Interceptor Group, 339th All Weather Squadron.

On June 26, John Muccio, U.S. Ambassador to South Korea, called for an evacuation of all American civilians and dependents. A great many of these lived in Ascom City near Seoul. They were instructed to take only what they could carry and one blanket per child.

The only ship available for this evacuation was the *Reinholte*, a Norwegian freighter. The ship's crew hurriedly unloaded its cargo of chemical fertilizer to make space for its human cargo. Despite having accommodations for only 12 men, the vessel took on close to 700 passengers that night – mostly women and children.

President Truman authorized fighter planes to guard the *Reinholte* on its grueling 40-hour voyage to Japan. Vernon Lindvig and pilot Darrell Sayre volunteered for the mission, as both their wives were on board.

The weather was still rough when Lindvig and Sayre returned to Itazuke Air Base in Japan, and they became disoriented in heavy fog. Their plane crashed, and both men were killed.[4]

When Emogene learned of her husband's death, she sailed for Hawaii with about 60 other women and children. She and five others were among the first widows in the Korean War, and when they reached Honolulu July 8, reporters were waiting for them. Exhausted and distraught, Emogene started crying, telling reporters she and Vernon were expecting their first child in October.

For unknown reasons, the circumstances of the plane crash were withheld. According to reporters, both Mrs. Lindvig and Mrs. Sayers believed their husbands were together on a C-54 transport ferrying supplies, and that their plane crashed into a mountain near Pusan, South Korea. It would be decades before this belief was corrected.

Another airman became Minnesota's first fatality the following day. Maurice Olson grew up in Battle Lake, Minnesota, where his father, Carl, worked as a butter maker for Land of Lakes Creamery.

They later moved to Sauk Centre, where Maurice graduated from high school, and then to Minneapolis.

---

[4]*The Laredo Times.* 9 July 1950. KORWALD Loss Incident Summary. www.dtic.mil/dpmo/pmkor/korwald_info_357.htm. Web: 19 Feb 2010.

After he turned 18 in 1944, Olson joined the Army Air Corps and served as a bombardier over North Africa and Italy in WWII.

His sister-in-law, Donna Olson, recalls: "He was really nice and was a very handsome young man. Everybody loved him. He went to work for the Minneapolis Street Car Company as a conductor after the war, but I'm not sure how long he was there, because then he reenlisted. He was a little bit on the restless side, and I think we were all a little disappointed when he went back in. And of course for him to be killed shortly after . . ."

Olson's nephew, Pat Hallisey recalls, "He had a deep love of flying. When you go back to that period of time, mid-40s, there weren't many people from humble beginnings that ever got to fly. But he did, and he loved it. He got a private pilot's license for small aircraft and then rejoined the military so he could spend time flying. He was based in Japan and, if I remember right, he wasn't very far from getting out again when the war broke out. He had told his mother that he was going to get out at the end of his enlistment. But that never happened." [5]

Maurice Olson circa WWII
(Courtesy Olson family)

When President Truman gave the go-ahead for air support in Korea, Olson started flying bombing missions as the tailgunner on a B-26B Invader piloted by Charles "Baldy" Avarello, from Buffalo, New York. They were credited with hitting a number of enemy tanks before they crashed ten miles northwest of Seoul at 5:00 p.m. on June 29.

The wreckage was spotted from the air, but the region was already in enemy hands. Search and rescue aircraft were not yet operating, so it

---

[5] Author interview Pat Hallisey and Donna Olson, Jan 2014; Also captured film footage: http://research.archives.gov/description/66171; *Air Intelligence Information Report No. (49)55-12-4*, 23 Jan 1951; *Additional Information Pertaining to Missing Air Force Personnel*. HQ Far East Air Force. 26 July 1951.

was several months before the crash site was investigated. Olson and Avarello's bodies were not found, and they were declared dead in 1954.

Recently, captured North Korean combat footage was made available on the National Archives website. The film included closeups of prisoners of war, and several of Avarello's relatives positively identified him as being in the group. It's unclear who decided a nearby prisoner was Maurice Olson, but various websites that have added this footage list him as being in the film. After viewing it, however, Olson's nephew and sister-in-law disagree.

"I don't see him," said Donna. "We don't know what happened. I have a feeling they took his body and, you know, threw it somewhere. For a long time he was listed as missing in action, and it was close to five years before his mother ever got the insurance."

Declassified intelligence documents provide several details of the crash, but they also raise questions. One report pertains to an investigation that took place November 9, 1950, and it reports the fuselage number of their plane was BC-339:

> **Cause of Incident**: While bombing an enemy railroad train carrying ammunition, the aircraft was hit by shells from the exploding train. The aircraft was disabled, and in an attempt to gain altitude, the aircraft hit electrical wires strung between mountains. Upon hitting these wires, the aircraft exploded.
>
> **Disposition of Crew**: The crew of the aircraft was killed instantaneously as a result of the aircraft's explosion. The bodies of the deceased crew were taken by enemy elements to the Munsan Ri Brewery. Three (3) hours later, the corpses were taken to the North Korean Army Headquarters in Seoul.
>
> **Degree of Damage to Aircraft**: The aircraft was completely destroyed.
>
> **Disposition of Aircraft**: Shortly after the aircraft had crashed, enemy soldiers appeared in the area, salvaged the more important parts of the aircraft, and transported them to Pyongyang.

The report states the plane was identified from a manufacturer's plate on the plane's seat drive. Investigators likely gained much of their information from civilians who did or did not know whether Olson or Avarello were dead, or just badly wounded, in the crash. The language barrier may also have caused difficulties, but the accompanying photo

(Courtesy Coalition of Families of Korean and Cold War MIAs/POWs)

(circa 1955) suggests the plane was fairly intact when it came down. Another report, dated July 1951, adds:

> A North Korean Newspaper [*Labor News*], dated 1 July 1950, captured at OKA-RI, Korea, 8 April 1951 . . . reveals information believed to pertain to Staff Sergeant Maurice A. Olson, gunner of B-26 type aircraft missing since 29 June 1950.
>
> The document contains a retouched picture which depicts an airman in complete flying equipment propped up against the wrecked wing of a USAF plane. The caption states that the airman was the "pilot" of the plane and that his name was "Olson Morris Arthur" and that he was dead. There are some discrepancies in the article such as referring to the plane as a P-38. These discrepancies are understandable in view of the fact that the incident occurred on the fourth day of the war. The sequence in which the name is given indicates that it was obtained from his identification tags. There is no mention of any other crew members, and this may signify that the other crew member survived and was later captured. Previous information, however, has been received from other sources

which indicated that both crewmen were killed. This plane carried a two-man crew on this mission.

Like thousands and thousands of men missing in Korea, and in all wars, the ultimate fates of Maurice Olson and his crew-mate will likely never be known, but their families still seek answers.

Emerson Huff and Peter Ternes

The second fatalities for both North Dakota and Minnesota happened the next day. Peter Ternes and Emerson "Paul" Huff Junior were both members of Company C, 71st Signal Service Battalion aboard a transport plane that was bombed on the runway at Suwon, south of Seoul.

Huff, from Aitkin, Minnesota, joined the Army in 1941 and met his Italian war-bride during WWII. He returned to Aitkin after his discharge but reenlisted in 1948 and was on occupation duty in Japan.[6]

Peter Ternes was from a large German-Russian family that farmed between Raleigh and Flasher, North Dakota. According to his brother Vic, "Pete was good in sports. He was an outstanding baseball shortstop."

Five of the Ternes brothers joined the service, three of them serving in WWII. Peter and his younger brother Roger both joined the Army later. Roger was accepted into the Army Band. "Out of all of us, he had the best job," Vic said.

Even after 60 years, Vic found it difficult to describe the day his family learned Pete was killed. "I remember the exact words," he said. "We got a notice that he was in the communications division, and when they asked for volunteers to go set up communications behind enemy lines, Pete and eight other guys volunteered. He died on a plane."

That plane was a C-54D Skymaster transport from the 22nd Troop Carrier Squadron, 374th Troop Carrier Wing.

Photos of the bombed plane were published on front pages across the nation, and the *Hamilton Daily News Journal* carried the caption: "An American C-54 military plane burns on a South Korean landing strip – possibly at the Suwon airdrome 25 miles south of Seoul – after being strafed by communist North Korean fighter planes. Several United States soldiers were wounded, and a parked C-54 was knocked out when Soviet-built Yak fighter-bombers swooped down on the Suwon

---

[6]*The Winona Republican-Herald.* 3 July 1950.

airdrome in waves of four."

An official statement claimed the burning plane was empty when it was hit, but declassified documents confirm the transport carrier was the one in which the two young soldiers died. All men on board – eighteen from the Army and five from the Air Force – were killed. The deaths of these men were disguised by a statement by MacArthur's Far East Command the following day, with one news report reading:

> ... a C-54 carrying 23 persons, including a crew of five, crashed on a hilltop *near Pusan, South Korea.* The announcement said there were no survivors of the crash. *There was no indication that the C-54 was carrying American troops into South Korea* (italics added). The announcement said the crash occurred yesterday (June 30).[7]

It was this misdirection that had led Emogene Lindvig to believe her husband Vernon had died in this phantom hilltop crash near Pusan (instead of in Japan). The report also led citizens to believe the crash(es) were on the southern tip of Korea instead of near the front lines.

Undoubtedly, the destruction of the C-54 that carried Ternes and Huff was covered up because their mission was secret, and it was also important to keep North Korea in the dark about their successful efforts to kill American servicemen.

Additionally, President Truman had committed air support for South Korea – but he had just *that day* announced the United States *would be* committing ground troops to the war July 1, a day after Ternes and Huff had already flown into Korea. There appears to be no logical reason for covering up the crash of Vernon Lindvig's plane in Japan, however.

Exhibiting a mischievous side, Pete Ternes left the plastic cover on his hat for this photo.
(Courtesy Ternes Family)

---

[7]*Winona Republican-Herald.* 1 Jul 1950.

Either way, these tragedies deeply affected the deceased men's families and friends.

"Pete was sent home in a welded-shut casket," said Ternes' brother Vic. "The Army staff sergeant stayed with us until the burial was over. We never got to see him. Don't think that wasn't hard for my parents and his family."

Chapter 3

THE BIG PICTURE

"If we are tough enough now, if we stand up to them like we did in Greece three years ago, they won't take any next steps. But if we just stand by, they'll move into Iran, and they'll take over the whole Middle East. There's no telling what they'll do if we don't put up a fight now." President Harry Truman, June 27, 1950

WAR CORRESPONDENT O. H. P. KING and other reporters traveled 180 miles from the crucial port of Pusan to the front lines in those opening days. Snaking through a sea of overwhelmed South Koreans, King was seeing firsthand the result of American and South Korean unpreparedness for war.

North Korea's element of surprise, as well as their state-of-the-art weaponry, initially devastated South Korea's inexperienced troops. Many were quick to accuse them of "bugging out" rather than putting up a fight, but some of this is unfair and inaccurate. King, for example, describes "several battalions of completely uniformed South Korean troop trainees, all carrying rifles that used to belong to the Japanese Army. But the rifles all were minus their vital bolts."

Sadly, lack of adequate weapons and ammunition would plague South Korean and American units for months into the future.

Conditions in Korea proved to be among the worst ever experienced by U.S. troops. Korea is ruggedly mountainous, and the weather rivals North Dakota's hottest summers and coldest winters.

Flat terrain was predominantly covered with the sucking mud of rice paddies, and tanks were almost useless anywhere but on roads. Monsoon rains during the summer left ground troops without air or artillery support much of the time, and mud and ice sent untold numbers of vehicles over the edges of narrow mountain roads.

As he traveled north, King spotted a much more serious problem, but he didn't recognize it. He reported seeing "thousands of bewildered civilian refugees – some trudging in one direction, others going the opposite way. All are laden with pitifully small bundles."[8]

Friendly troops would soon learn the refugees "going the opposite way" were seldom civilians. Beneath their white peasant garments, most were young enemy soldiers carrying weapons and ammunition. They were masters of guerilla warfare, and in the days and weeks to come, this group of "refugees" would prove to be the undoing of many brave attempts to stop the enemy's relentless march.

Early intelligence reports indicated Soviet and Chinese soldiers were also intermingled with North Korean infantrymen. Those suspected of being Chinese communists wore "mixed" uniforms. The Soviets were identified by their grey uniforms, and airman strafing northwest of Seoul estimated they killed 35 men "dressed in grey." U.S. pilots were also seeing a new type of enemy plane. American intelligence officials were unable to identify these aircraft, but they appeared to be Soviet-made and were being flown by Soviet pilots.[9]

Truman, Eisenhower & MacArthur

On July first, President Truman, a democrat and WWI combat veteran, announced he was committing American ground troops to help the hard-pressed South Korean Army. Four days later, Truman's decision was heartily supported by a republican and WWII combat veteran who was to become the next president. As described in newspaper accounts:

Gen. Dwight D. Eisenhower says the U.S. decision to assist South Korea in resisting "outrageous invasion" was inescapable. And, Eisenhower told 47,000 Boys Scouts at their second National Jubilee . . . the decision "must be carried to its conclusion by whatever means are necessary." . . . Eisenhower gave the boys no soothing words . . . "That you may not in your young manhood be sacrificed to war," he declared, "is indeed the primary purpose of our foreign policy today. And you shall not be if the pledge of allegiance stands always before the world

---

[8] *The Oakland Tribune.* 5 July 1950.

[9] Asst. G-2 Captain Lozano. *G-2 Journal.* HQ 24th Division. 29 June 1950.

as the guiding light of our national life."[10]

As American soldiers prepared for combat, other members of the newly organized United Nations took similar steps. But throughout the war, Americans outnumbered all other nations, other than South Korea.

World War II warrior, General Douglas MacArthur, was in charge of the Allied Far East Command, including Japan and Korea, and with the breakout of hostilities, he took charge of all Allied troops in Korea.

MacArthur had achieved remarkable success in rebuilding Japan after WWII, and now, just five years later, Japan was a democracy that embraced free enterprise, freedom of religion and educational reform. Because MacArthur was to become a controversial figure in the Korean War, a bit of background is in order. David Valley, a member of MacArthur's honor guard in Japan, writes:

> Building democratic societies took place over many years in other countries. In Japan, the change from a totalitarian state took place in a period of months when its Meiji Constitution was revised. It was not by choice, but by order of conquering nations after Japan's defeat in World War II. If not for masterful management by General Douglas MacArthur, Supreme Commander of Allied Powers, the outcome of the Potsdam Declaration, which decreed terms for Japan's surrender, could have been a fiasco.
>
> The linchpin of MacArthur's success in Japan, starting with the revision of their constitution, was keeping the Russians the hell out, for which he had to even out-maneuver our own State Department. If he hadn't, it would have been a fiasco like that in post-WWII Europe, and Japan would still be suffering the bad effects.[11]

Throughout his command of troops in Korea, General MacArthur remained in Tokyo. The man who actually took charge of Eighth Army on the ground was Lieutenant General Walton "Bulldog" Walker, a tough WWII veteran from Patton's Army.

---

[10] *The La Crosse Tribune.* 5 July 1950.

[11] Valley, David. *Bright Life, Framing Japan's Constitution.* Sektor Publishing. 2009: back cover.

Chapter 4

TASK FORCE SMITH

"I decided to open a can of C-rations, and that's when we saw the tanks. I just dropped the can. What the hell was this? Nobody told us about any tanks." Robert Roy, 21st Regiment, 24th Division

OF FOUR ARMY DIVISIONS serving as occupation troops in and around Japan, the 24th Infantry Division was the first to be deployed to Korea. It was to be the second time this division earned its slogan, *First to Fight*. The 24th and 25th Divisions (previously the "Hawaiian Division") were the first Army units to take up arms in WWII – they were stationed at Schofield Barracks, Oahu, when the Japanese carried out their surprise attack on Pearl Harbor December 7, 1941.

Now, in Korea, the 24th Division was entering one of the bloodiest phases of its illustrious history. When the word came down, the division consisted of three infantry regiments: 19th, 21st and 34th. Each of these was under-strength, with only two battalions instead of three.

Joe Langone & Paul Larson

Joe Langone had just gotten paid, and the young New Jersey soldier was on his way to town to celebrate.

The night before, there had been a scare in Japan, and Langone's 21st Regiment had been ordered to assume blackout conditions while a rumor spread that the Soviets had dropped paratroopers into Tokyo. Now, on the night of June 30, all seemed well. Other than the threat of rain, the evening passed in the manner of most payday celebrations.

I was returning from town at around 10:30 p.m., and as I entered the main gate, the MP on duty asked what company I was from. I told him Baker Company, and he said to get back to the barracks immediately. Within an hour, we were assembled in formation in our company area outside. We received no instructions of what was happening. It started to rain, and we pulled ponchos out of our packs.

At 3 a.m., Army transport trucks pulled up, and we were instructed to climb aboard. Some of the boys lit cigarettes and settled back.

Then the flap on the back of the truck was suddenly pulled open, and an Army chaplain asked, "How many of you boys are Catholic?" A number of us raised our hands. The Chaplain said, "Make a good Act of Contrition. I'm going to administer the Last Rites."

Even an atheist knows the meaning of those words. The boys stopped talking, and we stayed that way for the long 75-mile drive. We were told nothing. Words such as *war* or *battle* were not mentioned. All we knew was that we each had 120 rounds of ammunition and two days of rations.[12]

Paul Larson, from Duluth, Minnesota, was also on this uneasy journey. Larson and Langone were both in Baker Company, with an estimated strength of about 200 men. Larson was in a different platoon (40 to 50 men), but they were best friends. Langone writes:

Trying to describe a relationship between two young men is difficult. He was my buddy, and I was his. We met at Camp Wood sometime in 1949, and it was probably when we were preparing for our corporal's test that we really got to know each other. We had both loved soldiering since we were young, and he was brought up like me – playing Soldiers and Marines rather than cowboys.

We worked very hard studying, and when we found out that we both made corporal, we went to town to celebrate. Paul wasn't really a drinker. I think the only time he would drink beer was on payday night. One night he had too much, and a soldier from his platoon came over to my platoon to get me to bring Paul under control. He was a big guy and strong. I sat on the edge of his bunk and talked to him as though I was his mother,

---

[12] Langone, Joe. Unpublished memoir and emails shared with author 2012.

and he calmed down. "I'm okay, Joe," he'd say. "Go back to bed."

Paul, like me, went to church every Sunday morning. We always went together. But living the life young soldiers lived, we both stayed away from the confessional. We talked of home a lot, and things we did, but he never discussed old girl friends. I always felt he was shy when it came to girls. But with his good looks, I know many of the young girls looked his way.

We loved doing crazy things together. Sometimes we would go to town and try to let the brass on our collars shine into the sun and then move our shoulders to reflect the gleam. We were both 6 feet tall, strong, and in good physical shape. Not many people challenged us when we were together.

As their column sloshed through the rainy night, they had no idea they were about to contribute a new chapter to their division's history:

Most of us soldiers really had no way to know that the North Koreans had invaded South Korea. Newspapers and radios, believe it or not, were not readily available for troops pulling occupation duty.

The Task Force Deploys

Task Force Smith was named for Lieutenant Colonel Charles "Brad" Smith, 34, commander of the 21st Regiment's 1st Battalion. He was already at Itazuke Air Base, the mystery destination for the convoy carrying Joe Langone and Paul Larson. His orders were clear – *get to South Korea as quickly as possible*. His mission once he arrived, however, was still a bit murky.

Dawn was approaching, but the rain blocked the sunlight as his men scrambled to round up tools of war and load them onto transport planes. The division's war diary reports:

News of this move came as a complete surprise, and as a result many emergency requisitions were necessary. Some items such as individual weapons, very large, and very small sizes of individual clothing were almost impossible to obtain due to existing shortages . . . Some vehicle parts were impossible to get, and as a result vehicles were left in ordnance shops when the unit left Kokura. New or used vehicles were drawn as replacements for the above, but in many cases, these vehicles were in worse shape than vehicles that were left behind.[13]

Weapons, ammunition, field rations, armored vehicles – almost all were lacking in quantity and/or quality. Communications equipment was of particular concern – radios, phones, wire – much of these were obsolete or in disrepair.

With the threat of a full-blown typhoon moving in, the weather hovered between bad and worse as Smith's troops began arriving at the airbase. Several troop transports became airborne, but landing at their destination of Pusan, South Korea, became impossible for a time.

Colonel Smith was forced to scale back the number of men he could take over, and his temporary loss of Company A (Able) and critical sections of Company D (Dog), the battalion's heavy weapons company, proved crippling several days later.

Fortunately, a stripped-down version of the 52nd Field Artillery Battalion would cross over by ship, bringing along a handful of howitzers (cannons) to provide supporting fire.

Task Force Smith ended up going to war with roughly 500 men. An exact accounting of who was in this unit will never be known, because battalion records were lost in combat.

Still a bit uncertain about his precise mission, Smith met with General William F. Dean, commander of the 24th Division, later saying the objective Dean gave him was "the most general, widespread, far-flung order that a battalion commander ever had." General Dean told him, "When you get to Pusan (Korea), head for Taejon. We want to stop the North Koreans as far from Pusan as we can. Block the main road as far north as possible. Contact General Church. If you can't locate him, go to Taejon and beyond if you can. Sorry I can't give you more information. That's all I've got. Good luck to you, and God bless you and your men."[14]

Norman Fosness

"We found out later they meant for us to set up road blocks to delay the enemy until more troops could get over there," said Norman Fosness.

---

[13] 24th Inf Div War Diary for the Period 29 June 1950 5o 22 July 1950: Summary.

[14] Davies, Colonel William J., U.S.ANG. *Task Force Smith – A Leadership Failure?* U.S. Army War College. 1992. P 3.

"When we went over there, they told us it was just a few bandits crossing the 38ᵗʰ Parallel. We thought it was gonna be over in two weeks. We wasn't expecting what we got. There was some WWII guys, including my sergeant, that I listened to talking when were going up to the front line. He said, 'In two weeks, it'll be over with. This is gonna be nothing.' That's what we were expecting. We were sure wrong."

Fosness was from a large family that farmed in the vicinity of Barton, North Dakota. Although he was only 19, he had already been in the Army two years. Like Joe Langone and Paul Larson, Fosness was in Baker Company; he carried a heavy Browning Automatic Rifle (BAR), two hand grenades, and 240 rounds of ammunition.

Fosness was aboard one of the air transports that couldn't land in Pusan on July 1. Returning to Japan, he and some friends decided they would hitch a ride into town rather than spend the night at the air base, but military policemen spotted them and sent them back.

It was then that he realized his helmet and his .45 handgun had disappeared. He was able to replace the handgun, but he went into combat without a helmet, saying, "I felt like a turtle without a shell."[15]

Major Walter Pennino, previously a writer for the *Boston Globe*, writes:[16]

> There was little joy among this meager, jittery vanguard of the great army that was to halt the Reds. The men were wet, tired, bewildered. Swept from a quiet spot in peaceful Japan, they were being tossed to an enemy they knew nothing about, in a sickening country, in a confusing, mysterious war. And yet this under-strength battalion and its 19 jeeps represented the hope of 53 United Nations countries to hold back the Red forces plunging toward Pusan.
>
> Only about one in seven of the men were combat veterans; the rest were green. The bulk of the riflemen, machine gunners and mortar men were 20 years old or less. But the battalion had reached its peak of training; in Army parlance, 1ˢᵗ Battalion, 21ˢᵗ Regiment, was "red hot."

---

[15] Fosness interview with author 2004; "Osan, South Korea, July 5, 1950." *The Taro Leaf*. Summer-Fall 2007. P 29-33. Courtesy Norm Fossness and Lisa Sholl.

[16] Pennino. "7 Bloody Hours That Saved Korea". *Real* (magazine). Oct-Nov 1952. Web:6 Dec 2012. http://www.koreanwar-educator.org/topics/pusan/.

After reaching Taejon, the task force was split up to guard two different roads, while Colonel Smith and his principal officers jeeped north to get a look at what they were facing. The farther they drove, the more they encountered panicked refugees and demoralized South Korean soldiers. Several miles north of Osan, the officers came upon a cluster of hills with excellent positions for guarding the road and railroad lines out of Suwon. Smith decided this was where they'd make their stand.

Task Force Smith headed north to prepare their positions during the night of July 4. Norm Fosness's squad leader ordered him to dig his foxhole about 40 feet in front of a powerful 75mm recoilless rifle. His job was to protect the recoilless with his BAR.

"We got there about 3 o'clock in the morning, and we dug in," said Fosness. "I couldn't see another G.I. or foxhole anywhere around us. I could hear the guys on the 75mm gun talking behind us, though. We were spread really thin. The ground was hard and rocky, and we had to chip away with our trenching tools. It began to rain – real hard.

North to Suwon   South to Osan

Task Force Smith delayed North Korean's 4th Division along this road. The enemy came from the north (left), broke through the line along the ridge, and engaged the artillery farther south (right). (DoD)

"Just at the crack of dawn, enemy tanks came through around the bend. First I saw one. I thought, *That's no problem, we can take care of that.* Pretty soon another one. Then a second, and a third, and they just kept coming. This wasn't just a few bandits crossing the 38th parallel. And they didn't run when they saw American uniforms. We didn't have anything to knock them out with. Our bazookas, our shells, just bounced right off them. They were as effective as a bb-gun."

Reports vary, but between 31 and 40 tanks, spaced out in groups four to eight apiece, advanced toward the foot soldiers and took aim. These tanks were new Soviet T-34s with exceptionally heavy armor – virtually nothing could pierce them.

Peter Kalischer Account

United Press correspondent Peter Kalischer became trapped behind enemy lines with other survivors of the task force, and during the next two days, North Korean radio broadcasts claimed they had captured him.

When he reached safety on July 7, Kalischer could transmit only half his story before his allotment of telephone time was used up, so his full story didn't emerge until July 8. By then, other reporters had scooped him and moved on. Thus, his first-hand report is less well known but also more authentic. He reports:

> The American battalion, only two companies strong . . . opened up with everything it had – mortars, bazookas and new recoilless 75 mm rifles. For the most part, it was like hitting them with ping-pong balls . . . In the next terrible five hours... only three tanks were crippled. It took daring bazooka teams, running up to within 50 yards of the tanks and scoring four hits on the treads, to do this . . .
>
> Officers told me the tanks fired 88 mm guns (reported elsewhere as 85 mm), the all-purpose gun with which Nazis punished American troops in World War II. They also said the tanks were new and tougher armor, which made them almost immune to the American anti-tank equipment used that day. [17]

During the opening hours of the fight, New Jersey soldier Joe Langone and his platoon were defending a lower hill west of the road, and his foxhole was right next to the road. He writes:

> Anything and everything that came down that road had to pass me. It was unfolding like a movie. In frustration, I actually stood up in my hole and shot my rifle at a tank. I could hear my

---

[17] *San Antonio Express.* 8 July 1950.

bullets hitting, they were that close, but the damage was laughable, especially to those enemy tankers inside.

The T-34s reportedly broke through the infantry's positions by about 9:00 a.m. Now, they were rumbling farther south to engage the big guns of the 52nd Field Artillery. But the threat was far from over for the front line. When the rain eased, Colonel Smith could see almost all the way to Suwon with his binoculars. His stomach must have lurched when he realized a six-mile-long enemy convoy was snaking toward them.

It was later estimated Smith's men were outnumbered eight-to-one, with Joe Langone writing:

> It was just as well that we on the smaller hill, with just one platoon, didn't know the odds we faced. Our sergeant yelled to us not to fire at the advancing infantry until he gave the order. We watched as they advanced, standing almost upright, almost as though they didn't know we were there.[18]
>
> Each one of us singled out an enemy soldier, and when the sergeant yelled *Fire!* the single shot rifles, being fired in unison, sounded as though it was machine gun fire. The soldier in my sights dropped immediately to the ground. Did I actually shoot him, did somebody else shoot him, or did he accidentally fall? I'll never know.
>
> Our lieutenant, fearing we'd be overrun, ordered us to move to the larger hill where the rest of the battalion was fighting.
>
> I informed my squad we were leaving, and grabbing a can of machine gun ammunition, I ran like Hell across the road and started to climb the hill. I took the ammunition to the gunner who had set up on high ground overlooking rice paddies. The North Koreans were running across the paddies on small dirt pathways where our machine gunner, a corporal named Gonzales, was 'mowing' them down like those "Kewpie dolls" you see at a carnival. (Mexico's Florentino Gonzales received the Distinguished Service Cross for his action. Later in the day, he became a POW.)

After his platoon crossed to the east side of the road, Langone stumbled

---

[18] A captured enemy officer confirmed the North Koreans were surprised to see the Americans. Apparently, they had no communications with their tank column.

upon Paul Larson, his friend from Duluth:

> During a lull in the battle, Paul and I sat in a hole sharing my one lone Phillip Morris cigarette that I had broken in half. Neither one of us discussed fear. In a way, it was weird. All the killing and dying, the rain still coming down, artillery and mortar fire still coming in, and we're sitting there calmly smoking a cigarette.
>
> Soon the gunner on the enemy mortar was finding our range, so we got up and ran to a position higher up on the hill. We jumped into a Korean grave, a raised mound inside a deep hole, and started firing at the enemy advancing towards us.

Langone and Larson (Courtesy Langone)

> All of a sudden I heard a sound like something being slapped. I looked at Paul, and he had been mortally wounded with two shots [to the head] and one almost directly into his heart. I think at that very moment I gave death a very close look. We were fighting side by side, yet Paul was hit, and I wasn't.
>
> The only thing I could say was, "Start praying Paul." Paul replied, "I am." They were his last words.

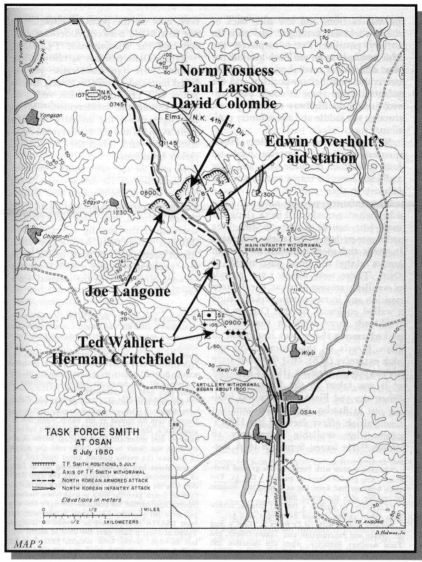

(Base map courtesy Center of Military History)

Tanks Versus Artillery

The 52nd Field Artillery's howitzers were meanwhile engaging the enemy in a direct tank-artillery battle a mile or so farther south.

Official records indicate the artillerymen lost all five of their howitzers, mainly because they ran out of ammunition, and the big guns had to be destroyed to keep them out of enemy hands.

The war diary states the artillery strikes on the T-34 tanks "seemed to have no effect." This was not about the tanks' armor as much as having the wrong type of ammunition for the howitzers.

When *Task Force Smith* was formed in Japan, only 18 rounds of antitank ammunition (HEAT) were available for the entire 24th Division – and only five or six of those rounds were now here on the battlefield.

Lieutenant Colonel Miller Perry, commanding the 52nd Artillery, gave all the HEAT to a one of his crews and sent them – as the only true antitank weapon he had – about halfway up the road to where the tanks were breaking through. This howitzer crew was on its own as an outpost.

Herman Critchfield & Edward Wahlert

It was midmorning when the T-34s started rumbling toward this forward gun. As they rolled, they blasted away any transport vehicles they spotted along the way – there would be no motorized retreat for the foot soldiers up front.

Herman Critchfield, Columbia, Missouri, was on this "outpost" and is the only person who can say what actually happened that day.

Critchfield previously served as an artilleryman with the Marines during WWII. "My family had just bought a small farm in Rocheport, Missouri," he said. "My father loved the soil, and this was his dream. But I was never a farmer. Just shortly out of the Marines and no job, I was just looking for something to do, so I joined the Army."

He was looking forward to occupation duty in Japan, but the day he arrived he went to the supply room to obtain linens and was instead handed a rifle. He was going to Korea.

As the new guy in Battery A, Critchfield was an unknown, but he had direct-fire experience (firing at visible close-range targets rather than long-range fire called in by a forward observer). So he was chosen to head up the crew on the forward howitzer. He writes:[19]

I was the ranking man in the section and was to be the Chief of Section/Gunner of the section. We set up forward of the main firing position just beyond a hill. I do not remember who picked the position out, but I assume it was Chief of Fire.

---

[19] *Statement of Herman V. Critchfield Re: 5 Jul 1950.* Hard copy shared with author January 30, 2013. Also email communications February 2013.

We did not dig the howitzer in – just made spade holes and shot from there. The prime mover (truck) was parked immediately to our right rear with a little cover of hanging tree branches. There was a telephone exchange building, stucco, to our immediate rear, and you could hear the relays clicking. There was an elderly man working in the building. I don't remember seeing him but once. He just disappeared.

We had wire communication with the main battery. After we had bore-sighted the howitzer in, we offloaded the five rounds of HEAT ammo and improved the position, and we were notified of tanks coming. I had previously asked if we could knock the small bridge out just to our right and about 50-75 yards to our front. This was denied. I was thinking I would have a much better shot at the tanks if I could see their belly.

There was no sense of anyone being afraid. As I look back, this point amazes me. How could these people, me included, have reasoned that we would get out of this situation alive? We just went about our job as trained. No one questioned the way I had set it up. All the men were good soldiers, and we were just lucky to get out of that alive.

We saw three tanks come around the bend about 400 yards up the road. They were buttoned up and slowly moving along. The morning was damp and misty with rain. I explained to the crew that I would get the first tank just short of the bridge and block it. I thought this might make the others pass him and go into the streambed and climb out.

When he was in range we fired, and he spun out off the road and stopped. We reloaded and fired on the second tank. I am sure he was also hit, as he also spun out. We loaded and fired at the third tank, but I don't know the results of that round. Firing at that [low angle] made so much smoke out in front of the howitzer that it was impossible to see.

We tried to load the next round, but it jammed; the brass shell casing crimped in the tube. This happens sometimes if the projectile is not properly seated in the brass casing.

About this time I heard small arms (rifles) popping around us. I do not think the tanks saw us, but they knew we were nearby. I thought it was too dangerous to have someone go out in front of the howitzer and – with a bell rammer – knock the round back out of the tube.

It was at this time that I ordered everyone back to the main battery. We went across the hill behind us, following a path that was slick and wet. Arriving at the main firing position, we saw the battery was busy turning their howitzers to the right, toward the road, getting ready for the tanks coming down the road. They could not see them yet because of the hill in front of the guns.

From this time on, for this day, things are a blur. . . . This is the way I remember the first day of combat in Korea, 5 July 1950. I am sure it is fairly accurate, as I have reminisced this day many times with others who were there at the same time and yes, asked the question, "How the hell did we get out of there alive?"

Herman Critchfield (right) in Korea (Courtesy Critchfield)

One of the men in Critchfield's crew was Private First Class Edward "Ted" Wahlert, the son of a truck driver from Dexter, Iowa.

"I couldn't have asked for a better dad," said Wahlert's son Randel. "He finished 8th grade and then had to go to work. He was strong as an ox, and many of his friends say they would never mess with him. He was 6'1" and built like – like the old saying, *like a brick shit-house.* But just the nicest guy you'd ever meet in your life. We had this freight route we did when I was in high school, and he'd sit there with people and talk and talk and talk. Everybody knew him. Everybody liked him. He was just a lovable guy. But the war is something I never ever found out about. I remember time after time trying to get him to talk about the war, and he wouldn't. He absolutely wouldn't."[20]

This is not surprising, given the severity of the fighting the 19-year-old experienced. A month later, Ted wrote to his fiancé, Kay:

I received a letter from you a couple of weeks ago, but haven't had time to write to you till right now. I arrived in Korea the night of the 2nd of July. We went up on the front lines the fifth of July. And that day we had a tank attack. My section and howister [sic] was on an outpost, and my section got the first tank that day. From there we had to withdraw from that position and we traveled about twenty-five miles that night, and we stayed in a schoolhouse that night.

(Courtesy Wahlert family)

Edward Wahlert was the first regular Army soldier from the upper prairies to be decorated for valor in the Korean War.

Corporal (then Private First Class) **Edward E. Wahlert**, *Battery A, 52nd Field Artillery Battalion, 24th Infantry Division, is awarded the* **Bronze Star Medal with V Device** *for heroic achievement on 5 July 1950 at Osan, Korea. Private First Class Wahlert was manning a 105-millimeter howitzer in a forward position when enemy tanks advanced toward his outpost. His*

---

[20] Author correspondence with Randel Wahlert and Rosanda Thompson, Dec 2012. Edward Wahlert's letters reprinted by permission.

section knocked out two of the tanks. Four other tanks took his section under fire, and Private First Class Wahlert continued to man his section, delivering counterfire until all ammunition was exhausted. Private First Class Wahlert drew back under enemy fire to his battery position and assisted other sections until directed to withdraw.

It was the war's first tank vs. artillery showdown, and at a certain point, their ammunition dump – some 300 rounds – received a direct hit. At about 3:30, they learned Colonel Smith had ordered a withdrawal. Now surrounded, the artillerymen disabled their howitzers and headed for transports they had parked on the outskirts of Osan. Critchfield writes:

> The Korean Captain who was assigned to us for training acted as our interpreter and got us out past the tanks by using cow paths. This Captain is now a retired Major General, Seung Kook Yoon, from the Korean Army. We got to a small village and occupied a school awaiting orders and new howitzers and other equipment.

Escaping to the Rear

Several hours into the battle, the North Koreans worked their away around the flanks of the infantrymen at the front, and North Dakotan Norm Fosness and his BAR assistant, George Pleasant, wondered what would happen if they were overrun:

> We took turns looking over the edge of our hole. There were bushes two to four feet high in front of us, and I discovered the North Koreans had camouflaged themselves to look like a bush. It was still raining, which made them even more difficult to see. But when I saw a bush move, I opened fire, and sometimes I just fired at anything in front of me. All the while that 75 continued firing. Then it stopped and I heard someone yell that it was hit.

By this point, communications between the different units had fallen apart. Telephone lines were severed, radios failed, and connections between the infantry and the artillery dissolved. Fosness got the word at about 3:30, when he heard a company runner yelling, *Retreat! Every man for himself!*

I fired my BAR as Pleasant jumped out of the foxhole and headed to the backside of the hill. I pulled the pins on my two grenades and threw them down the hill. Then I jumped out of the hole and ran to the rear side of the hill, where I thought I would be safe from rifle and machine gun fire.

Fosness and others became trapped in a ditch next to a rice paddy.

I heard Pleasant yell, *Come on Fosness,* and he took off running in the rice paddy. He hadn't gotten more than 75 feet when a machine gun opened up on him. He fell head-first in the paddy with a hailstorm of machine gun bullets spraying the water around him. I was sure he was dead! Then, after maybe a couple of minutes, I saw him unhook his ammo belt and push his rifle to the side. He began crawling away on his stomach through the paddy.

Someone else decided to make a try for it. He took about three steps from the bank. Again the machine gun splattered the water a couple of feet in front of him. He froze and then came back.

Then, I decided to make my break. I ran as hard as I could, but after only about 50 feet, I fell flat on my face. Running in rice paddies is impossible. You sink in mud almost to your knees.

I crawled on my stomach in about eight inches of water for about 100 yards, all the while bullets spraying around me. I came to a ridge about two feet high and found I was able to crawl without exposing myself too much. I couldn't see anyone else around me; for all I knew I was the only one left.

He eventually linked up with about 20 others, including three of his buddies, in a drainage ditch, writing:

It was then that the shock of the last eight hours hit me. The horror seemed unbelievable. None of us had a map or compass. We talked about going to the coast and hijacking a boat back to Japan. We didn't know if there were any more American troops coming over, or what was going to happen to us few G.I.s that were in Korea.

Fosness and his group found their way to a village, but they kept moving when they spotted enemy tanks. When they stopped to rest that night, he fell asleep, but luckily he woke up when someone tripped over him. They walked for the rest of the night, and the following day Fosness, his buddy Pleasant, and another man slipped in with a group of refugees fleeing south. When they finally made it to friendly lines, several officers whisked them into a tent to ask about other survivors:

> They wanted to know about Colonel Smith, whether he escaped, and if he was bringing out some more men. I told them as far as I knew, we were the only ones.
>
> I hadn't eaten in two days, but I couldn't eat. I took about three spoonfuls of beef stew and just couldn't eat any more. I thought about the last two days and felt like throwing up.

Fossness and Pleasant (Courtesy Fossness)

David Colombe

Among those who had been to war before was 34-year-old David Colombe, a Lakota-French Sioux warrior from Rosebud, South Dakota. David and two brothers had served in World War II. David was in the Army and Lester joined the Navy. Fred, a paratrooper, was killed in action at Luzon.

David's son Leonard says he does not believe his father joined the military out of economic necessity.

"He was working, and Mom was working, so I think they were surviving okay. I don't think it was that. That was '43, so the depression was all over with. So I don't think that was it. I think there was a call to duty. A lot of Native Americans were a warrior type personality – it was kind of like their duty. Probably he and his brothers weren't any different. They all volunteered and went in."[21]

David made the Army his career, but his wife and children remained in South Dakota throughout. Thus, Leonard did not really get to know his father until he became an adult. He remembers his dad as, "A good country boy. He grew up with guns, so he was a good shot. He was probably about 5'11". By the time he got out of the service, he was more like 5'10". He probably weighed about 180 pounds, if that. Very slim. Very greased lightning type."

Late in life, the elder opened up about his violent combat experiences. One notable action took place in Germany in 1944.

"It was a machine gun nest," Leonard explains. "They were firing at the Americans in this town, and Dad was knocked unconscious from some type of blast – artillery or something. When he woke up, his weapon was destroyed. He found a dead soldier with this trench knife, and he used it – he didn't have anything else. He killed two soldiers in a machine gun nest, and he killed a bunch of them when they were retreating from the town. He cut off their retreat, because this machine gun nest was kind of in their backup area. He was behind their military lines and was stopping them from retreating, and they surrendered in that town. He got credit for that. They were surrendering, not being able to retreat."

Although David Colombe was very highly decorated for this action, some felt he should have been awarded a Medal of Honor. Leonard says his father wasn't concerned about medals, however. He felt medals should go to those who lost their lives. One cannot argue, however, that this tough South Dakotan certainly deserved his prestigious award.

*The **Distinguished Service Cross** is awarded to Private **David L. Colombe**, Infantry, U.S. Army for extraordinary heroism in connection with military operations against an armed enemy while serving with the 414th Infantry Regiment, 104th Infantry Division, in action against enemy forces on 26*

---

[21] Interview with author December 2012.

November 1944, in Germany. Armed only with a trench knife after his rifle had been shattered by shell fragments, Sergeant Colombe leaped into an enemy foxhole and single-handedly captured two Germans. Securing a hostile automatic rifle from the emplacement, he voluntarily worked his way behind enemy lines. As pressure was exerted upon the enemy stronghold by his company, Sergeant Colombe killed seven Germans and wounded many more as they attempted to withdraw. His deadly fire demoralized the enemy force, resulting in the collapse of their defenses . . .

Sergeant Colombe had just joined the 21st Regiment when *Task Force Smith* made its stand north of Osan. During the retreat, Colombe and Corporal Van Bullman, from Alexander, North Carolina, headed into the hills together. Five days later, reporters were on hand when these two men walked into friendly territory.

Bullman spoke for both of them, telling reporters,[22] "When the order came to retreat, we started down the reverse side of the hill. We were under fire all the time. Sometimes we laid in rice paddies and played dead until they stopped firing. When we stood up to run, they opened up on us again. We ran, crawled and played dead some more."

That first night, Colombe and Bullman reached a village where an English-speaking teenager hid them in his family's home. Toward dawn, the boy's uneasy parents asked the soldiers to leave. Thinking they could circle around the enemy's rear positions, Colombe and Bullman climbed a ridge and headed north. But the enemy columns reached to the horizon, so they reversed course and headed south – they would have to move directly through enemy territory if they hoped to reach safety.

Later that day, Colombe and Bullman joined forces with five South Korean soldiers who were similarly cut off.

"The Korean captain, Dad said, is what really helped them," said Leonard, "because he could talk with refugees and civilians along the way and get them a little bit of food and some clothes. They dressed up like refugees is how they got out. They had to get rid of their weapons and their G.I. clothes, their boots, and stuff. It took them four or five days to get back to American lines, and they walked barefooted, so when they got back to American lines, Dad's feet were in pretty bad shape."

Official reports indicate they didn't make it back to their unit until July 10. The Army evacuated Colombe because of his injuries, and on

---

[22] *Chicago Daily News.* 10 July 1950.

July 12, he wrote to his wife, Josephine, in Winner, South Dakota:

> It wasn't long after I went to the 21st Infantry that I was on my way to Korea, and it has been pretty rough there. Was in one of the first Companies to get to Korea and into combat.
>
> Our two Companies were overrun and we were trapped behind their lines. Me and one of the boys were together, and it took us 4 days to get back to our lines. I had to go to the hospital with my feet but am leaving now and will probably go back to Korea again. Have been lucky so far and don't know how long it will last, so if I go back again pray for me.
>
> But if anything should happen don't you feel too bad. Just remember that I love you, and tell the boys I said hello.
>
> Jo, there has been a lot of young boys die in the last two weeks, but that's the way things go when there's a war on. I just hope it doesn't last too long. I sure wish I could be home with you right now. Well, I can wish can't I?
>
> You know the Korean soldiers aren't taking any prisoners, so I won't let them take me if I get back there again, and you know what I mean.
>
> That country is hard to fight in. All there is is rice paddies with water in them, and there isn't but a few roads. Most of the country is mountains. All I can say is that it's very rough, but will try and make it home again I hope. I suppose this mess will bring some more back into the army, and I'll bet they won't like that.
>
> Oh yes, forgot to mention that I am in the hospital in Japan with my feet. Just walked too much and will be leaving here this evening and will probably go to another outfit and back over to Korea . . . it's rough over there, so do some praying for me if I have to go back to Korea . . .
>
> Tell Broken Leg that it's rough over in Korea and to stay away if he can.

The following day, Colombe's immediate future was still heavy on his mind when he again wrote to his wife:

> Well my dear, am still lying around the hospital so thought I would write a few lines before going to bed. Am getting along fine and my feet are pretty well healed up so I suppose I'll be going to an outfit and then back to Korea. It's not that I really

want to, but if they say I'll have to go up, I guess I'll just have to. I just hope my luck holds out, but I guess a person can't live forever. Jo tell the boys I said hello and for them to be good. And I hope they never have to come into the army.

I hope this mess over here doesn't lead into another world war, but I suppose it will. It looks like that's all they want to do now is fight, and this fighting is rough. The other day you came near being a widow, just by inches, but like I said before, only the good die young. Guess I'll live to be an old man from the looks of things. Tell Broken Leg he had better stay away from over here as it's rough.

Oh yes Jo, the days I was behind the lines I learned to eat Korean meals. At first I could hardly choke it down but learned to eat it when I got good and hungry. Most of their stuff is hot and dirty. I've never seen people like them before. And they don't own anything except their rice paddies. It's Russia that has this mess going . . . Just let the folks know I am ok, and tell Lester to stay out of the army and navy.[23]

Colombe was indeed sent back to Korea to rejoin Baker Company, 21st Regiment, and some two weeks later, his worst fears materialized.

"They got overrun again," said his son Leonard, "and he got wounded and captured.

"When they retreated, it was at night, and he walked into two guys and said something like *B Company*, or whatever their call was. The guy hit him with the butt of the rifle and knocked him down. Dad pulled the guy down and ripped his nose, and then beat him with his cartridge belt.

"The other North Korean ran away, and Dad thought he was gone. But when he stood up, the second guy was laying down a little ways away and shot him twice – once in the chest and once in the back – and paralyzed him.

"They were in like a rice paddy type of thing, and the guy came over and put the gun to his head. But he didn't shoot him. Dad played dead, and the second North Korean dragged his buddy away.

"The next day, Dad said, the bugs were bothering him so bad that he had to get away from the water, and he crawled up to this old shack. He had scars on his arms and knees and stuff from crawling on the

---

[23] Letters David Colombe to Josephine Colombe 12 and 13 July 1950. Courtesy Colombe family. Some minor edits were made by author. Reprinted by permission.

rocks, because he couldn't walk," said Leonard.

"And then North Koreans came by and took him prisoner. They took his clothes and boots and his dog-tags. They took everything and just left him in his G.I. shorts. They had him for about four days. Some Americans were moving in – they were artillery – and the Koreans left.

"Dad thought they would kill him, but they left him alive. He couldn't walk, he was paralyzed, and they weren't going to carry him, I guess. They just left him. Then, the Marines came through after a day or two and picked him up. He was very lucky there.

"Mom got a letter saying he was missing in action and presumed dead at that time. Dad had a sister, Velma, who was a military nurse, and she found him in a hospital in Japan. She contacted us and let the family know that he had been found, and he was alive and doing okay.

"He recuperated and everything. Just the shock of the shells going through – it didn't hit him in the spine, but he had stuff that was still in his spine after he got out of the service. It was just too close to the spine to operate. He had two good-sized holes in his back shoulder and lower back where he was shot. He got the Purple Heart for that."

When asked why the North Koreans didn't kill his father, Leonard said, "He always thought that – maybe – the Orientals had kind of a feeling for Native Americans. The Indians were supposed to be descended from Chinese, so in a way they have an affiliation with Native Americans in a historical context. And he was very Native American. You could tell it by looking at him that he was Native American. He was Rosebud Sioux. And he thought that well maybe because of their feelings toward Indians. Who knows?"

(Courtesy Colombe family)

David Colombe's "million-dollar wound" got him transferred back to the States August 15, and he remained in the Army until retirement age. Given his history as a combat warrior, maybe it wasn't – as he suggested to his wife – that he was not *good* enough to die young. Perhaps he simply refused.

Chapter 5

EDWIN OVERHOLT AND THE WOUNDED

"You learned without reservation that as long as wars are possible and you wear a uniform, learn first to fight, then to practice medicine. " Alexander "Pete" Boysen, 21st Regiment

JOHN GLENN and other fighter pilots honed their flying skills in Korea long before they trained to become our first astronauts.

On February 20, 1962, when Glenn became the first American to orbit Earth, a number of physicians monitored his vital signs from the ground. One of these was Dr. Edwin L. Overholt, who grew up in Decorah, Iowa.[24]

Some dozen years earlier, Dr. Overholt was directly involved in another *first* when he was abruptly attached to *Task Force Smith*. Working in a slimy mud pit to save the wounded, his aid station bore no resemblance to Glenn's sterile space capsule.

Overholt went to medical school after graduating from the State University of Iowa in Iowa City. By early 1950, he was completing his residency in Denver as a member of the Army Medical Corps, writing:

In January of 1950, we were informed there was an acute shortage of physicians for dispensaries in Japan . . . 42 Army

---

[24] Overholt, Edwin L. Manuscript: *Korea – Task Force Smith – 5-7 July 1950 and the Medics During the War.* Biographies collection, 1998.74.40, Office of Medical History, U.S. Army Medical Department Center of History and Heritage, Ft. Sam Houston, TX; Cowdrey, Albert. *The Medics War.* Center of Military History, U.S. Army. 1990: p 74-76; *Army Medical Department in the Korean War: Colonel Edwin L. Overholt, Task Force Smith & the Medical Company in Combat in Korea.* 28 Jan 1966; http//history.amedd.army.mil/booksdocs/korea/TaskForceSmith/Overholt.html

physicians were to be chosen from our teaching hospitals. This was to be a 90-day [temporary tour of duty]. Having never been overseas, I looked upon this as a great opportunity! We were flown via commercial airlines. On arrival in Tokyo, three of us were "pipelined" to the southern island of Japan (Kyushu) occupied by the 24th infantry division.

No hint of the upcoming war existed when Overholt arrived. Of the troops of the 24th Division, he wrote:

> Their purpose was to insure against any resurgence of Japanese militarism. They were not combat units. Moreover, General MacArthur skillfully instituted common sense rules for the conduct of the troops, as well as a strict, kind, orderly life for the people of Japan. His public respect for their Emperor was a masterful move. Indeed when I arrived in Japan in April 1950, I felt very comfortable with the Japanese people!

When the war broke out two months later, Dr. Overholt was tasked with caring for American dependents, including North Dakota's Emogene Lindvig, who were evacuated from Korea. Overholt remembered them arriving on *The Reinholt*, calling it "a stinking Norwegian fertilizer ship."

At about 10:00 p.m. June 30, Overholt received a call from division headquarters ordering him to report to the Itazuke Air Base by 6:00 a.m. He was to prepare to set up a full medical aid station, because he would be serving in combat as a surgeon.

Because his tour in Japan was temporary, Overholt had not been issued full field equipment, so he spent the rest of the night finding what he needed with the help of another medical corpsman, Captain Douglas Anderson (later captured and died in captivity). By morning, the only personal item Overholt still needed was a set of combat boots.

Raymond "Bodie" Adams had been officially in charge of the medical platoon, but Colonel Smith assigned him a different role and put Overholt in command of the unit of about 30 officers, medics, litter bearers and aid station personnel. Adams was proud of these men — they had received the highest marks in the entire Eighth Army during recent field exercises.

Despite the quality of Adams' men, Overholt (now promoted to Captain) was worried. There would be no rapport or trust between him and them, and Overholt had not received training for the experience they were facing, writing:

> My first act on the C54 transport was to introduce myself to the
> aid station personnel. To this day, I vividly recall looking at
> these young men and knew that few were well trained for
> intense combat. I also noted that each solider had an extra pair
> of boots strung across the back of their neck. My first action
> was to ask who wore 8½ C boots? The raise of a hand by a
> PVT prompted the loss of his extra boots so I could go into
> Korea wearing appropriate footwear.

Overholt went forward from Osan with Colonel Brad Smith to scout
the area where the task force would fight.

> I chose to put the aid station on the back slope of the same hilly
> area where the troops would be on the forward slope. I carefully
> marked out where to put the aid station and discussed it in
> some detail with [Smith], who agreed with its position. It was
> not placed on the roadside, because it would have been at least
> two to three miles from the forward position of the companies.
> This is too far to litter carry a man who needs help, also too far
> to carry a man even if one had plenty of men, which we did not.
>   It was known that the North Koreans had tanks and, should
> they get through the road blocks, the aid station would be in
> direct view and be rendered ineffective if it were near the road.
> Also at this point, we had no organic transportation to get
> wounded men down the road. It was for these reasons that the
> aid station was close to the front lines and off the only available
> road.

Overholt positioned two old trucks at the closest roadside point for
evacuating the casualties. The plan was for serious casualties to be
driven to Pyongtaek, farther south. From there they would be evacuated
to the city of Taejon via a self-propelled rail car called a doodlebug.

   "The subsequent circumstances never permitted this chain of
evacuation to come into existence," Overholt wrote.

> On the evening of the 4th of July, under steady rain and pitch
> dark, we moved out of Pyongtek and three miles beyond to
> Osan, our blocking position. The Korean drivers would not go
> north, so we had to drive the old worn out Korean trucks that

we had commandeered. Exhausted from the events of the past days, the two companies immediately began moving into position under darkness. It was known that the tanks would be coming down the road, and the instruction was to shoot for the treads to stop them. The acute bend in the road would leave them ideally exposed.

Edwin Overholt, carrying his medical bag, leads members of the Army Medical Corps at the Taejon train station on July 2. (U.S. Army)

The medics were the last in the transport line. I was in the lead truck. The radiator overheated causing us to repeatedly stop and fill the radiator with water. The heavy rain made water easily available. Because of this difficulty, we were at least an hour behind the two companies of infantry. Fortunately I had marked our departure point off the road with white gauze. . . . I had also left markers along the way because I knew we would have to find our area under total darkness and we would have to traverse across several rice paddies to get into position.

Initially, the medics were reticent to follow me. Only a few were willing, but as morning light began to filter through the

rain, more and more of the medics fell into position. We were
unarmed and there was fear that the North Koreans might
already be in position. Also, there was no contact with the two
infantry companies ahead. Recall that I had not known these
troops and had never been in a field exercise with them. As a
27-year-old Captain with no prior combat experience, I was an
untried leader.

Overholt's aid station was a dugout about twelve-feet by twelve feet,
and about five-feet deep. To keep out the rain, they covered it with a
canvas tarp. He described himself as "very busy" during the main thrust
of the battle:

> We were in position by 0600 hours. About 8 o'clock and over
> the next frantic few hours, 33 Russian tanks lumbered down the
> road, and as they made that hairpin turn they exposed their
> bellies to our well-positioned bazooka teams. Unfortunately, the
> 2.36 inch bazooka was ineffective in stopping these Russian
> tanks, a fact I later learned had been known by our Army
> leaders since World War II. Certainly our bazooka teams with
> their second lieutenant officers did not appreciate this fact.

Of the actual medical procedures they used, Overholt wrote:

> First aid was rendered, that is, splint the part, stop the bleeding,
> and give the patient reassurance, morphine if indicated,
> appropriate tags, etc. These simple procedures were difficult
> because of three factors:
>
> (1) We were out in the rain. Tape would not stick, so all
> bandages had to be tied on. Our modest supply of such
> bandages rapidly became exhausted. We had the standard, well-
> equipped kits for aid stations.
>
> (2) Several rounds landed in our area and often scattered the
> corpsmen into their foxholes.
>
> (3) General confusion. This was their first combat!
> Nevertheless, we were able to take care of all the casualties in a
> satisfactory fashion as far as first aid is concerned. I did
> anticipate that we would not be able to hold the North Koreans,
> so I directed all walking cases to take off south through rice
> paddies and off the main road in the hope of getting to medical
> care. For example, all individuals with fractured arms and hands

from bullet wounds, whose bleeding was stopped and arm splinted, and individuals who had relatively deep soft tissue wounds who were not in shock and had the use of all four extremities. Perhaps 25 or 30 such individuals were so directed south. There rained an additional 25-30 men who were litter cases.

After several hours of battle, usual medical supplies were exhausted and we improvised with T-shirts, etc. It didn't really matter what you put on the wounds, etc., because they rapidly became soaking wet and muddy anyway.

When Colonel Smith ordered the withdrawal, he delegated two medics to remain behind with the wounded. Overholt didn't know this, writing:

Suddenly a lieutenant came running over the hill and stopped dead in his tracks when he saw the aid station surrounded by many seriously wounded soldiers. He yelled, "What the hell are you doing here?" You could imagine what I told him. We were well aware of imminent capture, and I had decided to stay with the wounded. However, in a matter of seconds, North Korean troops came around the hill and began to open fire on us despite the fact that our Red Cross markings were clearly exposed, and we had no weapons. As I knelt over a severely wounded soldier, I remember him looking at me and yelling that all was lost and I should get the "hell out of there."

I grabbed Chaplain [Carl] Hudson and made a break across the rice paddies. It was impossible to sustain a run, because. . . balance failed, and we repeatedly fell into the rice paddies. Fortunately the North Koreans were not interested in immediately chasing us . . .

In our retreat, I came upon wounded G.I.s and treated them as best I could . . . The roads behind me, where I had positioned trucks to evacuate the wounded to the rail station, were blocked by Russian tanks.

I purposely remained at the end of the retreat line to encourage as many of the disheartened soldiers not to give up. All were discouraged and extremely fatigued. I was often delayed and had to depend on friendly Koreans to send me in the direction of the retreating and larger group. On later reflection I am certain that this was worthwhile, since several soldiers joined me in our effort to reach Ansong.

*The **Silver Star** is awarded to Captain (Medical Corps) **Edwin L. Overholt**, U.S. Army, for conspicuous gallantry and intrepidity in action at Osan and Ansong, Korea, during the period 5 July to 7 July 1950. Working in rugged mountainous terrain with improvised facilities, hampered by rain and under constant enemy fire, Captain Overholt undoubtedly saved the lives of many wounded soldiers. In all instances his care of battlefield casualties was characterized by exceptional skill, calmness and deep personal concern without regard for his own comfort and safety. When forced to withdraw from Osan Hill, Captain Overholt assisted in carrying the wounded over mountainous terrain for a distance of approximately forty miles. During this journey, he remained behind with several litter cases who could not be carried further, satisfying himself that every possible aid had been given to each of the wounded men before he rejoined the unit. Immediately upon reaching Ansong, Captain Overholt, without food or rest, assisted with an emergency operation on an American soldier, and then he undertook to treat the wounded men of a unit that had lost its surgeon in combat. Captain Overholt's professional skill and selfless devotion in caring for the wounded with complete disregard for the hazards of battle exemplify conduct that is in keeping with the highest traditions of military service.*

General Harry Offutt presents the Silver Star
to Overholt March 13, 1951
(Courtesy *The Daily Iowan*)

Chapter 6

RICHARD STEPHENS & CHARLES ALKIRE

"Those who raised their hands to surrender were shot dead by as savage a foe as Americans ever faced." Keyes Beech, *Chicago Daily News,* regarding fighting at Chonui.

COLONEL RICHARD STEPHENS, the overall commander of the 21ˢᵗ Regiment "Gimlets," grew up in Pierre, South Dakota. His father Louis was an attorney whose most prominent client was Standard Oil.

After attending high school in Pierre for two years, Stephens attended the Shattuck Military Academy. They decided he was a good candidate for an appointment to the United States Military Academy, so he was soon transferred to West Point, where he was described as "sophisticated and disillusioned" and "one already old in experience." In his senior year, "Steve's" entry in the *Howitzer Yearbook* reads:

> His aptitude for the modern languages and his readiness to assist the less fortunate have been the means of retaining for the service many who otherwise would have fallen. A loyal friend and a true gentleman, Steve is bound to carve for himself a fair name in the field of achievement.
>
> . . . Steve's rendition of "Annie Laurie," during the reign of the Mad May Moon . . . gave promise – or warning – of a latent talent which was to become his sole conceit during the following year. However, under excellent tutelage this gift of joyous song proved to be his crowning glory . . . combined with the feline grace of a mountain lion . . .

In Europe during WWII, Stephens commanded the 119ᵗʰ Regiment, 30ᵗʰ Infantry Division, rising to become that division's Chief of Staff. By the time the Korean War broke out, Stephens was considered a somewhat unconventional but also immensely capable officer. Of his three regimental commanders, General William Dean is reported to have "much preferred Stephens."[25]

The 21st Regiment's code name was *Diamond*, and the call signs for its three battalions were *Red, White* and *Blue*. As commanding officer, Stephens was *Diamond 6*, but his men took to calling him "Big Six."

Stephens proved unflappable in combat, and he seemed to have little need of spit and polish to gain his men's respect. Harry Maihafer, an officer in Love Company in 1950, writes:

> The staff people at the CP (command post) looked worn out, but nevertheless businesslike. They said the regimental commander, Colonel Stephens, would want to talk to us personally. Stephens had been up most of the night, but was now awake and would see us in a few minutes . . . He appeared, wearing a faded old bathrobe. He was Richard W. Stephens. . . short, compact, leathery, exuding an air of tough professionalism.
>
> Somehow the bathrobe was reassuring. Wearing a robe, or merely having one available, was only a minor amenity, but it made one feel Stephens was a man who moved with confidence and who planned on staying around awhile. I found him not only impressive, but more than a little intimidating.[26]

Norton Goldstein served under Stephens while they were still in Japan. "One of my original jobs," he said, "was testing all the phones in the command post, so I was in his office every morning. Actually, he wasn't a colorful man. He was a very proud man, a very dignified man. He was a fantastic leader in combat."

Goldstein described Stephens "skylining" himself when they reached Korea – meaning he would allow his profile to rise above a ridge line so the enemy could see him.

"He would do that, because in the beginning we were just a bunch of dumb kids that didn't know our butt from a hole in the ground. And he would skyline himself to show us we had nothing to really fear. He

---

[25]Blair. *The Forgotten War, p 92-93.*

[26] Maihafer. *From the Hudson to the Yalu. . .* P 28-29.

was just an amazing leader. Nothing bothered him. He did whatever he felt was the right thing to do. He had no sense of worrying about how it might've looked to anybody. If he thought it was the right thing to do, that's what he'd do."[27]

After the disaster at Osan, Colonel Stephens ordered the survivors of *Task Force Smith* south to Taejon to reorganize and reequip.

The 24th Division's 34th Regiment, which had been positioned behind Smith's group on July 5, fought the next series of delaying actions at Pyongtaek and Chonan.

By the end of July 8, the 34th suffered at least 135 casualties, including the loss of the regiment's commander, Colonel Robert R. Martin, who was killed in action. Until another commander could be brought up, Colonel Stephens was ordered to take command of both the 34th and the 21st Regiments.

To beef up the 34th, Stephen's brought forward the 21st's 1st Battalion troops who were forced to stay behind when *Task Force Smith* deployed from Japan. This group numbered about 500 men, primarily from Able and Dog Companies. Now designated as *Task Force A*, these men sailed to Korea aboard the *William Lester*, captained by a Merchant Marine.

Task Force A was commanded by Captain Charles Alkire, 36, from Missoula, Montana. The son of a railroad man, Alkire had worked for (or as) a shoemaker before joining the Army in February 1941.

On July 9, 1950, Alkire and his men were ordered to take up blocking positions near Chonui. After seeing the terrain, Alkire positioned his men along a three-quarter-mile stretch below Chonui. The right (east) sector included positions along the Cho-ch'on River, the main highway between Seoul and Pusan, and a vital railroad line needed for bringing up supplies and evacuating the wounded.

Alkire's left flank was anchored on a hill east of these features. Due to lack of manpower, this isolated position was defended by a mere platoon (about 40 men).

Alkire positioned his only armored vehicle – one light tank – behind a hill to challenge T-34s that might make it around the bend. (This friendly tank actually ended up capturing an enemy tank.)

The enemy appeared on the horizon that afternoon. Of three war

---

[27] Goldstein, from Ohio, changed his name to Goldy Norton while later working in California. He wrote the first *Official Frisbee Handbook* for Whammo™ in 1972.

correspondents who dug in with *Task Force A*, Homer Bigart was the
only one who made it out alive, writing "the highway northward for a
distance of ten miles was crawling with enemy vehicles."

From his forward position, Alkire counted eleven tanks and 200-300
infantrymen leading the enemy convoy. Unlike the first day of combat,
the weather was clear enough for the Montanan to call up air strikes.

Artillery and mortar strikes were also effective, and by 5:00 p.m.,

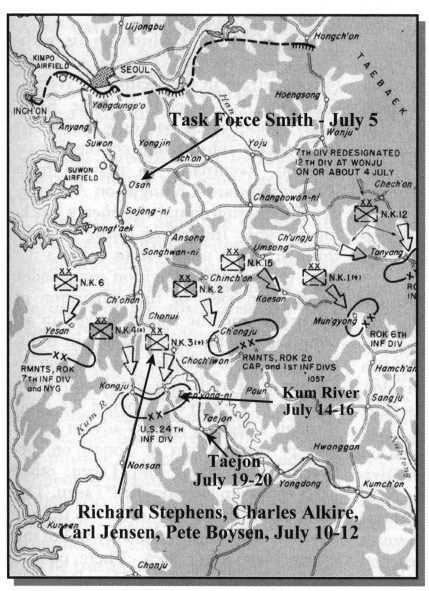

(Background map courtesy Center of Military History)

five of the eleven tanks were burning. Black smoke rose from the hills northwest of Chonui, and aerial observers reported about half of the 200 enemy vehicles north of Chonui were destroyed or burning.

Colonel Stephens to the Front

Richard Stephens joined Alkire and his men while the air bombardment was taking place and announced he would remain throughout the night. Security concerns prevented Homer Bigart from naming high-ranking field officers, so he referred to the South Dakotan as the *Old Man* when he wrote the colonel's presence brought a "noticeable boost in morale. Somehow, troops always feel [less] expendable when the Old Man is around, sticking his neck out just like any G.I."[28]

The air and artillery strikes had slowed the enemy considerably, and illumination from the burning city kept enemy advancement to a minimum throughout the night. But as the sun rose, a heavy ground fog lay before them.

Bigart jumped into a foxhole close to Colonel Stephens and thus provided a detailed account of what happened. The troops could hear, but not see, the North Koreans moving up.

"Not until 8 o'clock was the curtain lifted," wrote Bigart, "and by that time the enemy was in position to deal the death blow."

Between 15 and 20 tanks spearheaded the enemy attack, supported by 2,000-3,000 infantrymen. Four of the tanks breeched the forward positions and overran friendly mortar positions, forcing survivors to abandon not just their positions but also their weapons.

Stephens started calling for air support at 8:30, but it took three hours for the fighters to arrive. Meanwhile, North Koreans poured around both flanks and established road blocks to cut the Americans' routes of withdrawal.

In the 21st Regimental War Diary, Colonel Stephens reported: *"A" and "D" Companies held their ground admirably.*

About five hours into the fight, artillery fire was landing on the friendly units, and unfortunately it was coming from American positions. It appears artillerymen thought the front had been overrun, and they were intent on catching the enemy. Communication to the rear was compromised, so Stephens ran about a hundred yards to the rear to his radio jeep to call off the artillery. But it didn't work.

---

[28] *Winnipeg Free Press*. 10 July 1950. All Bigart quotes are from this article.

Shortly after, the isolated platoon west of the road reported they were surrounded. Most of these men were later found dead in their foxholes.

Homer Bigart reports it was five minutes past noon when Colonel Stephens finally ordered the task force to withdraw into the hills:

> He shouts an order that no small arms will be thrown way. "It's a long walk back, and we will probably meet the Communists on the way." On signal from the Old Man, we leapt from our holes and ran, crouching and dodging, across open ground to an orchard sloping down to rice paddies.

Charles Alkire in 1961 (Courtesy Gonzaga University Archives)

*Captain **Charles Alkire**, Infantry, United States Army, is awarded the **Silver Star** for gallantry. On 10 July 1950, near Chonui, Korea, Captain Alkire displayed gallantry in action while commanding Company D. Companies A and D were in defensive positions. They were subjected to intense fire from small arms, mortars and artillery, as well as infantry and armored attack by overwhelming numbers of the enemy. There were no weapons in the Company capable of destroying the enemy tanks. However, as a result of Captain Alkire's gallant example, his men remained in their positions in spite of direct attack by four tanks, which were from fifty to three hundred yards distant. By personally directing the fire effects of his command, Captain Alkire caused heavy casualties to the enemy. After his Company had been seriously depleted, he was ordered to withdraw. Passing the order onto his men, he personally directed the withdrawal and did not leave the position until every other man had escaped to safety. During the withdrawal, he constantly moved about the position in the face of extremely heavy fire. Due to his gallant and resourceful leadership, his company's mission was accomplished, and it was able to again enter combat with the enemy the next day.*

*Colonel **Richard W. Stephens** has been awarded the **Silver Star** by Major General William F. Dean for gallantry in action in Korea, the GHQ Public Information reported in a communique Friday. The citation said that on July 9 and 10, Colonel Stephens, as commanding officer of the 21st Infantry Regiment, by his "coolness under fire and personal leadership inspired the inexperienced officers and troops of elements of his command to effectively delay a determined attack conducted by numerically superior infantry and armored forces. Despite enemy fire, Colonel Stephens remained at front line positions during operations and*

Richard Stephens at West Point, 1924

personally directed the improvement of positions, placement of automatic weapons and the coordination of artillery and infantry fire. Learning that an enemy armored and infantry attack was imminent he returned to position and skillfully directed the conduct of the defense from an observation post in advance of the main defensive position. After his position had been surrounded on three sides by numerically superior forces of the enemy, he organized and conducted an orderly withdrawal to new defensive positions. He was the last man to leave the exposed and overrun position . . . (Stars & Stripes. 22 July 1950.)

Chapter 7

CHONUI TO CHOCHIWON

"The seats in Hell closest to the fire are for Army officers who knew the Bazooka didn't work and did not alert our soldiers to its inability to kill tanks, while keeping the larger, much more effective, 3.5-inch rocket launcher back in the States." Carl Bernard, 21st Regiment

CHARLES MUDGETT, JR., the 21st Regiment's executive officer (second in command), was at the port of Sasebo, Japan, at 3:00 a.m. on July 2. His immediate orders were to get his regiment's 3rd Battalion to Korea. (The 21st Regiment lacked its 2nd Battalion at this time.)

Carrying out his mission was complicated and all-consuming, so he was likely unaware of a news story running in Stateside papers that day. It would have deeply chilled him to know the ramifications of the report:

> Chinese Nationalist intelligence spotted approximately 200,000 Chinese Communist soldiers massing at the border between North Korea and China, and they appeared to be preparing to cross the border to support the North Korean troops.[29]

Failure by senior officials in Tokyo to take this and other such reports seriously would prove catastrophic several months into the future, but for the moment, Mudgett had his hands full with trying to find a way to transport an entire battalion to Korea without using aircraft.

The 40-year-old lieutenant colonel grew up in Valley City, North

---

[29] *Winona Republican-Herald.* 1 Jul 1950.

Dakota, and would go on to become a brigadier general after fighting in three different wars.

After graduating in 1933 from the University of North Dakota, Grand Forks, 6' 2" "Fritz" followed in his father's footsteps. Charles Mudgett Senior had commanded Company G, 1st North Dakota Volunteers, during the Philippine Insurrection (Spanish-American War) and was also decorated in WWI. The elder officer also served as a state senator, directed the Bank of North Dakota, and was appointed a U.S. Marshal by President Calvin Coolidge.

Fritz himself had fought as a battalion commander in Italy during WWII, receiving a Silver Star for gallantry in that war.

As for Korea, Mudgett disagreed with those who believed the upcoming "police action" would be short and simple. He felt the severe downsizing of the military after WWII had left American troops under-prepared, writing it was "sad, almost criminal, that such under-strength, ill-equipped and poorly-trained units were committed . . . " (It should be noted that other than raw recruits straight off the ships, many combat veterans of Korea object to the assessment that they were poorly trained.)

The 3rd Battalion arrived from Camp Wood, Japan, with seven or eight hundred men. Mudgett was able to get them out to sea the following morning only because he was able to commandeer three "filthy" Japanese freighters for their transport.

"It was a hell of a way to go to war," he said.[30]

Alexander Boysen

Doctor Alexander "Pete" Boysen did not learn until July 3 that he, too, was on his way to Korea. As a member of the Army Medical Corps, he was going into combat with the 21st Regiment's 3rd Battalion.

Born on Christmas Day, 1923, Pete grew up in Pelican Rapids, Minnesota, where among other things he became an Eagle Scout. Both of his parents were Danish, although his mother, Ellen, came to the States by way of China.

Boysen's father was a physician, and young Pete, although rebellious, followed in his footsteps. After getting his medical degree from the University of Minnesota in 1948, he accepted a commission from the Army and was assigned to Ft. Lewis, Washington, to begin a

---

[30] Blair, Clay. *The Forgotten War*. Anchor Books. 1989. P 93 & 96.

family practice residency – the military's first such program.

Like Dr. Edwin Overholt, who ended up in *Task Force Smith*, Boysen had volunteered for a 90-day tour of duty in Japan that spring. Boysen was promised he wouldn't be deployed beyond this stint in Japan, so he was similarly surprised when he was suddenly on his way to Korea. He later described the confusion of the situation:

> . . . routine processes involving leaving or transferring were non-existent. Personnel offices had been closed, Finance Officers were not operating, there was no chance to arrange for transportation of baggage, depositing of funds, or any of the normal things expected when changing posts.
>
> We were ordered to a briefing meeting at which time we were to meet a major who supposedly was sent to specifically brief us as to what the future meant. This was done by an Army Major who told us that we would be going into Seoul and to be sure to bring along all dress uniforms, civilian clothes, plenty of cameras, and that after the firefight was over we would be enjoying the peace and tranquility of South Korea.
>
> Following this, we promptly returned to our quarters, packed a field pack, placing the rest of our belongings in a foot locker to be sent home, changed our uniform to fatigues and, in effect, prepared to go to war. This is of interest mainly because of a tendency to not face reality. [. . .] It has been my experience that people are much more grateful for hard cold facts than they are for someone who misuses his sympathy and does not inform them with these realistic facts . . .[31]

Boysen caught up to the 3rd Battalion on July 6 outside of Pusan, Korea:

> We saw the results of the briefing Major's folly as we were bivouacked close to a barbed wire fence inclosure containing all of the goodies and the excess baggage that had been shipped with G.I.s and officers in a barbed wire inclosure, stacked twenty to thirty feet high. Troops were busy trying to find guns

---

[31] Letter LTC Alexander Boysen to 1LT David Wheeler, military historian, U.S. Army Medical Corps. 8 Dec 1965. Courtesy Research Collection, Office of Medical History, AMEDD Center of History and Heritage. Other info from Boysen's obituary, *Athens Banner-Herald*. 2 Apr 2002; Boysen *Written statement*, circa 1954, possibly a POW debriefing. Courtesy Dr. Dirk Boysen.

and ammunition. We were busy trying to locate guns, ammunition, and medicine. We had carried with us two "disaster chests" from the division in Hakada filled with worthless medications, long spoiled, and these had been sent to the bottom of the ocean . . .

We remained here that night, and the next morning was spent cussing at a pouring rain, trying to learn how to fire weapons, as well as holding a routine sick call. This was one 24 hours that began to explain the meaning of many arguments you had heard before. How many times had you heard medical students, interns and doctors tell you the futility of wasting your time at a medical field school? "Get your education first, the field work will come by itself." It may have, had you had someone to teach you at the time; the only catch was, there was no one to teach and no time to learn. You learned without reservation that as long as wars are possible and you wear a uniform, learn first to fight, then to practice medicine.

The evening was spent loading the train for a move north. We had managed to get about a dozen morphine syrettes and three or four bottles of penicillin to supplement our meager supply. Men had been stripped of all equipment except battle equipment while in Pusan. They continued to be apprehensive and wondered when and if they would receive more rifles and ammunition.

We slowly made our way northward, passing numerous trains headed south. Masses of human beings clung to any part of the train that was big enough to hold a hand.

On occasional stops, our canteens were filled with hot water or tea made by the local civilians. One small village had the entire population out, including their band, to wish us luck.

About noon we reached Taejon and met American officers who had preceded us. They had little information except that we were to go about twenty miles north by train and take up positions there.

By 1500 hours in the afternoon, we had talked to some South Korean soldiers who were looking for guns, food and more diligently, for a way south, and were on our way east of the village of [Chochiwon] to set up a position. By dusk we were back in town, having set up on the wrong road. The "gooks" were not coming on that road but on another road directly north.

This was to be our Waterloo in the next 72 hours.

Carl "Cliff" Jensen

Lieutenant Colonel Carl Jensen, 38, was the commanding officer of Doc Boysen's 3rd Battalion, 21st Regiment.[32]

Jensen grew up in Kimball, South Dakota, where his Danish immigrant parents ran a creamery. Carl, better known as "Cliff," graduated from high school in 1929 and went on to attend South Dakota State College in Brookings.

Jensen's daughter, Barbara Vanek, recalls her father as "brilliant, handsome and a born leader." Although she was young at the time, she remembers her father working in an agriculture-related job and believes the family lived in several North Dakota towns including Carrington, Fessenden, Devils Lake, Fargo and possibly Harvey.

When WWII came about, Jensen entered the Army from Carrington. Because he had completed Reserve Officer Training Corps (ROTC) in college, he was activated as an officer.

Jensen was not a combat soldier in WWII. Instead, he participated in a unique mission to establish a secret base in Greenland, where extreme weather, terrain and shifting ice packs limited travel choices to planes, skis and dogsleds.

In the summer of 1941, months before the bombing of Pearl Harbor, American forces realized the world's largest island would be "an essential springboard for any Nazi air-and-sea assault on the North American continent."[33]

But domination of Greenland was essential for another reason, as well – knowledge of Greenland's weather allowed the Allies to determine when conditions would be optimal for air strikes on Germany. Therefore, weather stations were needed there.

Because visibility was so poor, it wasn't learned until 1943 that the Germans, too, had established a secret weather station. Theirs was on Sabine Island, just off Greenland's east coast.

Ordered to destroy the enemy facility, the Army Air Force

---

[32] Clay Blair states the 3rd Battalion commander was Del Pryor, saying Pryor choked and had to be replaced by Jensen. The regimental war diary doesn't support this.

[33] Balchen, Bernt Balchen, et el. *War Below Zero*. Houghton Mifflin: 1944.

undertook the very first bombing of German installations on the west side of the Atlantic. This mission was also the farthest north the Air Force had ever attempted a bombing raid. On May 25, 1943, U.S. planes successfully destroyed the German facility and scored a bonus strike on a 300-ton German supply trawler that had frozen into the ice.

After 11 months in Greenland, Jensen was transferred to Italy for the remainder of WWII. After the war, he returned to North Dakota, where he spent about a year in Fessenden before choosing the Army as his career. By the time the Korean War broke out, he had risen through the ranks to become a lieutenant colonel.

Jensen at Chonui

On July 9, when Charles Alkire's *Task Force A* was engaging the enemy at Chonui, Cliff Jensen's 3rd Battalion was digging in behind them and registering its heavy weapons.

The following day, when Stephens gave the order for *Task Force A* to withdraw from Chonui, he simultaneously ordered his fellow South Dakotan to bring up his 3rd Battalion to counterattack and recapture the lost ground. This Jensen did, and that afternoon his men regained most of the positions, as well as weapons that had earlier been lost.

*The **Distinguished Service Cross** is awarded to Lieutenant Colonel **Carl Clifford Jensen**, [who] distinguished himself by extraordinary heroism in action against enemy aggressor forces at Chonui, Korea, on 10 July 1950. On that date, when a numerically superior enemy force, supported by artillery and armor, attacked the 3rd Battalion's position, Colonel Jensen displayed outstanding leadership ability and personal courage. He voluntarily exposed himself to the intense artillery, mortar, and small-arms fire and reorganized small groups of withdrawing troops and replaced them in the defense line. By his calmness under extremely heavy enemy fire, he inspired his men to the highest possible degree of determination and*

(Courtesy Barbara Vanek)

confidence. When the order to withdraw was issued, Colonel Jensen remained behind and personally directed the withdrawal of all units of his Battalion. When the withdrawal was complete, he himself began to withdraw from the forward position, collecting stragglers as he withdrew. As he led his small group of stragglers from the forward positions, they were pinned down by heavy enemy automatic weapons fire. Colonel Jensen once more exposed himself to the enemy fire, placing his men in positions from where the most effective fire could be delivered. He himself then took up a position and attempted to destroy as many enemy as possible. His utter disregard for personal safety, his exceptional leadership ability, courage, and devotion to duty, were directly responsible for saving the lives of many of the men in his command.

LTC Jensen (in sunglasses) in Korea. The only available maps were printed in Japanese. (Courtesy Barbara Vanek)

Jensen's men also rescued ten trapped soldiers and discovered the first known atrocities committed by the North Koreans against captured Americans. Lieutenant D.C. Gates told a reporter: "When I arrived on the spot, I found my four men and three mortar men, their hands tied behind them and a bullet fired into each face."[34]

This news spread like wildfire, and for every soldier who heard about it, the war became suddenly personal. And surrendering was no longer an option.

Jensen and his men held the recaptured ground at Chonui the rest of the day, July 10, finally withdrawing from the ridge just before midnight.

When they returned to their previous positions north of Chochiwon, they were surprised by enemy soldiers who had taken over foxholes in K Company's positions. After battling another hour, the North Koreans were finally booted out, and the exhausted men of the 3rd Battalion collapsed where they stood.

As it turns out, it was a tragic mistake to remain in these positions, because the enemy now had intimate knowledge of the battalion's layout. As had happened to Charles Alkire the previous morning, enemy tanks advanced through thick fog at dawn on July 11. Perfectly coordinated mortar fire started falling on the battalion's positions, and within a very short time, Jensen and his men were surrounded by approximately 1,000 enemy soldiers.

Captain Leon Rainville, a World War II veteran from St. Paul, was later interviewed by war correspondent Keyes Beech, of the *Chicago Daily News*:

We could hear their tanks moving up into position in our rear. They had automatic weapons and they brought their infantry up to the front in trucks. The firing first broke out on our right flank, then on our left, then in our rear. I was up on the hill at the observation post when [Colonel Jensen] ordered me down to get more mortar ammo. I went down but never got back up.

Ralph "Eli" Culbertson, of Love Company, relates:

We were surrounded and attacked with direct charges up the hill to our fox holes. Our [Company Commander], Capt. Odean

---

[34] *The Fargo Forum*. 10 Jul 1950.

Cox, ordered me to call the Command Post and report our situation. Col. Jensen ordered us to hold our positions at all costs. We fought off repeated assaults until about 10:00 a.m. I telephoned Lt. Jacques, Bn S-3, and was informed to withdraw the best we could. Capt. Cox ordered me to take the men at the company command post while he went to get Lt. Mitchell and his platoon. We fixed our bayonets at the [command post] to take as many of the enemy as we could . . .

We could see the men from K Company being shot and killed as they tried to escape by crossing the river. It was like shooting ducks in a gallery. I presented to Lt. Jacques a plan of following the river south, using the bank as a cover, as a means to withdraw. He agreed. We told the men of the plan. I was to lead and Lt. Jacques was to bring up the rear. I never saw Lt. Jacques again.

We continued downstream for about 200 more yards and came to another, yet wider, opening in the river bank. Here I saw about twenty [North Korean] soldiers about five feet away, pointing their rifles directly at ten of us who had made it that far. We then became prisoners of war.[35]

Second Lieutenant Carl Bernard, from Borger, Texas, headed west with a handful of men, later saying: "We were defending against what the official history later called 'one of the most perfectly coordinated assaults ever launched by North Koreans against American troops.' Our defense was later described as 'the most impressive performance yet of American troops in Korea.' Small comfort to the company's men, given its costs. Hell, no, we didn't hold. I lost nearly 101 men killed or captured out of a rifle company of 130 people. Thirty-three men died in captivity."[36]

Lieutenant Edward James, of Columbus, Georgia, was just as angry as Bernard, telling Keyes Beech, "Tell people how *(blank)* useless it is. I have been in the army eight years, and I've never fought without flanks."

The official 21st Regiment War Diary reads:

---

[35] Culbertson, Ralph E. "The Korean War – A Former POW's Story." *Ex-POW Bulletin.* March 1993. Web: 18 Feb 2010. www.lovecompany.org/pdfs/LoveBook.pdf.

[36] *Newsweek Magazine.* 8 March 1999. P 57.

The enemy tanks moved directly through the Battalion area and the infantry flanked both sides of the position in a double envelopment. As the attack progressed, enemy infantry increased in number to an estimated 2,500. Heavy Mortar fire continued to fall throughout the attack, seemingly concentrated in the Battalion at the Command Post area, blowing up the Battalion ammunition supply point, communications center and inflicting heavy casualties on Battalion Headquarters personnel. The Battalion held their ground until they were completely surrounded. Roads to the rear were cut off and there could be no resupply of ammunition or evacuation of the wounded. Approximately four hours from the time the attack started, the Third Battalion began to fight their way southward toward Chochiwon in small groups.

As the battered remnants of the Third Battalion began to assemble in the vicinity of Chochiwon shortly after noon, it was found that the Battalion Commander, Lt. Colonel Carl Jensen; the S-1, 1st Lt. William Cashour; S-2, 1st Lt. William Jester; S-3, 1st Lt. Leon Jacques and the Commanding Officer of Company "L", Captain O'Dean Cox, were missing in action. Through the following days hope remained high that these gallant officers who remained behind to direct the final operations of their command would return. But no official information has been received as to their whereabouts or fate.

Boysen is Captured

Following the disaster north of Chochiwon, it was eventually determined that Colonel Carl Jensen had been killed in action. But nobody knew until later the young physician from Minnesota was captured. As one of the fortunate few who survived the war, Pete Boysen wrote about the fighting and his capture:

A porch of a mud hut became my bed for a few hours before I was awakened by one of my medics. Our orders had been changed, and we were to go back. He explained to me that his men had found him a jeep and they were able to gather up some supplies from another unit and was prepared to go back in. They had 3 carbines, and we could shoot while we went through the valley we had come out of.

Besides all of that, *I heard a company screaming for medics on the radio, they are my buddies Doc, and we have got to help them in any way we can. I know they say it's a suicide mission, Doc, but my buddies are there and need us.*

I listened and tried to gather my wits. It was not that I had not been in pressure plays before, a rebellious student, ship jumping while an ordinary seaman, a history of telling the world that I could survive on my own, but was I up to this new development?

The thoughts raced through my head as the medic begged me to go if he would. It all came into play, a mission with no return, why me, the promise by the Medical Corp that I would not be shipped from Yokohama if I volunteered to go (to Japan), few letters from home since leaving, and why did this all have to be!

But if I didn't go, could I face my new enlisted friends, my own friends at home, or more important, could I face my family and myself? My God had been good to me throughout my escapades, surely he wasn't about to let me down now. My answer came quickly but not easily, as I said a prayer and joined my medic in his jeep that was headed north on a "suicide mission."

I wondered why there was no guidance from other medical officers, questioning where they were, and why we had not seen or heard from anyone connected to the division medics. No one had seen them, and they were supposed to still be in Taejon waiting for reinforcements.

I really had no idea of what was going on when we were stopped by the MPs at the base of the mountain ridge. We were told not to go back since the other side of the mountain was loaded with gooks and they were "thick as flies" waiting for morning. We argued, and they finally conceded that we were going to go on, so they began giving us the "lay of the land," explaining to us the area where we would receive fire, and how to coast quietly down one area and then "give her hell" until you reach another larger hill.

They were right, and as we gunned the jeep for all it had, the tracers flew by us as we emptied carbines up on to the ridges. A fast and rough ride but we made it. The driver was proud of his accomplishment as he excitedly recounted his skill in keeping the jeep upright when it careened on two wheels after hitting a hole in the road. He was entitled to every compliment he received!!

We arrived back at the site of our aid station. It was a mass of rubble. Wounded men were lying around, so we dressed their wounds as best we could, stopping every vehicle going south to load them on it. I wonder if they made it back. At least the driver knew what he had to do and was confident he could run it one more time.[37]

The enemy attacked at dawn, and Boysen was unable to get out, writing:

An attempt was made to take walking wounded and stretcher cases out. We were unsuccessful in this and we were under heavy machine gun and mortar fire, and eventually it was every man for himself.

Groups of us made it across the machine gun crossfire,

Boysen is the tall blond officer behind the American officer who is arguing with their North Korean guards. (Courtesy Boysen family)

---

[37]Letter: LTC Alexander Boysen to 1LT David Wheeler, military historian, U.S. Army Medical Corps. 8 Dec 1965. Research Collection, Office of Medical History, AMEDD Center of History and Heritage. Also Boysen account to his family.

crossing a river and a railroad track and waiting for the firing to stop. The troops involved were without fire power whatsoever. Men had guns and no ammunition, and the reverse existed. There was no artillery or mortar fire present.

The entire area was overrun . . . the old trick of playing possum worked and several hours later, I was able to take off alone into the mountains only to run into [an enemy] patrol 24 to 48 hours later. I was taken with the troops for a matter of days forward and eventually ending up, however, with most of the prisoners of the 21st Regiment and 34th Regiment of the 24th Division, in Seoul, eventually in Pyongyang.

Boysen later ended up in the Tiger Death March. Because the communists provided little to no medical care, Boysen and other captured medics, at great risk to themselves, secretly cared for fellow prisoners. They even practiced rudimentary surgery by fashioning tools from whatever could be scrounged, including a crude scalpel made from the steel arch support of a combat boot.

Close of Week One

Following the loss of Cliff Jensen and his 3rd Battalion, Colonel Stephens brought back Brad Smith and his 1st Battalion to once again delay the North Koreans. But July 12 brought another overwhelming attack through the morning fog. With his men hopelessly outnumbered, Stephens contacted General William Dean, commander of the 24th Division, at noon:

Am surrounded. 1st Battalion left giving way. Situation bad on right. Having nothing left to establish intermediate delaying position am forced to withdraw to river line. I have issued instructions to withdraw.

Late that afternoon, Richard Stephens' 21st Regiment – which should have numbered some 6,000 men – was down to roughly 325. Only 64 survivors from Cliff Jensen's 3rd Battalion were still able to fight.[38]

These sacrificial lambs had managed to stall the enemy for three critical days, for which they have never been adequately recognized.

---

[38] Appleman. *South to the Naktong.* P 99.

War correspondent Frank Conniff, a veteran reporter of WWII actions, arrived in Korea two weeks later. And even though the numbers of American fighters had tripled by then, he was shaken by what he encountered:

> ... our troops are fighting with bravery and skill against odds so desperate that the American people can even now hardly comprehend the bitter days that still lie ahead. . . . Never in recent American history have so few been asked to accomplish so much with so little. [. . .] But no outfit in the world can juggle 10, 20 and 50 opponents for each of its own personnel and still hold the line. . . . If this is merely a "police action" give me a nice, tidy, well run war.[39]

*The **Distinguished Service Cross** is awarded to **Colonel Richard W. Stephens**, (Infantry) U. S. Army, for extraordinary heroism . . . in action against enemy aggressor forces near Chochiwon, Korea, during the period from 9 through 13 July 1950. During the early stages of the Korean conflict, Colonel Stephens was assigned the mission of delaying the advance of the North Korean People's Army pending the buildup of United Nations forces for a counteroffensive. Making a personal reconnaissance of the area, he chose a delaying site in the hills north of Chochiwon, where he personally directed the construction of defensive positions and emplacement of automatic weapons, mortars and supporting artillery. When the enemy assault on the delaying position began, he, seemingly oblivious of the intense enemy fire, moved forward of the regiment's main line of resistance and established an observation post from which he directed the defense of his regiment's positions. When the observation post was encircled by the enemy, he organized a few men into a combat group and personally led them in an audacious attack on an enemy of overwhelming strength, successfully breaking out of the encirclement and reaching friendly lines. During the entire engagement, he exploited every possible means of stemming the enemy advance and his courage, fearless bearing, and aggressive leadership were largely responsible for the magnificent delaying action fought by his hopelessly outnumbered troops. (This award supercedes Stephens' previously awarded Silver Star.)*

---

[39] Conniff, Frank. *Tyrone Daily Herald.* 26 July 1950.

Chapter 8

DEVELOPMENTS IN THE SKIES

"All through the night, B-26 light bombers and rocket-carrying fighters took off at regular intervals. They roared over the area between Pyongtaek and Chonan and let the northerners have it."
William Jorden, reporter

ONE BRIGHT SPOT emerged during the first bleak week of the war. It started about the time Cliff Jensen's 3rd Battalion was recapturing lost ground at Chonui. Twenty-five air miles to the north, American fliers dropped down out of the clouds and had a field day, as described by Army historian Roy Appleman:

On the afternoon of 10 July American air power had one of its great moments in the Korean War. Late in the afternoon, [they] found a large convoy of tanks and vehicles stopped bumper to bumper on the north side of a destroyed bridge. Upon receiving a report of this discovery, the Fifth Air Force rushed every available plane to the scene – B-26's, F-80's, and F-82's – in a massive air strike. Observers of the strike reported that it destroyed 38 tanks, 7 halftrack vehicles, 117 trucks, and a large number of enemy soldiers. This report undoubtedly exaggerated unintentionally the amount of enemy equipment actually destroyed. But this strike, and that of the previous afternoon near Chonui, probably resulted in the greatest destruction of enemy armor of any single action in the war.[40]

---

[40] *South to the Naktong.* P 94-95.

During this 24-hour foray, reporter William Jorden hitched a ride on one of four bombers led by Captain Allen Blum, who grew up on a farm near Ashland, Nebraska. Blum, a champion skeet shooter, joined the Army Air Corps in 1942 and flew active missions in the South Pacific during WWII.[41]

Blum's formation took off from Japan that afternoon, with each plane carrying a thousand-pound bomb. Jorden writes:

> When we took off, we knew we were going to the Chonan area and that we were going to work over North Korean concentrations reported there. But we were told to contact American observers in the target area to get our specific target.
>
> As we neared the target area we heard odd snatches of conversation over the radio from the planes already working over the enemy.
>
> "You're too far south. Go north of Chonui and give 'em hell," an excited observer instructed some fighters.
>
> "What happened to that man that was flying off my right wing?" a pilot called out. "He's right behind you and above," another answered. "Roger. I see him."
>
> One fighter pilot roared over the enemy and then shouted, "I got two rocket hits on that first tank. Did you see it?"
>
> "Good boy," a liaison man answered. "Give 'em hell."
>
> An observer plane had spotted a group of Red tanks along the road just north of Chonui. That's where we were told to put our bomb load.[42]

John Murphy

Directing aircraft in close air support in the mountains of Korea was extremely difficult, and the liaisons/observers referred to by Jorden were key to why the air runs on July 10 were more successful than in previous days. Much of the credit for this goes to a North Dakota man.

Lieutenant Colonel John R. Murphy, Fifth Air Force, was born in Minot in 1918. He grew up in Fargo, and after stints at North Dakota State University and Notre Dame, he was appointed to the United

---

[41] Blum obituary, *Kansas City Star*. 2 Oct 2005.

[42] Jorden, William. *Charleston Daily Mail*. 10 July 1950.

States Military Academy at West Point. After graduating in 1942, he received flight training with the Army Air Corps, and he logged 305 combat hours flying a P-47 Thunderbolt over Europe during WWII. Decorated numerous times, he received the Silver Star for unflinching performance over Germany:

*The **Silver Star** is awarded to Lieutenant Colonel **John R. Murphy**, Air Corps, 365th Fighter Group for gallantry in action on 21 October 1944. On this date, Lieutenant Colonel Murphy led three squad runs on a highly successful fighter sweep in the Bonn-Dusseldorf area. Under his skillful direction, the squadrons engaged two formations of more than thirty enemy aircraft each, and in the course of each engagement, Lieutenant Colonel Murphy destroyed one enemy aircraft. During the course of the two engagements under his brilliant leadership the group destroyed twenty-one enemy aircraft, probably destroyed one, and damaged an additional eleven.*
(Ninth Air Force GO 48, 27 March 1945)

A younger pilot who flew with Murphy later said:

> Colonel Murphy was a lead-by-example type. He always led the group when the target was the most heavily defended. He was a leader but also a teacher/professor for young officers. After listening to comments from staff or subordinates, he would make his decision and, typically at that point, explain his decision rationale that was very instructive for junior officers. His decisions were based on conviction, not opinion of the moment or what he thought his boss might want. If he was under pressure from his superiors (and we knew at the time he was) he never passed that pressure down. The buck stopped with John Murphy.[43]

Communicating via Mosquitos

By the end of October 1950, Murphy would be commanding the 49th Fighter-Bomber Group, the first such unit to receive the Presidential

---

[43] *Lt. Gen. John R. Murphy biography, U.S. Air Force.* 15 Jan 1974; West Point memorial. http://apps.westpointaog.org/Memorials/Article/12949/: 15 May 3013. In WWII, Murphy commanded 388th Squadron, was Deputy commander 365th Fighter Group, and commanded 404th Fighter Group, flying 139 missions. Murphy's final military duty before retiring was Chief of Staff, U.S. Forces, Korea.

Unit Citation in Korea. The 49th was also the first jet fighter group to completely move its operations to Korea, rather than flying its missions from Japan.[44] But all of this happened later. Murphy's first mission in Korea was accomplished from the ground.

It happened when Murphy, with nine officers and 35 men from the 8th Communications Squadron, moved from Japan to Taejon, Korea, July 5-6 to set up a Joint Operations Center with the 24th Division. The plan was for the air force and army to develop a better method for directing air strikes in support of ground fighters. Up to that point, almost no means existed for directing air strikes from the ground.

Murphy and his men found themselves quite alone in the "joint" venture, as the situation on the ground was so fluid and chaotic that their 24th Division counterparts often could not say *where* their combat troops were at any given time.

Since aircraft had to be flown all the way from Japan, any strikes called in from the front lines could be completely changed by the time the planes arrived – and poor communication equipment (estimated to be faulty 75% of the time) often meant losing contact between the men in the air and the ground observer.

To deal with this, the commander of the Fifth Air Force started sending over F-80 fighter jets every 20 minutes when daylight and weather allowed. If immediate targets could not be identified, the planes kept flying north to hit "targets of opportunity."

On June 28, the air force had tried to set up two Forward Air Control (FAC) teams in Korea. Each team consisted of an experienced pilot and several other airmen using jeeps and jeep-mounted radios left over from WWII. Because there was no method for operating these radios remotely, these teams were hampered by several problems.

First, if a radio gave out, the entire jeep would need to be replaced by driving back to Taejon. This happened frequently, as these radios were fragile, and the rough terrain of Korean roads shook them to pieces.[45]

Second – also because the radios were attached to the jeeps – there was no way to observe enemy positions without exposing each team and its jeep to the full view of the enemy. Again, there was no option for

---

[44] *Pacific Stars & Stripes.* 13 Jan 1951; 2 Apr 1951.

[45] Ent, Uzal W. *Fighting on the Brink: Defense of the Pusan Perimeter.* Paducah, KY: Turner Publishing. 1996: p 121-122.

operating the radios remotely, so this job was exceptionally dangerous.

The official history of the Air Force in Korea indicates nobody is completely certain who came up with the idea to use spotter planes instead of FAC teams on the ground. But the credit appears to go to John Murphy.

On July 9, Murphy requested an operations officer and five pilots to fly reconnaissance missions in Korea. Two pilots, James A. Bryant and Frank G. Mitchell, came over with two L-5G liaison planes. Their radios were modified so they could accommodate four-channel VHF radios, but the radios weren't working. So they borrowed rides on two L-17s that were flying for the 24th Division.

Throughout the remainder of the day, Bryant and Mitchell each identified ten enemy targets during their reconnaissance missions. Normally, their reports would have been handled from the ground, but using their aircraft's radios, they were allowed to directly contact airborne jet fighters, and the resulting air-strikes were carried out with excellent results.

Another discovery took place when Bryant's plane was attacked by two YAK fighters. The smaller plane was able to deftly evade being hit.

John Murphy declared it "the best day in Fifth Air Force history," and a system was quickly developed in which T-6 pilots would receive pre-mission briefings, and once they were airborne, they would scout for likely targets. If the pilot spotted something – perhaps a camouflaged enemy tank – he would call fighters or bombers to the site and guide them directly to the target, often at great peril to himself.

On July 15, three such spotter planes were given code names beginning with the word Mosquito. The name stuck, and all spotter planes eventually became known simply as *Mosquitos*.

Alexander Macdonald

"Alex" Macdonald later became The Adjutant General of North Dakota, but as a young pilot, he flew a Mosquito in Korea. He started life in Braddock, North Dakota, where his dad operated a grain elevator, and his mother was a school teacher. Sadly, she died from complications from a tubal pregnancy when Alex was just two years old.

"Of course at that time, things were a lot different," he said. "That was 1931. My aunt and my grandparents came for her funeral, and they brought me home and raised me on their farm outside of Davenport, North Dakota.

"My dad came down here and worked around, and subsequently got remarried. He had three additional children, but I never lived with him and my stepmother. I was always with my aunt and my grandparents. They all ended up living in Davenport, including my dad and his three kids."

When asked how he ended up flying, Macdonald said, "During WWII, I was enthralled with the whole thing, because I was just a kid. But after I got out of high school and was going to NDSU [then North Dakota Agricultural College], I'd be out working on the farm in the summer time. The North Dakota Air National Guard had started in 1948, so I'd see them practicing up there in the air. And that seemed like the kind of thing I'd like to do. I had flown with my uncle, who was in the Civil Air Patrol, and I loved it. That's how it started."

Macdonald took part in Reserve Officer Training Corp at NDSU but dropped out after his sophomore year, because they were Army only. He wanted to fly, so in 1951 he joined the Air National Guard.

"I went off to train in Wisconsin, and it was kind of a funny deal. I was the assistant for the crew chief of the F-51. He didn't like to get up in the morning, so he checked me out on how to go out and conduct pre-flight and get it warmed up so the pilots could fly it. I did that for about a week and decided, *Gee whiz, how come they get to have all the fun, and I gotta do all the work?* So I went in and found out I could join the Air Force and go for pilot training.

"After I got out of pilot training, I served a year with the unit, and I went to Korea from there. I went over as a P-51 pilot, but by the time I got there, they didn't need P-51 pilots. I didn't have any jet time, so the only place I could go, without an extensive training schedule, was to the Mosquitos. I was with the 6147th TCG (Tactical Control Group). We flew the two-seat T-6. It was a 180-mph single-engine airplane that was used to train pilots. That's the first plane I ever flew when I was in the Air Force. It was good for handling enemy attacks."

Mosquito pilots flew roughly 20 missions, and then they alternately spent 90 days on the front lines calling in air strikes for the Army.

"We were right up at the forward observation positions," he said. "When we served in forward air control, we had our own men as radio operators, not infantrymen. Depending on what we were doing, we'd have to find a good position. We'd usually go up with the artillery observers – that was always a good place to go. You could see a lot. But normally, we were a ways back from them, because we had to set up radio antennas. We'd have a radio jeep with all our radio equipment, and it was a little hard for us to get too far out."

When Macdonald got to Korea in 1953, the program was still using the basic Mosquitos, but they were now outfitted with weaponry. "We put rocket rails on the plane to carry white phosphorous rockets. We used them to mark targets if people couldn't see them or the artillery couldn't put smoke on them with some of their white phosphorous. We would go in with FAC (Forward Air Control) airplanes and show them exactly where the targets were.

"We were out there all by ourselves. The front was split up into five areas, and you had a Mosquito in each one of those areas from sunrise to sunset. We'd be in contact with the army, and if the Army had a target, we'd try to get airplanes in.

"Sometimes the airplanes would come up, and we'd ask them if they had a target. If they gave us some coordinates, we'd go over, circle around and take a closer look. And they would come in and drop ordnance on that target.

"Once in awhile, we'd act as spotters for the Navy. The Navy would come in with the *USS Missouri* and lob their big guns. We'd watch the explosion, and then afterwards we'd go in and give them an assessment. *Well, you hit the target. You didn't hit the target. Here's what you destroyed or damaged* or whatever."

Macdonald flew 36 missions in Korea. "Those last months, the enemy realized the war was going to stop. So they got rid of everything. They shot artillery, I couldn't believe – just tons of it. Up to that time, they'd been fairly sparing. During the last mission I was in, I saw more anti-aircraft than I had ever seen before. I never got hit, but I had some close calls. One of my enlisted guys was killed standing right in front of me. But as for myself, nothing ever did touch me."[46]

---

[46] Macdonald, Alexander. USAF Major General (ret.) Author interview 25 Spt 2011.

Chapter 9

MISDIRECTION AND TRUTH

"The swiftness with which reinforcements were rushed to the scene once the crisis was recognized is a tribute to the resourcefulness of the United States Army, Navy, and Air Force. It cannot make up for the men who are dead and who might at least have had a fighting chance to live had we been prepared."
Maggie Higgins, war correspondent

"CASUALTIES EXAGGERATED," read a July 13 headline. This startling statement, issued by General MacArthur's Headquarters, reads:

> Losses sustained by the American forces in Korea have been greatly exaggerated in press reports from the front. This is the result of an experiment being tried perhaps for the first time in modern combat; that of avoiding any military censorship or undue restriction of the movements of war correspondents.
>
> Reports of warfare are, at any time, grisly and repulsive and reflect the emotional strain normal to those unaccustomed to the sights and sounds of battle. Exaggerated stories obtained from individuals wounded or mentally shocked have given a completely distorted and mis-representative picture to the public.
>
> The total American losses to the present time are less than 500, amounting to 42 killed, 190 wounded and 256 missing. Many of the missing are undoubtedly men who in the confusion of fighting have lost touch with their own units and will eventually return.

This press release was rather bizarre. Declassified records confirm casualties at that time were more than double – possibly triple – what MacArthur stated.

Some suggest his motive for this misdirection was political. Others say the general was trying to keep Washington from shying away from aggressive action. Either way, just one week later, the 24th Division's handful of surviving commanders could account for only 8,660 of 15,965 soldiers who were initially committed to combat.[47]

Under normal wartime circumstances, the 24th Division would have been pulled out, probably to Japan, to rebuild. But circumstances were anything but normal.

Meanwhile, correspondents continued to report the realities facing the troops. Stunned recriminations were boundless: the government had allowed the military to fall into a pitiful state of preparedness, and boys on the ground were paying the price.

Marguerite "Maggie" Higgins spoke at a forum conducted by her newspaper, the *New York Herald Tribune*. Willowy, smart and beautiful, Higgins was legendary among the G.I.s who had the great fortune of spotting her on the battlefield. (Her beauty aside, Higgins fought hard to gain a woman's right to report from the front lines, and she earned a Pulitzer Prize for her work.)

Higgins was among the very first correspondents to land in Korea, and she was at Chochiwon the day South Dakotan Cliff Jensen was killed, stating:

> Unpreparedness is hearing a battalion commander like Colonel Jensen bitterly predicting on a hilltop observation post: "This position will be untenable in 24 hours," and hearing his operations officer interrupt with, "No, sir, about 24 minutes. Enemy tanks are breaking through."
>
> Nor do I ever want to talk again to an embittered young American like Lt. Edward James of Columbus, Georgia, who, after seeing his outfit decimated by the Communists, asked us, "How can the United States throw us into such a useless, hopeless battle with so little to back us?"

Higgins' comments were reprinted in an editorial in the *Peoria Journal Star*, which also published a revealing letter from a gold star mother:

---

[47] *HQ 21ˢᵗ Infantry Regiment Unit Report No. 6: 131700 July to 141700 July 1950.*

He was on the front line for 25 days straight, lost 82 pounds in that length of time. He weighed 192 pounds when he went across; when he was killed he only weighed 110 pounds. He said he had but very little to eat and was sleeping in mud. I just can't get over it.[48]

Higgins' example of troop support was unfortunately countered by others that were hurtful – and those negative sentiments would plague Korean War veterans for decades to come. Sadly, these came from their older comrades in arms, with various veterans of WWII declaring this new generation of soldiers was substandard, because they were losing ground. Those who indulged in this line of thinking were disregarding the reality that troops in Korea were initially there for the sole purpose of delaying the enemy until more troops arrived. There simply weren't yet enough men for counterattacks or offensives.

Arrival of General Walker

One of the most important developments in this dark period took place July 13, when Lieutenant General Walton Walker arrived in Korea to take over ground operations as commander of Eighth Army.

A veteran of both WWI and WWII, he had commanded XX Corps in General George Patton's Third Army, and with good reason, Patton referred to Walker as "my toughest son of a bitch."

Walker was plain-spoken, compact, barrel chested, and ferocious – qualities that led many to refer to him as "Bull Dog."

---

[48] "Price of Unpreparedness." Editorial, *Peoria Journal.* Undated clipping.

Chapter 10

DONALD LeMATTY & JAMES BOLT

"When we went into Europe, our units were trained. We were equipped. We were not suffering. In WWII, we were not overwhelmed with an enemy except, of course, the Battle of the Bulge. But no comparison. Korea was much worse." Leonard Becicka, 29th and 35th Regiments

Donald LeMatty (Courtesy Keokuk High School)

CORPORAL DONALD LEMATTY, 21, disappeared July 14, 1950. Two years earlier, he was freshly graduated from high school in Keokuk, Iowa, where his father Alfred was a barber. Donald participated in track, football, K Club and Hi-Y and was, in short, a quintessential small town boy. His experience is used here to represent thousands of men who went missing in Korea.

Most of the missing have largely faded from view, some of them forever. But for many such soldiers, there can sometimes be found one veteran who cannot forget or let go – a veteran who makes it his mission to bring the fates of the missing to light. In the case of Donald LeMatty, that person is James Bolt, a fellow member of the 63rd Field Artillery Battalion.

LeMatty was in Battery A (Able), and Bolt was in Battery B (Baker). They didn't know each other, but they went through hell together. Their battalion was largely wiped out near the Kum River, where the 24th Division was staging another action to delay the North Koreans, and by sharing his story, James Bolt provides a background by which to remember LeMatty. He begins with problems they faced while still training in Japan prior to the war.

> I was assigned as the number-two man on the number-three Howitzer. My job was to load the shell into the Howitzer tube, and then remove the spent shell casings and reload after the shell had fired. If they were firing a time fuse, I had to check to be sure the time was correct before I loaded the shell. I spent four weeks in the field learning how to be part of an artillery unit. This was hard, because we were so short-handed. Most crews had five men in the crew, but the TOE (regulations) called for 14 men in a crew.
>
> Because of the shortage of funds for spare parts, we did the best we could with what we had to do it with. We held things in place with wire and tape (we used a lot of it). Just to do a day's training took half the night to be sure we could move out in the morning. We had to take parts off the mess truck or use the ammunition truck as the prime mover for the Howitzer.[49]

The 63rd was providing support for the 34th Regiment. Artillery positions were typically far to the rear of the main line of resistance, so it might be assumed they were less likely to be in direct contact with the enemy. Such was not the case for Bolt and LeMatty. Bolt writes:

> The 24th Division was under strength; we received replacements from the 1st Cavalry, and the 7th and 25th Divisions. By the morning of [July] 21st, most of them would be either dead or missing in action. We didn't even learn their first names.

Like the infantry units, the artillery units didn't have enough manpower to prevent them from being surrounded. And if they had to fall back, their ability to support the infantrymen with artillery fire disappeared.

---

[49] Bolt, James. Interview with Lynitta Brown, 2006. Web: 14 Aug 2010. http://www.koreanwar-educator.org/memoirs/bolt_james/#GoodLife. (Reprinted by permission.); Bolt's "Cannoneer Korea: My Time with the 63rd Artillery in July 1950." *Taro Leaf.* 24th Inf. Div. Assn. Vol. 61, P 41-43. (By permission.)

They were also plagued by communication malfunctions. Bolt writes:

> Our field radio batteries lasted about two hours, then they had
> to be replaced. They were made in 1942-1945. Without
> communications, the commander could not move his unit to
> the places that they were needed. One can be brave, but not
> suicidal.

The 34th Infantry and the 63rd Artillery were in constant action from July
7 to 11. At that point, they were ordered to cross the Kum River, the

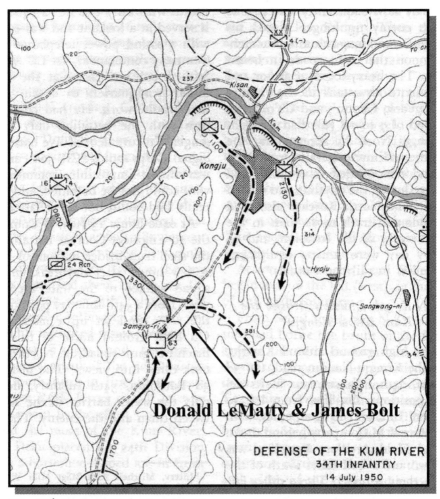

**The 34th Regiment was holding the northwest corner of the Kum River
perimeter when it was struck from both the north and the northwest.**
(Inset courtesy Center of Military History)

first major water barrier they could put between them and the enemy. The 63rd, with only three batteries instead of four, was positioned near the village of Samgyo-ri, about three miles from the Kum.

> Our Commander came by each howitzer and told each Section Chief, "Dig everything in deep." The Kum River line was to be held at all cost. We spent the next three days preparing our positions, putting in outposts, and running wire so that our switchboard could talk with a crank of the handle. We dug high-angle firing pits for each Howitzer; at the same time we fired a mission on the river line.

By July 13, the artillerymen were prepared. Their ammunition was replenished, and they all knew how their fellow soldiers would react under fire. But, Bolt said, the strain was starting to show.

> While I was on Howitzer guard duty around [11 p.m.], one of our outpost guards began screaming and throwing rocks at the other guards. Some of the HQ people ran him down, tied him to a stretcher, and carried him back to the rear . . . One became edgy after being on alert for 24 hours a day and all the tension in the air. If a frog was croaking in the rice paddy and a crane flew in, the frog would stop. You'd strain to see if there was human movement. This builds up over time, and you're drained until you become numb to everything that goes on around you.

The following morning, July 14, Bolt had a cup of coffee with a buddy he would never see again. He writes:

> All that morning, there was a Korean on the hill above the Battery. When we approached him he would wander away, but he would be back on another hill as soon as we went back to our positions. We were told he was just a farmer checking his rice crop. But it seemed to me that his clothing was too clean to be a farmer. He turned out to be an advance scout from the [North Korean 16th Regiment, 4th Division]. Since we had (previously) mistakenly had a firefight with the South Koreans, we had become gun shy. Our orders from above were: *Don't shoot till they shoot at you.* That was fine, although when they walk into your position, it's a little too late to start a fight when they're right on top of you!

The weather was hot, humid and full of stink rising from the rice paddies. Men were suffering from dysentery, and the 63rd Artillery was also dealing with the loss of key leaders.

The entire 24th Division was now in Korea, although each of its units was still seriously under strength. The 21st Regiment was in the rear rebuilding, while the 19th Regiment took up positions east of the 34th Regiment along the Kum River. The 19th was still untried, and with the 24th's heavy losses thus far, the entire Division amounted to little more than 2,000 men defending a squiggly river frontage 34 miles long.

In several cases, gaps of a mile or more were reported between units – ample room for enemy infiltrators. It's a bit surprising, then, that the North Koreans chose to cross the river the following morning in broad daylight. Whether they were acting as decoys is unclear, but they knew what they were doing.

It was about 1:30 p.m. when enemy soldiers approached an outpost held by Donald LeMatty's Able Battery. As James Bolt said, they had been told to hold their fire until they determined if the approaching soldiers were friendly. By the time they figured it out, it was too late. The North Koreans captured the outpost, as well as its machine gun, which they turned on nearby Headquarters Battery. At the same time, mortar started raining down on both Able and Headquarters Batteries.

A short time later, North Koreans swarmed across a rice paddy, and LeMatty's Battery A retaliated with rifle fire. The first wave of attackers moved into nearby hills, while a second wave attacked from a slightly different direction. The only thing that stopped the second wave was an enemy mortar round that hit a fully loaded American ammunition truck.

Meanwhile, coordinated mortar rounds took out Headquarters Battery's switchboard, medical section, another ammunition truck, and the command post's radio truck.

A short time later, the Americans were forced to get out any way they could. Dodging enemy fire, as well as their own exploding artillery rounds, few got out safely. The North Koreans had already cut off their escape routes.

James Bolt came off guard duty at about noon and headed for Baker Battery's mess tent. He writes:

> The cook broke open the C-ration carton and put a can of beans and franks in some boiling water to heat and also gave me a can of fruit cocktail. We lost contact with HQ Battery a little after 1300 hours, and the Battery Commander sent a jeep over

with one of the new men that had arrived the night before. Joe Duran was at the wheel, and James Thomas was riding shotgun. As they left, Joe shouted *I will try to find some extra C-rations.* I wouldn't see Joe again for 54 years, when I retired from the Army in 1969. He told me Thomas and a Lt. were killed in a road block and, though shot in the face, Joe was able to fight his way out.

I sat on the trails of the howitzer to eat; an empty shell casing was my table. I had finished the beans and franks and began to open my fruit cocktail. But the empty bean can slipped off and fell, so I set the cocktail can on the shell casing and bent over to retrieve the fallen can. In that instant, a sniper's bullet exploded my can of cocktail throwing sticky juice all over me! I thought for a moment that I was hit!

Men in the Battery began screaming "Sniper" and in just a short time some of them would be wounded. After the sniper fire stopped, the wounded were sent on to HQ Battery, but all were killed at a roadblock on the way . . .

A Sergeant from L Company (34th Regiment) reached the 63rd and told an officer about the [North Korean] crossing, but the officer paid little attention. By 1300 hours, the 16th Regiment slammed into the right flank of HQ and A Batteries . . . Mortars took out all communications with the other batteries and set fires in both HQ and (Donald LeMatty's) A Battery. By 1400 hours both batteries were overrun.

Then the North Koreans turned their fury on B Battery. By 1500 hours the 63rd had lost 11 officers and 125 enlisted men, ten 105mm Howitzers, and 60-80 trucks and trailers. In total, [our] losses were 23 killed in action, 24 missing in action, and 89 prisoners of war.

It was not learned until many years later that Iowan Donald LeMatty was captured that day. Like Doc Boysen, LeMatty ended up with roughly 750 other prisoners in the Tiger Death March, so named for its sadistic North Korean leader.[50]

After the fall of Taejon, the 63rd pulled out and retreated to Taegu, the North Koreans' next major objective.

---

[50] Donald LeMatty died between Manpo and Chunggang-jin, North Korea, November 1, 1950, the second day of the march.

We looked like vagabonds. I slept most of the way. There was a small creek running through our bivouac area creating a large pool of water maybe 10-12 feet deep, just like a large swimming pool. We dismounted and fell in to listen to the Battery Commander.

A small truck drove up and handed out a package from the Red Cross. A Service Battery truck drove up and unloaded C-rations. I took my ration and package and walked to the pool of water. I took off my boots, and with all my clothes on, I waded into the water with a bar of soap. I tried scrubbing away the blood, dirt and the memories of the last 14 days.

The blood and dirt I was able to remove, but the memories won't go away. Nor do they fade. They remain with me still today; as strong now as if it had just happened. It's as if time stands still – so long ago and in a place so far away, called "The land of the morning calm."

James Bolt cleans the breech block for the howitzer he used July 14. (Courtesy Bolt)

Chapter 11

CHICKS AT THE KUM RIVER

"The battle of the Kum on 16 July was a black day for the 19th Infantry Regiment. Of the approximately 900 men in position along the river, only 434 reported for duty ... the next day." Roy Appleman

THE 24th DIVISION'S remaining regiment, the 19th, was next in line to delay the North Koreans. Arriving in the Far East only recently, they had undergone customized training to prepare them for Korean-style combat, and a lot hinged on how they performed in their first battle.

The 19th Infantry Regiment received its *Chicks* moniker when it became known as the *Rock of Chickamauga* during the Civil War.

Like its two sister regiments (21st and 34th), it arrived with only two of its authorized battalions – the 1st Battalion (Companies A, B, C and D) and the 2nd (Companies E, F, G and H).

On July 12, the 19th moved up to the Kum River to relieve the 21st Regiment, which was falling back in the aftermath of the Chonui and Chochiwon disasters.

Lieutenant Ralph Harrity, a forward observer for the 13th Field Artillery, would soon be responsible for calling in artillery strikes in support of Charlie Company, 19th Regiment. In his book concerning their travails that summer, Harrity writes:

Just as the 19th column halted, several trucks from the 3rd Engineer Battalion, carrying infantry, sped across the bridge from the north. The men had been engaged in mining bridges and otherwise preparing obstacles along the road beyond the river. The trucks came abreast of the 19th column and stopped, the men dismounting. Then, in what appeared to be a weary, agonizing moment, the dust-covered men comprehended the significance of what they saw, that their eyes had not deceived them. They were looking at fresh troops, men sent to relieve them and carry on the struggle.

Almost unanimously the tired men of the 21st gave what soon came to be known as a "Thank God" cheer – softly, firmly, but [no drama].

Harrity and his fellow soldiers were taken aback by how gaunt and haggard these men were. Even their clothing – mismatched filthy rags – was alarming. One weary soldier caught Harrity staring and told him replacement clothing was nearly impossible to find. Harrity writes:

> Duffle bags had been indiscriminately ripped open by supply personnel and appropriate clothing confiscated and distributed as needed. The 21st was reaching the bottom. The 19th had arrived just in time.

Harrity watched as these men prepared to move to the rear to rebuild. Of the 21st Regiment leader from South Dakota, he wrote:

> Their commander, Col. Richard W. Stephens, seemed at great pains to exude optimism, dashing about in his jeep and never failing to stop and speak with or nod in respect to officers under his command. His presence was noted as one not wearing a steel helmet. Those who wondered about this were informed that this was his way of instilling confidence.[51]

The Chicks were right to be apprehensive. A week from now, their own ranks would be thinned by almost 800 casualties.

Battle of Kum River

The 19th Regiment's 1st Battalion was selected as the first to meet the oncoming enemy. The 2nd Battalion was to be in reserve, and when things got too hot, the 1st would withdraw through the 2nd's positions,

---

[51] Harrity, Ralph Derr. *Q Clan*. Dorrance Publishing. 2005, p. 70-72.

thereby keeping up a solid defense – a tactical maneuver that never materialized.

The initial plan was sound except for one key factor. The killing field laid before them like a wide shallow bowl of rice-paddy soup, but they weren't prepared for an attack from the hills behind them.

North Korea's 3rd Division already had men moving up behind the Chicks, and many were already switching their disguises from peasant garb to American uniforms. Others carried white flags to lure friendly troops into the open. The Regimental War Diary for July 13 reads:

> The Regiment was disposed along the river. Companies were given extensive areas to defend and did not have the men or means to cover the territory. There were tremendous gaps between companies. For example, between C and E Company along the river's edge there was a gap of 4,000 yards completely undefended. It could not be [done] with the force available. After losing its 63rd Field Artillery, the 34th Regiment pulled back ten miles on July 14, leaving the 19th Regiment's left flank unprotected. This ultimately made it necessary for the Chicks to commit both of their battalions to cover the two-mile front – there would be no troops left in reserve for backup actions.

The first incoming fire came from enemy tanks moving toward the north bank of the Kum the afternoon of the 13th. A confusing situation soon arose with "numerous reports of so-called enemy refugees crossing the river." Despite the probability that many of these refugees were actually North Korean infiltrators, requests to stop them from crossing the Kum were denied. As explained in the previous chapter, at least 500 of these hit the 63rd Artillery alone.

Air support was good, but it disappeared when the sun went down. At about 9:00 p.m., heavy concentrations of tank and artillery fire started landing along the friendly side of the river. With fears that the North Koreans would cross the river under cover of darkness, troops gained permission to set abandoned buildings on fire for illumination.

As the sun rose on July 15, reports came in that four boatloads of enemy soldiers had tried to cross into the positions vacated by the 34th Regiment to the west, but these were foiled by machine guns and renewed air strikes.

It was evident the main thrust would soon occur, and aircraft bombed and strafed the oncoming enemy troops throughout the day. Additional air support for dropping flares was promised for the night, but the planes all but disappeared by 8:00 p.m. The 19th's diary reads:

> Enemy tanks then moved onto a knoll in front of the 1st
> Battalion positions across the river. 15 tanks were counted.
> These opened fire on the 1st Battalion positions. Heavy (enemy)
> artillery at the same time was firing on the rear areas. Air
> support was requested but only two planes arrived. These planes
> and our artillery destroyed two enemy tanks. The main positions
> took a terrific shelling while enemy troops moved to the river
> in trucks. The enemy also moved up automatic weapons to the
> river's edge.

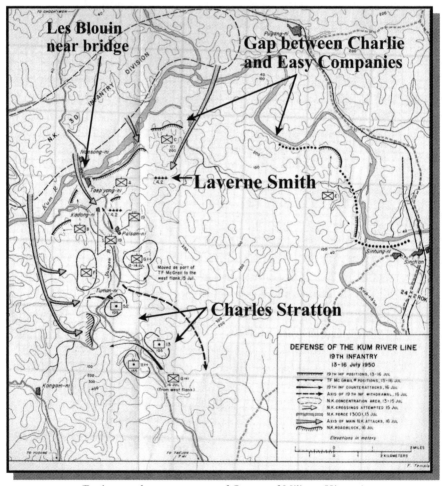

(Background map courtesy of Center of Military History)

At midnight, Charlie Company reported enemy troops were crossing the river and moving through the 4,000-yard gap to their right. The main enemy assault was now upon them. Details of what happened during the next 24 hours are scant, with the entire war diary entry reading:

This summary of events is compiled from memory of the operational staff of the 19th Infantry. The dates, times and figures are approximate [because the] journal of the 19th infantry was lost in action and destroyed by fire Sunday 16 July.

At this time the 19th RCT consisted of the 1st and 2nd Battalions; Company A, 3rd Engineers; Platoon Company A 78th Tank Battalion; 13th Field Artillery Battalion, and 24th Ambulance Platoon.

At 3 a.m. a flare dropped by an enemy plane was apparently a signal to start the attack. Heavy tanks, artillery, mortar and small arms fire was received along the entire front. Enemy troops repeatedly made Banzai attacks against the river defense line.

Our forces called for all artillery and mortar. Everything in supporting weapons was called for and used.

Enemy troops were unable to cross against our dug-in positions along the river. Numerous enemy crossings were made in the gap between Charlie and Easy Companies on the right center flank. These enemy forces hit the right platoon of Charlie Company and forced it back to some extent. It was this gap that the enemy used as the main crossing area.

Two more attempts were made to cross by enemy troops. They were successful in getting through at some points in the C and B Companies after repeated storming of positions. Many enemy troops were able to infiltrate into the rice paddies behind the dike on our side of the river.

The 1st Battalion command post was attacked, but the enemy was driven off in a charge led by Major John Cook, Capt. (Allen) Hackett, Lt. Hall, and Lt. Col. (Otho) Winstead. Major Cook and Capt. Hackett were killed in this action.

During all of this time enemy troops continued to cross through gaps on the flanks of B and C Companies. A report was received that 1,000 enemy troops were moving south, with some of them turning toward the main supply route.

A counterattack force was organized from Regimental Headquarters Company. It consisted of all company officers, the Security Platoon, cooks, clerks, drivers, and mechanics. This force went forward to assist in driving the enemy from the rice paddies. Col. Meloy (19th Regiment commander) moved forward with a tank and a half-track from the 26th Anti-Aircraft Automatic Weapons Artillery to assist in the attack. The situation at this moment was improved. The counterattack forced a large number of enemy troops to move back across the river. There was great difficulty however encountered in the evacuation of our casualties.

A young WWII veteran from Woodbine, Iowa, was a player in this counterattack:

*Private First Class **Jerry J. Butcher**, Coast Artillery Corps, U. S. Army, a member of Battery A, 26th Antiaircraft Artillery Automatic Weapons Battalion, 24th Infantry Division, is awarded the **Bronze Star with V device** for heroic achievement on 16 July 1950, near the Kum River, Korea. With support from one tank and infantry elements, Private Butcher and three companions moved their half-track vehicle forward in the face of artillery and mortar fire and the small arms fire of securely entrenched enemy infantry. The [friendly] tank was forced to withdraw. Private Butcher and his companions remained in their exposed position and delivered telling fire on the enemy for a sufficiently long period to allow the accompanying infantry to withdraw to cover. During this firing, the companions dismounted and destroyed it in spite of extremely heavy enemy fire. They then evacuated a wounded companion and, upon rejoining friendly infantry elements, volunteered to go on patrol to destroy the enemy machineguns that were delivering a devastating cross fire on our troops. By his heroism Private Butcher brought great credit to himself and the military service.*

The war diary continues:

At 10:00 a.m., the Commanding Officer 1st Battalion (Otho Winstead) reported to the command post that enemy flanking forces were slowly closing in on Charlie Company. He stated that he could hold the river line, but he had no forces to use in the rear area or, for that matter, elsewhere.

By this time, Fox Company positions on the left flanks were under fire. Baker Company was in trouble on the extreme left flank. Reports were received that the enemy was attacking across the main supply route as far as three miles to the rear.

Ammunition supply was stopped by the enemy road block. No 4.2-mortar ammunition was left in the position.

A directive from division was received to prepare withdrawal positions. The commanding officer (Guy Meloy), S-3 and Assistant S-3 moved back towards the rear. At this time, the 52nd Field Artillery was receiving heavy fire in their position. One battery was out of commission. The 11th Field Artillery and 13th Field Artillery reported sniper and machine gun fire to their rear. It was at this stage that the withdrawal order was issued.

On their way to the rear, Colonel Meloy and S-3 ran into the enemy road block established by heavy automatic and light anti-tank fire on the main supply route. The road was congested with vehicles for four hundred yards. The machine gun fire was a crossfire pinning down any personnel that moved. Colonel Meloy was hit in the leg while trying to organize the clearance of the fire block.

At noon, tanks were again dispatched to break the block. The initial movement for a withdrawal began with Baker Company dropping back. The withdrawal was made under great difficulty. The covering force of Fox Company was attacked from all sides.

Meantime the road block was reenforced by the enemy. Casualties continued to pile up in our aid station and could not be evacuated because of the roadblock.

Baker Company was ordered to knock out machine guns on the left side of the block. Attempts were made to maneuver tanks into position to fire. The 1st Battalion was trying to fight its way out. Planes were called to help.

Elements of the friendly force broke off and worked their way into the hills.

At 5 p.m., the S-2 loaded all the wounded on vehicles, planning to place tanks at the head and rear of the column to push through. Captain (Edgar) Fenstemacher, assistant S-3, returned from the head of the column and reported a push through was impossible, as the road was then completely blocked by vehicles. At 7 p.m., S-2 and Captain Fenstemacher ordered all personnel out of the vehicles, and the wounded were placed on litters for cross-country movement around the blockade.

An estimated 500 men, including walking wounded and litter patients, moved uphill and south for cross-country escape.

At least 75 vehicles had to be abandoned on the road.

An attempt was made by a force under command of Lt. Col. Thomas McGrail, commanding officer of the 2nd Battalion, to break the block from the south. This force was withdrawn from the extreme west flank on the river. It was made up of two tanks and four (26th) Antiaircraft Artillery halftracks armed with heavy machine guns and some 37mm guns.

Late in the afternoon, this force broke through the block to the point where the Regimental Commander, Colonel Meloy, was wounded earlier. Here the anti-aircraft vehicles, which were road-bound, proved prime targets for the light antitank weapons being used by the enemy. A heavy firefight between the enemy and this force did create some diversion, but they were unsuccessful in their mission of breaking up the enemy block. After firing up their ammunition, this force withdrew. Those vehicles that could move provided transportation and cover for the wounded in the immediate area. The Commander of the force, Lt. Col. McGrail, remained in the road block area and guided some other men out of the immediate danger area just before dark . . .

One note of interest available is that the 4.2 Mortar Company fired 1588 rounds of ammunition from 3 p.m. July 15 to 4 a.m. on 16 July 1950.[52]

It was another devastating blow for the 24th Division, with the 19th Infantry losing its regimental commander, its 1st Battalion commander, and hundreds of other officers and enlisted men.

But the men who fought at the Kum River resisted magnificently, with roughly 80 men receiving awards for heroism. A whopping 16 distinguished service crosses (DSCs) were awarded – possibly a record for one regiment in a 24-hour span, especially for one that was seriously under-strength in its very first combat action.

Charlie Company was particularly hard hit, losing 122 men out of 171.[53] PFC Charles Tabor, from Louisville, Kentucky, was a mortar man for the company and was among the DSC recipients. After the enemy

---

[52] All information this section is from *19th Infantry War Diary for the period 29 June 1950 to 22 July 1950.*

[53] Appleman. *South to the Naktong.* P 144.

knocked out two 60 millimeter mortars by small arms fire, Tabor stayed at his position with the one remaining mortar and continued to fire. When the base plate of that mortar was destroyed, he held the hot tube in his hands and continued to fire it until all the ammunition was exhausted. His citation reads, "During this heroic action he suffered a broken arm." Of far greater consequence was that the 18-year-old was also killed in action.

Laverne "Corky" Smith

Positioned immediately to the rear of Tabor's Charlie Company was another mortar man, Laverne "Corky" Smith, a member of Heavy Mortar Company. By the end of the day, Smith would have the tragic distinction of becoming the first Iowan to die in Korea.

Smith's father was an electrical lineman, and Corky and his brothers often went along with him while he repaired power lines in their area. He had served during the Spanish American War and again in WWI, and all of his sons followed in his footsteps.

Corky attended schools in Waverly, Clarksville, and Shell Rock. He enlisted in August of 1949 from Waterloo and arrived in Japan in January 1950.

The 20-year-old was awarded a silver star at the Kum River, but many might agree he and his comrades more aptly deserved higher awards for their ultimate sacrifices.

Laverne Smith
(Courtesy Richard Smith)

*The **Silver Star** is **Posthumously** awarded to Private **Laverne N. Smith**, Infantry, U.S. Army. On the morning of 16 July 1950, the Second Platoon, Heavy Mortar Company, 19th Infantry Regiment, was in support of*

Company C, which was subjected to a number of attacks by enemy infantry. After a number of such attacks had been repulsed, the enemy succeeded in flanking the position of Company C and attacked between the rear of that organization and the heavy mortar position. Since the enemy was inside heavy mortar range, the platoon defended its perimeter position with small arms fire. When the position became untenable, the Platoon Leader gave the order to withdraw. Private Smith and three other soldiers, although unwounded and perfectly able to withdraw, volunteered to remain in the platoon position and hold off the enemy while the rest of the platoon withdrew. During the time the platoon was withdrawing, Private Smith and his companions repulsed two assaults, killing at least nineteen of the enemy. Defying odds of about thirty-to-one, these soldiers enabled the main body of the platoon to withdraw and take their wounded with them. On the final enemy assault, their position was overrun and all were killed.[54]

Leslie Blouin & Charles "Wild Bill" Stratton

As a communications operator for Headquarters Company, 13th Field Artillery Battalion (FAB), it was Leslie Blouin's job to make sure the artillery battalion could communicate with the 19th Regiment.

Blouin grew up in the town of Delamere, North Dakota. As a middle child with six siblings, young Leslie became close to his dad by riding along on his father's rural mail delivery route. As a teenager, Blouin quit school to service and build power lines for an electric company. After his dad died in 1948, he joined the Army.[55]

"I went to radio repair school," he said, "and then I went to Japan, and they put me in the 13th Field Artillery. I had enlisted for the Signal Corps with my electric and communications background, but they said, 'You're in communications. That's what you wanted.'"

The 13th FAB provided general support for the entire regiment, with each of its firing batteries assigned to one specific infantry battalion.

"Each of those batteries put a forward observer up with the infantry battalion," Blouin said. "The artillery headquarters, which I was in, provided the communications link to the forward observers, who were up with the infantry. We would lay wire lines up to the back of the

---

[54]Smith's comrades were Lee Killingsworth, Oklahoma; Leonard Schlinghoff, Arizona; and Dennis Nyhan, Long Island. Although Schlinghoff's mother was notified of his death, he was returned during the prisoner exchanges in 1953.

[55]Interview with author, Sep 2010.

infantry battalion and then lay wire lines up to the three forward observers who were up in front. We generally had a switchboard. They also had radio communications, but wire was more secure.

"The forward observers would ring our switchboard, and we'd connect them with wherever they wanted to be connected. Sometimes it was back to the battalion commander, sometimes it was to personnel, but in most cases it was back to FDC – Fire Direction Control."

Blouin was manning his switchboard during the early morning of July 16, when trouble erupted.

"The fighting started on the afternoon of the fifteenth and went through the night," he recalled. "The 19th Infantry was at a bridge they were guarding. From where we had our forward switchboard set up by the Kum River, we could see the battle for the bridge during the night of the fifteenth. By the morning of the sixteenth, the North Koreans had crossed somewhere else, and they were working their way through the hills to come in behind us.

"We started getting overrun when our line back to our battalion went dead – I don't know if it was hit by artillery or what. Harold Golnick, from Michigan, and I went with our wire truck to run a new line. We thought we could go down to find where it was blown out and just splice on to it with a new line."

Blouin and Golnick threw equipment into their three-quarter-ton truck and moved out – one driving and the other one running behind stringing out wire in the ditch, so it wouldn't get tangled up with traffic. They abruptly came under fire when they reached a roadblock caused by enemy crossfire.

When their vehicle was hit, Blouin and Golnick jumped into the ditch. The enemy had heavy weapons, which allowed them to stay out of range of the Americans, who had only M-1 carbines. Their sergeant, Alan R. Sharp, was just making his way up to them when he was hit. "He was just a little ways from us," said Blouin, "and I think it was an AK-47, because there's not many guns as accurate as that one. He had twelve slugs that made a hole in his belly about the size of a half-dollar."

At some point, Blouin and Golnick spotted a small tank carrying an infantry officer, as well as the commander of the 13th Field Artillery.

"He was Colonel Stratton – *Wild Bill Stratton* – the best commander I ever had," Blouin said. "He was in one of the division's reconnaissance tanks, and there was a rocket-propelled grenade, I think, that hit the side of that tank, and they got out and joined us in the ditch. There were a lot of people caught in that roadblock; we weren't the only ones."

Charles William Stratton, 45, had ties to Blouin's home state, having spent several years with North Dakota's 185th Artillery prior to WWII.[56]

Ralph Harrity, the forward observer who called in artillery coordinates for Charlie Company, described the "old man" as "wiser than many thought."

Prior to Korea, the men of the 13th FAB observed Stratton under peacetime conditions. A West Point graduate, the colonel's sandy hair was greying, and he was developing a paunch. But, writes Harrity, his blue eyes "pierced when angry," and he was a man of action in combat:

> When in battle dress, his irrepressible hustle was so disheveling that any press or distinction to his uniform vanished almost from the moment he donned it. Further, he was never able to make his [helmet fit]. More often than not, as he faced one way, his helmet faced obliquely another direction or was perched comically on the rearward side of his crown.
>
> Yet . . . Stratton was in his element in a battle situation, constantly thinking ahead . . .

Harrity writes of one other quirk that endeared Stratton to his men:

> Stratton also had a rather unorthodox way of saluting and responding to salutes that were sources of amusement yet comfort to his men. When departing on one of his frequent jaunts, he would invariably give last-minute instructions, [his subordinate would salute], he would respond with a wide sweeping motion of the right hand to the side of his helmet. . . with a well-mouthed "Good-o" . . . and be off in a cloud of dust. More than once, in extremely tense situations, this drama would elicit smiles all around. Lt. Col. Charles W. Stratton was a soldier's soldier.[57]

Stratton was soon beloved by not only his own artillerymen, but also by the infantry units who profited from his fire support. Stratton faced danger head on and, Harrity learned, "would never abandon the foot soldiers, no matter the circumstances."

---

[56] *The Bismarck Tribune.* 8 Jan & 12 Feb 1938; 17 Jun 1939.

[57] Harrity. *Q Clan.* P 118-119.

At the Kum River, Stratton ended up with responsibility for more than his own 13ᵗʰ Artillery. He assumed provisional command of the 52ⁿᵈ and 11ᵗʰ FABs, as well.

*The **Distinguished Service Cross** is awarded to **Charles W. Stratton** . . . While at the command post of the 19ᵗʰ Infantry Regiment, Colonel Stratton received a message from the commanding officer of the 52ⁿᵈ Field Artillery Battalion that their positions were surrounded by enemy infantry. Colonel Stratton left the regimental command post immediately to effect relief and withdrawal of the artillery units which were surrounded. Commanding a tank, Colonel Stratton worked his way through to the forward position area of Battery A, 52ⁿᵈ Field Artillery Battalion, which he found well organized, and effectively beating off the enemy attack with artillery and small-arms*

Stratton at West Point

fire. He then proceeded to the position area of Battery B, where he attempted to clear fire blocks which prevented withdrawal of the battery. During this action his tank was knocked out by enemy fire, killing the tank driver and seriously wounding the tank commander. Colonel Stratton dismounted from the knocked-out tank and proceeded on foot. Upon arrival at the B Battery area, he took personal command of the area, since the battery commander had been killed by enemy fire. He fearlessly directed the howitzers in direct fire against enemy infantry and three enemy fire blocks of an estimated two machine-guns each. The battery at this time was under intense enemy mortar, automatic weapons and rifle fire. Colonel Stratton remained in the area for six hours fighting off infiltrating enemy infantry and attempting to reduce enemy fire blocks in order to effectively withdraw friendly infantry and artillery units. Later, taking complete command and effecting complete coordination, Colonel Stratton organized the remaining personnel of the 19ᵗʰ Infantry Regiment and the 52ⁿᵈ Field Artillery Battalion in this area and led them in fighting through enemy installations and through the hills to friendly forces. By these actions Colonel Stratton saved numerous lives.

North Dakotan Leslie Blouin escaped with Colonel Stratton, saying, "We had to get out over the hills. We mostly had to walk, because it's difficult to run in rice paddies. We went around behind a sort of stone cliff, and Colonel Stratton stuck his head out to see what it looked like going across the paddies. A couple bullets ricocheted off the rock." Blouin chuckled, "He pulled his head back and says, 'Those pecker-heads see my rank on my helmet! Give me your helmet!'

"Evidently it was just some wild rounds, because I didn't give him my helmet, and nobody shot at him when he looked back around."

Chapter 12

OUTSIDE LOOKING IN

More war correspondents have been killed in the Korean War than in the first year of World War II. Eight are dead, and four more are missing and may have been killed . . . But still correspondents are pouring in. Fargo Forum. August 15, 1950

WAR CORRESPONDENT Philip Deane flew 11,000 miles from Greece to "cover this little war, and I am anxious to get to it in time."

Upon his arrival in Korea, Deane learned it would take at least 24 hours to reach Taejon by rail, so he hitched a ride aboard an unarmed L-5 Piper Cub – one of John Murphy's Mosquitos.

Lieutenant John Stanton, from Exeter, Missouri, was the pilot, and Deane got a first-hand look at how well the Mosquitos worked, writing, "One hour after we leave base we strike gold. That, at least, is how Stanton puts it."[58]

Below them was a long enemy convoy with "some strange, large objects optimistically camouflaged to pass for haystacks." Stanton called over the radio to fighter jets, code named *Utah Dogs*, and minutes later, Deane was startled by silver streaks whooshing past. Stanton meticulously instructed the Utah Dogs when to bank or turn, and when to pull the trigger. "One after the other, eight trucks go up in the air, and the twenty or so others burst into flames," Deane reported.

On their last run, the Dogs used rockets on the haystacks, which turned out to be enemy tanks.

Stanton then flew on to Taejon, where Deane thought the city's

-----

[58] John Stanton received three Distinguished Flying Crosses prior to being killed in action on October 16, 1950.

airfield looked more like a vacant city lot.

From the landing strip, he hitched a ride in an ambulance carrying four severely wounded soldiers and a medic who Deane described as "a child pale and shocked." As they drove over pocked and cratered roads into Taejon, Deane did what he could to help the young medic deal with tourniquets, gaping chest and abdominal wounds, and administering plasma.

Fans of the television comedy M*A*S*H would find no resemblance to the medical realities Deane found in the heart of Taejon. Inside a large public building "deodorized by gallons of disinfectant," stretchers covered the floors of all rooms, corridors and stair landings. Medical staffers were haggard from exhaustion and numbed by the sheer numbers of wounded. Deane writes:

> Doctors operate ceaselessly, their hands bare, blood spattered down their fatigues. No rubber gloves, no white smocks here. Stitch this, clip that, sponge, stitch, clip, saw – faster, faster, faster, there are more waiting.

Back outside, Deane found his young medic sitting against a wall with his face in his hands. "Thick tears streak the blood caked brown on his fingers, and disturb the flies," he wrote.

Deane offered the boy a drink from his flask and learned he and his four patients were the only ones in their medical team who weren't killed when a shell landed on their aid station. After having seen the conditions of the other men, Deane feared the young soldier might end up being the sole survivor of his team.[59]

Philip Deane's given name was Gerassimos Svoronos Gigantes, and he was no stranger to war. Although he was Greek, he was decorated in WWII while serving with the British Navy, and his present job was writing for the *London Observer*. A true world citizen, he later served in the Canadian Parliament, as well.

He had journeyed to Taejon to report on the 24th Division, and although he would spend the majority of the war as a POW, the few articles he posted before he was captured provide valuable insights into

---

[59] Philip Deane quotes and descriptions come from his book, *I was a Captive in Korea*. W.W. Norton:1953. Also from the daily International News Service reports he filed between 17 and 24 July 1950.

the situation in and around Taejon as the city fell to the North Koreans.

Deane's first impression of the roughly 5,000 Americans in the city was a sense of hopelessness about fighting off "fifteen divisions, four hundred tanks, thousands of howitzers, armored cars, antitank rifles."

It was July 16, and casualties were flooding in from the action at the Kum River. To get out to the front lines, he hitched a ride with Major Wade Heritage, the divisional surgeon, who was headed northwest to Kongju to see how his medical teams were coping.

As they passed through masses of refugees, they noted numerous healthy young Korean men, "heads held high, arms swinging. They are the only ones with smiles on their faces," he wrote.

Shell fire increased when they reached an advanced aid station where Deane thought Lt. Parker Pratt "looked as if he would pass out on his feet any minute."

Pratt told them the North Koreans had blown up their previous aid station with three artillery salvoes. As they watched aid men carry six wounded survivors into the new position, Pratt told Heritage, "Christ, those kids had acted so cheerful, feeling their troubles were over now that they were in the hands of medics."

Heritage patted the lieutenant on the shoulder and said: "How would you like for me to send someone to replace you. You've had it too long up here," Deane wrote. Pratt and his assistants had not slept for a week. But they declined Heritage's offer, and turned their attention to an arriving soldier with a broken back.

The road became more and more deserted as they drove on to the outer perimeter. They were stopped by Lieutenant MacCarver, a sandy-haired Canadian-American commanding the 3rd platoon of King Company, 34th Regiment. MacCarver and his 36 men were in charge of guarding a front three miles wide – or as MacCarver put it, the "rearguard platoon, of the rearguard company, of the rearguard regiment in this here shooting war."

MacCarver advised the major to turn back. They'd learned there were two enemy patrols in the vicinity, and their mission was to capture a North Korean for questioning. Heritage had other aid stations to visit, and Deane was in pursuit of his story, so MacCarver agreed to allow the reporter to tag along if he protected himself with more than his camera.

The reporter said he became a buck private at that moment, and he soon had second thoughts. "With an occasional bullet whizzing overhead, with the gooey muck of rice paddies in my shoes, and with leeches sucking at my ankles for all they were worth, I thought I would rather be a banker. But even then I wasn't so sure, because that would have denied me the privilege of meeting these kids."

One of those kids was Gerald Nelson, "a freckle-faced youngster" from Halma, Minnesota, who wasn't old enough to shave and whose appetite was enormous. Nelson complained to Deane that a card he sent his mom for Mother's Day took weeks to reach the States.

MacCarver, a veteran of fighting in the South Pacific during WWII, told Deane: "Two weeks ago when I was given this squad of schoolboys I thought, 'Christ, I can't go into battle leading a nursery school.' But they are tough and every bit as good as their older brothers were in the Pacific."

During a subsequent firefight, MacCarver captured his North Korean soldier, and Deane thought he looked remarkably similar to the smiling young men they'd observed among the refugees.

They began working their way back to Taejon, with combat engineers blowing the bridges after they crossed. At some point, intense enemy shelling wounded several of them, including Deane, who was hit in the shoulder. The reporter bandaged his own wound, got himself a shot of morphine, and gamely continued on with Macarver's platoon.

Up the road, they found young Americans who had collapsed and fallen asleep in the road, "their shoes flung aside to ease their bleeding feet. They have reached the point in human endurance where exhaustion brings first heedlessness, then oblivion."

Macarver's men stuffed these soldiers into the back of their truck, "packaging them tightly so that they cannot fall out" while the teenagers continued to sleep.

This group arrived back in Taejon before dawn July 17. Deane found the latest news confusing, but he was quite certain the city would soon be evacuated – but not before the G.I.s "pushed back again and again the tanks, heavy artillery and waves of expendable infantry hurled at the thin American line."

Deane Meets Colonel Stephens

Deane was impressed by these men, and he lamented the enemy's inability to understand the essence of American soldiers like the 21st Regiment's commander, Richard Stephens from South Dakota. Deane recalled standing with some of Stephens' men listening to the colonel lecture them on how to get into a foxhole with dignity.

"When you hear shells," Stephens said, "you walk nonchalantly off the command post, walk to the foxhole or nearest ditch, and get down into it feet first without disarranging your uniform."

Moments later, incoming shells had them diving for the ditch.

"From the ditch," Deane wrote, "we watched him walk across to us, look down at us, and shake his head sadly."

When the time came for Deane to get out of Taejon, a flaming road block flanked by enemy snipers cut the 24th Division's southern escape route. The city was surrounded, and heavy enemy fire came from every direction. Of the many deaths Deane observed, he wrote there was "not one of which the Democratic world need be ashamed." Faced by insurmountable odds, "these kind young kids . . . fought like their brothers on Bataan and Guadalcanal."

During the eventual evacuation, Philip Deane rode out in a column of tanks flanked by Lieutenant MacCarver's men. In the short time since they first met in no-man's land, MacCarver had been bumped up from leading a platoon to commanding all of King Company – the previous commander had since become a casualty.

From Taejon, the wounded reporter hitchhiked south to Taegu, where he was captured several days later. He was accused of being a spy and was severely tortured before eventually being joined to a group of civilians to endure the Tiger Death March.

Chapter 13

THE FALL OF TAEJON

"Americans in 1950 rediscovered something that since Hiroshima they had forgotten: you may fly over a land forever; you may bomb it, atomize it, pulverize it, and wipe it clean of life – but if you desire to defend it, protect it, and keep it for civilization, you must do this on the ground the way the Roman legions did, by putting your young men into the mud." T. R. Fehrenbach, *This Kind of War*

SIFTING THROUGH CASUALTY lists can be a dry and detached task. But there are times when something starts nipping at your mind, and a gradual recognition of something unusual seeps in.

It starts with a noticeably high number of casualties for a certain day. And then the list gets longer. Much, much longer.

You remember all these names are not just statistics. They were fresh-faced boys out to see the world. Some enlisted so their mothers could feed their siblings back home. Others, with families of their own, hoped to make the Army their career. Still others were grizzled war horses fighting in their second or third war, because this was their calling.

More than a thousand casualties in two days. . . Even General William Dean, the commander of the entire 24th Division, became a casualty. *What in God's name happened here?*

Buildup to the Battle

General Walton Walker, commander of the Eighth Army, had set up his command post in Taejon, which lies roughly midway between Seoul and the port town of Pusan in the south. Strategically, the city encompassed a web of critical supply routes, an airstrip, and key railroad lines for moving men and supplies from Pusan to the front lines.

Generals Walker and Dean near Taejon (NARA)

It's no surprise the North Koreans were anxious to capture such a jewel, and by July 19, the situation in and around Taejon significantly intensified. This was the 24th Division's fifth major delaying action, and it included a two-day street-fight that ultimately trapped thousands of soldiers in a flaming inferno.

The engagement primarily involved the dwindling 34th and 19th Regiments, the 11th, 13th and 63rd Artilleries, the 3rd Combat Engineers, and other critical units. (Richard Stephens' 21st Regiment was in reserve south of the city, where it continued to rebuild and prepare to re-enter battle.)

By the end of the second day, Walker's total American casualties in Korea would top out at more than 3,000 men. About one-third of these were from July 20 alone.[60]

---

[60] National Archives. *Records on Korean War Dead and Wounded Army Casualties*, documenting the period 2/13/1950 - 12/31/1953. NARA includes only Army, so airmen are not included in the reported total of 3075 casualties.

Historians point to several costly mistakes made by top commanders, beginning with General Walker telling General William Dean, the 24th Division's commander, to hold the city *two more days*, until he could bring forward newly arriving elements of the 1st Cavalry Division. Some believe Walker meant for Dean to pull out July 19, but it appears Dean believed he needed to hold until July 20. Either way, the attempt to withdraw came much too late.

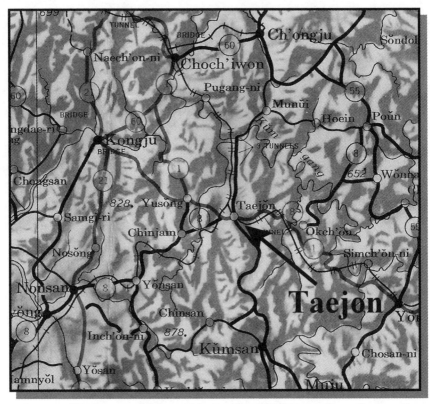

Taejon was like a spider web with five roads and three railroad lines converging at its heart.

General Dean later wrote:

> In the days before July 20, I was getting intelligence reports from Korean Army sources and some of my own Korean agents. My private agents had said days earlier that the Communists would not attempt a direct attack on Taejon but would move around it to the west and south. It was also

reported that civilians in captured areas had been ordered to make thousands of suits of typical Korean white clothing, in which North Korean soldiers would infiltrate our lines at Taejon itself. Then these, plus the turncoats already in the town, would capture it without a frontal assault.

I discounted this information in preparing for the Taejon defenses; but there is no denying such thousands of infiltrators did come into town and confuse the situation.[61]

With the town crawling with enemy snipers, the battle was taking place everywhere at once by July 20. Communications all but disappeared, and there were crucial points when commanders could not be located, and nobody of sufficient rank was authorized to give orders in their stead.

The situation was complex, confusing and chaotic. Indeed, the loss and subsequent recapture of Taejon merits a book of its own, but the following personal accounts provide vivid examples of what the warriors of the battle experienced.

George Kristanoff

The 24th Reconnaissance Company had been in and around Kumsan, south of Taejon, on July 17 and 18. Their mission was to keep an eye on the 24th Division's south flank and to keep the road open as a withdrawal route for the troops fighting in and around Taejon.

Lieutenant George Kristanoff, commanding the Reconnaissance Company's 2nd Platoon, was the son of Dimitri Kristanoff, a Yugoslavian immigrant who worked first as a baker, and then as a miner, in the vicinity of Calumet and Bovey, Minnesota. Dimitri had built a three-story log home with two spacious porches where he and his wife raised their six children.

George began his Army career as an enlisted man in 1943, and although he got married – and liked living in Minnesota – he rejoined the Army soon after his discharge following WWII. He was selected for Officer Candidate School in Ft. Benning, Georgia, but as the son of a working man from Minnesota's iron range, he felt socially out of place as revealed in a letter he wrote to his parents:

---

[61] Dean, William. *General Dean's Story*. NY: Viking Press. 1954. Quotes are taken from pages 30-46 and will not be further cited.

We finally got assigned to a class. I'm sure glad that we are getting started . . . Don't be surprised someday after I finish this course that I might want to join the paratroops. Nothing definite. Just a thought.

Mom, I wish you would cash a couple bonds for me and send me the money. I don't want you to get worried that I have done something wrong or intend to, because I don't intend to and I haven't.

Here is the story. I want to become an officer the worst way now. But Mom, I've got to be able to get into the social life of an officer. You know that at home I wasn't able to go out much and now I can't go with the rest of the fellows and bowl and play tennis and such things. As that, I've got a bad case of inferiority. At least I feel that way. I'm actually afraid to go out and ask a girl to dance. It just isn't any fun being that way. I don't want you to think that I want the money to go on a good spree. I don't. I want it so I can go out and bowl and dance, things like that.

I feel like I've got to get out in this world – meet people and do the things they do instead of saying, "I'm sorry, I don't know how." I'd probably get by with it if I remained a buck private, but Mom, if I want to be an officer, I've got to be able to meet people. I can't do that now.

I don't want you to think that I have been shut in by myself all the time. I've certainly acquired barracks buddies, but I haven't felt quite equal to them because I didn't feel I could do the things they did. I've got to get confidence in myself and I can't do it by sitting around the barracks on weekends. Don't forget, Pop, if I get to be an officer I'm getting up into somewhat higher social society, and if I do, I have to be able to meet it.

It's hard to get into words what I want to get across to you. I guess that is quite a bit to ask for at once, but there are so many turned back here, because they don't have the experience, and they aren't just recruits fresh out of basic training . . . I know I can do it if I get more confidence in myself. I hope you understand.

It's uncertain whether his parents cashed in his savings bonds for him, but Kristanoff successfully became an officer, and he and his wife had their only child, Mary Lou, at Ft. Benning. She writes, "I was born in

November of '49, and Dad went over, I think, in January of 1950. I don't even have a picture of the two of us, which just breaks my heart."

When asked how her father ended up in Officer Candidate School, she said, "At the very end of WWII, he was going to start a mink farm, and that didn't happen. He tried to join the Air Force, so he could be a pilot, and he didn't pass that. They put him into the Army again, and he went through officer training.

"He was a pretty neat guy, from everything I've heard of him. My mother had only one sibling, and that was her sister Leona who lived close to Father and Mother. She often tells me the story that when she was very pregnant, one day my father stopped by her house and ended up scrubbing her kitchen floor, because it would have been too difficult for her to do the work. I don't know of many men that would have done something so kind for my aunt."[62]

It had been ten days since Kristanoff had overseen the offloading of a dozen precious vehicles at the port of Pusan. The cargo – including seven tanks – was shipped north and unloaded at Chochiwon, and at dawn July 8, Kristanoff's 24th Reconnaissance Company drove north to support the 34th Regiment.

General Dean gave orders for the Reconnaissance Company to provide in-depth defense along the battalion's right flank, and by 9:00 a.m. Kristanoff's 2nd Platoon moved into position. Fifteen minutes later they were in combat.

After an all-day fight, Kristanoff and his men provided cover fire as the 34th Infantry pulled back. Late that night, they crossed the river right before the 3rd Combat Engineers blew the bridge. The transmission went out on one tank, so Kristanoff had his men strip it for parts.

It was the morning of July 14 that George Grim, a Minneapolis journalist, first met Kristanoff. They were between Taejon and the Kum River. Grim writes:

> He was calm in the early hours of a damp morning. That day would see his tank move into combat. He knew the limitations of that tank, its inability to move through the mud of a Korean rice paddy.
>   . . . In the last moments before our outfit pushed off, I noticed [he] was shaving with his mirror propped up on a tank

---

[62] Interview author with Mary Lou Kristanoff, July 2013.

tread.

"Look at him shaving!" said a corporal. "At least we're gonna have one clean face in this outfit!"

It appears Grim met Kristanoff by accident. Sometime before dawn, Grim and another reporter lost their ride and ended up wandering into the recon team's positions in a school yard. Grim writes:

> We slept on the ground. The men shared their early dawn coffee with us. I met half a dozen Minnesotans, a boy from La Crosse, another from Valley City, N.D.
>
> They knew what faced them, but they had confidence. Of course they were uneasy. Bravado exists in operettas but not in the heart of a soldier at dawn.
>
> As George's tank lumbered north, his wrecker went back to Taejon for supplies and offered me a lift. That was the last I saw of him.[63]

Forty Men Stop Four Hundred

On July 19, a message came in from the 34th Regiment ordering the 24th Reconnaissance Company to send a platoon toward Nonsan to see if the enemy was moving toward Taejon from the southwest.

It was midmorning when George Kristanoff led his platoon on this mission. They made it only several miles before coming up against some 400 enemy soldiers aiming straight for the heart of the city. Immediately engaging Kristanoff's men, these enemy troops made a determined effort to sweep around both of the 2nd Platoon's flanks.

Corporal Robert Watkins, from Union, Mississippi, was in the lead vehicle, which fortunately had a 30-caliber machine gun mounted on the right front side. He inflicted at least 50 casualties while giving the others time to move to better defensive positions. From there, Kristanoff's men inflicted more than 300 additional casualties while taking only one themselves.

Reinforcements arrived at about 9:00 p.m., allowing Kristanoff and his men to withdraw.

Several hours later, they received orders from the 34th Regiment to send a patrol back down the south road toward Kumsan to see if it was

---

[63] Grim, George. "I Like it Here." *Minneapolis Star*, clipping circa mid-1950.

still open as an escape route for troops fighting their way out of Taejon. Kristanoff headed out with nine men and four jeeps just before midnight.

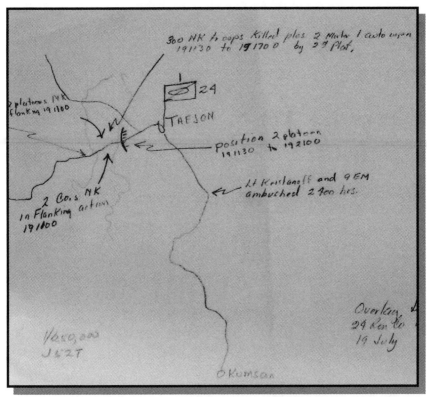

Map from 24ᵗʰ Reconnaissance Company's war diary shows the location of Kristanoff's 2ⁿᵈ Platoon on the road to Nonsan (left/west) during the day, as well as the site of the ambush at midnight.

Six miles out, this patrol was ambushed by an estimated five enemy machine guns firing from both sides of the road. Kristanoff kept up a steady report about the enemy trap until radio contact was lost . . .

Thomas Kilfoyle, who entered the military using the name Joseph W. Doyle, was a Brooklyn boy who had just turned 19. He was a great admirer of his platoon leader, writing[64]:

There are not enough words to describe what a great Officer

---

[64]Email communication Kilfoyle with author 11 Dec. 2012.

and Gentleman and all around good guy Lt. Kristanoff was. He was a really great guy and a great Platoon Leader. I had the pleasure of driving the Lieutenant from June 26, 1950, until July 18, 1950.

Under ordinary circumstances, Kilfoyle would have been in the ambush that night. He later described the events in a memoir:

> During this time period we were working almost around the clock. I had taken ill, and I told PFC Frank Knights that I was going get some sleep under one of our platoon's M24 Tanks. When Lt. Kristanoff came looking for me, [PFC Knight told him] I was ill, but he would get me for him. Lt. Kristanoff told Frank never mind, that I had been working hard, and he would get a volunteer to go.
>
> I awoke on the morning of the 20th of July blissfully unaware of the above events. I crawled out from under the tank and was greeted with surprise. Everyone wanted to know how I had gotten back and if there was anyone else with me. They told me I better see Captain Kearns right away, so I went directly to the CO, and as I walked in he said, "Thank God, is there anyone else with you?"
>
> I told him I didn't know what he was talking about. He asked if I was with Lt. Kristanoff, and I told him no. Then he told me to sit down, and he told me what had happened.

In early September, Captain Kearns wrote to Kristanoff's wife, Valerie, saying he would have written sooner but wasn't permitted to until proper notification was made to the family. Kearns described George's mission:

> It was a night patrol and we had contact with the group via radio. The last message we received was that the patrol was being fired on by the enemy. I attempted to get to the area from which his message was received but by this time it was in enemy hands.
>
> From an observation post I could see the vehicles in which the patrol was riding the next morning. We could positively identify four American bodies lying around the vehicles but could not identify individuals.

I don't want to be hardhearted about the whole thing, but I wanted you to know exactly what happened. Wish you would keep the information I've given you within your immediate family.

George was well liked by the officers and men of my company and I considered him as one of my best friends, as well as one of the most courageous officers I've ever known. The only thing for us all to do is to pray that he might have been captured alive by the Koreans and is now in an internment camp.[65]

*First Lieutenant **George W. Kristanoff** . . . 24th Reconnaissance Company, 24th Infantry Division, is awarded the **Silver Star** for gallantry in action near Taejon, Korea on 19 July 1950. Lieutenant Kristanoff was given the mission of determining the strength and location of an enemy unit which was reported as operating 6 miles south of Taejon. With a patrol of 10 men in 4 jeeps, he proceeded about 6 miles when he encountered an enemy road block. During this time he maintained radio contact with his company command post. His patrol engaged the enemy*

(Courtesy Mary Lou Kristanoff)

road block and during the engagement he reported that he was also attacked from the rear. With complete disregard for his own safety, Lieutenant Kristanoff remained at his radio and gave full information as to the enemy's disposition and location. As a result of the information given by Lieutenant Kristanoff, reinforcements were dispatched to the scene of the action and held off the enemy during the night, thereby gaining valuable time in the defense and evacuation of Taejon . . .

Every member of Kristanoff's patrol was listed as missing, believed dead, including Sergeant Robert L. Martin; Sergeant Hugh Townsley; Corporal Norman Fontaine; Corporal Hershall Newell; Private First

---

[65] Letter John A. Kearns to Mrs. George W. Kristanoff. 11 Sep. 1950. Courtesy Mary Lou Kristanoff.

Class Robert Agard; Private First Class Robert Blair; Private First Class William Boyd; and Private First Class David Monphor.

Private First Class Clyde Steele, from Charles City, Iowa, was also missing, and Tom Kilfoyle believes it was Steele who volunteered to take his place as Kristanoff's driver that night. Unfortunately, nobody will ever know for sure. The only man whose remains were found and returned home were those of Hershell Newell.

As Captain Kearns had hoped, George Kristanoff, as well as Clyde Steele and one other man, are known to have been captured. But it would be decades before their families learned this – and that it was not necessarily better to be captured than be killed.

John Stepanek

John Stepanek was also a member of the 24th Reconnaissance Company, but he was in a different platoon. Stepanek had fought in WWII, getting wounded in fighting at Saint Lo, France, and also during the Battle of the Bulge. Like Kristanoff, he had since gone through Officer Candidate School and was commissioned as a lieutenant.

Stepanek left the Army in 1945 and returned to his hometown of Cedar Rapids, Iowa. He got married and worked as a commercial artist to supplement his V.A. disability payments related to the aftereffects of his wounds. The Stepaneks started a family, and they also adopted the son of John's brother Les, who was killed at Normandy.

Life was good, but after several years, Stepanek's love of the Army was nagging at him, so he visited the local recruiting office in the spring of 1949. With his disability issues, 34-year-old couldn't pass the physical that would have allowed him to reenlist as an officer. So he gave up his job and disability compensation and reenlisted as a Sergeant First Class.

By that fall, Stepanek and his growing family were stationed in Japan, where they grabbed attention as the new caretakers of Ricky, a small, perky-eared mutt adopted by an Air Force unit in Germany in 1944. Ricky ended up in Japan where he enjoyed life as the Fifth Air Force's mascot. After flying on 52 missions, Ricky was transferred to 24th Reconnaissance Company in October 1949.

Stepanek later told reporters,[66] "Ricky was really given to my platoon, but he soon adopted me and has been with me ever since. That is, all except the time I was in Korea. The CO wouldn't let me take him

---

[66] *Cedar Rapids Gazette.* 1949; *Pacific Stars and Stripes.* 7 Feb 1951.

there." The little dog rode shotgun in Stepanek's tank. "He doesn't mind the noise a bit and even tries to chase the bullets."

The fact that Ricky chose Stepanek said a lot about the Iowan. Throughout his military career, Stepanek proved he was a man to be trusted. Four years prior to his death at age 56, Stepanek, fondly known as "Desert Fox," was invited to share his seasoned perspective with a graduating class of newly commissioned officers. Speaking from the point of view of a noncommissioned officer, he told them:

I feel a tinge of regret that I am not young enough to be sitting out there as some of you. You have so many years of challenge and adventure to look forward to. So many of these years are behind me.

Soon you will meet your platoon sergeants, your first sergeants, your sergeants major, your other noncommissioned officers, and your troops. What do we expect from you as officers, commanders, leaders?

We expect of you unassailable personal integrity and highest of morals. We expect you to maintain the highest state of personal appearance. We expect you to be fair – to be consistent – to have dignity but not aloofness – to have compassion and understanding – to treat each soldier as an individual, with individual problems.

And we expect you to have courage – the courage of your convictions – the courage to stand up and be counted – to defend your men when they follow your orders, even when your orders are in error – to assume the blame when you are wrong.

We expect you to stick out your chin and say, "This man is worthy of promotion, and I want him promoted." And we expect you to have even greater courage and say, "This man is not qualified, and he will be promoted over my dead body!" Gentlemen, I implore you, do not promote a man because he is a nice guy, because he has a wife and five kids, because he has money problems, because he has a bar bill. If he is not capable of performing the duties of his grade, do not do him and us the injustice of advancing him in grade. When he leaves you, or you leave him, he becomes someone else's problem!

Gentlemen, we expect you to have courage in the face of danger. Many of you will soon be in Vietnam where there are no safe rear echelons. During your tour, opportunities will arise for you to display personal courage and leadership.

Opportunities could arise from which you may emerge as heroes. A hero is an individual who is faced with an undesirable situation and employs whatever means are at his disposal to make the situation tenable or to nullify or negate it.

Do not display recklessness and expose yourself and your men to unnecessary risks that will reduce their normal chance of survival. This will only shake their confidence in your judgment.

Now Gentlemen, you know what we expect from you. What can you expect from us?

From a few of us, you can expect antagonism, a *Prove yourself* attitude. From a few of us who had the opportunity to be officers and didn't have the guts and motivation to accept the challenge, you can expect resentment. From a few of us old timers, you can expect tolerance.

But from most of us, you can expect loyalty to your position, devotion to our cause, admiration for your honest effort – courage to match your courage, guts to match your guts – endurance to match your endurance – motivation to match your motivation – esprit to match your esprit – a desire for achievement to match your desire for achievement . . .

We won't mind the heat if you sweat with us. We won't mind the cold if you shiver with us. And when our cigarettes are gone, we won't mind quitting smoking, after your cigarettes are gone.

Gentlemen, you don't accept us, we were here first. We accept you, and when we do, you'll know. We won't beat drums or carry you off the drill field on our shoulders. But, maybe at a company party, we'll raise a canteen cup of beer and say, "Lieutenant, you're O.K." Just like that.

Remember one thing. Very few noncommissioned officers were awarded stripes without showing somebody something, sometime, somewhere. If your platoon sergeant is mediocre, if he is slow to assume responsibility, if he shies away from you, maybe some time not too long ago someone refused to trust him, someone failed to support his decisions, someone shot him down when he was right. Internal wounds heal slowly. Internal scars fade more slowly.

Your orders appointing you as officers in the United States Army appointed you to command. No orders, no letters, no insignia of rank can appoint you as leaders. Leadership is an intangible thing; leaders are made, they are not born. Leadership is developed within yourselves. You do not wear leadership on your sleeves, on your shoulders, on your caps, or on your calling cards. Be you lieutenants or generals, we're the guys you've got to convince, and we'll meet you more than halfway . . . [67]

John "Desert Fox" Stepanek (Courtesy Stepanek family)

---

[67] Stepanek, John G. "As a Senior NCO Sees It." *Army Digest*. Aug 1967:P 5-6.

John Stepanek gained this wisdom the hard way. And when he spoke of heroism, he could have been describing himself.

Several days before the fall of Taejon, it was learned that during a withdrawal of the 34th Regiment, a medical unit had not gotten word and was now trapped behind enemy lines. Stepanek led a patrol of four jeeps to find and rescue these medics and their wounded.

On July 19, the Cedar Rapids man again displayed the leadership qualities he requested of those new young officers in 1967.

*Sergeant First Class **John Godfrey Stepanek**, Infantry, U. S. Army, 24th Reconnaissance Company, 24th Infantry Division, is awarded the **Silver Star** for gallantry in action on 19 July 1950 near Taejon, Korea. The scout section under the command of Sergeant First Class Stepanek was protecting the left flank of the company during its withdrawal when the order was given for the scout section to withdraw. He ordered the section to withdraw, and he remained with four men who had been wounded. With disregard for his own safety and under heavy artillery and automatic weapons fire, he obtained a jeep to evacuate them. After the company had withdrawn and the wounded evacuated, he remained in the area searching for other wounded until a tank was sent out to bring him back to the unit. The act of gallantry displayed by Sergeant First Class Stepanek reflects great credit on himself and the military service.*

Escape From Taejon

(Courtesy Lou Repko)

Louis Repko, of Lorain, Ohio, was a jeep driver in the 34th Regiment, and before this day was over, almost 600 of his fellow soldiers would be added to the 34th's already lengthy casualty lists.

Being in combat had not been part of Repko's plan when, at age 16, he persuaded his mother to alter his birth certificate so he could join the Army. His four older brothers had come home safely from WWII, so his mother agreed, and he ended up being stationed in Japan. In his account of what happened at Taejon, Repko writes:[68]

We kept moving south until we were told to hold up in a town called Taejon. We arrived there on the 18th of July. We were told that the 19th, 21st and 34th Regiments would have to hold our positions for as long as possible.

On the morning of the 20th, enemy tanks moved to the center of town and started firing at everyone in the school yard. Stewart Sizemore and I had a small bazooka, a 2.6 I believe, and we tried to knock out a tank, but it just wasn't enough power. We found a can of gas from the jeep, filled a couple of bottles full and made it across the street to a big building. Then we made it to the top of the building. The tanks saw us on top and tried to fire at us, but the guns wouldn't raise that high. Before we could throw the bottles of gas, the tanks moved out.

By this time the town was on fire, and we were given word to pack up and get out. *What you can't get in the trailers – burn.* HQ Company was going to pull out on the 19th, but General Dean said we had to hold one more day.

I didn't know what road to follow going out of town, there was so much fire. Just about then a 2½-ton ammo carrier was going through, and I followed it to the other side of town. I don't know how we made it. The town was burning so badly that we couldn't even see where we were going. When we got to the end of town, the 2½-ton truck turned to the right. I turned to the left, and about five minutes later was under fire.

There was a small hut to the right, about 100 yards down the road, where there was a machine gun set up firing at everything that moved. Trying to get out of the line of fire my jeep got the tires blown off the right side. I lost control of the jeep, it turned over and I fell out, landing on the road.

Trying to get to cover from the machine gun still firing, it became silent. Someone had knocked out the gun. As I was trying to cross the road to run for the hills, another jeep was coming down the road. I didn't see it in time and was knocked down. My right leg was hit by the bumper [but] I was too scared to feel the pain.

A big man got out of the right side of the jeep. He didn't

---

[68] Repko, Louis. *A Soldier's Story*. Unpublished memoir shared with author 2007.

have his helmet on, but I did see his sidearm. He was carrying a chrome-plated .45, so I knew it was General Dean. Just then we started to get fired on again. There were ten G.I.s laying on the edge of the road.

Dean said, "Come on men, we have to try and make it to the bottom of that mountain on the other side of the rice paddy." We had to crawl most of the way. We could see the enemy coming down the road and rice paddy. When we made it to the bottom of the mountain there were eight to ten more G.I.s already there from the 34th Infantry who were lost.

There was one sergeant in the group, and Dean put him in charge. Dean told the sergeant to get all the men to the top of the mountain and dig in until morning. Then we'd see how we could get out of there. He told the sergeant that he had to go back and find his aide. I thought the aide had been with us the whole time. This was at 9:00 p.m. on July 20, 1950, and it was the last time I saw the general.

The next morning we could see from the top of the mountain that the city of Taejon was still burning. The fighting had stopped, but the damage had already been done. We waited until around 9:00 a.m. before we started to move down from the mountain. About half way down we spotted another group of G.I.s from the 21st Regiment. We tried to stay together as much as we could. We had about 30 men in our group, and about half had some type of wound. No medic was in our group, so we did the best we could. By this time my leg was really burning. The top of my boot was rubbing it pretty badly, but the other men had worse wounds than mine.

Night started to set in, and we found a small cove to rest in for the night. We heard the enemy patrols all night, but we were lucky, and they stayed on the road. The next day we walked until we couldn't go one more step. This was the evening of the 3rd day, and we ran into a South Korean patrol. They took us to a small village and gave us some food and a place to rest for a couple of hours. At midnight they came, got us up, and told us they were leaving. That's all they said. We started walking until we came to a river. I didn't know what river it was, and I didn't care . . . I just wanted out of there.

By this time we only had six men. The rest had fallen back. The Korean patrol said not to worry about them. They would find them and get them to safety. About an hour later we saw a boat coming. It wasn't a very big boat, and I didn't think it was going to get us across to the other side. But, it did. When we landed on the other side we were given directions as to which way to go. We rested that night, and about 11:00 a.m. we spotted one of our patrols, and we were all taken to a first aid station.

Arthur Clarke & General Dean

Three days after the fall of Taejon, Lieutenant Arthur M. Clarke, a pastor's son from Boone, Iowa, emerged from a ditch with his hands up. He was wounded in his right shoulder, and the heels of his boots were worn off, but he was alive, and so were 18 others – some badly wounded – he brought out with him. Since fleeing Taejon, these men had traversed 35 miles of mountains and rivers, moved through artillery and, now, came under friendly rifle fire.

"Don't shoot," he called out. "We're Americans."

It was noon on Sunday, July 23, and the soldiers Clarke was calling to were from the 1st Cavalry Division near Yongdong.

As the cavalrymen came to aid his group, Clarke tried in vain to pay a South Korean man who had guided them to safety. A camera man caught the moment on film, and soon there was a burst of excitement when it was learned Clarke knew General Dean got out of Taejon alive.

Clarke, 28, disliked attention and tried to avoid the reporters, but they finally cornered him. It was then that he learned his boss was listed as missing in action.

Clarke was officially an artilleryman, but during WWII, he had served as a flight instructor, and it was partly for his flying skills that General Dean selected him to be his aide five months earlier.

Clarke briefly told them what he knew – that he had last seen Dean the night they got out of Taejon, and at that time the general was unhurt. He also told them how he, Dean, and a handful of other men hunted and destroyed an enemy tank before the withdrawal. After several failed attempts, they finally managed to destroy one by shooting into it from a second-story window.

"You could hear screaming inside the tank," Clarke said. "A second shot into the tank stopped the screaming. We put a third into it to make sure the tank was out of action."

Two years later, a reporter back in the States coaxed Clarke into saying a bit more about what happened that day. Bernard Horton writes:

Clarke's eyes seemed to light up a little as he recalled that the 3.5 bazookas got their first tryout that day.

"We knocked out two tanks at the entrance to Taejon, blocking the road," said Clarke. "After the fires died down from those two, more tried to infiltrate. We chased four of these and were able to knock out one.

"In the afternoon, we were reported surrounded, so we started scouting for routes of departure. At about 5:30, we formed a column of vehicles loaded with wounded and other personnel and started movement from the town, which was burning by that time. We ran several road blocks, until about five miles south of town we could go no further."

. . . From there on, Clarke's story became sketchy, as though he would rather not talk about his part in the battle.[69]

Indeed, Clarke took little credit for his actions, as seen in the official "certificate" he prepared a month after Taejon fell:

At approximately 7 p.m. 20 July 1950, the withdrawal from Taejon was affected by General Dean and party. I do not know at what position in the column the General's party was located. Approximately 2 miles from Taejon on the Kumsan road the General dismounted and loaded his jeep with wounded and other enlisted men. The General refused to either get on his jeep or on mine, which was just behind his, but waved us on and said to keep going.

Approximately one mile further down the road I was wounded in an ambush and after another mile or two, we were stopped by disabled vehicles covered by machine gun fire blocking the road.

General Dean later provided more details:

We drove through, careening between the stalled trucks. It was a solid line of fire, an inferno that seared us in spite of our speed. A block farther on, my jeep and an escort jeep roared straight past an intersection, and almost immediately [Arthur] Clarke, riding with me, said we had missed a turn. But rifle fire

---

[69] Newspaper clipping, *Wyoming Eagle*, 1952. Courtesy Clarke family, 2012.

still poured from buildings on both sides, and turning around was out of the question . . . So we bored down the road in the general direction of Kumsan, while snipers still chewed at us from both sides of the road.

We were all by ourselves. Our jeeps tried to barrel through the snipers' fire, but it blocked us time after time.

It was at this point that they stopped to load up walking wounded. After Dean signaled Clarke to keep moving, the general grabbed a ride on an overflowing artillery vehicle. Dean wrote he was "hanging by precarious toe and handholds."

As they came to an S-curve leading to a bridge, Dean spotted his Headquarters jeeps ahead. They were abandoned, and enemy machine gun fire was pouring from within a jumble of wrecked vehicles.

Dean and the other men tumbled off the truck into a ditch. The general then realized he no longer had a weapon; his trademark pistol holster "dangled empty at my hip."

Dean and Clarke found each other in that ditch. Clarke had been hit in his right shoulder, and since he could no longer shoot, he gave his weapon to the general. Returning to Clarke's narrative:

> . . . together we crept through a bean patch to comparative safety behind the house bordering the road and into a garden.
>
> At this point I remained in the garden, and the General crept on into a bean field next to it. I lay approximately 1 yard from Capt. Rowlands in the edge of the garden (in a hemp patch) from 8:30 to 9:30 p.m. at which time the General and the rest of us moved out through the bean patch.
>
> At the edge of the patch, General Dean held a conference appointing a right, left, and rear guard, as well as a rifleman to guard the forward sector. After this, at about 10:30, we crossed the stream, bordered it for 100-200 yards and then headed up a draw into the hills. Approximately 50 yards up the hill the group of 18-20 stopped while several men returned to the stream to get water.
>
> As we started up the hill, the General returned to the base of the hill to aid a man with a wounded leg up the hill. Capt. Rowlands and his group moved on up the hill leaving seven of us, Gen. Dean, the wounded man, four other enlisted men and myself, in the rear.
>
> Climbing the hill, the six of us without leg wounds aided the

wounded man in climbing the hill.

It might be noted here that General Dean wrote that it was pitch black, and it was Arthur Clarke who worked his way forward to let him know about the wounded man. Dean went back with Clarke to help the soldier, who was wounded in both legs. Two men were already carrying him and, Dean writes, "Another man staggered along beside them. At the first opportunity Clarke used his first-aid kit to bind the man's leg wounds, although his own shoulder still had not been treated."

The hill was covered with loose sand and rubble, making it difficult to carry the man.

"Hell," Dean told the others, "get this man up on my shoulders. I can carry him more easily that way by myself."

But the general's 50-year-old body failed him. "We went back to the two-man carry," he wrote, "and even then it seemed as if my turn came around every five minutes."

They were trying to move silently to avoid detection from possible enemy patrols. But the wounded man, writes Dean, became "more or less delirious; he drank all the available water and then called for more."

They reached the crest of the mountain's "shoulder" at about midnight. Dean told Clarke he was going back down for water, but the aide talked him out of it because they had spotted an enemy patrol using flashlights behind them.

Since the Rowlands group had outdistanced them, Clarke took the initiative of scouting for any trails they might use. It was now almost 1:30 a.m., Clarke wrote.

> I found no one was following me, and no noise to the rear. So I returned to find five men asleep on the ground. I called for the general, and one of the men answered that he had gone for water. As I figured the round trip could be made in an hour, I set the goal of two hours as the maximum time that we could wait. The general didn't take a canteen or a helmet, so I assumed he was going to try to find some stragglers rather than to get water. At 3:15 a.m. I woke the men and we headed to the top of the hill, arriving just before dawn.

Dean, it turns out, did go down to get water, because he thought he could hear some trickling in the darkness. But he lost his footing, tumbled down a steep slope, hit his head and passed out. Clarke writes:

Just as it was beginning to get light, I had the men spread out and posted two as guards for one-hour shifts. I figured we'd at least be able to see what killed us, as we had no weapons. I no sooner posted the guards when I checked and found them asleep. I awoke them and asked them if they wanted to be killed. I don't remember their exact answers, but they were to the effect that they didn't care whether they were killed or not. So I stood guard until they woke up. At daylight I searched the area with my field glasses, saw that our vehicles were gone, and three Koreans were sitting on top of a hill to the northeast of us. We spent the day where we were, on top of the hill. It was scorching hot. We had the shade only of a few bushes about a foot high. During the day the men almost turned against me, because I wouldn't let them start off until it got dark. As it did begin to get dark we started south along the ridge . . .

It was still dark when the general had regained consciousness that morning. He didn't yet know he'd gashed his head; his first realization was that his shoulder was broken and he had severe pain in his abdomen.

He was lying in a dry creek bed, and although he was dazed and groggy, his thirst drove him to search for water. He finally found a tiny trickle of muddy water in some rocks and then passed out again.

When he awoke, a patrol of eight to ten North Koreans passed within 10 yards of him. There was faint light from the approaching dawn, but they didn't spot him. They passed by and started climbing the steep incline where he had tumbled during the night.

I thought, "Oh-oh, this is the end for Clarke and the others. They're gone now." That was the lowest moment I've ever had in my life. I could see all those people on the hill being killed; and the realization that Clarke didn't even have a pistol – I had his – made me feel even worse.

It turns out Dean had been thinking about reassigning Clarke and another aide, because they were both family men, and he felt it was unfair to keep them in a combat zone, writing:

. . . my experience with aides and drivers for division commanders in wartime is that they are very likely to get killed. I felt I shouldn't have men with young children taking the risks they had to take . . .

They were both very fine men, and I'd never been so proud of Clarke as in the last few hours when he'd been organizing that column and keeping people together.

The general resolved to decorate the Iowa officer for his actions, but three years later, when the North Koreans released him from captivity, Dean found his division had already taken care of it.[70]

*First Lieutenant **Arthur M. Clarke**, Field Artillery, U.S. Army, Headquarters, 24th Infantry Division, is awarded the **Silver Star** for gallantry in action on 20 July 1950 near Taejon, Korea. When withdrawing from Taejon with elements of the 34th Infantry Regiment, the motor column which Lieutenant Clarke was accompanying came under intense enemy machine gun fire which destroyed the leading vehicles and halted the column. The entire column was then brought under intense enemy automatic weapons fire which caused numerous casualties. Lieutenant Clarke with complete disregard of his own safety removed several of the wounded to places of relative safety. Later he organized and led a group of soldiers over thirty-five miles of enemy infested and mountainous terrain to rejoin their units. The group of men he led carried a wounded soldier over this distance, despite the fact that this action delayed their withdrawal and endangered their safety. During the course of these acts, Lieutenant Clarke was wounded. . . .*

Almost 900 men were listed as missing in action at Taejon.

General Dean evaded capture for roughly five weeks before two supposedly friendly civilians gave him up to the North Koreans for the equivalent of five dollars. As the communists' most highly prized prisoner, Dean spent the remainder of the war in isolation.

Rumors emerged that he'd been captured, but it wasn't until December 1951 that the world learned he was alive, when Wilfred Bruchett, a reporter for a communist newspaper in Paris, snagged an interview with the general. When Bruchett told Dean the Army had awarded him a Medal of Honor, he balked; he didn't feel he deserved it.

---

[70] *General Dean's Story.* P 30-44; *Mason City Globe-Gazette.* 24 July 1950; *Pacific Stars & Stripes.* 24 Jul 1950; *IA City Press-Citizen.* 18 Dec 1951. Clarke's "certificate" is dated 23 August 1950 (no further information), courtesy Clarke family, 2012.

After continued contact with Bruchett, Dean was grateful to learn his wife now knew he was alive.

But what gave him equal comfort was learning that his aide, Arthur Clarke, had also survived.

While his wife looks on, Arthur Clarke, wearing his Purple Heart and Silver Star, receives another award from the governor of Wyoming circa 1953. General Dean holds Clarke's daughter, Artelyn, right. (Courtesy Artelyn Clarke Harris)

Chapter 14

CLARENCE LACKNER

"Others often look down on infantrymen, finding them lacking in civility, intellect, or morality. However, throughout history it has been infantrymen at the critical place and time who have made the difference between success and failure, between victory and defeat, between freedom and servility . . . It is infantrymen who go the final yards." Sam Holliday, 35th Regiment, 25th Infantry Division

CLARENCE "GACK" LACKNER, a rugged combat veteran of WWII, was one of the Army's most decorated combat veterans by the time he left Korea.

Lyle Conaway, who would himself earn the Navy Cross several months later, was Lackner's neighbor in Finn Town, a section of the northern mining town of Virginia, Minnesota.

"I knew who he was, but he was a lot older than I was," said Conaway. "I would've been about eleven, and he was draft age when Pearl Harbor was attacked. My brother-in-law, Walt Aho, lived in a place in Finn Town called the Mehan Apartments. I went up there on that Sunday afternoon when the news came out, and all those guys were there – Gack, Walt and Wally – all of them were about 19, 20-years-old.

"They were discussing it in a very serious manner. They all knew they had to go in the service, but where were they going to go? There were conversations like *I don't want to go in the Army and live in a hole in the ground. Well, I don't want to be on board a ship down in a hole when it sinks. I don't want to be on a bomber when it's burning.*

"But they had to make up their minds where they wanted to go. I remember one guy saying, 'I'm in the CCCs (Civilian Conservation Corps), I might as well pack and go right now.' They were having some beers at the time, you know?"

Lackner and his friends had worked as bodyguards for a small-time hustler during the depression. "Gack was a big guy, and he pushed his weight around," Conaway said. "All those guys thought they were pretty tough, you know? They had to be, or they wouldn't have gotten hired. They were all into gambling and enforcing, but on a small scale. Nothing like Chicago or New York or anything. At that time, I think there were 13,000 people in Virginia (Minnesota).

"There are two lakes right in the middle of Virginia, Silver Lake and Bailey's Lake. That summer I was coming home from Silver Lake, which had a public beach. It was about four o'clock in the afternoon, and I had to walk past the south shore of Bailey's Lake to where I lived in Finn Town. I saw an old car pull up – nobody could afford new cars, these were 1920s, '30s cars. This car pulls up with at least four or five guys. One guy got out and yells, 'They're not gonna draft me!' and he goes running off into the lake. He tried to drown himself, but the water was only about three feet deep out about a hundred yards. So he was having one helluva time trying to drown himself. They were drunk, you know?

"This other guy gets out and takes his clothes off – that was risqué in those days – all but his shorts. And he goes running out after this guy in the water. The guy's still hollering 'They're not gonna draft me!' They wrestled out there a little bit, and he starts dragging him to shore, and the police show up. Well, that was Gack Lackner who went in after the other one," Conaway said.[71]

Men like Lackner were ideal candidates for combat, as North Dakotan Harold K. Johnson personally attested.[72] Johnson later became Army Chief of Staff under President Lyndon Johnson, but as a fresh young 2nd Lieutenant out of West Point, one of his first assignments was overseeing men in the Civilian Conservation Corps (CCC) camp on the Mesabi Iron Range in northern Minnesota. It was 1933, times were hard, and the federal program was aimed at putting unemployed young men to work on reforestation and land reclamation projects.

The camp couldn't be operated under military rules, because it was a civilian program, and in this region, Johnson said, most participants

---

[71] Conaway interview with author 2012.

[72] Sorley, Lewis. *Honorable Warrior*. University Press of Kansas. 1998. P 17.

were Finnish immigrants like Gack Lackner. "They were *tough*," Johnson said. Most of them carried knives and were *"wicked"* in a fight.

Gack Lackner ended up choosing the Army, and he made a substantial contribution during WWII. As a member of Company F, 18th Regiment, 1st Infantry Division in Europe, he earned a Distinguished Service Cross, the Croix de Guerre from France and Belgium, at least two (possibly three) Silver Stars, and possibly one Bronze Star for Valor (it is unknown if the Bronze and one of his four Silver Stars were awarded in WWII or Korea). One of his Silver Stars was awarded for actions near Mosles, France, on June 7, 1944:

During the confusion of battle, a supporting tank mistakenly opened fire upon one of the company's platoons. Sergeant Lackner, in the face of withering enemy fire, voluntarily advanced to the tank and notified the crew of its grave error. His exemplary action undoubtedly saved many of his comrades' lives and earned him the praise of all who witnessed his deed. (1st Div GO 28, 9 Sep 1944)

Lackner's **Distinguished Service Cross** was awarded for actions a few months later, on November 26, 1944:

When his company was halted by superior enemy fire, Technical Sergeant Lackner moved through intense hostile fire and located two friendly tanks. From an exposed position atop one of the tanks, he guided them toward the hostile positions and directed devastating fire upon the emplacement. As the tanks moved forward, Technical Sergeant Lackner, armed with a submachine gun, personally killed nine Germans attempting a bold maneuver. Observing a wounded soldier in direct line of hostile automatic rifle fire, Technical Sergeant Lackner dismounted from the tank, moved through the withering fire and evacuated the wounded man to safety.

In Korea, Lackner was a platoon sergeant in Fox Company, 35th Regiment, 25th Division. They had been in reserve while the 24th Division's situation played out at Taejon, and now, on July 21, they were on their way to the northwest sector of the perimeter to relieve exhausted South Korean units. They began digging in near the village of Sangju that day.

South Korea's 6th Division was to their north, between the villages of Hamchang and Mungyong, fighting along the north edge of a swift stream gushing out of the fearsome Taebak Mountains. Army historian

Roy Appleman described the current as so strong it was "rolling large boulders along its channel."

Word soon came down that Lackner's Fox Company was to be detached, sent north to the other side of this river, and inserted into the center of the South Korean unit to bolster its position.

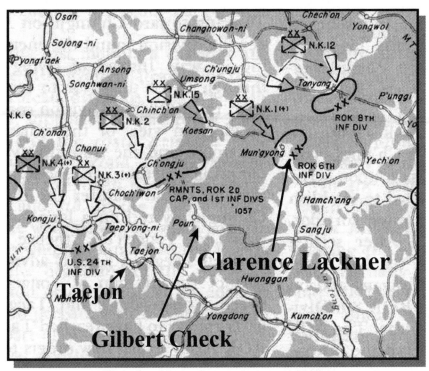

(Map inset courtesy Center of Military History)

The battalion and regimental commanders both protested this division-level order, saying they didn't want this untried company depending on the stability of an unknown unit during its first combat experience. Nonetheless, Lackner and the other 160 or so men of Fox Company were soon on the north side of the river, where a ridge behind them further isolated them from the rest of the 2nd Battalion. The 35th Regiment's War Diary reads:

> Late that afternoon, Fox Company was attacked by an estimated two battalions of enemy, making the odds roughly 8-to-1. Fox Company fought off the enemy, inflicting heavy casualties. It was raining, and immediately to their rear, the river began to rise.

Communications – bad as they were – were even worse in this scenario because of the language barrier between Fox Company and the adjacent Korean units. Reports are confusing, but it appears that at a certain point the South Koreans may have believed their relief had shown up, and the arrival of Fox Company meant they could depart. Roy Appleman writes:

> On 22 July the North Koreans attacked. The South Koreans withdrew from their positions on either side of F Company without informing that company of their intentions. Soon enemy troops were firing into the back of F Company from the hill behind it. This precipitated an unorganized withdrawal. The swollen stream prevented F Company from crossing to the south side and the sanctuary of the 2nd Battalion positions. Walking wounded crowded along the stream where an effort to get them across failed. Two officers and a noncommissioned officer (believed by this author to be Lackner) tied a pair of twisted telephone wires about their bodies and tried to swim to the opposite bank and fasten a line, but each in turn was swept downstream where they floundered ashore a hundred yards away on the same bank from which they had started. Some men drowned in trying to cross the swollen river. The covering fire of a platoon of tanks on the south side held off the enemy and allowed most of the survivors eventually to escape.

Appleman called this a "fiasco," and historian Clay Blair wrote that Fox Company "bugged out." Neither of these descriptions seems accurate. The river had by now torn away all wire communications, and Appleman's statement that the "North Koreans attacked" is wholly inadequate. The 35th Regiment's war diary reads:

> For three long hours the company stood up to the assault, but at the end of that time, with the position penetrated, the company split, and casualties mounting, with the swollen river preventing resupply and evacuation, there was nothing left to the harried company commander but to attempt a withdrawal.
>
> Under the circumstances there was no possibility of maintaining perfect control of the movement. Formations became confused. Men were drowned trying to swim the river. Some men were able to move downstream under cover of the river bank and make a safe crossing. Some distance

downstream, "B" company, 65th Engineers, attempted to place a raft in operation, but the swift current foiled the project. The saving factor turned out to be the tanks of a platoon of Company "A" 79th Heavy Tank Battalion, which appeared on the friendly banks of the river and placed covering fire on the attacking enemy and thereby enabled "F" company to complete its crossing.

Lackner and others were later interviewed by AP reporter Tom Lambert, who titled his news story: *Minnesotan in 60-Hour Korean Battle*. A company sergeant told him, "They used practically nothing but automatic weapons, which can really spit lead. We were temporarily backed off our hill for about ten minutes, so Sergeant Clarence Lackner of Virginia, Minn., went back to investigate."

Lambert writes that when Lackner returned, he assured his platoon there were only two or three enemy soldiers left, "So, we took the hill again," the sergeant said.

Clarence Lackner told Lambert: "The Reds continued to harass the company all night. A heavy rain Friday added to its trouble. Saturday morning the Reds attacked early, first feinting toward the South Korean army-held lines."

It was at that point that Lackner spotted eleven enemy tanks approaching. These tanks "shelled at almost point blank range, while the Red infantry maneuvered until mid-afternoon," Lackner told Lambert. "Then the Red tide rolled forward. For about two-and-a-half-hours there was savage close-in fighting."

Lambert concluded his report with, "The tired men who got out do not look defeated. Lackner was among them."[73]

Master Sergeant Lackner is believed to be the first man from the 25th Division to be decorated in Korea.

A Second Bronze Oak Leaf Cluster in lieu of a **Third Award of the Silver Star** *is awarded to Master Sergeant* **Clarence Lackner**, *Infantry, U.S. Army, for gallantry in connection with military operations against an opposing armed force while serving with Company F, 35th Regimental Combat Team, 25th Infantry Division, in action in Korea on 22 July 1950. While Company F, 35th Infantry Regiment, occupied a position near Mungyong, a superior*

---

[73] *War Diary, 12-31 July 1950.* Headquarters 35th Infantry; *Narrative 12-31 July 1950.* Headquarters 35th Infantry Regiment; Lambert acct. *Winona Republican-Herald.* 24 July 1950.

Lackner is one of Minnesota's most decorated combat veterans.
(Courtesy Lackner family)

number of enemy forces attacked the right flank of the Second Platoon, making the company's position untenable and forcing its withdrawal. Rallying his comrades, Sergeant Lackner led his platoon in a successful counterattack, regaining the high ground, and consolidated the position while under heavy artillery, mortar and small arms fire. When his company was forced to withdraw a second time, Sergeant Lackner remained in position and covered the withdrawal by delivering effective and deadly counter fire until every member of the company had withdrawn. The aggressiveness, undaunted courage, and outstanding leadership by Sergeant Lackner was an inspiration to his comrades and reflects great credit on himself and the military service.

What's missing from Lackner's citation is that Lackner also pulled off a repeat performance of that long-ago day in Finn Town, when he splashed into the lake to save his friend who wanted to drown rather than be drafted. The *History of the 25ᵗʰ Division*[74] reads:

> At the height of the action, while his comrades were going down before enemy slugs, Sgt. Lackner cooly aided the wounded, and others who could not swim, across the bullet churned waters of the stream.

---

[74] *Twenty-fifth Infantry Division: Tropic Lightning, Korea, 1950-1954.* 2002. P 19.

Chapter 15

ENTER THE WOLFHOUNDS

"Some people are exhilarated by combat. They love it. They seem to thrive on it. I knew people like that. Most people though, ninety-nine percent of them, are scared to death. Including myself. It's only after it's all over that the grand design falls into place, and you begin to see what you had a hand in doing." Uzal Ent, 27th Infantry Regiment

WHEN THE 25th DIVISION set sail from Japan to Korea, its 27th Regiment *Wolfhounds* were the first to deploy. Like the other early units, they had only two of their three battalions when they arrived on July 10.

Upon reaching Pusan, the regiment met its new commander, a handsome charismatic Californian who fought as a paratrooper in the 101st Airborne during WWII and also served as senior aide to future president Dwight D. Eisenhower when he was Army Chief of Staff.

Colonel John "Mike" Michaelis had since been stationed in Japan and didn't learn he was to take command of the Wolfhounds until 45 minutes before his plane departed for Korea.

"I remember sitting there one afternoon, thinking how lucky I was in this fat desk job," he said. "I had seen enough of war to last me a lifetime. I was thinking of getting me a little flag to put on my desk and a little sign saying: '*Go get 'em, boys. We are all behind you.*' The next morning I was on a plane bound for Taejon. Three days later, at the docks in Pusan, I took command of the regiment."

Michaelis found his new situation "pretty depressing." His second in command was new, and some of the officers he inherited were too spooked for field command. These had to be identified and replaced. He also learned most of his troops were green recruits.

"They came in with their duffel bags loaded down," he told reporters. "The officers carried foot lockers. As a paratrooper, I learned that you have to travel and fight lightly loaded if you are going to fight at all. [. . .] We had all kinds of special-services gear – violins, banjos – God knows what all. There must have been eight carloads of junk shaken out of the regiment before we started north. But when we started out, we traveled like a fighting soldier ought to travel. Each man had his weapon, his ammunition, his blanket, shelter half, mess gear, razor, soap and towel and an extra pair of socks. That was all, and that was enough."[75]

Gilbert Check

Lieutenant Colonel Gilbert Check, from Williston, North Dakota, commanded Michaelis' 1st Battalion. "Gil" was the middle of three high-achieving brothers, all of whom became war heroes; Raymond and Leonard were killed and highly decorated in WWII.

The Check family, which included sisters Kathleen and Bernice, grew up around the corner from Gil's future wife, Thelma Hofengen. When asked when she first met Gilbert, Thelma said she could not recall a time that she didn't know him.

Gil's father, John, was a Polish immigrant who worked as a road-master for the Great Northern Railroad, and the family moved around North Dakota several times before settling in Williston. Leonard was born in Churches Ferry in 1911; Gilbert was born in Berwick in 1912; and Raymond was born in Granville in 1917.[76]

Gil's sister-in-law, Bernice Haakenson, recalled, "Those three boys were kind of tough, and their mom was strict." Indeed, Lena Check, a German-Russian immigrant, was known to wield a broom when she felt they needed it.

All three boys attended the University of North Dakota (UND) in Grand Forks. Gil studied law and went through the Reserve Officer Training Corp (ROTC) program, and during summer breaks, he worked

---

[75] Martin, Harold. "The Colonel Saved the Day." *Saturday Evening Post.* 9 Sep 1950.

[76] Captain Raymond Check was in the Army Air Corps flying a mission over France when he was killed June 26, 1943; he was celebrating his 25th, and final, mission that day. Leonard Check was a fighter pilot in the Pacific, where he became an ace, downing 12 enemy aircraft. He was killed in action 4 Jan 1945 and was the recipient of a Navy Cross, Silver Star, Legion of Merit and two Distinguished Flying Crosses.

in a Williston creamery. After getting his law degree from George Washington University, he returned to North Dakota to work for the Department of Agriculture.

Gilbert Check (front left) and future wife, Thelma Hofengen (back left), as sophomore class officers; Gil was treasurer, Thelma was secretary. (Williston High School yearbook 1931)

Raymond and Leonard were airmen, but Gil moved up through the Army ranks. By 1946, he was a lieutenant colonel acting as the executive officer with the Prosecution Division of the Supreme Commander of Allied Powers' Legal Section.

"Gil never saw a shot fired in anger in WWII," said his son-in-law, Jack Dorr. "He had passed the bar and was highly educated, so he was siphoned off to help prepare for the Japanese war crime trials."[77]

In 1946, Check was awarded a Bronze Star for "meritorious service in connection with military operations from 24 October 1944 to 2 September 1945." His citation reads:

As Assistant Chief of Staff, G-3 and as Executive of the G-3 Division,

---

[77] Author interviews Gilbert Check's wife, sister-in-law and son-in-law, 2010.

Headquarters, Replacement Training Command, he initiated, organized and subsequently guided the training program through which over 150,000 replacements were processed.[78]

Check planned to retire from the Army after the war trials, but the Army offered him a regular commission and allowed him to return to North Dakota to oversee the ROTC program at UND.

In contrast to his larger-than-life boss, Colonel Michaelis, Check was a smaller man, quiet spoken, deliberate and unassuming. But Check had since been sent to the Army War College and proved himself a very capable commander. Although they had very different personalities, the two officers were a good match in Korea, and their men appreciated both of them.

Lieutenant Addison Terry served directly under Check, and it's through his eyes that the North Dakotan comes to life. "I can't talk about Colonel Check without getting emotional," he said. "He was a great soldier and a true gentleman."[79]

Terry was the forward observer for the 8th Field Artillery, which was attached to the Wolfhounds. He had received almost no field training and had called in (fired) an artillery strike only once before being deployed. Worse, his training was obsolete – since his ROTC training in 1948, the artillery had switched to a grid system, and he had to learn his job while under fire in Korea; Gil Check was his teacher.

Terry lasted longer than most, making it to early September before getting his million-dollar-wound (a combat injury serious enough to require evacuation). While recuperating in 1950-51, he wrote a vivid and often humorous memoir titled *The Battle for Pusan*, which provides a compelling insider's view of Gilbert Check's command early in the war.

As soon as the regiment hit Korean soil, Check's 1st Battalion was rushed north to support a South Korean unit near Uijong. Luckily, the ROKs held, allowing the Wolfhounds to shake out their jitters on patrols and smaller skirmishes.

Four days later they were at Andong, where his superiors inspected his forward position. Terry writes:

---

[78]"Lt. Col. G. J. Check Awarded Bronze Star." *Stars & Stripes*. 25 April 1946.

[79]Author interview with Terry 2010; Terry, Addison. *The Battle for Pusan*. Written 1950-51, published Presidio Press, 2006. Excerpts reprinted by written permission.

Colonel Check was a slight little man with a quiet confidence about him . . . Colonel Michaelis was tall and slender. His hair was a silver gray, his skin as clear and smooth as I have ever seen on a man. He was extremely alert and spoke distinctly . . . The two stood above my hole and discussed the campaign, and I eavesdropped for all I was worth.

The regiment moved out that night at about 10:00 p.m., forming a motorized column "at least five miles long."

In all the towns, the civilians were lining the road, even after midnight, in tight little groups, watching us roar past. They made no sound and no one waved. They just stood solemnly at the side of the road and watched with poker faces as we rode by.
. . . By 0200 it started to rain, and this not only added to the misery of the trip, but also to the hazard. We were in a particularly mountainous region, and the rain had made the red clay roads deathtraps of oozing mud and water. Two trucks were lost over the edge of a precipice, and most of their cargo of men were lost.

An hour later, they entered a large city. Terry spotted a drenched MP and asked what town they were in.

"Taegu," came back his muffled voice. I looked around at the others in my party in surprise. What the hell were we doing back in Taegu?

The column headed out and continued moving until 4:30 a.m. They sat in the rain until dawn and then drove until mid-afternoon.

Because we had learned of none of the unfortunate battles at the Han River, Suwon, Osan, and so on, we had no idea of the critical state of our position. . . . We completely turned around twice, and by 1400 I don't believe there was a soul in the outfit who had any idea where we were. The significant thing, as I saw it, was that there was more and more military traffic as we moved forward, and all the vehicles were from the 24th Division.
Another condition that pointed toward our nearness to

some action was the thousands of refugees who streamed east and south. It was obvious that things were not going too well. A few of the troops of the 24th had been questioned by our men at rest breaks, and the tales they told turned our blood cold. They told of tanks, artillery, and mortars that supported thousands of yelling North Koreans who charged on toward them indifferent to their own casualties. They told of entire battalions being wiped out, and artillery positions and regimental CPs (command posts) being overrun. They told of the aid stations being run through by tanks, and of the enemy shooting the G.I. wounded as they lay on litters. . . . Frankly, seeing and talking to these troops from the 24th frightened us.

The convoy continued moving until nearly midnight. At 6:00 a.m., the word came down that the North Koreans were pressing hard on the 24th Division at Taejon, and the Wolfhounds were going to move up on their right to prevent them from being flanked via a secondary road.

Meanwhile, Colonel Check kept Lieutenant Terry nearby and in his classroom manner taught the young forward observer the crucial steps for directing the fire of the artillery weapons far to their rear.

"Of course the mission of the artillery is to lengthen the battlefield and to disperse the enemy formations before they can get in small arms range," Terry said. "So whenever we went into a new position, it was very important that we pick out avenues of approach, and have preplanned concentrations on those, and record the range and deflection and so forth.

"Colonel Check would look through his field glasses, and I would be standing beside him. I would look through my field glasses, too, and he'd say, 'Well, Lieutenant Terry, see that draw over there? I think that's an obvious avenue of approach.'

"I'd agree, and he'd say, 'Okay, we'll call that concentration one.' And then he would say, 'That ridge over there is obviously a defilade. I think we ought to plan some high angle fire so we can get rounds on the backside of that hill.'"

Terry chuckled as he remembered trying to sound self-assured. "Yes sir, we sure ought to do that," he answered. "But by doing this, he led me to know what to look for."

Upon arriving at their critical position east of Taejon, Check ordered Terry and his crew to set up an observation post on a mountain that he and his crew quickly dubbed a *bare-assed son of a bitch*.

The battalion spent the rest of the day digging in and preparing defense positions.

Meanwhile, four fresh enemy divisions had bypassed Taejon, and one struck Gilbert Check's battalion at dawn, writes Terry in his memoir:

> It was 0540 on the dot, for I had just looked at my watch, when the crap hit the fan below. The sun had come up in a big orange ball and with its light we could see for miles – but not below us. There was a thick fog or mist clinging to the valley, and we could observe only about two or three hundred feet down the hill . . . Below in the white fog there was a helluva firefight in progress.

When the fog lifted, Terry tried his radio, which had been obsolete since 1946. It was inoperable, as was a different model used by another soldier.

> Here we were on this hill for the sole purpose of keeping the battalion informed of the situation to the front and the left flank, and we could not even communicate with them. If there were enemy tanks coming down the road, I could not even get the artillery to fire on them for lack of communication. I cussed.

As they waited for wire to be brought up for a telephone connection, they turned their field glasses on Taejon, about 15 miles distant.

> I gulped. There was an air strike in progress and it looked as though a dozen or so planes were giving the place the once-over. Smoke was beginning to spiral up into the sky, and if I listened carefully, I could hear the "booms" of artillery or bombs – I was not sure which [. . .] mortar and artillery rounds were bursting all over the road and rice paddies over which the 24th was trying withdraw. I watched this scene with horror. The sergeant had his glasses on the road to Taejon also, and his only comment was, "There goes the 24th."

In 1953, Army historian Roy Appleman conducted an extensive interview with Check and used the North Dakotan's first-hand account to describe this battle for *South to the Naktong, North to the Yalu*. Check wrote:

General Walker had begun the quick and improvised shifting of troops to meet emergencies that was to characterize his defense of the Pusan Perimeter. The 27th Infantry's mission at Hwanggan was to relieve the decimated [South Korean] troops retreating down the Poun road.[80]

Check moved out early on July 23 and took up defensive positions that evening near a mountain village called Sangyong-ni. Check's objective was to find the enemy's positions, so he turned to the exhausted South Koreans his men were replacing, writing:

> I was unable to get from [the South Koreans] a statement on the enemy. The South Koreans appeared rather orderly in their movement to the rear but did not indicate to me the size of the enemy following them.

Check sent out a 30-man patrol led by 1st Lieutenant John Buckley of Able Company. Moving north toward Poun, the patrol spotted a column of enemy approaching. Buckley sent his men up onto the terrain on either side of the road, and when the North Koreans were nearly abreast of them, they opened fire. The enemy soldiers reacted with a certain amount of confusion, which gave the patrol the opportunity to break off and head back. When they returned at 4:00 a.m., six of their men were missing, writes Check:

> Lt. Buckley did come back after his contact with the enemy, and we did therefore have notice that we would be soon engaged. We had rather strong defensive positions on small ridge lines through the center of which ran a road. I had a Company on each side of the road on the high ground.
>
>   In the early [morning] the attacks commenced in a rather heavy fog. This fog enabled the enemy to come extremely close to our positions before we were able to observe him. The attack was preceded by mortar and artillery fire on our positions, and then tanks rumbled down the road and were successful in penetrating our position on the road.

---

[80] Gilbert Check letter to Maj. Gen. Richard W. Stephens, Chief of Military History for U.S. Army. 25 Nov 1957. Includes notes on original manuscript of Appleman's *South to the Naktong. . .* (See footnote 48, page 201). Copy of letter provided by John Dorr.

My Command Post was immediately behind Baker Company. The tanks, in penetrating this position, fired into the Battalion Command Post from the road. In the meantime, both Rifle Companies were extremely heavily engaged in repelling the foot elements of this NK Division. Heavy fighting lasted all morning.

Several of the tanks were knocked out by artillery, bazookas and certainly by the Air Force, which arrived in the nick of time to knock out several more tanks. [The Air Force] also succeeded in destroying several of my jeeps and killed my Medical Officer. I cite this in order to show that our vehicles and enemy tanks were in extremely close proximity.

When the North Koreans finally withdrew, Colonel Michaelis theorized they would try to encircle Check's battalion during the night, so he ordered Check to quietly withdraw his men through the 2nd Battalion after dark. Check writes:

Later that evening, the enemy again struck full force, but our redisposition on new ground surprised him and we were able to inflict many casualties. Heavy fighting continued until late in the evening at which time we disengaged and moved to the rear to new positions . . . I should like to state that a disengagement at night under full attack was an extremely difficult maneuver. My troops, new as they were to battle, accomplished this in a veteran manner.

. . . I consider [this battle] extremely important, because this was the first fight of the Wolfhounds, and the first battle where the Koreans were really fully stopped for a day, even though they were equipped with tanks.

Colonel Michaelis later recalled: "The kids won a battle – won it big – and that was very important for the outfit. They developed that all-important confidence right away. In fact, they became so cocky they were almost intolerable."[81]

He also acknowledged Check's leadership for this action.

---

[81] Appleman. *South to the Naktong, North to the Yalu.* P 200-202.

Silver Star: *"**Colonel Check**, a battalion commander in the 27th Regiment of the 25th Division, was cited for heroic action in rallying his unit to repel an overwhelming attack by superior numbers of enemy infantry and tanks when defeat seemed imminent. In the action, enemy tanks penetrated his positions and attacked the battalion command post. Although soldiers of his unit were untried in battle, they were inspired by his calm direction of defense and personal bravery to withstand the three-hour attack and inflict such heavy casualties on the Red Korean enemy they were forced to retire, according to the citation accompanying the award."* (*Pacific Stars & Stripes*. 8 Aug 1950.)

Addison Terry agreed with Michaelis's assessment, saying, "Colonel Check was absolutely unflappable. When everybody else was hiding in the ditch, he was standing up there saying, *Do this, do that, do the other.*"

Chapter 16

MAJOR GENEVIEVE SMITH

Major Smith had a premonition of disaster, saying that she "wouldn't come back from Korea." A Concise Biography of Major Genevieve Marion Smith, ANC

LIKE MANY OF her contemporaries, Major Genevieve Smith had accomplished a great deal since dropping out of high school. But her brilliant career ended the night of July 27, when the Air Force C-47 in which she was flying exploded while en route from Japan to Korea. Only one of the 23 passengers aboard survived. The others, including the plane's crew, were lost at sea.[82]

Smith's newest assignment – Chief Nurse of the Eighth Army in Korea – would have been the crowning touch in her 22-year career.

One of six children born to Thomas and Mary Smith, Genevieve decided early that farming was not the life she wanted. Her siblings often recounted her telling them, "As soon as I'm old enough, I'm getting out of here."

Smith had three years of high school, attending Visitation Academy in Dubuque and Cascade High School in Cascade, Iowa. Focusing on a career as a nurse, she left high school to begin her training at Mercy Hospital in Dubuque, becoming a registered nurse in 1925. Four years later, she entered the military as a 2nd lieutenant in the Reserve Army Nurse Corps, and it was during a subsequent five-year assignment at

---

[82]Smith information based on various sources, chief of which is: *A Concise Biography of Major Genevieve Marion Smith, ANC*, prepared by Genevieve K. Comeau; General Reference and Research Branch, Historical Unit, USAMEDS; Walter Reed Army Medical Center; April 1962. *Lubbock Evening Journal*, 1 Aug 1950; Also various newspaper reports from Iowa newspapers, 1950;

Fitzsimons General Hospital in Denver that she found time to finish her high school graduation requirements.

In the mid-1930s, Smith began a string of assignments as Chief Nurse, first in the States and then during WWII with the 189th General Hospital in Europe during the Rhineland Campaign. During the occupation period following the war, she served as Chief Nurse at the Philippine Scout Hospital in Manila and the 155th Station Hospital in Yokohama, Japan, in July 1949.

Remarks from Smith's efficiency reports found their way into a short biography written about her in 1962. These tend to agree that she was cheerful, tolerant, "neat in appearance," quietly efficient and "admirable"in her ability to cultivate solid relationships with her fellow workers. She was also described as "businesslike and thoroughly professional in bearing, judicious in speech and ideas."

When Smith volunteered to go to Korea with the advance party of nurses, Brigadier General James E. Graham was key to getting her assigned as Chief Nurse, with her biographer writing:

> During a telephone conversation on 13 April 1962, General Graham reminisced about Genevieve Smith. He recalled that her position as Chief Nurse did not prevent her rolling up her sleeves and going to work like anyone else. He said that he had never known a nurse who could do "so many things so well without getting bogged down." He called her "a tremendous woman" and explained that she had been selected for [Chief Nurse Eighth Army] because she was "the most capable person to organize the nursing service in Korea."

Vivian Shepherd Moore, Smith's co-worker, was also interviewed. While the two women worked closely in Japan, there was another connection between them. Moore was married to another Iowan – Colonel Ned Moore – who was just taking command of the 19th Infantry Regiment at the time of Smith's death. The biographer wrote:

> Mrs. Moore . . . said that Major Smith was "one of the most wonderful" Chief Nurses she had known, and deemed it a privilege to have worked under her. She felt that one reason for the high morale among the nurses was the fact that Major Smith never interfered or held a tight rein if the nurses were performing their duties conscientiously and well. However, if they failed to live up to the high standards which she set for

them, she did not hesitate to reprimand them and take corrective action. But even as a disciplinarian she was tactful and just, so that she did not incur resentment or insubordination.

Genevieve Smith. (Courtesy Ed Horsfield)

Mrs. Moore also recalled that Major Smith had a premonition of disaster, saying that she "wouldn't come back from Korea." She was not afraid of death but, true to her general character and specific sense of responsibility, she hoped to retire at the end of the Korean War. Her sisters and brothers had been caring for their aged mother and she felt that it was now "her turn" to shoulder the obligation.

Thus the tragedy of 27 July 1950 deprived a family in Iowa of a fine and loyal member and cost the Army Nurse Corps one of its most outstanding administrators.

Ed Horsfield, Genevieve's nephew, was a teenager at the time of her death, and he recalled the night the dreaded telegram arrived at the Smith farm near Epworth, Iowa. "About nine o'clock, a taxi brought it out. It said she was missing," he said. "The plane went down, and there were no survivors."

Fifty-eight years later, Horsfield visited Arlington Cemetery, saying, "There wasn't a sound in the whole area. It doesn't take much to break down crying."

It was then that he realized Genevieve was never provided a headstone, saying, "I knew she was out there some place, and somebody had to know."

Using her service number, Horsfield set out to have his aunt properly memorialized. After a great deal of effort, Major Smith's military records were discovered to have survived the great fire of the National Archives in St. Louis, MO. With those documents in hand, Horsfield was able to secure a headstone for Genevieve at Arlington in May 2008, saying it was placed on a peaceful hillside facing the Washington Monument.[83]

Other Uncounted Casualties

The number of dead Americans incurred due to the Korean War will often appear as two very different numbers. The official count of dead is often shown as 36,576, while others insist the total number is 54,246. This disparity is attributed to those who were killed "in theater" as opposed to all American servicepeople who died during the three-year war. Training accidents and other nonbattle deaths are included in the larger number, but for some reason, Genevieve Smith and others who died in the July 27 crash aren't included in either tally.

---

[83] Reber, Craig D. "A headstone for Genevieve." *Telegraph Herald*. 12 Sep 2008. *Pacific Stars & Stripes*. 10 Apr, 31 May, 23 Sep, 2 Oct, & 14 Oct 1950; *Dubuque Telegraph Herald*. 30 Jul 1950; *The Fargo Forum*. 2 Aug 1950; *The Charleston Gazette*. 2 Aug 1950; *Winona Republican Herald*. 29 July 1950. *The News* (Mt. Pleasant, IA). 1 Aug 1950; *ASN Aircraft accident Douglas C-47D 44-76439 O-Shima*. Aviation-Safety.net. Web: 18 Oct 2012.

Another Iowan killed on this flight was Major Frederick Engel, who grew up in Hubbard. The son of an Evangelical pastor, Engel took Reserve Officer Training (ROTC) in college and was the band teacher at Lincoln High School in Des Moines for 13 years before being activated for service in WWII. After the war, he was transferred to Japan, where he worked with the Army's Troop Information and Education division (TI&E). Part of his job involved working with *Pacific Stars & Stripes* newspaper, and his flight was related to that assignment.

Another victim, Lieutenant Colonel Wilfred Jackson, 47, served in Europe during WWII. In August 1947, he moved to Fargo, North Dakota, where he was a military science instructor with the 411th Infantry Organized Reserve. The bespectacled officer developed a deep interest in the life General George Custer, and at the time of his death, he was writing a book about Custer. Colonel Jackson was one of MacArthur's staff officers who regularly commuted to Korea on "undisclosed" military missions.

A bit of mystery surrounds Matthew C. Moravec, 35, from Winona, Minnesota. He was in the Army from 1940 to 1946, serving Stateside, in Europe and in Alaska. He served as a court reporter during war crime trials and had since been employed as a civilian by Army occupation forces in Japan. He was reportedly working for the provost marshal, the Army's law enforcement branch, at the time of his death at sea.

*The **SOLDIER'S MEDAL (Posthumous)** is awarded to Sergeant First Class **Melvin F. Schultz**, Corps of Engineers, U. S. Army, while a member of Company B, 13th Engineer Combat Battalion, displayed heroism at Camp Fuji, Honshu, Japan, on 25 August 1950. On this date, Sergeant Schultz was in a trench with members of his platoon acting as instructor in hand grenade throwing. Upon seeing an enlisted man accidentally drop an activated hand grenade in the trench, Sergeant Schultz ordered his men to safety and at the same time, with complete disregard for his personal safety, dived for the grenade in an attempt to clear it from the trench. As he grasped the grenade, it exploded and inflicted injuries so severe that Sergeant Schultz died immediately. By his courageous action, he saved his men from possible death or serious injury. The heroism and self-sacrifice displayed by Sergeant Schultz reflect the highest credit on himself and the military service. Home of record: **Fosston, Minnesota**.*

The Soldier's Medal is a non-combat equivalent of the Medal of Honor. Schultz is not considered a casualty of the war.

A recent letter to a friend in Winona indicated he was working, as a civilian, on a criminal investigation. But Moravec's family received a letter from him that made them wonder if he had reenlisted. He wrote it shortly before his flight to Korea: "Yesterday I received orders to proceed to Pusan, Korea. Expect to leave Yokohama tonight at 12 midnight by plane. I will wear an Army uniform but with no insignia."

Moravec informed his family he was sending home two boxes – one containing clothing and the other photographs: "I will keep some civilian clothes in Yokohama as I am ordered to Korea only temporarily ... If everything goes all right, I'll be in Pusan tomorrow morning."

Moravec's actual mission is not known to have ever been publicly revealed.

Chapter 17

WALKER VERSUS MACARTHUR

"We were part of Lieutenant General Walton H. Walker's 'mobile defense.' The strategy focused on using a small number of soldiers to form a thin screen while the bulk of the force waited to counterattack. The idea was unheard of in the 1950s and considered a 'theory' at best, but Walker used it to perfection."
William Richardson, 3rd Battalion, 8th Cavalry

GENERAL WALKER WAS a cavalryman during WWII, serving as one of General George Patton's chief officers. When the 1st Cavalry Division arrived in Korea, it was led by another of Patton's officers, Hobart "Hap" Gay. Thus, Walker gave the division an extra warm welcome.

As with every unit that had arrived in Korea, the Cavalry immediately took some hard hits. The division steadied itself by July 26, but Walker's line was still too thin, and too many holes still needed plugging. He had given the exhausted 24th Division a fleeting moment to rest and regroup, but the situation was still so dire that he was forced to almost immediately send them back to the front.

With his lines stretched so thin, he could see only two choices – find more men or shrink his perimeter. The Army was requesting 100,000 draftees be selected in September and October, but that wouldn't help him here and now. His only logical choice was to focus on tightening his perimeter, and he wanted to do it by consolidating Eighth Army troops along the Naktong River, a natural barrier that arcs around the southeast portion of the Korean peninsula. Since this river was in friendly territory, bridges could be prepared for demolition as soon as allied troops crossed over, and North Korea would be denied easy avenues of pursuit.

Walker phoned General Edward "Ned" Almond, General MacArthur's right-hand man, at general headquarters in Tokyo, Japan. While Walker had come up the ranks under General Patton, Almond was a loyal admirer of General MacArthur. In this triangle of command, Walker was the odd man out.

From his distant vantage point – 700 miles from the battlefield – Almond perceived Walker as having a defeatist attitude and warned him that a withdrawal to the Naktong River would almost certainly lead to "a Dunkirk."

After hanging up, Almond urged MacArthur to fly immediately to Korea to light a fire under the Eighth Army Commander.

MacArthur had his heart set on an amphibious assault half way up the west coast of Korea at Inchon. Due to lack of troops, however, he had been forced to postpone this landing. Thus, he was unhappy with Walker's declaration that the current delaying strategies were too costly.

The following day, MacArthur and Almond, along with selected reporters, arrived in Taegu for Almond's proposed pep talk with Walker. It was MacArthur's first trip back to Korea since the war began.

The meeting lasted approximately 90 minutes. Historian Clay Blair describes it as MacArthur doing most of the talking, "speaking as much to the 'unseen audience' and history as to Walker."[84] MacArthur did not discuss Walker's wish to tighten his perimeter. He spoke, Blair writes, "grandly and loftily of Eighth Army's role in history and the defeat of communism. Ultimate victory was near at hand."

In short, Walker's plan to consolidate his troops along the Naktong was denied. This was not surprising to those who knew the Supreme Commander. On June 28, General Dwight Eisenhower had met with General Omar Bradley's principal assistants, General J. Lawton Collins, General Wade Haislip, and General Matthew Ridgway.

In his desk journal, Ridgway noted: "In commenting upon General MacArthur, Ike expressed the wish that he would like to see a younger general out there, rather than, as he expressed it, 'an untouchable' whose actions you cannot predict and who will himself decide what information he wants Washington to have and what he will withhold."[85]

After dismissing Walker's concerns, MacArthur returned to his

---

[84] Blair. *The Forgotten War*. P 167.

[85] Ibid. P 79 and p 996 n 41.

private plane, telling reporters, "I have a feeling of optimism after this inspection today." He told them his trip "completely confirmed" his statement to President Truman the preceding week – that the quick and valiant actions of combat troops in Korea had "bought the precious time necessary to build a secure base" and "ended the chance for victory by the North Korean forces. That does not mean that victory passes to us instantly or without a long hard row and the most difficult struggle,"

General Walker (rear) wearily accompanies General MacArthur to his plane after the meeting. (DoD)

MacArthur said. "That we will have new heartaches and new setbacks is inherent in the situation, but I have never been more confident in victory – in ultimate victory – in my life than I am now."[86]

The following morning, MacArthur released an enthusiastic communique regarding the situation west of Pusan titled: "U.S. Forces are preparing to move into Hadong when the town stops burning as a result of aerial strikes by U.N. planes." *Pacific Stars & Stripes* elaborated:

> Putting the brakes on the unopposed Communist walk through the southwestern quarter of Korea, fresh American troops were reported in action for the first time on the southern coast 70 miles west of Pusan Thursday, as a firm west wall for the United Nations' beachhead began to take shape. A U.S. 5th Air Force spokesman in Korea said the Yank infantrymen, whose outfit was not identified, were prepared to move into Hadong, 20 miles west of Chinju, after jet planes set fire to the river port occupied Tuesday by what GHQ (MacArthur's General Headquarters) called Red "marauders rather than consolidated columns." The situation now has "solidified," said a GHQ spokesman, and there no longer is any doubt that the United Nations' forces will be able to hold their beachhead in the southeastern quarter of the peninsula.

This statement was utter folly, and any secrecy that might have protected the upcoming mission to Hadong had just evaporated.

---

[86]Don Whitehead (AP). *Indiana Evening Gazette*. 27 July 1950.

Chapter 18

THE TRAP AT HADONG

"Comparing service in Korea with World War II, he says there is no comparison in hardship endured. He said the Korean situation is much more serious for the men in action." Twin Falls reporter about Chester Brumet, recipient of a Distinguished Service Cross, two Silver Stars, and three Purple Hearts.

THE UNIDENTIFIED "FRESH TROOPS" referred to in MacArthur's press release consisted of two battalions of the 29th Infantry Regiment, which had just sailed from Okinawa to Pusan. The unit was officially the 29th Regimental Combat Team (29th RCT) because it was lacking its 2nd Battalion and wasn't at full regimental capacity.

A high percentage of these men were raw recruits who had just sailed to Okinawa from the States. The 29th RCT was to have paused in Japan for additional combat training, but the situation was too desperate. The 29th instead swerved toward Korea, and the men went directly to the front lines in support of the 19th Regiment.

The 29th's 1st Battalion was rushed to Anui, while the 3rd Battalion headed west, paralleling the southern coast, toward Hadong, where it was to cover a southwestern highway route into Pusan. Allied intelligence failed these men who believed they would face a handful of "marauders," as described in MacArthur's communique. The 3rd Battalion was moving straight into the jaws of North Korea's crack 6th Division, which had slipped, apparently unnoticed, down the west coast of South Korea.

Morris Breed, Dale Kutz & Jim Yeager

Morris Breed later lived and worked as a millwright in open pit mines on the Mesabe Iron Range near Aurora, Minnesota. After retiring, he said, "I moved to Alaska to warm up."[87]

Breed was a member of Headquarters Company. "I'd just left the states," he said. "I was gonna go to Okinawa for occupation duty. We were in the middle of the Pacific when we heard, on board ship, that North Korea attacked South Korea. The second day, they announced the Air Force was bombing North Korean installations, and we knew.

"We went to Okinawa, and there was a typhoon. There was another shipload of men coming in, but they finally made it.

"We knew that it's possible we would be going to Korea. We were sitting in our barracks, and somebody walked in and made the announcement that if we had personal items, we were to dispose of them – for example, ship them to the States through the military post office – because, we were going into combat.

"Well, our hearts – we actually died right there on the floor. Nobody talked. You know, we'd been trained to be soldiers, but it was peace time. Second World War had just ended and, you know, *we were safe*. We were just occupying Japan. Everything was okay. But now here we're faced with we're going into battle, and it took us by shock. Later on we realized we had to keep living, and so we just moved on.

"On about July 21st, we got on this Japanese cargo ship, and from there we went to Pusan. There was only [living] space for 12 men on that Japanese ship. They had just unloaded cement. It was just nothing but a big tank – what I mean is no bunks, nothing, just a hole. I was one of the last guys to go down in there. You had to climb down a rope ladder into the hole. It was all dark down in there, and there was water on the floor. Somebody told me that where I was standing, that was my place. I looked up the ladder, and there was nobody coming, and I told my buddy, 'I'm not staying here.'

"All of our trucks and equipment was tied down up on the upper deck, so I went back up the ladder, and him and I stayed in the anchor port, up in the bow of the ship," said Breed.

"That's where we stayed 'til we got to Pusan. Nobody argued with us. Somebody probably figured we were guards on duty. It was such a mixed up mess, nobody knew what was going on."

"I had been on Okinawa for a year the day the Korean War started," said Dale Kutz, of Allentown, Pennsylvania. "I was supposed to leave the next day, on the 26th – on my birthday – to come home. And

---

[87] Author's interviews with Breed, Kutz and Yeager conducted 2008.

because of the war, I had an extra year in Korea instead.

"They were really professional in telling us about it – especially those of us who were due to leave the next day. They called us all in, we had a meeting with the regimental commander, and he told us what happened. He said, 'Right now, nobody's going home. We're all going to Korea.' I was disappointed not to be going home, but everybody took it real well. You know, we were amazed that the North Koreans had invaded South Korea, but more or less I'd have to say I think everybody was gung-ho, ready to go."

Kutz recalled arriving in Korea. "Things were so hot and heavy, and the North Koreans were making so much gain, that when we arrived in Pusan, they put us on a train immediately, and we went to Masan. As soon as we disembarked from the train and got our vehicles ready and all, we left for Hadong. We were all in trucks and jeeps and what have you. Up toward Hadong is where we started to run into the refugees. This is when things got bad. We were under the impression we were going to fight a few hundred guerillas. But they were waiting for us."

That night, the battalion dug in near the village of Huangchon, about five or six miles east of Hadong.

Jim Yeager and a handful of men in the battalion's S-2 (intelligence gathering) section drove toward Hadong on a reconnaissance mission that night.[88]

Yeager grew up in Colorado, where his father trained him from childhood to be a soldier, even taking his son along for National Guard training on weekends. The youngster fired his first gun at age five, and he was thoroughly educated on almost every hand-held military weapon by the time he joined the Navy in 1947, when he was 17. During his year with the Naval Reserves, he also qualified on a number of specialized weapons, including antiaircraft and onboard heavy weaponry.

The military was scaling back at this time, and his unit was deactivated, so in 1948, Yeager joined the National Guard, where he qualified on additional weaponry, including machine guns and mortars. The following year, he enlisted in the Army. He was a squad leader

---

[88] Yeager, James "The truth about what really happened at Hadong." *The Graybeards*. Korean War Veterans Association. Vol 18, No 1. Jan/Feb 2004: P 27; Yeager's unpublished memoir, *My Trip to Hell and Back*. No date. Author interview 2008. Excerpts identified by "he wrote," and interiews quotes as "he said."

throughout his training, and after completing basic training, he was selected to attend the leadership academy. He ended up in Okinawa on occupation duty.

Because of his background and keen interest, Yeager was exceptionally suited for reconnaissance. In the case of Hadong, accurate intelligence was sorely lacking, as he soon learned.

About his 3rd Battalion commander, Yeager wrote, "It is interesting to note that Col. Mott had previously told the troops that there were only about 300 peasants armed with pitch forks and clubs in Hadong. They were causing trouble, and we were going to kick the shit out of them."

The evening of July 26, Yeager and his good friend John Toney accompanied the battalion S-2, Captain William Mitchell, on a patrol of the road up to the Hadong Pass.

"We were probably about five or six miles distant from Hadong," he said. "We had to go up over a mountain pass to get into Hadong. A typhoon had been screwing things up and had washed out a main road, and Fat Chae[89] had us take this secondary road to go toward Hadong. Captain Mitchell took Toney and I, a driver, and an interpreter. I don't know where this interpreter had come from, but he was a Korean.

"We went forward that night after dark. As we drove down the road – now visualize this – we're going into a horseshoe-shaped valley. As you're looking to the top of the horseshoe, that's where the pass is. [We'd be using a one-lane] road just basically wide enough for a jeep or 2½-ton military truck. The trucks would be right on the edges of the road – the big trucks. On your right-hand side is mountains. On your left-hand side the road drops off into large rice paddies. On the other side of those are another bunch of mountains. We were walking into a horseshoe-shaped configuration," he said.

"Now . . . we get about three-quarters of the way, or half the way up this valley, and there was a hut over on the right-hand side at the base of the mountains. As best as I can remember, there were only one or two huts there.

"Just before we turned off to these two huts, or Korean houses, we passed about six or seven young Koreans. Now these kids had almost bald heads, their hair was so short. They were in the native white

---

[89]General Chae Byong Duk, South Korea's Army Chief of Staff, accompanied the 3rd Battalion as a guide, interpreter and advisor. He had recently been relieved of command, and the Americans reportedly called him "Fat" because of his girth.

clothing. White pants and shirt. They were squatted down in the ditch on the right-hand side of the road, there. There was no visible weapons, but these kids were in shape. They looked to me like – of course it's hard to tell an Oriental's age – but they looked to me like they were 18, 19, 20-year-olds. And they weren't starving to death, either. I mean they were in good, good shape.

"They were all bunched up, squatted down in the ditch like they'd been coming down the road in a column of twos, and they saw us coming. Of course we were running without our lights on. We had our blackout lights on, but we didn't have our headlights on, just the blackout lights. These men didn't make any gestures or anything as we passed. Some kind of looked at us and smiled. Others didn't.

"Shortly after we passed this group, we pulled over and talked with an old man in one of these huts through the interpreter," he said. "I looked forward while this conversation was going on between the

(Map courtesy of Center of Military History)

captain, the interpreter and this old man. And I could see cigarettes lighting up all through this area ahead of us. I mean it wasn't one or two. It was like I was looking at a darked-out baseball stadium full of people who were smoking, drawing on their cigarettes," said Yeager.

"The old man told us, 'If you keep coming, tomorrow there'll be a big battle.' That's what he told us. He already knew we were coming some way or another. They knew what was going on.

"So Captain Mitchell says *all right*, we get back in the jeep, and we go back to the battalion. By that time, it's one or two o'clock in the morning. He reports to the battalion commander, Lieutenant Colonel Mott, and tells him what we discovered up there.

I don't know what the whole briefing was from the Captain, but the next morning, they don't have any flankers out, no scouts out on the flanks, or out on your right and left sides. No one was out there running the ridges or down below the military crest, to see what the hell's ahead there on those mountains. Nothing like that."

The battalion column of roughly 900 men approached the Hadong Pass about an hour later.

The Trap is Sprung

Morris Breed was near the front of the column. "Before the battle started, I'm standing next to my lieutenant – Lieutenant Sykes from Sykes, Pennsylvania. We would do anything for him. He was a great man.

"There was an American colonel there, I believe his name was Mott, and one of my own buddies was his jeep driver. Next to him was a Korean general in American uniform [Chae], and we were in a little tiny village of four or five huts. We were preparing to attack, and these officers are talking and arguing amongst themselves.

"There was an old Korean woman, she came out of one of the huts. She put her hands together in front of her face as if to pray, and she came up to the Korean general and said we should not move, because the mountains were saturated with the enemy.

"The Korean general suggested to [Colonel Mott] – now you gotta remember, the general's a Korean – he's more or less a guide – he's saying we shouldn't go forward. I'm standing right there, probably within 10 feet of all these men, and I heard them talking.

"The colonel said we go forward. And the general was doing everything he could to tell us no, because of the information this woman was giving him.

"Pretty soon they told us to march," said Breed. "We started marching into the battleground, and I remember this woman walking parallel to me. She was crying and praying, and all of a sudden, it started raining. The rice paddies were boiling. It sounded just like a heavy rain hitting all around us. But it wasn't rain drops. It was bullets."

"Somebody shouted at us, *get down!* Well, the only place you could get down was to lay in the water. You know, there's no place to hide, because at this spot, we're on a flat road. As soon as you leave the road, you're immediately in the water – in the rice paddies.

"I'm assuming the old woman lived right there, but I have no way of knowing for sure. The only one who could understand her language was the general. Nobody else listened to her. They couldn't understand her. She walked right into battle with us. She walked beside me, and when those bullets started coming, we ran for cover. I have no idea what happened to her. It's a memory I'll never forget."

Jim Yeager, who had seen the glowing cigarettes the night before, wrote in a memoir:

At approximately 0900 hours, the S-2 section was riding in the jeep [fifth in line of the vehicles] when we heard 75mm recoilless fire. Mott went forward with some of the Battalion staff and the Korean general. In a very short time they returned, and after the general got seated in his jeep (we were all sitting in our vehicles) all hell broke loose. The general took a round and was bleeding like a stuck hog. Two of his body guards tried to get him out of the jeep. The [battalion's second in command] Tony J. Raibl was seriously wounded.

When the battalion officers went forward, they had encountered a group of people approaching from farther up the road. "Fat Chae called out to them, and they all jumped off the road," Yeager told this author. "He apparently called to them – of course I wasn't right there – but he must have called to them in Korean, because he recognized them as Korean people, and some of them had on G.I. uniforms.

"We all jumped from the jeep and took cover in the ditch on the right side of the road. There was a small bank where the road had been cut through. A captain jumped up on the weapons carrier that was right behind the jeep and tried to get the [50-caliber machine gun] into action, but he received several rounds of machine gun fire and fell off the truck.

"The ambush had been sprung, and the North Korean troops were in place on the high ground from where they placed concentrated fire on us, and we had no place to take cover. At this point Col. Mott came driving his jeep back down the road like a mad man, yelling, 'Every man for himself, it's a trap!' He had blood on his face and nose."

Yeager harbored bitterness toward the commander, saying, "Everything is in high gear, running a hundred miles an hour, and Mott comes down the road, he's been clipped across the nose, and he's yelling, 'Every man for himself!' That S.O.B. went to the rear. Now, can you imagine a battalion commander going to the rear and starting to unload ammunition? Well, that's what he did. And he dropped a case of .30 caliber ammunition on his foot and broke it.

"Now, here Tony Raibl was all shot to hell, and Mott wanted him to take over the battalion! Raibl refused to do it because of his gunshot wound."

Yeager maintains that after Mott broke his foot, a soldier dug a foxhole for him, and the colonel stayed in it for the rest of the battle.

"That's where he ended up. As he went back down the line, after he passed with his jeep going full bore, that's where he ended up."

After Mott left the front, a veteran master sergeant ordered Yeager and Toney to turn up a small hollow to take up firing positions. The two of them fought from this position for the rest of the day.

"We went up the hill on our right, and there was kind of a military crest there," said the Coloradan. "I stopped there, because there was a medic there, and they were pulling back a squad that they had sent out across an open area. One of the machine guns that were firing on us was situated out there, and they had chopped this squad up – they were like Swiss cheese.

"An Air Force forward observer had followed us in a yellow jeep, and his radio wasn't working that day.[90] The weather had kind of closed in, and he wasn't able to get air support in for us. He came up – and he was a captain – but he was working as a rifleman with us.

"These kids were totally demoralized when I got up there, and Toney and I just took over. We'd been up there for quite awhile, and I had spotted where this machine gun nest was, but it would be like assaulting out across a football field – from our position to where this machine gun was. It would be like running from one goal to the other, and I wasn't about to go out there and become a casualty.

---

[90]See section on Laurence "Pat" Martin.

"A first lieutenant came up, and I don't know who he was. He was a big tall guy, and he was standing, and he yelled at us. I turned around and looked, and he's standing holding a tree and his knees were rocking together. He yelled, 'Attack that hill! Attack that hill!'

"I said, 'Lieutenant, there's a machine gun nest up there. Get me a .60 mm mortar or something up here to take this thing out. Then I'll attack your hill.'"

While Yeager waited for a mortar crew, he studied the "camouflaged trees" of the enemy machine gun nest. It must be noted that at this point in the war, the Soviet Union had vehemently denied involvement in Korea, but Yeager noted otherwise when a Soviet momentarily stepped out from the emplacement.

"He was in their field uniform. He had on the Russian riding pants-type trousers and the smocked jacket, and of course, the soft-cover Soviet cap – similar to the caps the Air Force guys wore in the B-29s. He stepped out. He wasn't camouflaged at all, and that was his mistake. I killed him.

"Then a mortar crew came up. This guy apparently had been a WWII boy – a sergeant – and he had a .60-mm crew. I showed him where the machine gun nest was and fired my rifle – which I got from the sergeant, because my carbine fell apart and was inoperable. I fired at this machine gun nest and told him where it was. He fired about six rounds, and he got clear off to the right.

"I said, 'You're firing over on K Company. Stop it,' and he broke up and started crying. He grabbed his helmet and ran off the mountain, and his crew followed him. They weren't demoralized, but he was. Some of these boys had seen too much in Europe, and that was just too much. So I'm not chastising him for his action," Yeager said.

"Then a kid came up with a 3.5 rocket launcher, and I've been in several arguments over this, because the 3.5s didn't really show up much until later.

"But I know what bazookas look like. Like I told you, I was in the National Guard, and this was a new weapon they had. An antitank weapon. I told this short, little, sawed-off kid where the machine gun nest was. 'I'll fire out there and show you exactly where it's at,' I told him. He said, 'Well, I only got two rounds.' And I said, 'You better make them do it, then.'

"He fired the first round, and that was the end of the machine gun nest. White clothes, uniforms, machine gun parts and everything else went sky high."

Laurence Martin

"They were rationing our ammunition," said Laurence "Pat" Martin of Munich, North Dakota. "If you got a hand grenade, you could figure yourself very lucky. You'd get two bandoliers of ammunition. Well, two bandoliers isn't going to last long. We had M-1s, then I started carrying a carbine."[91]

Martin managed to live through the battle of Hadong without becoming a casualty, saying, "The first day into combat, we lost our communications chief. He was killed. He was a sergeant first class. I was a private first class. Our company commander, our first sergeant, and our communications chief all got killed. The captain called me in and said, 'We lost our communications chief. You're it.'

"I thought *Holy cow! I'm a pretty young guy.* I says, 'You think I can handle it?' He said, 'Damn right, now get out of here.'

"A very, very good friend of mine, his name was Kenneth A. Oshinski, he was my repair man. There was about seven of us. Communications in the infantry is the next thing to a (medical) corpsman, because they gotta string the wire right alongside the corpsmen that's picking up the wounded, and they gotta make sure these lines are open.

"Now, with the communications they have today – just looking in on the new equipment – they're unbelievable. Those old radios we had, you'd get over the hill, and you couldn't hear them. [. . .]

"We really got clobbered. They could put a mortar in your back pocket if you gave them a second chance. They pulled us into like a horseshoe hill, and why we didn't look it over first – I hate to admit it, but we were all greenhorns. The older guys in the Army – the WWII vets – kept saying, *This isn't right.* But I didn't know. I was just a punk kid, you know? So we got caught in there."

Martin understood why the Air Force liaison ended up fighting as a rifleman beside Jim Yeager. "The first shell missed the Air Force jeep," Martin said. "We had communications between the Air Force and the fighter pilots. But the second one got it. They went right on down the line. We were in a convoy [. . .] and they went right on down the line. Our communications truck was probably the fifth or sixth – maybe as

---

[91] All references to Lawrence "Pat" Martin are from *Kriegieland: Conversations with Ex-POWs*. Video interview by Elmer Lian, 22 Jul 1997. Produced by UND AeroSpace Network. Edward and Elmer T. Lian papers, Elwyn B. Robinson Dept of Special Collections, Chester Fritz Library, UND. By permission of Martin family.

far back as the tenth. They skipped several vehicles, and they hit us. And man, there went all our communications. Hit by mortar.

"Us communications boys, we grabbed a rifle and went to help our boys out. Everything we had was gone. There were a lot of them lost that day. There were some bad calls made. I hate to be the judge, but some of our officers blundered."

Harbinger of POW Treatment

Private Alfred Meek was next to General "Fat" Chae's jeep when the firing began that morning.

"The general was hit bad, and he died quick," Meek told a reporter. "Just before he died, he said: 'I think this is a trap. You'd better get out.' Everybody scattered, and a lot of boys went down."

When Private Meek found himself alone, he scrounged for a compass, extra ammunition, and a pair of binoculars. He then took cover on a nearby hill.

Meek told the report that because the road was too narrow for vehicles to turn around, many men headed toward distant foliage along a river. Most of these men were killed or captured while trying to run through the sucking mud of the rice paddies. Meek witnessed the torture and murder of some who were captured.

"About eight of the enemy came up the road," Meek said. "About ten of our men, who were trying to help the wounded, put up their hands."

Through his binoculars, Meek watched as the Americans were stripped of their clothing, boots and socks and then forced to "run up and down over sharp gravel. I know that gravel was sharp," he said. "I had felt it even through my boots. Pretty soon one of our men fell, and the enemy all shot at him and killed him. Pretty soon another went down and they shot him, too."

After about three hours, all the prisoners were dead, Meek said, "and the enemy went away."

Meek made it out of the pass and, after a 10-mile search, he met up with others from his unit.

Four days later, he was killed in action.[92]

---

[92] Johnston, Richard J. H. "G.I. sees 10 buddies tortured, killed." *The New York Times*. 31 July 1950.

Pennsylvanian Dale Kutz was toward the rear of the convoy during this time. As a machine-gunner in Mike Company, the battalion's heavy weapons company, he and his buddies were doled out to support the rifle companies where needed.

"I happened to wind up with the mortar platoon that day. We were on the road, and the rest of us – we had a machine gun platoon, and we had .75 recoilless rifles – they were with the rifle companies.

"The truck I was on, we were carrying mortar ammunition, and we were pretty far back in the convoy. When they opened up, we were right in a bend in the road. Actually, the bend protected us from direct tank fire where we were. But if you went up the road maybe 50 yards, you were in direct fire.

"They were waiting for us. They were prepared. The road was cut in along the side of a mountain. On the right-hand side of the road, there was a mountain that went almost straight up – from where I was, you know? In other words, you wouldn't even try to climb that mountain.

"But maybe two or three blocks, maybe half a mile, before we got that far, there was a valley that went up toward the mountain. That's where a lot of the troops started up that mountain when this thing started. They were headed up that way, but we were on the road, and you couldn't even get off the road. It was narrow and dirty. There was no way you could've got off it.

"When the fighting broke out," said Kutz, "we handled our own for a while. Then they evidently brought in their heavy weapons, because we were getting heavy weapons fire. But we couldn't get the truck turned around to get it out of there, because the road was too narrow.

"Now, that particular truck – we were taking fire, and I was squatted in the middle of the road firing back at some of the North Koreans. We had a supply officer, his name was Nazario. He came, and he tackled me and pushed me off to the side of the road. 'You wanna get yourself killed?' he said to me – he and I were good friends.

"We laid there beside the road and returned fire, but it got so heavy that we had to start moving back down the road. We hadn't gotten too far, and a mortar round or something came in and had a direct hit on that truck. It just blew it to bits. [93]

"They were trying to cut the road behind us," said Kutz, "but we

---

[93] Kutz suffered burns and a severe concussion. Seven weeks later, he was back with the unit when it went back to Hadong to recover their dead. About one-third of the battalion's soldiers were killed, and roughly 100 others were captured.

made it out. There were some firefights along the way, you know, but we got out before they had their main group there to block the road."

In a different part of the battlefield, Lieutenant Sykes sent Minnesotan Morris Breed and his unit up a mountainside and told them to hold it.

"Our belts were full of bullets, and we had a few bandoliers, which is a kind of a cotton sack we kept our rifle rounds in," said Breed. "We threw those over our shoulders, and that was it. There was no artillery. There was no aircraft, no tanks. We didn't have any of that stuff. All we had was just men. Just plain rifles and hand grenades. That was our first day of battle, sent into a horseshoe mountain. We walked through the door of the mountain, and when we got in, they just closed us off."

As the horrific day ground on, Breed realized a retreat was taking place in his vicinity.

"Our job was to handle the battalion ammunition. We ran back down the mountain to where the ammunition was, and they had unloaded our truck! I couldn't hardly believe it. They'd taken our ammunition and unloaded it on the ground and then moved the trucks away. I figured that alone was a stupid move, you know? To unload the ammunition on the ground. But they must have figured well, this is a secure place. The enemy must have sat over there and laughed as they watched them unload, knowing that they were gonna wait until the whole outfit got into that trap. You know, like the mouse and the cheese, and then they'd spring the trap after we got in.

"Somebody told us to get that ammunition back on the trucks as fast as we could. The ammunition we couldn't get on the trucks, we were to blow up, because we had to get out of there. M-1 ammunition weighs 113 pounds per box. I'm just a little skinny fella, and those truck-beds are up to your armpits high. And this one truck, the reverse gear didn't work in it. You gotta realize our equipment was old Second World War junk. There was absolutely nothing new. Well, this truck would go forward, but the rear gear was gone. So we had to take this ammunition and carry it several hundred feet to the truck.

"I got to the truck, and I was so weak I couldn't lift the box. Well, a little short fella comes up next to me with a hole in his neck, and he's squirting blood out of his neck." Breed couldn't think of this moment without becoming emotional. "I saw him put that ammunition box on that truck, and I figured if he could do it, so could I. I don't know how many I threw on after that . . .

"When we got the trucks loaded, they loaded the wounded on top of the ammunition. The ones who could, they climbed in by themselves.

And the other ones we just placed in on top of the ammunition.

"Then the rest of us climbed up on the trucks, some hanging on the outside of the racks. You're hanging onto a piece of metal, and you're riding on the outside. We had to shoot our way out, and the enemy was coming at us. Naturally some of us made it, and others didn't," Breed said. "Since then, I've had nightmares about it.

"Some of us escaped in all different directions. It took a couple weeks before we were actually all reassembled. It's fortunate that that many of us were recovered. Some of them were captured, and others . . . you know.

"That battle of Hadong was chaos. You know, they told us it was a police action. And America, as big as we are, we think we know it all. We take America, and we look at a little tiny country, a little peninsula called Korea. And then we think of a smaller section. North Korea. Why sure, that'll be just a police action. But, we found out they had more strength.

"So, America went over there with a – now, this is my opinion, don't get me wrong – we went over there and figured, *Well, we're big daddy, and we'll stand on the street corner and tell you boys you can't do this. You go back home.* But it was a little more serious than that."

Yeager & Toney are Captured

As evening approached, Coloradan Jim Yeager and his buddy John Toney were still fighting up near the pass. Yeager had fired his rifle so much that his shoulder was deeply bruised, and he had to switch to his opposite side.

"The firing started to subside," Yeager said. "I started looking around and man, we were right in the middle of the North Korean Army. I gathered up what kids were there and said *let's go.* We started down to the road, and I booby-trapped a BAR (Browning Automatic Rifle) – took the bolt out of it and threw it away. Then I scooped out a hole for my high explosive grenade, pulled the pin on it and spread the receiver over it – so if anybody picked it up, it would go off and get them.

"Then, I went down on the road and booby-trapped a 4-x-4. Raised the hood and hooked it up so that when they started it – the pin was already pulled, but you know – it would cause the grenade to go off.

"Then we started across this dry bean field next to these paddies, and they started shooting at us like crazy. We ran up this mountain. The Air Force observer was still fighting with us, and Toney was ahead of this observer.

"I hit the ground, because they were really concentrating in on us, and when I hit the ground, I thought I got hit in the chest. Well, everybody else kept running, and I was trying to figure out what I was gonna do with a sucking chest wound. I slowly and gently pulled my hand in to check my chest, and I discovered I'd landed on a rock. Of course I was a little disgusted at myself.

"I jumped up and caught up with the group, and they were still firing at us. They shot the heel off the kid's combat boot in front of me. I just kept right on going, because some of them were slowing down.

"I finally caught up with the Air Force captain and Toney. We got clear up on top of this mountain. We were all so exhausted that we laid down on the ground. The kids were strung out behind me, Toney was in front of the captain, and another kid was in front of Toney. We were right up on top of this mountain.

"I had a map, because I was a scout observer, and I had that in my helmet liner. I also had field glasses, you know, because that's my job.

"The captain is kneeling down – he's sitting on his heels in front of me. I could reach out and touch him, that's how close we were. I was at the base of a scrub cedar tree, and all of a sudden I heard a round go off. They shot him right through the heart, and he rolled over backwards. I was at the base of this tree, where people couldn't see me – inborn from playing soldier all my life; I just automatically did this.

"I looked to my left, and here's three North Koreans raising up out of grass about knee-high – two burp-gunners and a rifleman.

"I still had the M-1 that I had picked up on the hill there on the right. Now, the M-1 has a clip with eight rounds of ammunition. I put 16 rounds in those boys before they could hit the ground. We were close enough that I could see the blood spurting from them, and it looked like they were being hit in the chest with a sledge hammer from the impact of the round hitting them. So that gives you an idea of how close we were.

"During this fire fight that I had, when that clip ejected after the eight rounds were expended, I shoved another one in. I was firing that thing like a machine gun. Some people might doubt that, but believe me, I can fire an M-1 that way. If you needed a demonstration, I still have an M-1.

"While this transpired, the kids behind me threw their rifles down and dropped off the side of the mountain. These kids ranged in age, but most of them were 16, 17, 18. I was 20-years-old. I was an old man! The one guy that was up ahead of Toney, he just disappeared. I don't know whatever happened to that man.

"Toney and I got together, and we were scouting out on this mountain. We got to looking down, and there was a humongous rice paddy way down to our right. We could see way out, a thousand yards at least, and there were Americans trying to get to a river.

"There was a machine gun firing on them, and we looked down immediately below us, and low and behold, here was these kids that had run off to the left of us when I got into that firefight. They're walking down a little old path on the edge of this rice paddy. There was a finger of ground sticking out on some more of the mountains down below us where this machine gun was firing.

"I told Toney, 'My God, they're gonna run into that machine gun if they don't stop. We better go down and stop 'em.' And that's what we proceeded to do. We came tearing down off the mountain, and we got about 30, 40 yards – or 50 yards at the most – and they were on the road, no weapons or nothing. They had stripped themselves, all they had on was their fatigues. About that time, too, North Koreans jumped up out of the ditch there – between them and the rice paddy – and they were camouflaged up. They looked like moving trees.

"These boys said to us, 'You better throw your rifles down, or they're gonna shoot us and you, too.'

"I turned around to say something to Toney, and here was a whole platoon of North Korean soldiers raised up out of the grass. Well, I threw my rifle down, and so did Toney. I took my helmet off and gave that one heck of a throw – it had that map in the top, and I knew I'd be in for a bad time if they found that map on me.

"We went down the road, and they lined us up and started jerking dog tags off of kids and throwing them in the rice paddies. I'd seen what was happening, because Toney and I were at the rear of this column that they had assembled. So I stuck mine in my pants. When they came up to me – they had made me take my shirt off, and here I am, all I got on is a pair of pants. They took the carbine and a bayonet that I had in my boot, and they frisked me. They didn't do a real good job, and they missed a couple of things that I had on my person that they found later on.

"They marched us into Hadong then that night."

Contrary to what some historians have written, the men at Hadong are proud of how hard they fought that day. Most of the dead were found still in their positions when discovered many weeks later. They did not turn and run. Until ordered to withdraw, they fought to the death.

Chapter 19

PRISONERS OF WAR

"Those of us who were in the service at the outbreak of the Korean War, and committed to prevent the loss of South Korea, suffered terrible unforgivable losses. Of approximately 1500 men of the two Battalions of the 29th Infantry Regiment that came from Okinawa, some 500 to 600 men were casualties within a week." Leonard Becicka, Able Company, 29th Regimental Combat Team

LAVERN GOHL, from Williston, North Dakota, was a member of George Company, 19th Regiment, when he was reported missing after the Kum River action.

Wilbert "Shorty" Estabrook had gotten to know Gohl earlier, in Japan, when their companies were side by side for a time. They found each other again after they became prisoners of war.

"When a person is thrust into a situation like being captured," said Estabrook, "they usually seek out people from their home state and their military unit. I was looking for guys from the 19th Regiment, and so was he. We were captured on the same day, and what a day that was.

"I remember Lavern as looking very young and bewildered. He was very quiet. We talked about other guys in George Company I knew.

"Capture is such a horrible and terrifying event. You don't know what will happen to you. We had already seen men with their hands tied behind them and shot in the back of the head. You think that you, too, will be shot after being tortured. All of us were beaten soundly as we moved back through the enemy's front lines. Attempts were made by their front line troops to hit or stab us.

"It was very hot and humid the summer of 1950," Estabrook continues. "The smell of battle and flesh was all around. We were fed millet and maize grains and a thin soup of Chinese cabbage. But the worst thing was being thirsty. We drank from highly polluted sources such as rice paddies and soon we were all sick with stomach pains. Thirst can drive a man crazy, and drinking from those rice paddies proved fatal for many of our group."

Bill Henninger & Joe Monscvitz

William "Bill" Henninger and Joe "J.T." Monscvitz were both captured at Taejon.

Henninger was the oldest of three children. Born in Saint Paul, his family moved to Florida until 1930, when his mother died. Bill was six years old. That year, the family moved back to Minnesota, where his grandparents helped raise him and his siblings.

Henninger was a veteran of WWII. He liked the structure of military life, and three years after he was discharged, he reenlisted.

He was with the ill-fated 34th Regiment when it deployed to Korea. During the battle of Taejon, he was hit with shrapnel and later removed six pieces of metal from his arm after applying a poultice he made from tobacco.

During the retreat from the city, he was separated from his unit, so he crossed a rice paddy, hid in some brush, and then crossed a nearby river. On the far side, he met up with a South Korean who told him he was going the wrong direction. Bill wrapped a rag around his head to disguise himself and headed down some railroad tracks with the man. About five miles outside the city, communist sympathizers confronted them and shot the South Korean when he took off running. Bill was spared and marched back to Taejon.

"On the way they wanted me to hurry," he said, "and I wasn't gonna hurry. I was gonna take my own sweet time. When we got into Taejon, they took us right to the building where they had all the wounded and so forth. We were all pretty much from the 24th Division."[94]

J.T. Monscvitz grew up on Tony's Road (named for his father) in Cecil County, Maryland, and is one of a very small handful of prisoners captured in the opening weeks who lived to tell about it. He was with the 3rd Combat Engineers and had been carrying out his duties in the heart of Taejon since his arrival in Korea.

---

[94] Avery, Pat McGrath and Joyce Faulkner. *Sunchon Tunnel Massacre Survivors.* P 10, 11, 31.

"We got to Pusan on the 4th of July," he said. "They threw us on a train, and we moved the equipment up to Taejon, and we set up a water point there. My job was water supply, and I was a technician. There was another technician, myself, a truck driver, and a corporal who was in charge of this water point. That was probably the 5th or so, and we worked there until the 20th.

"Up until July 19th, we were working 24 hours a day. Then suddenly the demand for water stopped. So what the hell, I'm 18 years old, I don't know what I'm doing anyway. It was the corporal's job to worry about what we were doing. But, you know, the demand stopped.

"The next morning, we still hadn't had any people asking for water. We were having some C-rations, and a big tank comes rolling up the street, and we said 'They're bringing in some big stuff, now.'

"That sucker started shooting up everything in the area, and when he turned around, we saw it was a Russian tank. We said *Holy crap!* and jumped over into one of these open sewers while the bullets were flying around.

"He left, and we were wondering what took place," Monscvitz continued. "After a bit, an infantry lieutenant came along with his squad, and he said, 'What are you engineers doing here?' We told him, 'We're here to supply water.' He said, 'Forget about that, we're surrounded. We're getting ready to fight our way out of here.'

"So we loaded up our truck, and by late afternoon we caught up with a part of the 34th Regiment, which was trapped in Taejon at that time along with the 19th. In the late afternoon, they started trying to lead us out, and something happened at the front of the column. The rumor that came back to us guys sitting in the back of a truck was that they had jammed a viaduct, and we couldn't get out. It stopped the column.

"Anyway, bullet holes started popping through the side of the truck, and my buddy and I got out and jumped over a wall. He went one way, and I accidentally went another way. I ended up with a small infantry squad during the night and crept out to the lines that the North Koreans had set up, and we got into the countryside."

The following morning, Monscvitz's group was engaged in a fire fight, and that afternoon they spotted the enemy searching the hills for them. Using only the sun and the stars for guidance, they headed south and evaded capture for more than a week.

"That was really not a good idea," Monscvitz said. "If we'd have had a map, we'd have known we should've been going southeast toward Pusan. Because as long as we went south, we were still in enemy territory. By that time, they had solidified the Naktong perimeter, and that was east of us. But we didn't know that."

Several days later, the group was hiding in a small community, and needing food, they approached some Koreans who betrayed them to the enemy.

"You don't really know who the enemy is," Monscvitz said. "But I assume that either Communist sympathizers or the North Korean Army sent out a squad of some sort. All I know is when the bullets started flying, one guy got hit, and I ended up as a rear guard as we were trying to get out.

"Afterwards, I couldn't find the squad, so I was by myself for the next several days – maybe about a week.

"Right now, I would agree that's not a good situation to be in. But I was too damn dumb to know that at the time. I knew it was difficult, but the idea was to get out, so I started using my skills. One thing they taught me in water supply – besides how to treat water – was good map-reading. If I'd have had a map, I'd have really been in good shape, but I didn't have a map.

"You're hungry, you're losing weight, and you can't go anyplace without climbing a mountain. I traveled after dark, but one afternoon I started out early, because no one was around up in the mountains. I ran into a South Korean, and I thought well gee whiz, maybe I can get some food or, better yet, I can get some directions. Well that turned out to be a tactical error, because he kind of assured me he was going to get me some food. But what he did was come back with the North Koreans.

"That was the end of my freedom. As they were marching me back into a town, they stopped under a tree, and I thought, 'They're gonna hang me. I am done. My time has arrived.' They got into a discussion of some sort. I couldn't understand it, but I like the way they settled it. They marched me on into a local jail."[95]

Burdett Eggen & Rodger Jones

"I was a cook, until one day they told me I was going to be a rifleman," wrote Burdett "Ace" Eggen.

During the tragic slaughter at the Hadong pass, Eggen feigned death

---

[95] Monscvitz entries are based on interviews with author in December 2008 and will not be cited further.

while enemy soldiers checked the bodies of his dead buddies for souvenirs. Unfortunately, he was lying face down in the mud, and when forced to come up for air, he was spotted and captured.

Eggen, who could speak some Japanese, asked his captor how old he was. The Korean replied he was 18 – the same as Eggen. The North Korean offered to let Eggen stand up to fight him, but the young American turned him down, because his captor was holding a weapon on him. The two developed a certain rapport, however, and Eggen was not subjected to the torture being shown to other captives.

Although Eggen was born in Fort Frances, Ontario, his ancestry traced back to Williston, North Dakota. His father Alfred joined the U.S. Navy and served with an intelligence unit in WWII. After the war, the family eventually settled in Los Angeles, where Eggen went to Hollywood High School at the same time as actress Carol Burnett.[96]

As a child, Eggen had a way with animals, and many sick or injured pets were entrusted to him. Eventually, he picked up work on a ranch that trained animals for movies. His job included working in the aviary, where his favorite bird was a cockatoo.

The family's military traditions traced back to the Revolutionary War, and when Eggen completed 11th grade, his father felt he should join the Army to gain a sense of discipline and build his character. Burdett was only 17, and his mother was reluctant. But she signed

(Courtesy Eggen Family)

---

[96] Burdett Eggen's account published in *Valley Times* (North Hollywood). 20 Jan 1951; Mary Lou Eggen-Castillo letter to author 20 May 2010. No further citations.

a waiver and her son became a soldier.

Eggen's daughter, Mary Lou, wrote that after Burdett was declared missing in action at Hadong, the decision to enlist the boy in the Army haunted his parents to such an extent that they later divorced.

On the night of their capture, POWs from the 29th RCT were marched into the town of Hadong, where they were packed into a small brick church. Among them was Rodger Jones, a spunky Pennsylvanian who fought in Italy during WWII. Jones was wounded multiple times before he was captured, including a hit to the left rear of his skull.

"A piece of my bone is still over there," he said. "I guess some anthropologist will find it and wonder what it is. But I'm a thickheaded Welshman, so it never knocked me out. But it caused me to go blind for about an hour or two. That scared the daylights out of me. It was a couple hours, and then the light started filtering in."[97]

Jones was also hit in both shoulders, as well as "about five to six inches up the right side of my back. But then the minor ones were powder burns all the way across the shoulders and a flesh wound on the inside of the left elbow. But that blindness scared the hell out of me."

Hadong Prisoners Bombed

A North Korean officer began interrogating the prisoners inside the church the following morning. It was a nasty introduction to life as a POW under the North Koreans.

"We were lined up in a column and called up one at a time," said Coloradan Jim Yeager. "I was the fourth one in line. The first man was a master sergeant. The officer asked him where our artillery was located. The sergeant just stated his name, rank and serial number. The officer asked him the same thing again, and once again he gave his name, rank and serial number. The officer became very upset and yelled something to the guards in Korean. The guards took the sergeant, pushed him up against the wall, and the officer took out his pistol and shot him in the head, splattering brains, bone and blood against the wall.

"The officer called the next man and asked him the same question. Actually, we had no artillery with us, but this man told him that we had a regiment and gave him a false location. The officer called the next man up and asked him the same question. This man told him the same

---

[97] Jones interview with author October 2008. No further citations.

story, so he motioned him to move on.

"Next it was my turn to be called up. The officer jumped up and jabbed his fingers into my chest and asked, 'What is your job?' I replied I was a jeep driver and made a motion like driving and turning a steering wheel.

"He said, 'You lie! You die!'"

The officer beat on Yeager's injured shoulders.

"After I had recovered somewhat from the beating, I yelled back at him, saying I was a rifleman and made a motion of firing a rifle and said, 'It's too bad I didn't kill more of you.'

"At this point he said something to the guards, and they dragged me to the wall like they had done the sergeant. I thought they were going to kill me, but they beat me with their rifle butts on my shoulders and head. They cold-cocked me. When I woke up later, the interrogation was over. I crawled to my spot on the floor and laid there.

"During the early hours of the day, the North Korean soldiers herded the townspeople past the church, having them look through the open windows, jabbering and pointing at us. We couldn't understand what was being said, but it was very evident the NKPA [North Korean People's Army] was showing us off for propaganda purposes," said Yeager. "We were exhausted, and most of the men were laying on the floor either sleeping or resting. There was 80 of us jammed into this small building."

"There was one recon plane up in the air," said Rodger Jones, "like a Piper Cub? He was just floating around. Nothing happened, and then all hell broke loose. I mean, we must have gotten hit by every type of plane our Air Force had. They were continuous for eight solid hours up there."

The WWII veteran became emotional when talking about this . . . "Pardon me," he said, "but I get angry, because people don't even talk about Korea, you know?"

"The day was hot and humid," said Yeager. "Shortly after noon, I was lying approximately three-quarters of the way back in the church. All of a sudden the town was being rocketed and strafed. A rocket came in the front of the church up by the pulpit. I was on the right-hand side of the church, with my left ear facing the pulpit. Noise from the explosion rendered me completely deaf at the time. (After several days my hearing partially returned.)

"The rocket entered the building at an angle, blowing a large hole at point of entry and a hole about twice the size of entry about midway down on the left wall. The roof collapsed, and timbers and masonry rained down. I had a difficult time getting the debris off me because of my back pain, but I managed to exit through the hole in the left wall before the next strafing run. I can still see the carnage. Body parts all over. One man in a sitting position was split wide open with his guts hanging out and still alive."

Burdett Eggen was hit by shrapnel and was partially blown through the wall. He reported 25 men were killed in the blast.

The survivors were herded through Hadong and up onto a mountainside, where Jones and others ended up in a cave. That evening, the North Koreans separated the seriously wounded from those who could walk. The group that could march numbered about 45 men, including Jim Yeager and his friend John Toney.

"We were formed up and marched off to the north," Yeager said. "After an hour, we turned off a narrow track into a farm yard. After a few minutes, we were pushed, kicked and butt-stroked into a small building resembling a corn crib about 8' x 12'. We were stacked up like a pile of hogs.

"The next morning we received a small rice ball, and a sake (rice beer) bottle with water in it was passed around. Again we were formed up and marched north. The roads were very primitive, only wide enough for a jeep. This was the routine over and over. Sometimes we were held in barnyards and slept on the bare ground. During this time we were marched from daybreak till late at night."

This routine would change when the North Koreans decided they no longer wanted to dodge air attacks during daylight hours. After that, POWs were marched primarily at night.

Meanwhile, Rodger Jones and other seriously wounded prisoners were moved back to Hadong and rehoused in a different building.

"It was like the agriculture center for the area," said Jones. "There was an old desk in there and some old chairs with no wheels, you know. They left 39 of us behind with our medic, Doc (George D.) Calender. After he was captured, they made him treat their wounded, and then they gave him back some sulpha powder, alcohol, a pair of tweezers, and a pair of scissors.

"Out of the 39 of us that were left behind, five men died, and that left us with 34, right? There was 23 of us that were ambulatory, and 11 who weren't. Some of them were in pretty bad shape. There wasn't much Doc could do for them; he could do just a certain amount of stuff.

"He had one kid out of his head named Remus Blackwood. I

remember his name. He was Blackwood from Greenwood, Mississippi. He was out of his head, and we couldn't find out what was wrong. We took all his clothes off him – because of his natural functions, he was messing them all up, you know? And one day Doc said, 'Okay, hold him down. I'm gonna check him from the bottom of his feet to the top of his head.'

"And he couldn't find a darn thing, you know? And he got up on the top of his head, right on the left side, right at the top, and there was a tiny hole. Like maybe a piece of shrapnel went in, huh? And one day he's sitting there looking at everybody, and he says, 'Hey, where's my rice?' Before that, he was out of it, right?

"Then the so-called Korean medical people came, and they didn't do nothing. There was a man and a woman with a red cross on their sleeve. When he saw them, he was happy. But after they left – they didn't even look at him – he went back into his same old way, and he passed away (Aug 20). He was 19-years-old.

"One kid couldn't keep his dirty fingers out of his wound, and he died, and one kid by the name of Alfredo Bracamonte died (Aug 21). Doc asked me and another guy to move him, so we moved him in the building. He was so heavy, and I says, 'Bracamonte, lift your cotton-pickin seat' but I didn't use that word. By the time we got him in there, he weighed a ton, and we laid him down. So I called the Doc, 'Hey Doc, come here.' And he came over. *He's dead.*

"I said, 'What the hell you mean, he's dead? He's only got a bullet hole in his leg.' That's where I ran into my first *shock*. He went into shock. I couldn't believe it, you know?

"One kid had a hole in his back, left shoulder blade, right? And the only way he could breathe was like – remember the old iron lung? It was like sit up, lay down, sit up, lay down. That's the only way he could breathe. He was laying by the door, and I walked in one day, and I looked at him and called the Doc. He had passed away.

"But none of the guys that were non-ambulatory were any problems. Never a complaint, no nothing, you know? They'd say hand me that, give me a can to go shi-shi, or have to go doo-doo, right? Or give me a match or a drink of water. That's all. They were great, great guys.

"They moved us out of that building into another building, which they said was the bus station. It was awful, because there were no windows or nothing. So we took all our rice straw mats and hung them over the windows downstairs [for protection during the night] and put these 11 guys down there, right? Of course we rolled the mats up during the day when it was nice.

"But, the rest of us were in one row upstairs. At night you'd hear somebody say 'turn,' and we'd all turn – laying on one side all the time, huh? The lieutenant, Kenneth Reid, was up at the end where all the rats were. You'd hear rats, rats, rats all night long.

"We stayed in that bus station for about a month," said Jones. "Finally, they said, *Okay, we're taking you north.*

"But before that, we had to go bury those guys who were dead in the church, huh? And that was a uh, uh . . . we had no gloves or nothing like that, right? And they laid up there in the heat and the sun for 10 days or more. How we did it was we'd take two boards and lay them crosswise. Then we'd take a shutter and lay them across those boards. Then we'd roll a body on a shutter. Four of us would pick him up and take him over to a hole the Koreans dug, go *one, two, three and drop.* We had the names of most all of them, right?"

Chapter 20

CHINJU, JULY 31

"They were just looking for cannon fodder. That's all we were. We were to delay the North Koreans until we could amass some sort of sufficient number of live bodies to stop them. There were not very many people with an infantry background. We were green as grass." Raymond Cody, 13th Field Artillery Battalion.

FRESH FROM ITS stunning victory at Hadong, North Korea's 6th Division started moving east toward Pusan. This division had been instrumental in seizing Seoul earlier in the month and had sustained only 400 casualties, killed or wounded, by July 28.

The enemy commander, Major General Wae Pang, was prepared to finish the fight when he addressed his troops: "Comrades, the enemy is demoralized . . . The task given to us is . . . the annihilation of the remnants of the enemy . . . the liberation of Chinju and Masan means the final battle to cut off the windpipe of the enemy."[98]

In a thinly manned north-south line, the 34th and 21st Regiments took up positions behind the Naktong River. The remaining regiment of the 24th Division, the 19th, was farther south near Chinju.

Ned Moore

The 19th *Rock of Chickamauga* Regiment had lost a great many officers at the Kum River. The newly arriving regimental commander was 43-year-

---

[98]"North Korean 6th Infantry Division," Inter Report 33-36, Allied Translator and Interpreter Service, Far East Command; Goulden, *Korea, the Untold Story of the War*. P 175 & 658(n)14.

old Ned Moore, from Guthrie Center, Iowa.

Colonel Moore was a 1930 graduate of West Point, and during WWII, he served with the administrative staff of the 101st Airborne Division in Holland and Normandy, France.

Siphoned from the 7th Infantry Division, Moore was brought in to replace Colonel Meloy, who was wounded at the Kum River July 16.

Historians infer Moore had not led combat troops before, but he was certainly in harm's way according to famed newscaster Walter Cronkite. Cronkite was a war correspondent in Holland when in 1944 he wrote:

> Lt. Col. Ned Moore, Guthrie Center, IA, and the private were in the same ditch, dodging the same German Tiger tank in the darkness near Zon, and it looked like curtains for them both until the shadow of a donkey saved their lives.
>
> This is how it happened: Moore took a patrol of 12 men to reconnoiter the strength of German tank forces moving toward the Wilhelmina canal bridge at Zon, across which supplies for Lt. Gen. Miles C. Dempsey were moving.
>
> Moore had started down the canal bank when he saw the tiger tank advancing, so he sent part of the patrol back into Zon for help. The patrol lost several others while maneuvering toward the tank to get a bazooka shot, and finally only Moore and 2 enlisted men were left. When they were within a few dozen yards from the tank, Moore ordered one man with a bazooka to slip up the canal bank and put a rocket into the tank. The G.I. missed and became so scared he dropped his bazooka and fled. Then the second soldier dashed up the bank and plunked a rocket into the tank, but the tiger rolled right along. Moore had one rocket left.
>
> "I decided to have a pop at the tank with that, because he was getting pretty close by that time, but that damned rocket jammed and I didn't get my shot," he said.

Cronkite reported that as the enemy tank came abreast of Moore and his remaining companion, they crouched down along the bank. They were hoping to stay out of the gun's firing line but then realized the tank was followed by two "German infantrymen dog-trotting along behind it with rifles."

Farther along the canal, the tank rolled to a stop to lob some shots into the town of Zon. But the two German soldiers remained behind, effectively pinning down Moore and the other man until evening.

Moore spotted a nearby building, and after darkness closed in, they edged toward some woods to screen themselves from the Germans as they made their way to this potential shelter. As they neared the building, the tank scored a hit on it, and Moore his companion were lit up. Cronkite writes:

> Afraid the Germans would spot their human silhouettes, Moore recalled a kid stunt and made a donkey head with his hands against the flickering flames from the house.
>
> "The fire threw the silhouette of the donkey, as big as a house, right in front of the tank," Moore said.
>
> "What do we do now, sir?" asked the soldier.
>
> "We lie low," Moore replied.
>
> "I'd like to know your name, sir," the soldier said. Moore gave him his name.
>
> "I'm J. J. McCarthy, sir, let's shake on it," said the private.
>
> By the light of the flickering flames, right under the noses of German guns, they solemnly shook on it. In a little while, the Americans knocked out the tank, and McCarthy and his colonel made their way to safety.[99]

Now, in Korea, Ned Moore was facing a potential collapse of the 19th Regiment he was inheriting, and he had a lot of catching up to do. Lieutenant Ralph Harrity, who had been in the fight at the Kum River, recalled his first meeting with the new commander:

> After being ushered into the command tent, the sides rolled up completely for air conditioning, (I) was introduced to a slightly stocky, somewhat diminutive man wearing a spotless white T-shirt and easing nonchalantly on a steel army-issue chair, watching and listening to members of the assembled staff as they worked. This was Col. Ned D. Moore.[100]

Moore arrived at the front at about the same time the 29th RCT was attached to his 19th Regiment. With the loss of Hadong and other

---

[99] *Mason City Globe-Gazette.* 3 Oct 1944.

[100] Harrity. *Q Clan.* P 163.

points, it now fell to him and his men to defend the final miles to the enemy's ultimate goal of Pusan. It was to be a very long and brutal fight.

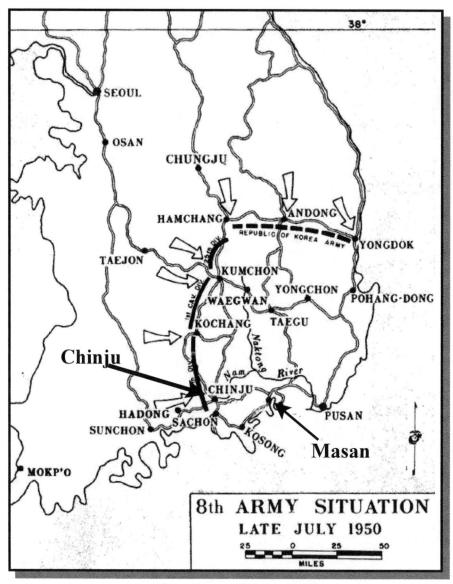

(Map Courtesy U.S. Navy)

Moore's first objective was to hold the town of Chinju. It was already the scene of heavy fighting, and processing new replacements was a very serious undertaking. Army historian Roy Appleman writes:

The 19th Infantry faced the critical test of the defense of Chinju pitifully under-strength. Its unit report for 30 July gives the regiment a strength of 1,895, with 300 men in the 1st Battalion and 290 men in the 2nd Battalion. Colonel (Ned) Moore, however, states that the strength of the 19th Infantry on 30 July, including the replacements that arrived that afternoon, was 1,544. The 3rd Battalion, 29th Infantry, still disorganized as a result of the Hadong battle, had a reported strength that day of 396 men.

Several hundred replacements arrived at Chinju for the 19th Infantry at this time – 175 on 28 July and 600 on 30 July . . . Of the 600 that arrived on 30 July, 500 went to the 19th Infantry and most of the remainder to the 13th Field Artillery Battalion.[101]

It was about 4:00 p.m. when the second batch of replacements left the regimental command post to be distributed into the front lines. Many of the units they were to join were currently under attack, but with the urgency of the situation, Moore couldn't wait for a lull in the battle to feed these new men into the line.

During the predawn hours of July 31, a Nebraskan and an Iowan each earned Silver Stars for handling the replacements assigned to Charlie Company, 19th Regiment. They didn't know each other, and both thought they were the only artillery forward observers positioned with the company. But their citations are remarkably similar.[102]

Harry Tincher

"I was a pretty good kid," said Harry Tincher, the artilleryman from Plattsmouth, Nebraska. "My dad was kind of strict. We lived on an acreage. We had chickens, and pigs, and a cow, but I worked in town. I shined shoes in a shine parlor, and then I sold shoes in a shoe store. At 16, I was a deck-hand on a Corps of Engineers boat on the Missouri River. That was during the height of WWII, so all the men who had those jobs were gone. That's how we were employed at 16."

After high school, Tincher went to the University of Nebraska in Lincoln for one semester. Tuition was a problem, he said, "So a friend

---

[101] Appleman. *Naktong to Yalu.* p 228-229.

[102] Author interviews with Tincher and Cody, Oct. 2011.

and I joined the Army, because they had the G.I. Bill."

The Army offered to send Tincher through Officer Candidate School, and commissioned as a young 2nd lieutenant, he started his 20-year career in Japan.

"I belonged to the 64th Field Artillery of the 25th Division the day the Korean War started," he said. "We were on amphibious maneuvers off the coast of Tokyo. We boarded LSTs and went back to Osaka, but some of us were called and went ashore on a small boat before we got into Osaka.

"They said, 'It's been nice knowing you.'

"We said, 'Are you going some place?'

"They said, 'No. You are.'

"They put us in trucks, took us back, and gave us an hour to get our stuff packed. Then they shipped us to the 24th Division to fill them up, and I was attached to the 11th Field Artillery. Replacements were few and far between in those early days."

One week before the battle of Chinju, Tincher's battery provided supporting fire for the 19th Regiment farther north at Yongdong. "We had a unit behind us that got hit pretty badly," he said. "We were in a retrograde movement, and we were in the shelling area. We were trying to find out where the shells were coming from."

*Second Lieutenant **Harry R. Tincher**, Artillery, U.S. Army, a member of Battery B, 11th Field Artillery Battalion, 24th Infantry Division, is awarded the **Bronze Star Medal with V device** for heroic achievement near Yongdong, Korea, on 24 July 1950. During an enemy artillery attack on his battalion's positions, Lieutenant Tincher, accompanied by an enlisted man, volunteered to go forward to locate the enemy's positions. Braving the intense fire, he remained in an exposed position until the necessary data could be obtained and relayed to his battery. From his valuable information, the enemy guns were silenced by the accuracy and volume of friendly artillery fire. While maintaining observation on the enemy gun positions, Lieutenant Tincher was severely wounded by the counter-battery fire.*

When asked about his severe wounds, Tincher said, "I know what it says, but it was minor, and I didn't even report it."

Now, on July 30, Tincher was dug in on a forward slope about four miles south of Chinju in support of Charlie Company, 19th Regiment. As a forward observer, Tincher was not back with his battery – he was up at the front with the infantrymen.

Young Sam Walker, son of General Walton Walker, had recently taken command of Charlie Company – General Walker had started out as a 19th Regiment "Chick" early in his career, and he thought it was fitting for his son to be attached to a regiment close to his heart.

Charlie Company was in the forward position for the 1st Battalion, and as Tincher watched from his observation post, he could see many soldiers climbing the opposing slope in front of him. He wanted to call in an artillery strike, but his request was denied, because the South Korean Marines were expected to be coming through those positions.

"I said, *Well, it seems strange they're digging in on this side of the hill*," said Tincher. "But nope, they said *They're friendly*. They told us to hold our fire. So we didn't shoot at them.

"But they didn't turn out to be South Koreans. At about two or three o'clock in the morning, they jumped off on the attack. It was during that attack that all of this happened. It was just before dawn."

The 19th Regiment's war diary states that at 5:30 a.m. "the 1st Battalion was attacked by enemy of unknown strength. Company C's positions were overrun, but a quickly formed counterattack repulsed the enemy and caused them to retreat. The cost to enemy, actual count, was 200 dead. The 1st Bn continued to occupy its positions."

It was during the midst of this fighting that the new replacements were undergoing their first experience in combat.

(Courtesy Harry Tincher)

*Second Lieutenant **Harry R. Tincher**, Artillery, U.S. Army, a member of Battery B, 11th Field Artillery Battalion, 24th Infantry Division, is awarded the **Silver Star** for gallantry in action on 31 July 1950 near Chinju, Korea. Attached to Company C, 19th Infantry Regiment as a forward observer for his artillery unit, Lieutenant Tincher, with utter disregard for his own personal safety, materially assisted the organization and deployment of new replacements received by the infantry company while under severe enemy attack. All during the enemy attack, he continued to deploy the new replacements effectively and assisted in their efforts against a numerically superior enemy. His gallant actions continued until*

*he was wounded by enemy small arms fire and was forced to crawl to the
rear for medical assistance. Due to Lieutenant Tincher's self-sacrifice and
actions beyond the call of normal duty, the infantry company was able to
rally and hold its positions.*

"What I was doing mostly was moving people around," Tincher
explained. "There were a couple guys got hit, and we tried to get those
into a position where they could be picked up and then cover the areas
where they had been."

When asked about the wounds mentioned in this second citation,
Tincher agreed they were very serious this time. "I was outside of my
foxhole when a mortar round landed," he said. "It picked me up, turned
me over and landed me back in the hole. I crawled, actually, to the aid
station, and they put me in an ambulance. That was in the days prior to
helicopter evacuation. It was 12 miles to Masan, where the field hospital
was, but it took almost 24 hours, because the enemy was between us
and Masan. So we had to go back up around to get there."

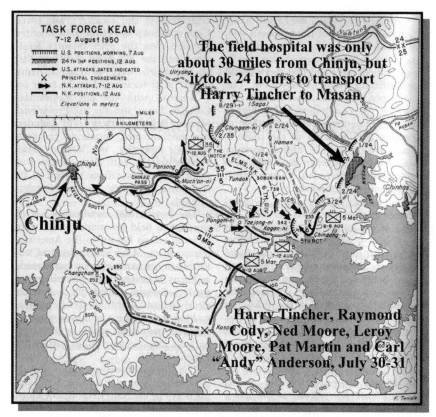

(Base map courtesy Center of Military History)

Tincher spent the next three months in a hospital. "The wound was in my back," he said. "I was very fortunate. It sheered the skin off my ribs. At first, they thought they'd need to send me back to the States for skin grafts. But one of the doctors thought he could close the wound. There were four operations to close it, but it kept breaking open. So I got a pretty good scar in the back, but fortunately there was no permanent damage."

Raymond Cody

"It was a gray, hazy, rainy, sloppy, terrible day," said Raymond Cody about the morning of July 31. As a forward observer for the 13th Field Artillery Battalion, Cody was also attached to young Sam Walker's Charlie Company, and like Harry Tincher, he believed he was the only forward artillery observer in their line that night.

When asked about this, Harry Tincher thought for a moment and said, "There may be something to it, because the 13th Artillery was the direct support battalion. The 11th Artillery was a medium support battalion, but we were detached and acting as direct support at that time. In other words, the batteries were separated. So it's possible that he could have been right close there, because we were all strung out along the area there."

Cody recalls that he wasn't calling in fire for the 13th FAB, however; the only battery he could fire that night was Tincher's 11th FAB. (The confusion of the situation is not solved within these pages.)

When asked about his childhood, Cody said, "I was born in 1927 in Dubuque, Iowa, and the family moved to Chicago during the Chicago World's Fair, which was between 1932 and 1933. We lived in Chicago until my father died in January 1938. We went to the funeral and then returned to Chicago to finish the school year, and then we moved back to Dubuque in 1938.

"When my father died," he said, "we were in rather dire financial straits. It wasn't a very great time in the economy of the country – the Great Depression lasted until the 1940s, and everything was going to hell in a bushel basket.

"I went out for football as a sophomore in high school, but my mother said *You gotta get a job*. I was the baby of three siblings, and we all worked. I shined shoes, worked at a packing plant, at a box factory, and what was then called North Home Industries. They manufactured upholstered furniture. I also had a newspaper route, and at one time I was distributing the *Chicago Sun*, the *Chicago Tribune*, the *Chicago Examiner* and the *Telegraph Herald*. Dubuque also had a Catholic paper called *The Tribune*, so I went with all of those," said Cody.

"I was raised Catholic, which is a very structured religion, a very hierarchical religion. And so I was really good at taking orders, and if somebody said do something, I just did it. If something had to done, I had the feeling that *if I'm here, and I'm available, I ought to do it.*"

Cody enlisted and went on active duty with the U.S. Coast Guard in 1945. A year later, he got out and went to Loras College in Dubuque.

"There was an officer procurement program in 1948 that authorized applications for combat arms commissions for people who had a year of previous experience and two years of college," he said. "I had served over a year in the Coast Guard during WWII, and I had two-and-a half years of college. So I applied for a commission. I took a mental, a physical, and an oral exam, and that's how I got the commission.

"Unfortunately, Congress forgot to fund the Officer Procurement program that year," he said. "So I didn't go on active duty in the Army until May of 1949."

Of the situation south of Chinju the night of July 30-31, Cody said, "When I arrived with Charlie Company, the 1st Battalion of the 19th received some astronomical number of replacements. The only people with authority were the company commander and the company sergeant major, a man named Ray Point. And all of a sudden, we had all these replacements."

The artillery was still under a "no-fire" order because of the expected South Korean Marines in front of them. So Cody left his two-man crew at his observation post and volunteered to help with the replacements.

"We were under fire, and somebody had to get them into the holes," he said. "I was a commissioned officer. I was supposed to be doing something, and I couldn't fire artillery, so I offered my services to the company commander and Sergeant Point. They said to start placing people.

"I don't know why the colonel from the 1st Battalion insisted on placing these people, because we were the forward company, and we were under fire when these people arrived. I don't know if there were a hundred of them or how many there were, but somebody had to do something, so I got up and helped. We had to walk down some ridge line forward of the reverse slope and put them in foxholes," Cody said.

"I believe company rear was together with company forward, so the company was using kitchen help, and motor pool people, stuff like that.

A company is normally about 200 men. I think we had only about 40 or 45 effective men left in the company – only about a platoon. And all of them were dug in holes. So I took my share of new replacements and put them in these holes alongside existing members of Charlie Company. But we had more replacements than we had holes, so a lot of the replacements had to dig their own holes or double-holes.

"I was a lieutenant, and I had a pistol on my hip, and as far as they were concerned, I was some *old man*, because I was about 23. One of the replacements said to me, *Lieutenant, I don't have the cosmoline cleaned off my gun.* You know, he had an M-1 rifle. Another one said, *Lieutenant, I don't know my whatchamacallit from a hole in the ground.* My friend – Charlie was his name – said they were radar people."

Toward daybreak, Cody was told the 11th Field Artillery was the only artillery he was allowed to fire. "They told me they had received march orders. They were up north in Chinju, and they were about to be overrun. They had orders to move out, so I got my last fire out of the 11th.

"North Koreans are really great at attacking at night," said Cody. "We were on a gently sloped hill, to the west and south, and they were attacking from the south and west and running up the hill. When you're in a hole, and somebody is running up at you – even though it's rainy and messy and dark – you can smell them and see them.

"There were a lot of casualties. The corporal in my forward observer crew was hit. It was an abdominal wound, and you can't dink around with something like that. You gotta get them to a medic in a hurry. So we put something on him, and my driver and I started carrying him down the hill on a poncho.

"As I came down the hill, Sergeant Point asked, 'What are you doing?' I said, 'I'm taking my guy back to the medics,' and he said, 'We got a whole bunch of people down here who are wounded.' He had a jeep and a trailer, so I took a whole load of wounded people back to an aid station.

"Point asked me to bring back some ammo, because they were almost out. So after we delivered the wounded, I picked up a load of ammo at the ammo depot, and my driver and I went back to Charlie Company. By that time, the firing was down to sporadic and not very organized.

"There were a lot of new men killed before they even got on the company rosters. You know, dog tags come in two. So you take one and put it between a guy's teeth, and you grab the other one. And I know they were doing that when we got back with the ammo."

Cody's Silver Star citation states he evacuated an officer, but other than the company commander, he doesn't recall any other officers being there. But there *was* another officer there, and he *was* severely wounded. Perhaps it is feasible that the officer Cody evacuated was Lieutenant Harry Tincher – the *other* "only forward observer with Charlie Company" that night.

As Cody said, "We only had a worm's eye view of the world, each different person in combat."

*Second Lieutenant **Raymond J. Cody**, Artillery, U.S. Army, a member of Battery B, 13th Field Artillery Battalion, 24th Infantry Division, is awarded the **Silver Star** for gallantry in action against an armed enemy on 31 July 1950, near Chinju, Korea. As forward observer for artillery supporting Company C, 19th Infantry Regiment, Lieutenant Cody volunteered to leave his observation post and assist in the effective deployment of replacements brought up to the infantry company position while that company was being subjected to intensive enemy fire. With complete disregard for his own safety, he continuously moved among the men, encouraged them when they seemed to falter, and supplied them with ammunition. Unhesitatingly he evacuated an officer and enlisted man severely wounded by the devastating fire to places of safety, although in doing so he heedlessly exposed himself to enemy fire. Although his battery could no longer give supporting fire and had been ordered to withdraw, Lieutenant Cody remained with the infantry and continued to inspire the men by his gallant actions and extreme devotion to duty. His complete disregard for personal safety in the face of overwhelming enemy odds reflects the greatest credit on himself and the military service.*

Carl Anderson & Leroy Moore

Friendly troops had dire need of tanks and other armored vehicles, but several of the first tanks to arrive at the front didn't go into action until almost a month later, as described by Colonel Arthur Connor, Jr:

Desperate to get some armored force into the fight in Korea to counter the North Korean T-34 tanks, Eighth Army formed the 8064th and 8066th Platoons on July 10, 1950 . . . Eighth Army scoured its depots and found three M-26 "Pershing" heavy tanks. All three tanks suffered from a variety of mechanical problems after 5 years of neglect. Desperate for anything that could stand up to the North Korean tanks, it was decided to rebuild the Pershings, form them into a provisional tank platoon (the 8064th), and crew them with men from the tank company of the 1st Cavalry Division.[103]

Meanwhile, the 8064th Heavy Tank Platoon was sent by rail, arriving in Chinju at 3:00 a.m. July 28. Unfortunately, their M-26 tanks overheated within just a few hours. Their fan belts started stretching, and no replacement belts could be found in the entire Far East. Efforts to replicate new belts in Japan failed, and after three days in Korea, the tanks were still in poor condition.

First Lieutenant Samuel Fowler, commander of the tiny 8064th, went to Colonel Ned Moore the morning of July 31 for instructions on how he and his 14 enlisted men should proceed. The enemy had hit the 19th Regiment very hard during the night, and Colonel Moore told Fowler that unless he could load the tanks on a train, they should try to drive them out of the city under their own power. Failing that, they were to destroy the tanks and try to get out of Chinju by truck or on foot.

One of Fowler's crew members was Carl "Andy" Anderson, a WWII cavalryman from Sioux City, Iowa. He was added to the unit at the last minute, according to Alvin Clouse, who told researcher Lynnita Brown: "There are two things not correct in [Arthur Connor's] information on the 8064th. The crews were from the 77th Tank Battalion, and only six where killed. I was supposed to have been with them, but Lieutenant Fowler replaced me with Anderson, because he was a mechanic."[104]

It was Anderson's description of events that Army historian Roy Appleman used when he wrote:

William R. Moore, an Associated Press correspondent, suddenly appeared and suggested to Fowler that he should check a body of men coming up the rail track. It was now perhaps an hour past noon. Fowler had an interpreter call to the approaching men. They were North Koreans. Fowler ordered his tank crews to open fire. In the fire fight that immediately flared between the tank .30- and .50-caliber machine guns and the enemy small arms fire, Fowler received a bullet in his left side. In this close-

---

[103] Connor, Arthur W. Jr. *The Army, Transformation, and Modernization, 1945-1991: Implications for Today*. The Strategic Studies Institute: 2002.

[104] www.koreanwar-educator.org/topics/brief/p_strategic_studies_institute.htm.

range fight the tank machine gun fire killed or wounded most of the enemy group, which was about platoon size. The tankers put Fowler into his tank and started the three tanks east on the road to Masan.

Two miles down the road the tanks came to a blown bridge. The men prepared to abandon the tanks and proceed on foot. They removed Fowler from his tank and made a litter for him. Fowler ordered the men to destroy the tanks by dropping grenades into them. Three men started for the tanks to do this. At this moment, an enemy force lying in ambush opened fire. A number of men got under the [blown] bridge with Fowler. MSgt. Bryant E. W. Shrader was the only man on the tanks. He opened fire with the .30-caliber machine gun. A North Korean called out in English for the men to surrender. Shrader left the machine gun, started the tank, and drove it close to one of the other tanks. He dropped the escape hatch and took in six men. He then drove back toward Chinju and stopped the tank a few feet short of the bridge over the Nam, undecided whether to cross to the other side. There, the overheated engine stopped and would not start again. The seven men abandoned the tank and ran into the bamboo thickets fringing the river. After many close calls with enemy forces, Shrader and his group finally reached safety and passed through the lines of the 25th Division west of Masan. The men back at the blown bridge had no chance. Some were killed or wounded at the first fire. Others were killed or wounded under the bridge. A few ran into nearby fields trying to escape but were killed or captured.[105]

Carl Anderson was among those who were captured and would soon be joining North Dakotan Pat Martin. They would end up with a group of POWs destined for the Sunchon Tunnel Massacre, but due to the resourcefulness of the Iowan, their path was going to deviate.

Leroy "Buck" Moore, of Pender, Nebraska, was a member of a newly formed unit that was also attached to Ned Moore's Regiment at this time. The 31-year-old corporal had been with the 55th Quartermaster Depot in Japan before he was abruptly transferred to the 8066th Mechanized Reconnaissance Platoon. Overnight, he went from being

---

[105] Appleman. *Naktong to Yalu*. P 231-233.

a sales clerk to being a machine-gunner on an armored car.

Returning to Arthur Connor's description of the small armored platoons, he describes how Buck Moore's unit was put together:

> . . . another provisional unit, the 8066th, was formed from men out of Kobe Base, Japan, who had previous armor experience. The platoon consisted of five M-8 "Greyhound" armored cars used by the military police in Tokyo for crowd control. The 8066th arrived in Pusan in the middle of July, with the [8064th's three Pershings] following on July 16, 1950.

M-8 Greyhound armored car circa 1952 (U.S. Army)

[. . .] Attached to the 1st Battalion, 29th Infantry Regiment, the 8066th was ambushed while participating in a reconnaissance in force westward from the village of Chungam-ni back toward Chinju on August 2, 1950. The North Koreans destroyed four of the five armored cars of the platoon and killed the platoon leader.

That platoon leader was Buck Moore, who was highly decorated.

*The **Distinguished Service Cross** is **(Posthumously)** awarded to Corporal **Leroy L. Moore**, U. S. Army, for extraordinary heroism in connection with military operations against an armed enemy of the United Nations while* *serving with 8066ᵗʰ Mechanized Reconnaissance Platoon attached to the 1ˢᵗ Battalion, 29ᵗʰ Regimental Combat Team, 24ᵗʰ Infantry Division. Corporal Moore distinguished himself by extraordinary heroism in action against enemy aggressor forces near Chinju, Korea, on 30 July 1950. On that date, Corporal Moore was a gunner on an M-8 Reconnaissance Car in support of an infantry company which was pinned down by heavy enemy machine-gun fire. Without regard for his own personal safety, Corporal Moore moved to an exposed position on a river bank, and with accurate fire from his machine-gun knocked out three enemy machine-guns, inflicting heavy casualties on the enemy. This action enabled the infantry company to withdraw to new positions. In a later action, on 2 August 1950, when his car was put out of action, Corporal Moore dismounted a 30-caliber machine-gun and attempted to move to the flank of an enemy machine-gun which was hampering the evacuation of wounded men. During this action Corporal Moore was killed by mortar fire.*

Laurence Martin Captured

Pat Martin (North Dakota) made it out of the Hadong battle in one piece, but his luck was shifting.

"We moved back maybe six miles and set up again," he told interviewer Elmer Liam. "The next day was a repeat of the first day. The trouble was we couldn't get enough ammunition. They'd ration it to you. Finally, after about the fourth day, we got back to Chinju – inland – probably seventy-five to a hundred miles southeast of Seoul."

Of the attack at Chinju, Martin said, "They hit us from all directions. They put us up on a hill, a kind of a range. What it turned out to be was an old cemetery.

"We were supposed to hold back the oncoming forces. Well, we got out on that hill, and they came from all sides. They were on foot, and they had a few tanks. All we had to fight tanks was an M-1 rifle. We had one bazooka and three rounds of ammunition."

It was now July 31. "That was the day Oshinski was killed in the foxhole I was in. He got hit in the spine, so I suppose it was another ten minutes. He kept saying, 'Pat, call a medic,' so I hollered *Medic!* But I knew there wasn't one within ten miles. I stayed with him until he passed away.

"Earlier, maybe 15 minutes, I got shot through the heel of my shoe. It was hot, man it burned. I took off my shoe and thought, *Boy, I lost my foot.* It was blood red, but there was no serious bleeding. I thank my lucky stars, because I was able to walk. We were out of ammunition, so I field-stripped my rifle and threw it away."

Martin took off into a ravine, where he hid for more than a day. Two other Americans soon joined him. "They were two real young fellas," he said. "I was young myself, but they were two years younger – they were 17. Their parents had to sign for them to get them in.

"While we were there, the firing up on the topside was getting less and less and less. You could hear the screams and hollers. The North Koreans were going out, and our guys who were hurt and couldn't walk, they murdered them right there. Once you couldn't walk, you were history.

"We were cut off. We were alone. We knew there was a railroad track going out of Chinju. So it was my idea that we try to find this track and head south. We would come to Americans sooner or later, because it came out of Pusan. We started over that direction, and that's when the North Koreans spotted us. They came over and got us. They were going through all kinds of motions. They were pointing a gun at our heads, and they were gonna shoot us. There was about a dozen of them and only three of us," said Martin.

"They put us in this room and blindfolded us. Before they tied our hands, they made us empty our pockets. I laid out everything, and my mother had given me a rosary and a watch with a green crystal. It was real pretty. It was a Longines Wittenhauer™ I'd been given for graduation. Well, that was gone.

"They took everything except my rosary. They don't believe in God, but they wouldn't touch it. They knew what it was, and they gave it back to me. I said, 'Thank you, I'll keep it.' And I did.

"In my billfold, I had a few pictures of my girlfriend and maybe my brothers and sisters. I stuck it in the crotch of my pants, and by golly they never found it. They searched me a couple times, and they never found it.

"They let me keep my dog tags as long as I was mobile, but if I'd have ever gone down, they'd have taken those.

"They were screaming and hollering, yipping and yapping. Finally, you get so scared – and I'm scared – you get to a point and . . . well anyway, this voice came in, 'Do not fear. We will not harm you.'

"I said, 'Who are you?' He said, 'My name is Michael Bark,' in English. He said, 'I was educated in Singapore with American children.' They took our blindfolds off and untied us, and we talked for a while. He was the North Korean interpreter. What he was after was information. He was trying to get us relaxed. He wanted to know where we were from, how many guys were in our outfit, where we came from, all this kind of stuff, you know? He wasn't bad at all," said Martin

"Then they took us over to like an old school, and that's where we met the tough boys. Higher up. They were asking us questions through the interpreter. They finally brought in another guy who could speak fairly good English. He would ask *what's your name*, and he talked like – I always thought – like a gopher. He would ask the same question over and over, hour after hour.

"One day I got so damn mad, I spit in this guy's face. I shouldn't have done it. He slapped me with a rifle, and I slept for a while. When I woke up, another guy said to me, 'Martin, when a lion has your arm in his mouth clear up to the shoulder, you better damn well pet him with your other hand.' There's a lot of truth to that. I learned to keep my mouth shut.

"The other two guys fared about the same. What was really sad was they wouldn't eat. We did get a cucumber apiece. I ate some of mine, but we had gotten diarrhea so bad. I don't know if it was the water, or the cucumber, or whatever, but it was tough.

"They gave us one rice-ball a day, when it was available. Black rice. It was kind of like a paste – semi-cooked, like glue, in a ball about the size of a baseball. One a day. If water was available, we'd get it.

"Every day they moved us from place to place, and the way we'd get the water, we had one canteen for 12 or 13 of us (POWs). One guy at the front would lay it down in a creek that came down from the rice paddies. Lay it down sideways. The guy on the end would pick it up and hand it forward. We tried to get a little water that way.

"Those two young fellas both passed away, because they wouldn't eat the food. They absolutely refused anything. All they'd do all night long was cry, 'I want a malt and a hamburger.' They were hysterical, but what can you do? One lasted a week. The other one lasted about nine days. They just got so weak."

End of the Delaying Actions

The terrible bloody month of July drew to a close, with many more brutal months yet to come. But those men who lost their lives, limbs and spirits had done the impossible. They had held back the entirety of the North Korean Army until more of their countrymen could be brought in to back them up.

For the families who lost sons, brothers and fathers, it may have been of little comfort, but South Korean and American troops were finally turning a corner. The arrival of more and more troops – from the States and also from other nations – would allow for the comparative luxury of counterattacking or even going on the offensive. For those men still standing, there were finally glimmers of hope.

Norton Goldstein summed up the fighting of July 1950 by saying, "We had 12,000 men in our 24th Division, and theoretically, in an infantry division, *one in seven* is a combat infantryman. Yet in three weeks, we had over 6,000 casualties.

"To this day, in place of what many people wear in their lapel, which is the flag, I wear the emblem of the 24th Infantry Division to honor all the guys who weren't as lucky as I was."

1949 basketball champs in Japan: Norton Goldstein, Len Cox (killed at Chochiwon) and Mike Danszak. (Courtesy Goldy Norton)

Part II

★

Holding the Naktong Perimeter

Chapter 21

ALONG THE SOUTH COAST

"No orders, no letters, no insignia of rank can appoint you as leaders. Leadership is an intangible thing; leaders are made, they are not born. Leadership is developed within yourselves." John G. Stepanek, 24th Reconnaissance Company

AFTER THE LOSS of Chinju, Eighth Army commander Walton Walker quietly moved the 27th Regiment Wolfhounds to the south coast from positions farther north. He filled the gap left by the Wolfhounds with newly arrived troops from the 1st Cavalry Division.

As one AP reporter wrote:[106]

> The good news swept through the Eighth U.S. Army Tuesday that fresh American troops have landed. Those were sweet words to hard-pressed infantrymen who have been slugging it out with an enemy without rest and with the barest reserves....
>
> The fresh Army forces looked well equipped and fit. The combat experienced veterans among them faced imminent entry into battle calmly but not with the cockiness of some of the youngsters who have yet to face realities of war.
>
> The unloading was continuous throughout the night. Like all new soldiers about to go into combat they were curious about what they would encounter in the coming fight. Several asked for confirmation of stories about North Korean atrocities on American soldiers.

---

[106] *Pacific Stars & Stripes.* 1 Aug 1950.

David Hurr

During the cavalry's difficult retrograde movement, the 5ᵗʰ Cavalry Regiment served as rear guard, blowing the main highway and railroad bridges while still engaged in heavy combat.

Among the cavalrymen bringing up the rear was 19-year-old David Alfred Hurr, the fifth child born to Bruce and Loretta Hurr.

David was of Ottawa descent and was a member of the White Earth Nation. He spent his early years in Ponsford, Minnesota, until the family moved to Detroit Lakes in 1940. In high school, David played football and was on the high school golf team, and he also worked as a caddy-master at the Detroit Lakes Country Club during the summers of 1948 and 1949.[107]

Hurr had been in the service only eight months. Much of what happened the night of August 1-2 is lost to us, but luckily, WWII veteran Ed Hendricks described the situation to author Donald Knox. Hendricks was in Fox Company, which was adjacent to Hurr's Easy Company that night.

> I lost a lot of kids – snipers, mortars, artillery. By the time we got to Taegu, everybody was either withdrawing, in the hands of the medics, or dead. Taegu had been bombed and shelled and was on fire. There was no transportation for us. Trucks were full up bringing back the dead.[108]

David Hurr received the highly esteemed Distinguished Service Cross for his ultimate sacrifice, but this author believes a Medal of Honor may have been more appropriate for the level of bravery displayed by this young buck private.

*The **Distinguished Service Cross** is awarded **(Posthumously)** to **David A. Hurr**, Private, U.S. Army, for extraordinary heroism in connection with military operations against an armed enemy of the United Nations while serving with Company E, 2ⁿᵈ Battalion, 5ᵗʰ Cavalry Regiment (Infantry), 1ˢᵗ Cavalry Division. Private Hurr distinguished himself by extraordinary heroism in action against enemy aggressor forces at Kumch'on, Korea, on 1 and 2 August 1950. During the late afternoon of 1 August 1950, Company*

---

[107] *Detroit Lakes Record.* 24 Aug 1950.

[108] Knox. *The Korean War, An Oral History, Pusan to Chosin.* P 65.

E, 5th Cavalry Regiment, to which Private Hurr was attached as a machine gunner, came under furious assault from hordes of enemy soldiers. In the bitter and intense battle that ensued, he was severely wounded in the stomach by a mortar fragment, but he refused evacuation and steadfastly continued to man his heavy machine-gun and deliver devastating fire into the ranks of the stubborn assailants. In the early morning hours of 2 August 1950, when the unit was finally ordered to withdraw in the face of increased and extremely intense hostile fire from this numerically superior enemy force, Private Hurr voluntarily remained at his position to provide protective fire for his comrades during the withdrawal. With indomitable courage and determination, he continued to sweep the assaulting force until his ammunition was expended. When last seen alive, armed with only his rifle, he was delivering deadly accurate fire into the charging foe. When the strong point was regained later in the day, his body was found beside his gun, with numerous enemy dead lying in his field of fire. The voluntary and heroic stand he took in the face of utmost peril resulting in his death enabled his comrades to make an orderly withdrawal and evacuate the wounded.

Ned Moore & John Michaelis

The enemy's next objective along the south coast was definitely Masan, the last sizable barrier between Chinju and their ultimate goal of Pusan.

Colonel Ned Moore, Guthrie Center, Iowa, was pulling his 19th Regiment back from Chinju when Colonel Michaelis and his 27th Regiment started arriving to support Moore and his men.

Moore and Michaelis had served together during WWII. When the 101st Airborne was surrounded at Bastogne, during the Battle of the Bulge, the chief of staff committed suicide. Moore moved up to temporarily fill the position until Michaelis could take over, pending recovery from combat wounds.

Late in the night of July 31, Moore and Michaelis met in Masan with General John Church, the new commander of the 24th Division, to discuss the battle plan for the following day.[109] Essentially, Moore was to continue defending the sector east of Chinju, while Michaelis moved the 27th Regiment into support positions behind the 19th Regiment at a mountain feature called The Notch. (See map page 210.)

---

[109] Accounts of The Notch/Chindong-ni are based on writings by Clay Blair and Roy Appleman, which differ. The author favors Appleman's account, because it was based on communications with Moore, Michaelis and Gilbert Check.

The next morning, Michaelis and his two battalion commanders, Gordon Murch Gilbert Check and, reconnoitered the ground around the Notch to decide how to position their troops.

Michaelis had deep concerns. The main road leading east out of Chinju split into a north road and a south road at a fork near the village of Muchon (hereafter called the Muchon Fork). In effect, these two roads could be likened to the rim of an ice-cream cone, with the scoop of ice cream representing a mountain mass rising from within the rim.

Ned Moore (U.S. Army)

Michaelis's concern was that if they lost control of the Fork, the enemy would have access to both the northern and southern roads to Masan, as well as all the high ground in between.

Ned Moore's men were played out, and if they couldn't hold at the Fork – and they fell back toward Michaelis – the two regiments would be double-teaming the North Koreans on the north road, while the south road to Masan and Pusan would be wide open.

Michaelis drove to the 13th Field Artillery command post, where he called Moore to discuss the situation. But at this point, Moore had his hands full.

A heavy attack was threatening to break through his 1st Battalion at The Notch. Air strikes failed to slow the enemy, and by mid-afternoon, the battalion was pushed back about ten miles to the vicinity of Chungam-ni.[110] The beleaguered Iowan was highly decorated for his handling of the crisis.

*The **Distinguished Service Cross** is awarded to Colonel **Ned D. Moore**, Infantry, U.S. Army, for extraordinary heroism in connection with military operations against an armed enemy of the United Nations while*

---

[110]Maj Gen John Church. *24th Division War Diary, From: 312400K July to: 012400K August.* P 29.

Commanding Officer of the 19th Infantry Regiment, 24th Infantry Division. Colonel Moore distinguished himself by extraordinary heroism in action against enemy aggressor forces near Chungam-ni, Korea, on 1 August 1950. During a visit to the command post of his 1st Battalion, Colonel Moore discovered that the positions were in grave danger of being overrun and that the defenses were rapidly nearing a breaking point. Without hesitation, he initiated prompt action to prevent a complete collapse. In spite of intense enemy automatic weapons, small-arms, mortar, and tank fire, which was falling throughout the entire area, he voluntarily undertook the task of making a personal visit to each of the exposed front line units. He immediately went forward to a position less than one hundred yards behind the foremost rifleman of Company C and, from this position, personally began to rally the wavering front line troops. Later, under his personal supervision, Company A was quickly reorganized, and it launched an attack that regained critical terrain which had been lost to the enemy. Colonel Moore remained with the forward elements of the battalion throughout the remainder of the day, directing the employment of heavy weapons and riflemen, until the enemy attack was completely repulsed. The calm demeanor, prompt decisions, absolute disregard for his own personal safety, fearless leadership, and the courageous example he exhibited were an inspiration to all members of his command and proved to be the turning point for our troops during this crucial engagement with the enemy.

With the southern route now in serious jeopardy, Michaelis tried to connect with General Church. When he was unsuccessful, he made a decision that could have ended his career. He boldly chose to divert his two battalions of Wolfhounds to cover the southern road – with or without orders.

After a grueling 27-hour truck drive from their previous positions, Michaelis directed his troops to set up camp in a schoolyard at Chindong-ni, a coastal village southwest of Masan. Meanwhile, he took Gilbert Check and Gordon Murch out along the southern route to size up the situation they would face. (The air distance between the Muchon Fork and Masan was some 20 to 25 air miles.)

According to Roy Appleman, General Church had since learned of Michaelis' desired change and agreed the Wolfhounds should protect the south road. But he again ordered both the 27th and the 19th to go on the offensive the following morning (August 2). Their shared mission was to converge at the Muchon Fork and then attack west through the Chinju Pass to recapture Chinju.

Church offered them only one bit of good news – each regiment would have with them a platoon from the newly arrived 8072nd Medium

Tank Battalion. Michaelis contacted Moore to tell him about the new attack plans, but Moore was dubious about whether his exhausted battalions could recapture the road back to the Muchon Fork. But he did agree to commit the 1st Battalion of the 29th RCT for the attack.

Michaelis ordered Lieutenant Colonel Murch to dig in his 2nd Battalion at key points along the south road, while Gil Check was to jump off with his 1st Battalion at 4:00 a.m. the following morning.

Check Leads his Men West

Check's men were euphoric about finally going on the offensive, and in the manner in which young men excel, they were itching to tangle with their opponents. As the tanks warmed their engines, trucks came from Masan to carry Baker and Charlie Companies. The men of Able

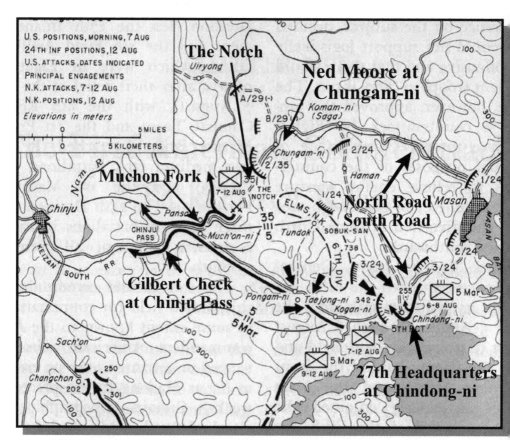

(Base map inset, courtesy Center of Military History, depicts troop movements a week later, but uses author's additions to depict the situation August 1.)

Company would ride on the tanks at the head of the column, along with Dog Company and their heavy weapons. Addison Terry writes:

> The men scurried around in the half light filling clips, snapping bolts, drawing grenades, and adjusting packs. The scene reminded me of paintings I had seen of events of the two world wars. *This would never be painted,* I thought. This probably wouldn't even be noted in the papers . . . This, to the rest of the world, was not noteworthy of mention, but for these weary, lean men and boys in the schoolyard, it was one of the most important moments of their lives, perhaps the last.

As forward observer for Battery A, 8th Field Artillery, Terry rode in the first jeep behind the tanks, saying they were old Shermans, but "they looked good to us."

All was quiet as they motored into the predawn darkness. The men began joking that the North Koreans had heard the Wolfhounds were coming and had fled.

One tank was suddenly disabled by an oil fire, and the crew assured the men they'd take care of the problem and catch up as soon as they could. "I never saw them again," said Terry.

Back at the schoolhouse in Chindong-ni, Michaelis grew nervous about the lack of enemy Check was encountering. What if he made the wrong decision? What if the enemy was concentrating only on the north road, and Moore's 19th Regiment gave way?

After a time, a spotter plane dropped a message for Gilbert Check that enemy troops had been spotted in the next village. Addison Terry wanted to be able to call in artillery fire if things got hot, so he climbed onto the second tank for a better view.

When they came within a thousand yards of the village, anyone still riding on tanks dismounted and moved off the road into rice paddies. Several enemy soldiers were caught trying to set up a machine gun; they surrendered without a shot. Terry writes:

> As we approached the group of huts, it seemed certain that a rain of fire would start the show, but none came. We reasoned that the hostiles were waiting for us to get into point-blank range, but it certainly seemed as though we were close enough now. There was a teeth-chattering silence that made everyone

slow down to a snail's pace. We felt just as though we were walking into the lion's mouth.

The first tank crept around a little crook in the road and looked straight into the courtyard of the largest house. There, kneeling around a cook-fire, were about fifteen enemy soldiers. The lead tank let them have it with three quick rounds of high explosive . . . We had evidently hit the advance guard of a larger force and had found them completely asleep. We all prayed the next group of North Koreans we met would be as careless.

The Wolfhounds progressed several more miles toward a cluster of hills.

A stray cow was peacefully grazing, but there was no other movement. The men of Able were starting up the hills from both flanks now, and we began feeling our way forward. At this moment, all hell broke loose.

Enemy small arms and mortars erupted. In turn, American tanks blasted machine gun positions, and the enemy scrambled to the backside of the hill. The tank on which Terry was riding lurched around a bend and caught enemy soldiers diving for the ditches.

From all accounts, it appears they had successfully reached the Muchon Fork. Baker Company went up to reconnoiter the area and quickly returned to report that an entire enemy column, possibly a full division, was approaching. The North Dakota commander immediately ordered a full assault, and his tanks pulled around the bend and opened fire. Terry recalls:

In front of us for several miles were oxen, oxcarts, infantry, and jeeps. Most of them had managed to get off the road and were struggling in the paddies. The second tank (my mount) and the third and fourth, as they came around into position, opened up with their .75s and .50s with small arms aboard, spraying the flanks. The first mortar rounds could now be heard starting their journey from our rear and shortly could be seen bursting on the road and in the paddies to our front. Their effect was extremely profitable and seemed to have a terrific effect upon the spirit of the Reds. They were on the receiving end of a rolling mortar barrage of perhaps a hundred rounds a minute, plus the flat-trajectory fire of our four tanks and several recoilless rifles that were now getting into action on the hill.

It looked like our first battalion was invincible. Many of the enemy were killed and practically all of their larger equipment was destroyed . . . We ran through them like a dose of salts, and in a matter of what seemed like a few minutes, we had reached a point where there was no more equipment in front of us, and the only foes conspicuous were dead ones except for some fast disappearing little black dots . . .

Check called for the men to regroup and resupply. To keep his trucks from falling into enemy hands, he sent all but the mortar and artillery transports back to Chindong-ni. With temperatures pushing 100 degrees, the men were feeling the effects of more than just their adrenaline, but their spirits were soaring. Terry writes:

There is nothing so essential to the morale of an army as success in the field. . . . The effect of this success had the effect of a bolt of lightning. From my perch, I could see this esprit de corps take hold, generate heat, and then erupt. I could feel it. We were an unbeatable team of killers.

It was time for their next objective – turn west and recapture Chinju. They headed up a twisting road through stands of dust-covered cane, ever smaller rice paddies, and a narrowing valley that became the Chinju Pass. The men started talking about driving straight up to Seoul, joking and laughing "like children on a hay ride." The first tank rounded a bend in a corridor flanked by cane, when Terry's tank was suddenly hit by antitank fire.

There was the ear-shattering sound of ripping metal. I don't remember jumping, but I am certain that I did, for people were already landing on top of me in the ditch on the right side of the road.

The third tank came under the same fire with three direct hits. The soldiers on the ground fired and threw grenades into the cane, and then rushed across the road where they finished off two "elephant guns" concealed just a few feet off the road.

The gunner from Terry's second tank was killed, and the remaining crew members were wounded. From the sounds coming from the third tank, he thought its crew was hit just as badly, if not more so.

From a cliff above them, rifle fire and grenades started pouring down. The fourth tank blasted the enemy from their perches, while the men dragged their wounded back to a safer spot by a rice paddy.

Colonel Check learned that although the second and third tanks were disabled, they were still operable, so he sent out word that he needed soldiers with heavy equipment experience. Several former bulldozer operators came forward and were given emergency training on how to operate the two crippled tanks, while several riflemen jumped on top to man the machine guns.

Check kept the pressure on, but the battalion gained only a few hundred yards during the next hour. Unable to communicate with his boss, Check sent runners back to Chindong-ni. None of them made it.

Meanwhile, on the north road, Ned Moore had deployed the 1st Battalion of the 29th RCT from the Notch that morning, but they immediately ran into a fierce wall of resistance. Moore ended up committing four different battalions to the fight, but the hills were crawling with enemy troops, and Moore's mission was stopped cold.

The enemy was, in fact, covering both roads to Masan, confirming Michaelis' earlier fears. Worse, the North Koreans had already gained control of the high ground between the north and south roads, and they could cut off Check's escape route in the same way they were now flanking Ned Moore's troops.

As the fighting heated up west of Muchon, Addison Terry lost his ability to communicate with the artillery and turned his attention to rescuing the wounded from rice paddies. It didn't take long before they were receiving fire from both their left and right flanks.

At about 2:00 p.m., Colonel Check drove up to appraise the situation in their position and told Terry to head back to Chindong-ni to get himself a replacement radio. He was also to pick up a captured North Korean officer and a promising load of captured satchels and documents to take to Michaelis.

Using a battered jeep with flat tires, Terry drove east feeling fortunate to miss the main clash at the Chinju pass. But the North Koreans had already established a road block behind the regiment. An hour later, he decided to push his luck by pairing up with a two-and-a-half-ton truck loaded with some 25 wounded and headed out again.

About ten miles down the road, they were stopped by six G.I.s who suggested they turn off onto "this little two-rutted trail running to the left" which would take them right back to regiment. Unfortunately, they were talking about the wrong regiment – the 19th.

"I realized later the Lord had his hand on my shoulder," said Terry, "because by getting lost we met up with a hospital train in the town of Haman." Terry and the truck pulled up alongside and delivered their wounded, some of whom were Terry's good friends, saying, "I learned years later that all the wounded ended up surviving."

Meanwhile, Lieutenant Colonel Check was unaware of the seriousness of his situation until about 5:30 that afternoon, when a liaison plane dropped a message from Colonel Michaelis. Cressie Johnson, a member of Dog Company, told historian Uzal Ent that he watched as Check opened the note, saying, "I could see his mouth tighten." The message read, "Return. Road cut behind you all the way. Lead with tanks if possible. Will give you artillery support when within range."

Fortunately for his men, Gilbert Check had recently been training troops on withdrawal techniques, and he knew what he was doing. He immediately disengaged and began fighting his men back toward Chindong-ni. He put his two damaged tanks at the front of the column and placed his two good tanks at the end of the column behind the mortar and artillery trucks. The foot soldiers moved along the sides of the ridges paralleling the road and withdrew under heavy fire.

As sunset approached, the Wolfhounds were still well short of reaching the Muchon Fork. Check knew he still had to contend with the enemy-infested south road, so he piled his infantrymen – some 100 men – into and on top of his vehicles and made a run for it. Draped with riflemen, these vehicles made juicy targets, but it was the only way for them to gain the speed they needed.

When it got dark, their air cover ended. At a certain point, however, they got within range of the friendly artillery, and as Michaelis had promised, a battery of howitzers shelled enemy targets along the sides of the road. The battalion finally made it back to Chindong-ni at about midnight.

Check went to see Michaelis, who was being interviewed by war correspondents John Martin and Maggie Higgins in the command post (the school's science lab). Martin wrote[111] that Check was "gaunt and

---

[111]Martin, Harold. "The Colonel Saved the Day." *Saturday Evening Post.* 9 Sep 1950.

tired, and he still looked more like a schoolteacher than a fighting man, but there was a great pride in him."

Check told Michaelis, "It was a firefight all the way – harassing fire from the rear. Once we hit a hole in the road and had to stop until it was filled. The kids in the back kept yelling to hurry it up, they were under fire. We had some wounded, and once we stopped the whole column until a medic could give a wounded man an injection of plasma. It might have been a fool thing to do, but – well, we had some good men killed today, and I didn't want to lose any more."

Cressie Johnson later said, "Colonel Check . . . with that thoughtful school teacher way about him . . . made the cool decisions that saved a lot of lives. I loved and respected that little man, and I believe the whole battalion did, too."[112]

(Courtesy Check family)

*The President of the United States takes pleasure in presenting the **Distinguished Service Cross** to Lieutenant Colonel **Gilbert Joseph Check**, (Infantry) United States Army, for extraordinary heroism in connection with military operations against enemy aggressor forces at Chindong-ni, Korea, on 2 August 1950. On that date, the 27th Infantry Regiment was ordered to attack in the vicinity of Chindong-ni, and Colonel Check organized a task force with the 1st Battalion as the nucleus. Throughout the day he remained at the head of his unit, constantly exposing himself to heavy enemy fire, as he led his force in an advance of twenty-two miles into enemy held territory. He consistently outmaneuvered the enemy, overran strong points and smashed roadblocks. When he was ordered to return for the purpose of consolidating the*

---

[112]Ent, Uzal. *Fighting on the Brink.* P 115.

regiment's position, he supervised the loading and evacuation of the wounded and returned in an orderly manner. The exemplary leadership of Lieutenant Colonel Check so inspired his unit that they disrupted enemy communications, destroyed road blocks and inflicted many casualties.

Surprise Attack in the Morning

The Wolfhounds made the news not only because of what transpired August 2, but also because a surprise greeted them the next morning. Regimental staff members, as well as the two visiting reporters, were eating breakfast when small arms fire from a nearby bluff shattered the windows of the school house. As the bullets poured in, the reporters crawled out a back window, and the officers made their way out to organize their men. After their arduous action the previous day, some were jolted from their sleep and were shoeless – a valuable lesson learned.

The enemy had gotten this close because of a misunderstanding about who was going to handle security measures the night before. And that morning, men on guard duty mistook several enemy soldiers for South Koreans – another lesson learned.

The Americans gained possession of the high ground using small arms, mortars and artillery fire.

The North Koreans brought up at least one more battalion when their initial attack failed, but the reinforcements were spotted in the distance and were dispersed by artillery.

The fight continued until early afternoon. When the North Koreans finally withdrew, they left behind 400 dead. Another 200 were estimated killed and carried out by their comrades. In sharp contrast, the Wolfhounds suffered 13 killed and some 40 wounded.

After weeks of grinding losses, U.N. troops had finally pulled off a resounding victory, and General Walker had found himself a fire brigade.

Chapter 22

TASK FORCE KEAN

"You have to imagine the chaos. All the roads were jammed with civilian refugees. Sometimes it seemed like everybody in the country was trying to go south. From one position we were on we overlooked a railroad, and we could see these trains coming through, with the outside of the cars just alive with people. They were hanging on the sides, on the roofs, they were jammed in over the couplings." Uzal Ent, 1st Battalion, 27th Infantry Regiment

CONGESTION, CONFUSION AND CHAOS posed a nightmarish situation for newly arriving troops along the five-miles between Masan and Chindong-ni, where Gil Check's men had just beat back the surprise enemy attack the morning of August 3.

Although it was a two-lane road, it was sandwiched between rice paddies and moderately high hills; turning around was nearly impossible, especially with the heavy amount of troop movement taking place, and making matters worse were thousands of refugees, as well as continuous enemy harassment of one sort or another.

Daily temperatures hovered at a hundred degrees or more, and the humidity and gagging stink rising from the rice paddies started buckling the knees of even the strongest warriors. Medics sent out emergency calls for salt tablets, and the 25th Division created an emergency holding station for men suffering from heat stroke.

Walker's Dispersal of Troops

Ironically, General Walker was pulling back to the Naktong River after all. The earlier decision by Generals MacArthur and Almond – to disallow Walker's request to consolidate his troops along the sprawling

Naktong – was exacting a grave toll.

The Naktong Perimeter (also called the Pusan Perimeter) now comprised a rectangle of real estate about 60 miles wide and 90 miles long on the southeast corner of the peninsula.

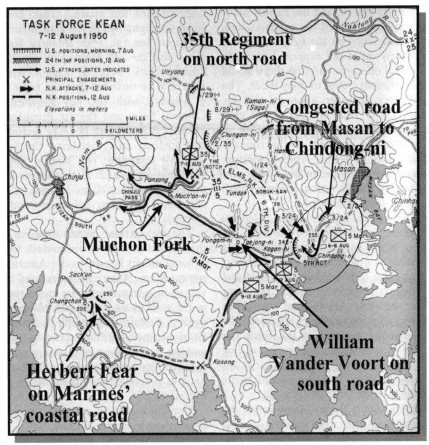

(Background map courtesy Center of Military History)

In the south, Walker was now pulling out the 27th Wolfhounds for use elsewhere, and he was also trying hard to give Ned Moore's 19th Regiment a much needed pause for regrouping. With the situation highly fluid, however, he was still shifting his troops on an hour-by-hour basis. The only positive thing in this sector was that the enemy had taken such a trouncing that it was having to also stop and regroup.

Four newly arrived regiments were negotiating the tangle of man and machine southwest of Masan:

- The 25th Division's 24th Regiment, an African-American unit, took up positions along this road to stop enemy infiltrators.
- The 35th Regiment relieved Ned Moore's 19th Regiment along the north road.[113]
- Hawaii's 5th Regimental Combat Team (5th RCT) moved toward the south road recently traveled by Gilbert Check's men. (This unit, more than any other, was in for some very rough days ahead.)
- The 5th Marine Regiment, operating as the 1st Provisional Marine Brigade, was to go even farther south, hugging the coastline to possibly fight the recently spotted 83rd Motorcycle Regiment.[114] (The Marines fortunately had a great many veterans of fighting in the Pacific in WWII.)

These new regiments and their support units were under the command of General William Kean, 25th Division commander, as *Task Force Kean*. Their mission was to launch an offensive August 7 to drive the enemy back past Chinju.

This plan had its drawbacks, but General Walker wanted to keep a sizable number of North Koreans tied up in the southern corridor, while the 1st Cavalry Division and the newly arriving 2nd Infantry Division helped South Korean troops fend off the enemy farther north.

The task force got off to a bad start, in part because of the traffic snarl, but more importantly because the threat was now right on top of them in the surrounding mountains.

North Korea was also preparing a major assault, and the race was on to see which side would jump off first. Excerpts from the 25th Division intelligence reports for August 4-5 read:

The enemy has vigorously felt out our lines all during the day. He is attempting to keep our forces fixed as he continues to build up for an attack. There are indications of movement of troops forward from rear areas, as well as recruiting of local men . . .

---

[113]The 1st Battalion of the 29th RCT – after a brief respite – joined the 35th and was later absorbed by that regiment as its third battalion, while the 29th's 3rd Battalion was likewise absorbed by the 27th Regiment.

[114]Variously called the 82nd Motorcycle, 83rd Motorcycle, or 83rd Motorized Regiment.

Coins sewn in the lining of clothing is a method of identifying enemy intelligence agents. These persons also sometimes wear South Korean police uniforms. Enemy troops infiltrate in groups of three to five and then assemble in rear of our lines at a predesignated spot. . . . Enemy troops occupy perimeters of large towns with very few elements located in the main area of towns.

An August 6 entry reads:

Enemy has emplaced artillery, prepared hasty fortifications, and has otherwise installed himself firmly in the front of the Division. Self-propelled guns have also been brought up. The enemy has continued to engage in vigorous patrolling. The air bombardment he has been receiving in closing with the Division front line troops is forcing the enemy to secure what gains he could in places not subject to air attack. Concentrations to the south flank are indications of probable presence of the 3rd Regiment, 6th North Korean Division in that vicinity. The enemy is becoming more cautious than before, now is infiltrating rather than just barreling into our positions . . .

Two of the regiments are composed mostly of veterans of the CCF [Communist Chinese Forces] Koreans sent back to Korea to join the North Korean Army. It is estimated that the unit has 25 tanks. This enemy is capable of launching a coordinated attack at any time, at a point or points of his choice, approximately the same time of our attack. He can inflict severe damage to our convoys and personnel along our route of advance and supply line by infiltrating small units and attacking from the heights using mortars and automatic weapons. Units of the 4th North Korean Division could be quickly shifted to this front.

Both Sides Attack

As predicted, *Task Force Kean* and the North Koreans launched their attacks simultaneously.

The 35th and 29th Regiments jumped off at 7:30 a.m. on August 7, but fog and heavy overcast prevented air support. They were soon in heavy combat between The Notch and the Muchon Fork, and by nightfall, they inflicted a reported 350 enemy casualties, captured four trucks of weapons and ammunition, and reached the high ground overlooking the critical fork. There, they dug in to await the arrival of the 5th RCT, which was slated to arrive via the south road.

Meanwhile, the 5th RCT had encountered problems almost immediately. After seizing their first objective, they ran into very heavy enemy fire, with the 25th Division's war diary calling it "their inauguration to the 'Holy Hell' of the Korean Battlefield."

This action was so near to Chindong-ni that the Marines could not bypass the action to reach their assigned route down along the coastal road. The Marines fought beside the 5th RCT to repel enemy attacks, while other units fought to keep open their supply route from Masan. During this time, the enemy successfully cut off and trapped a number of Americans who had to be rescued.

By August 9, both regiments were slowly making progress, but they were two days behind schedule – two days in which the North Koreans had been maneuvering into ever-better positions. In addition to the heavy fighting, badly drawn maps caused convoys from both the 5th RCT and the Marines to make wrong turns onto each others' roads. Had the higher-ups swapped their attack routes, things may have turned out differently than they did. But this was impossible, and a great deal of time was lost while each miles-long convoy had to back up and/or turn around.

Now, as each finally headed down their respective dust-choked roads, the excessive heat became a central cause of casualties, especially for the men who were climbing the ridges running parallel to their roads. Francis "Ike" Fenton, then executive officer of Baker Company, 5th Marines, recalled that when they ran out of water and couldn't be resupplied, they began dropping.[115] He writes:

> The troops that had passed out had to be left where they had fallen, since no one had the strength to move them. The men who had heat prostration, but [were conscious], tried to place themselves along the ridge where they could cover their fallen buddies in case of an enemy attack. The heat reached 114 degrees, and I personally don't believe that our men on the hill could have repulsed 10 enemy troops.

---

[115] Chapin, John C. *Fire Brigade: U.S. Marines in the Pusan Perimeter.* Marine Corps Historical Center. Washington, DC:2000. P 24-25.

Despite the conditions, both regiments inflicted damage on the enemy by nightfall, and General Kean ordered both to push throughout the night to join the 35th and 29th Regiments near the Muchon Fork.

5th RCT at Pogam-ni

At about 4:00 a.m. on August 10, the 5th RCT convoy, which included the 90th and 555th Field Artillery Battalions, was winding its way into the vicinity of Pogam-ni, about one-third of the way to the Fork. Here, they were stopped by an enemy ambush.

Pogam-ni was in a low area described by one man as resembling a rice bowl. Friendly units moved into positions along the bottom land and also on much of the surrounding rim, but the only way to go beyond was to climb a switchback and move through a pass on the far side of the bowl. And the North Koreans had that section firmly in hand.

Roughly an hour later, the 1st and 2nd Battalion gave cover for the 3rd Battalion to run the pass, after which those troops kept going. They were the only ones to make it all the way to the linkup at the Muchon Fork. The war diary reports "a virtually continuous attack and infiltration in the 5th RCT zone" from then on:

> The enemy maintained a constant harassment of our forces throughout the day with artillery, mortar, automatic weapon and small arms fire. Enemy infantry in small groups and organized units were scattered all over the area. They were conducting a well-coordinated action. The enemy was present on a fight-to-the-finish basis.

Twenty-four hours later, in the predawn darkness of August 11, the fighting continued. The diary reads:

> Enemy activity, which had been continuous and vigorous, exploded in the area north of [Pogam-ni. Elements of the 555th FAB and 90th FAB] were ambushed in the rear of the 1st Battalion 5th RCT positions ... in what appeared to be an all-out attack. Automatic weapons, mortars, self propelled guns, small arms, grenades and antitank rifles were used with devastating effect. Artillery positions in some instances were overrun. Congestion on the road hampered movement of vehicles and equipment. Six 105mm and six 155mm howitzers were lost ...

The disaster appears to have stemmed from pressure put on General Kean by General Walker – and by General Kean on Lieutenant Colonel Godwin Ordway, commander of the 5th RCT. Understandably, they wanted results.

Ordway estimated some 2,500 enemy soldiers were bearing down on them on August 12, and he requested permission to push his entire regiment through the pass. But Kean apparently didn't believe the danger was as imminent as Ordway claimed. Kean did give permission for Ordway to send his 2nd Battalion and its support units through the pass after dark, but Kean's second order alarmed Ordway and doomed many of his men. He was to keep his 1st Battalion in Pogan- ni until dawn and then have them run the pass in full daylight.

Sergeant First Class Edris Viers, 555th Artillery, was listed as missing in action on August 12. His remains were identified in 2011, and he was laid to rest in Swan, Iowa, in 2012.

At the point of receiving this order, Ordway's men were heavily engaged from all sides, and he balked at splitting them up and leaving half of them isolated. He protested, but Kean's only concession was that he would send a battalion from the 24th Regiment to support Ordway's men from the rear. (This promised battalion failed to show up in time.)

With deep misgivings, Ordway did as he was ordered. After dark, he sent his 2nd Battalion and their attached artillery units over the pass. The 1st Battalion and the remaining artillery batteries were now on their own in what became known as *Bloody Gulch*.

William Vander Voort

Among those who remained on the east side of the pass was William Vander Voort, who was born in Bijou Hills, South Dakota. His father passed away when Bill was only three, and he was subsequently raised by his mother, Ruby, and his stepfather, Garland Nelson, in Mitchell.

Vander Voort entered the Army from Rapid City in the spring of 1949. He was underage, but his mother granted her permission, later writing:

> He was a nice boy. He was only 19. He didn't drink or play cards. He saved his money. He wrote his mother regularly – wrote glowingly of his plans when he returned home. When he got out of the Army, Bill would write, he was going to use his money to buy livestock. Bill longed for the life of a rancher in western South Dakota.[116]

Now tonight, Ordway's men were lining up in hope of getting the word to move out, but shortly after midnight, the North Koreans again attacked in strength, and this time, it was a fight to the finish.

Thomas Roelofs, newly commanding Vander Voort's 1st Battalion, reportedly urged Ordway to go ahead and run the pass, but Ordway could not get through to General Kean to get his orders changed. After three critical hours, Ordway finally acted on his own and ordered his men to run the pass.

Advancing by jeep, Ordway made it across without incident. The majority of the foot soldiers followed, but behind them, a disabled vehicle blocked the road and stalled the artillery units and other convoy vehicles. As the sun rose, both artillery battalions came under heavy attack from three sides, and by midmorning, they were overrun.[117]

The Americans sustained some 300 casualties, and of those who were captured, the North Koreans murdered twenty men from the 90th Field Artillery.

Of Charlie Company's 180 men, 157 became casualties, including the young soldier who dreamed of becoming a Badlands rancher.

*The **Distinguished Service Cross** is **(Posthumously)** awarded to Private **William Vander Voort**, United States Army, for extraordinary heroism in connection with military operations against an armed enemy of the United Nations while serving with Company C, 1st Battalion, 5th Regimental*

---

[116]Locati, Trevor J. and Mitchell Bradley. Spearfish, SD. 21 May 2004. Web: http://koreanwarmemorial.sd.gov/SearchEngineForm/profiles/235.htm. Web: 9/9/2010.

[117] Toland, John. *In Mortal Combat.* P 142.

Combat Team. Private Vander Voort distinguished himself by extraordinary heroism in action against enemy aggressor forces at [Pogam-ni], Korea, on 12 August 1950. While participating in the defense of a strategic terrain feature, Private Vander Voort's company became engaged in heavy fighting, repulsing a series of attacks launched against the position by a determined enemy. During this action, and while repeatedly exposing himself to enemy fire, Private Vander Voort was wounded. He was placed in a foxhole for protection against enemy fire and to receive medical treatment. Launching a concerted attack on the company positions a short time later, the enemy lobbed a grenade into the emplacement occupied by Private Vander Voort and an aid man. As the result of the explosion of the grenade, he lost his life when his body absorbed its full blast.

Chapter 23

HERBERT FEAR AT CHANGALLON

"They walked ashore with boots dry, which spoke of the gallant men holding the Perimeter curving northward. Trained to war, masters of amphibious landing . . . those Marines of the First Brigade knew the value of their dry boots, and the price being paid by men somewhere over the mountains behind the port."
David Douglas Duncan, photographer *Life* magazine

THE CHANGALLON VALLEY was a bitter pill for Marines who were forced to withdraw before their job was finished. Among them was a seriously wounded private who was one week shy of his 21st birthday.[118]

Herbert "Skip" Fear was the youngest of eight children born to John and Verna Fear, who farmed near Hopkinton, Iowa. When his parents moved to Cedar Rapids in 1946, the husky blond joined the Marines. He would ultimately serve two tours in Korea and two in Vietnam, being highly decorated for both valor and merit along the way. But in August 1950, he was still a private who was about to experience his first major combat action.

After fighting side by side with the 5th RCT in and around Chindong-ni, Fear and the rest of his 5th Marine Regiment[119] were finally

---

[118]Email communications and support materials: Fear family, January 2014.

[119]The 5th Marines, the only Marine regiment in Korea at this point, was referred to as the 1st Provisional Marine Brigade. The 5th had all three of its battalions, but each of these was short one rifle company, and the heavy weapons companies lacked machine gun platoons. Fenton estimated his 1st Battalion numbered less than 600 men at this time.

able to head down their assigned route, a lesser road that hugged the coast. As members of *Task Force Kean*, their objective was the town of Sachon, where they would turn north toward Chinju.

By August 11, the Marines arrived at the town of Kosong, about halfway to Sachon. Here, where the long curving road turned west, they engaged the 83rd North Korean Motorcycle Regiment in what appeared to be no contest.

Francis "Ike" Fenton, executive officer of Herbert Fear's Baker Company, later wrote the fight lasted all day, with the Marines "hot on their heels" and Marine air support having a "turkey shoot."[120]

The North Koreans disappeared after this humiliation, and the 5th Marines had high hopes of reaching their destination without further interference. Unfortunately, the enemy had a score to settle.

The following morning, Baker Company, reinforced with five tanks and a detachment of 15 reconnaissance men, was designated as the advance guard for the column. Heading out in jeeps, these men were aided by spotter planes and helicopters checking the terrain on their flanks.

The column moved out at 8:30 a.m., and by 12:30, they were within four miles of Sachon. Still, the enemy was nowhere in sight.

About a half-hour later, reconnaissance men crossed a bridge into the little town of Changallon, which was situated in a narrow valley completely surrounded by high ground. Two enemy soldiers were spotted diving for cover, and the Marines opened fire. In turn, they received fire from nearly every direction.

The enemy's ambush was thus spoiled, but not entirely. The Marines had no means for turning around, and those on the road had no place to take cover. The North Koreans, on the other hand, were well camouflaged, with an estimated 500 soldiers dug in and concealed up on the surrounding ridges.

Captain John Tobin, commanding Baker Company, immediately sent forward two tanks and his 1st Platoon, led by Hugh Schryver, from Laurens, Iowa.

The others jumped into the bordering ditches and rice paddies. Lying in nearly two feet of water, wet radios immediately started failing, and platoon leaders ended up depending on runners for sending

---

[120]Fenton, Francis I. Jr. "Changallon Valley." *Marine Corps Gazette*. Nov 1951. P · 48-53; Further information is taken from *Special Action Report 2*, Period 2 August to 6 September 1950. 1st Battalion, 5th Marines.

messages over the next crucial hours.

Luckily, tanks farther back still had functioning radios, and an air strike was called in to hammer Hill 250, the ridge overlooking the road on the right.

South Dakotan David Cowling was ordered to take this hill with his 3rd Platoon after the air strike. When the Corsairs launched their attack, Cowling and his men dashed to the base of the hill and set to work cleaning the mud from their weapons.

After the strike, Cowling and his men climbed the hill against little opposition, but when they reached the crest, the North Koreans counterattacked from the reverse side of the ridge. This action was so furious and unexpected that the Marines were pushed halfway down the hill almost before they could react. Cowling lost two men killed and seven wounded. He himself took a bullet in his foot and was evacuated soon after.

Fanning into the surrounding hills, the fight went back and forth until evening before the Marines were able to get fully situated. With no food or water, not to mention the heat, the men were exhausted as darkness fell. Ike Fenton writes:

> All of us felt that if the enemy had any troops left in the area, we could expect a counterattack during the night. To be certain that we would be ready for them . . . we ordered 50 percent of the men to be awake at all times. This proved to be a fatal mistake . . . The men were just too tired to try to stay awake half the night.

Before the sun rose the following morning, the remaining men of David Cowling's 3rd Platoon were overrun as they slept. The enemy captured two machine guns and turned them on the Marines during the general attack that followed.

Fenton reported the Marine artillery and mortar men "will never be forgotten . . . It is impossible to adequately describe the pinpoint shooting they did."

Despite this heavy fire support, the enemy kept coming, and a short time later, Schryver reported the North Koreans appeared to be breaking through between the 1st and 2nd Platoons. Captain Tobin ordered Baker Company to fall back and prepare to counterattack at dawn.

Unfortunately, the counterattack couldn't be carried out. The North Koreans had breached the Naktong River farther north, and General

Walker needed the Marines to help push them back.

The Marines knew there were still eight of their own alive in those hills, and they begged for just one more hour to finish off the North Koreans and rescue their men.

But the situation was too dire, and the answer was no. Fenton writes:

> Getting the wounded off that hill and moving through those rice paddies was a pitiful sight. Everyone who could walk had to carry the more seriously wounded and dead back. Seeing a wounded Marine, badly hit but walking, trying to carry another wounded man who couldn't walk was like watching the blind leading the blind across New York's 5th Avenue. . . .

Among the wounded was Iowa's Herbert Fear, who saved the lives of four men during the withdrawal.

Fear with his mother, Verna, in 1951. (Republished with permission © 2014 SourceMedia Group, Cedar Rapids, Iowa)

*The **Distinguished Service Cross (Army award)** is awarded to Private First Class **Herbert H. Fear**, U. S. Marine Corps, for extraordinary heroism... At about 0730 on 13 August 1950, the squad in which Private First Class Fear served was ordered to break contact with elements of the 83rd North Korean Motorized Regiment on the Kosong-Sachon road, near the village of Changallon. As the unit was withdrawing, intense enemy fire from machine-guns, mortars, and small-arms covered the area, wounding Private Fear and four of his comrades. Refusing medical aid for the painful wound in his left shoulder, he held his ground to cover the evacuation of the wounded men and, when the enemy attempted to overrun his position, he killed three and deterred many others, gaining valuable time for the withdrawal of his comrades. During this action Private Fear was again wounded by mortar fire in the back and hips, but still refusing first aid he continued to fire until his squad had reached a safe place. Only then did he rejoin his unit, whereupon he collapsed from loss of blood and was carried to the aid station.*

Chapter 24

WARD NEVILLE, BUILDER-WARRIOR

"If we had to build a bridge or a road, we didn't even have picks or shovels. I remember building things, and the only thing we had to work with was our bayonets. We used them for shovels, and we used them for nail hammers – to pull nails, if there was such a thing. There was no saw in my outfit, because we lost everything we had so many times. The only things we managed to keep were the clothes on our back and our rifle." Morris Breed, combat engineer

LIEUTENANT WARD NEVILLE, Baker Company, 3rd Engineer Combat Battalion, had been blowing up bridges and laying mines ever since he arrived in Korea. He was well suited for the job.

Born in 1917, he was the youngest child of Orville and Maud Neville of Zap, North Dakota.

"Ward was a sturdy boy who played hard," his brother Robert later wrote. "He was one of the first daring kids to dive off the bridge into the creek right after the spring thaw. Despite the daring things that boys do, he had a compassionate and sentimental streak throughout his life. He was a protector of the underdog. One of the occasions that comes to mind was one of his teachers observed that a boy who was a slow learner was being taunted by most of the kids in town. Ward would protect this boy and dare the kids to take him on, too."

When Ward's parents moved to California during the depression, Ward moved to Minnesota to live with an aunt and uncle in St. Paul.

Neville's niece, Verna Oase, remembers him being a popular, fun-loving, energetic "rascal" who entered a room singing. He was particularly fond of Irish tunes and would prod people into singing along.

Ward Neville with mother and three older siblings. (Courtesy Verna Oase)

Neville played basketball for Park High School in St. Paul – a far cry from his experience in Zap, which had no gymnasium in the 1930s. In Zap, school desks had to be pushed aside to make room for indoor basketball games. There were no showers, although a resourceful coach drilled holes in the bottom of a washtub and nailed it to a wall. The boys could stand beneath it while he filled it with (unheated) water.

Robert Neville wrote that while in St. Paul, "Ward played hard and to win," recalling Neville played so aggressively his coach told him he had to take it easy, because he was injuring his own teammates.

After high school, Neville moved to California and found a construction job on Johnson Island in the South Pacific. When the Japanese bombed Pearl Harbor, he joined the Army.

Neville was commissioned as a 2nd Lieutenant in 1943, and he spent the next three years of WWII as an engineer in the China-India-Burma theater, where one of his assignments was working on the Lido Road.

He was discharged as a 1st Lieutenant in 1946, was reactivated in August 1949, and assigned to the 3rd Combat Engineer Battalion, 24th Division. Thus, he was one of the first American combat engineers to hit Korean soil. Among the many responsibilities assigned to him and his men were constructing and destroying roads and bridges; carrying out reconnaissance patrols; and laying and defusing mine fields – all while engaged in armed combat.

Philadelphian Robert Byrem served under Ward Neville earlier in Japan and also in Korea. Byrem was rebellious by nature and remembers

Neville "was tough and went by the book. And I can tell you, he and I didn't get along too well, because I was definitely not by the book, and he was." Byrem chuckled, "That doesn't mean he wasn't a good officer, you know. Most soldiers don't like to go by the book."

Byrem remembered the 3rd Combat Engineers debarking at Pusan. "They took us to a train station, and we were supposed to go to Osan, and from there, we were supposed to find whatever was left of *Task Force Smith*. Before we got about a mile from Osan, there were artillery shells coming in. The railroad station was on fire. We ran out of the train and ran into the station, and there were – it was a mess. There were people with their arms and legs off lying on the floor. What few medics that were there were trying to do something for them.

"From then on it was just chaos. We just took off in all directions. That was the first day. We weren't exactly ready for war, let's put it that way. Most of our equipment was Second World War surplus, and half of it didn't work," he said.

"In those first days, the enemy wanted the bridges intact, and we wanted to blow them up. Most of the time, it was a last-ditch stand. They'd tell us, *We have a few tanks up north of you. If you can, wait for them. If you can't, they're gonna get wiped out.*

"We blew everything we came across. In fact, I ran across a guy in my squad later on, and he said, 'Boy, you're lucky you left when you did, because everything we blew up, we had to rebuild.' (Byrem was wounded August 6.) That was a tough job, being a combat engineer. You were like an infantryman plus an engineer."[121]

On July 8, the 3rd Combat Engineers were tasked with blowing an important bridge near Chochiwon. It was Baker Company's first day of combat and also the first day Neville was decorated.

*The **Bronze Star Medal with Combat "V"** is awarded to First Lieutenant **Ward Orville Neville** . . . a member of Company B, 3rd Engineer Combat Battalion, 24th Infantry Division, on 8 July 1950 near Chochiwon, Korea. Hard pressed by a determined and numerically superior enemy, friendly troops were forced to evacuate their positions in face of the increasing superior fire power of the enemy. Given the mission of destroying a bridge after the crossing by the friendly troops, Lieutenant Neville exposed himself to the withering enemy fire with complete disregard for his own safety, prepared the bridge for demolition, and destroyed it in the face of the enemy advance. This courageous action deprived the enemy of a route to*

---

[121] Author interview with Byrem, November 2009.

pursue their attack on the friendly forces and permitted the troops to evacuate their untenable position with a minimum of casualties.

Continuing their missions of delaying the North Korean advance, the men of the 34th and 21st Regiments fought from new positions farther south, including the 21st's terrible ordeal at Chonui and Chochiwon. In support, the 3rd Engineers blew more bridges, planted more land mines, and created road craters to slow the enemy.

When the 21st Regiment withdrew, Neville's unit stayed behind to carry out a dangerous mission for which he was again decorated.

*The **Silver Star** is awarded to First Lieutenant **Ward Orville Neville**, U.S. Army, for gallantry in . . . action on 12 July 1950 near Chongju, Korea. The First Platoon of Company B, commanded by Lieutenant Neville, was performing the mission of laying antitank mine fields and preparing two road bridges for demolition in front of the 21st Infantry Regiment. After completing this mission he took one squad forward to place a new mine field when he noticed approximately three hundred enemy troops approaching his position. With disregard for his own safety Lieutenant Neville continued laying the mine field and then withdrew the squad and the remainder of the platoon and blew the bridges they had previously mined. During the withdrawal he had to take his platoon and its organic transportation through approximately twenty miles of enemy occupied territory. Due to his leadership and devotion to duty he was able to lead his platoon to safety and avoid possible capture.*

Of their escape, Neville's commanding officer wrote:

> One platoon of Company B, under command of Lt. Neville, which had been left north of the Kum River, returned through the right flank of the 24th Division by ingenuity and hard work. It followed trails and kept off main roads, and was able to reach the Kum River with all four (4) platoons, two ½-ton trucks and one (1) jeep. Since there was no bridge over the Kum River in their area, rafts were built and all vehicles ferried across without mishap. No men or equipment were lost.[122]

Robert Byrem recalled, "I had two South Korean soldiers that kind of

---

[122] Hyzer, Peter, Lieutenant Colonel. *3rd Engineer Combat Battalion War Diary: 122400/K July 1950 to 132400/K July 1950.*

hung around. I didn't know if they were assigned to me or not, but I couldn't get rid of 'em. They went everywhere with us. I never had any trouble with 'em, but they could've been North Koreans for all I knew. You couldn't tell who was who up there."

Toward the end of July, the North Koreans used this "lookalike" advantage against Neville, as reported by the Associated Press. Four enemy soldiers posing as South Koreans drove up in an American weapons carrier as Neville and his men were preparing to blow a bridge:

> Three spoke English, one quite well – "better than my interpreter," Neville said. They amiably discussed the bridge demolition job. One of them blew a whistle and about a dozen men in white came out from the enemy side of the bridge and helped put in the demolition charges. When the Korean blew the whistle again, the men in white left.

At that point, the men asked Neville if they could bum five gallons of gasoline, and Neville gave it to them. Only when the Koreans drove onto the bridge – headed for the enemy side – did he realize he'd been tricked. He fired a warning shot, and the North Koreans returned fire. While his men took the guerillas under fire, Neville blew the bridge.[123]

By the second week of August, the 24th Division's main supply route was threatened when North Koreans breached the Naktong Perimeter in several locations, and it was essential for every unit to carry out aggressive patrols to determine enemy strength and positions.

During the night of August 10, Lieutenant Colonel Peter Hyzer, commander of the 3rd Engineer Combat Battalion, crossed the Naktong into enemy territory near Chang-dong, southwest of Taegu. With him was a crew of four men, as well as a patrol led by Neville. The plan was for Neville and thirteen enlisted men to move four miles into enemy territory to Hill 489. There, they were to "observe enemy movement during the day, and return to the East bank of the Naktong the next evening."

Upon reaching the enemy side of the river, Hyzer, two soldiers, and a Korean interpreter moved behind enemy lines with Neville and his men. Upon reaching Hill 207, Hyzer felt assured the patrol hadn't been

---

[123]"Korean Reds Bum Gasoline, Then Battle Surprised G.I.s." AP, *Titusville Herald* (PA). 22 Jul 1950.

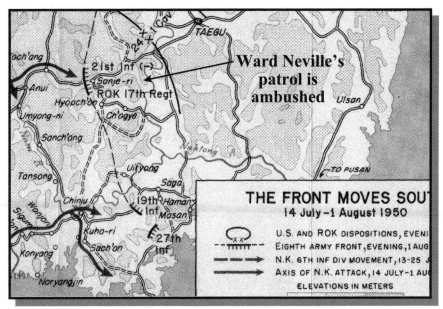

(Inset courtesy Center of Military History)

spotted and headed back. Unfortunately, the colonel was mistaken.

Neville's patrol continued toward their objective, but at daybreak they realized they had veered off-course some 600 yards, but whether they stayed there or moved to the preselected coordinates is unclear. At about 3:30 that afternoon, they spotted enemy soldiers. Hyzer's report reads:

> . . . when interrogators went to question them, they were fired on. At the same time, approximately 150 enemy troops, some in uniform and some in white clothing, were seen approaching the hill from the North, South and East. Lt. Neville and his patrol started withdrawing to the West, but were fired on, and Lt Neville was wounded. He instructed the rest of the patrol to make it to the friendly side of the Naktong River, and at this time, Lt. Neville was hit again. Lt. Neville remained behind to cover the withdrawal of the rest of his patrol.

Only five of Neville's men made it out alive. They arrived back at Hyzer's command post at about 5:00 a.m. the following morning.

The details of what transpired must be reconstructed from citations for valor that were issued. Colonel Hyzer's Silver Star citation indicates that when he and his three men returned to the river bank that night, they found a member of their boat crew had been killed.

With Hyzer were a Korean interpreter and two soldiers, including Private First Class John Bolster, from Chatfield, Minnesota, who was a member of Team 3 of the Reconnaissance Section. They noted nearby enemy movement and decided to forego using the boat; they would swim back instead.

They got out into the river about ten yards when the enemy opened fire. Hyzer's interpreter panicked and turned around to return to the enemy-held bank. Hyzer realized the interpreter had vital information about Neville's patrol, as well as the battalion's disposition. He couldn't let the interpreter fall into enemy hands, so he swam back to help him.

John Bolster started floundering at this time, so Hyzer let go of the interpreter and tried to save the Minnesotan. Enemy fire intensified, Bolster struggled against Hyzer, and the colonel was unable to save him.

Hyzer turned back for his interpreter but couldn't find him, so he swam to the friendly riverbank. The interpreter had made it safely across, but the remaining soldier with Hyzer also drowned.

Corporal Rosslyn Gresens from Hill City, Minnesota, was with Neville's patrol and was decorated for valor that day. His citation provides further details about what happened to the group.

*The **Silver Star** is **(Posthumously)** awarded to Corporal **Rosslyn E. Gresens**, U.S. Army, for gallantry . . . in action on 11 August 1950, in Korea. At this time he was a member of a patrol assigned the mission of penetrating enemy lines and observing location, movement, and strength. After proceeding 5,000 yards, the fourteen man patrol was fired upon from three sides by enemy riflemen of vastly superior numbers, killing and wounding several members of his patrol. Exposing himself, Corporal Gresens advanced on the enemy and killed two riflemen who were directly threatening the patrol from advantageous positions on the opposite bank of the Hoechon River. His effective covering fire during the river crossing accounted for at least fifteen enemy casualties and he was last seen following the patrol across the river firing his rifle at the enemy . . .*

A Silver Star citation for Private Jose Archuleta, Colorado, adds:

After proceeding 5000 yards, the fourteen-man patrol was fired upon from three sides by enemy riflemen of vastly superior numbers. In this fire fight the patrol leader [Neville] was wounded in the right leg and ordered the other members of the patrol to withdraw to the opposite bank of the

Hoechon River. Private Archuleta, after killing outright five of the enemy riflemen, worked his way to the wounded patrol leader and attempted to carry him across the river. Under a direct order to leave, he crossed the river and gave covering fire to the patrol leader until seriously wounded.

Three of five survivors received Bronze Stars for valor. The citation for Sergeant Q. Z. Goodwin, from Birmingham, Missouri, reads:

The small patrol of which he was a member, probing deep into enemy held territory, was attacked by a force estimated at company strength and its leader wounded. Assuming command, Sergeant Goodwin personally directed the patrol's withdrawal, and exposing himself to intense enemy fire, he covered its movement by effective fire. He remained in a forward position without regard for his own safety until assured that the patrol had safely withdrawn.

The citation for Franklin Pinkerton, Washington, Pennsylvania, reads:

The withdrawal was held up by heavy enemy small arms fire, and the patrol leader and several others were wounded. Corporal Pinkerton, observing three of the enemy advancing on the patrol, with complete disregard for his own personal safety, exposed himself and hurled a grenade killing all three. Assuming command, he then directed the withdrawal of the wounded. He continuously exposed himself and remained in a forward position in order to cover the withdrawal of his men to friendly positions by use of effective rifle fire.

Gene Timmerman, East Chicago, was the group's medic:

During the withdrawal they were held up by heavy enemy small arms fire which had wounded the patrol leader and several others. Corporal Timmerman, with utter disregard for his personal safety, while continuously exposed to heavy enemy fire, administered first aid to the stricken men until ordered to withdraw.

Ward Neville – in Korea less than six weeks – earned his third and final award for heroism:

*The **Distinguished Service Cross** is **(Posthumously)** awarded to First Lieutenant (Corps of Engineers) **Ward Orville Neville**, United States Army, for extraordinary heroism . . . in action against enemy aggressor forces near Hill 207 in the Republic of Korea on 11 August 1950. Lieutenant*

Neville volunteered to lead a hazardous patrol across the Naktong River and five thousand yards into enemy-held territory with the mission of observing enemy movement, strength, and location. At 1700 hours on 11 August 1950, the patrol, consisting of Lieutenant Neville and thirteen enlisted men, was attacked by a force of an estimated two hundred enemy riflemen. Lieutenant Neville, realizing the impossible odds with which his patrol was confronted, decided upon a desperate course of action. He personally led his patrol through a hail of enemy fire to the west, one thousand yards farther into enemy territory, to the east bank of the Hoechon River, without casualties. Upon arriving at the Hoechon River, the patrol was fired upon from the North and South by an estimated one hundred enemy riflemen. Lieutenant Neville was shot through the right leg and immobilized, and three of his patrol were mortally wounded. Vehemently refusing assistance from any of his patrol members, he directed them across the river and, after most had crossed, he dragged himself through the river to the west bank. During this time he was constantly ordering his patrol to shoot into the areas from which the heaviest enemy fire was coming and urging them on, lest they be captured. Lieutenant Neville, mortally wounded, dragged himself into a rice paddy and was last seen with a grenade in his hand, urging the patrol on to safety. His utter refusal of assistance from his patrol after he was wounded made it possible for five members of the patrol to return to friendly lines and safety.

Neville, Bolster and Gresens were declared dead at war's end. Bolster and Gresens remain missing in action, but Neville's remains were recovered in December 1951; he was laid to rest at Golden Gate National Cemetery, San Bruno, California, on November 1, 1955.

Chapter 25

GILBERT CHECK AT THE BOWLING ALLEY

"I dimly recall one of my grammar school teachers telling the class that if you were to flatten Korea it would cover approximately one-third of the world . . . After climbing a few of their hills, I feel that the teacher made a gross understatement."
Francis Fenton Jr., Baker Company, 5th Marines

AUGUST 15 MARKED the five-year anniversary of Korea's liberation from the Japanese. North Korean leader Kim Il Sung chose this "final victory date" for the reunification of Korea – with himself as ruler – and the level of determination of his troops became almost fanatical.

After the fall of Taejon, Taegu became Kim's next major target on the highway from Seoul to Pusan. As August 15 passed into history, Taegu was still in friendly hands, but just barely.

During this period, the battle-hardened South Korean Army had been primarily deployed along the top edge of the Naktong Perimeter to the east coast, while the Americans defended the west side of the perimeter south to the sea.

South Korea's 1st Division started to falter north of the Taegu on August 16, and Paik Sun Yup, a highly competent commander, was overjoyed when General Walker sent the 27th Regiment Wolfhounds to back him up the following day. Walker's orders were clear: *Taegu must be saved.*

Army historian Roy Appleman described the situation based on his interviews with North Dakota's Colonel Check:

In front of the 27th Infantry position, the poplar-lined Taegu-Sangju road ran northward on a level course in the narrow mountain valley. A stream on the west closely paralleled it. The road was nearly straight on a north-south axis through the 27th Infantry position and for some distance northward. Then it veered slightly westward. This stretch of the road later became known as the "Bowling Alley."

The following day, as he was trying to reach an observation perch overlooking the Wolfhounds' positions north of Taegu, Lieutenant Addison Terry cussed the medic who had sent him back into combat while he was still banged up.

He and his assistant found their spot at noon "after what seemed like hours of climbing straight up." They freshened their camouflage, ensured their communication wires were working, and settled in to rest.

That afternoon, Terry was warned to stay alert; an attack was expected that night. An hour before midnight, Terry received word of motorized traffic farther north, and a round of illumination was fired.

> I listened intently for motors, but because of my altitude I couldn't hear any. There was a report from the rear. The round whooshed above us and burst high over the valley a thousand yards out. There was a splendid silver spray of light and as the parachute opened and the flare burned to maximum efficiency, the entire valley was illuminated.
>
> I stared below shocked and frightened. There were tanks and self-propelled guns cluttering the road, bumper to bumper, scrambling toward our positions. Around these armored pieces were hundreds of NKPA infantrymen. I grabbed for the telephone and screamed for a fire mission. The [other forward observers] must have done the same thing, because I could hear the switchboard operator answering other calls along with mine. I yelled for him to tell the others to adjust on the rear and center of the column, and that I would get the leading elements. I gave my fire mission, hurriedly calling for battery three rounds to start off with. While I waited for the "On the way," I hoped that the batteries were really as well registered as I had been told they were, because there was no time for an adjustment now. I heard the rounds leave the howitzers in the rear and watched eagerly for them to burst.
>
> While my rounds were still in the air, I heard another battery sound off in the rear, which meant that the fire for the rear of the column was on its way.

There were big red flashes and explosions on the road to my left front now, and as I watched the eighteen rounds go in I gave a real old rebel yell because I got a direct hit on a tank and it started to burn . . . I looked farther down the column and gave another yell as I saw the rounds that Lieutenant Parker had fired crashing all over the enemy armor, starting several fires. In the meantime, the 60mm, 81mm, and 4.2 inch mortars had gone to work on the column and somebody had the sense to keep shooting star shells over the area (to keep it illuminated). The din from all the shooting had reached a constant roar now and I couldn't identify my rounds, but I saw them go in, all right. They hit the front of the column with a wide enough spread to saturate the rice paddies on either side of the road, which was thick with Reds.

[. . .] In the meantime, the Reds, seeing that they were discovered, started pouring the lead in our direction. The tanks and self-propelled guns on the road opened up on us, and the elephant guns and 120 mortars started firing at the battery positions to our rear. The sound of the artillery going back and forth through the air was hair-raising, and the awful explosions of the bursting shells were accentuated by the manner in which the sound waves were funneled up and down the valley. It was this sound of artillery shells rushing through the smoke-filled air and exploding with a terrible crash that prompted one G.I. to refer to the valley as the "Bowling Alley" when speaking of it to a correspondent the following day.

[. . .] Roberts was yelling at the top of his voice and beating on my back in wild excitement. . . . Here was U.S. firepower at its best. We were cutting them to pieces. But it was not a one-sided engagement.[124]

---

[124]Terry. *The Battle for Pusan*. P 166-182. Reprinted by permission.

Chapter 26

OBONG-NI RIDGE

"During World War II, every guy, who was healthy, was wearing a uniform, and those who weren't were making their contributions to the national effort. In [the Korean war], kids such as Herbert Fear are stumbling wearily across a battlefield while most Americans worry about prices, order a new car, or sit down with a contractor to plan a house." Lou Breuer, *Cedar Rapids Gazette*

WHEN THE MARINES were abruptly pulled back from their mission with *Task Force Kean*, they were shifted 26 miles north to what was known as the "Naktong Bulge" – a horseshoe of land bordered on three sides by the Naktong River.

The 24th Division, as well as the newly arrived 9th Regiment of the 2nd Division, had been holding back the North Koreans for eleven grueling days when the Marines joined the fray on August 17. The Marines took up positions on the Army's left flank with the mission of rousting the enemy from a series of hilltops the press labeled *No Name Ridge* – now commonly called Obong-ni Ridge.

Harold Twedt & Richard Olson

The entire 5th Marine Regiment fought hard in this action, but this chapter focuses primarily on the 1st Battalion, which included a significant number of participants from the northern prairies.

The most highly decorated of these was Harold Twedt, who was born in March 1930. In his early years, he and his parents lived on his grandparents' farm in Medicine County, Minnesota. Twedt's father and grandparents had all emigrated from Norway.

Twedt was in Able Company, along with another Minnesotan, Richard "Oley" Olson. Olson grew up in St. Paul, where he had a paper route and was a member of the Boy Scouts. From a very young age, he knew he wanted to join the Marines. His father had fought and was wounded in WWI, and Olson ended up in his dad's same unit – the 5th Marines – in Korea.

Richard Olson

Twedt and Olson joined the Marines at the same time, in July 1948. "The local recruiting station was having a drive to get up a *St. Paul Platoon*," said Olson. "There were twenty-five or so who signed up, and we went to San Diego and went through boot camp together." Olson writes:

> After boot camp we went back to St. Paul for a ten-day leave. Harold and I double-dated a couple times while there. I lost track of him after that and didn't even know he was in my company in Korea. In combat, the scope of your awareness is very limited.
>
> Harold was killed during our first move up on the Naktong River. We suffered lots of casualties that day taking back ground the Army had lost.
>
> The Army had been dug in on the high ground overlooking the Naktong River, and the Koreans had crossed the river, attacked the Army, and the Koreans took over. MacArthur had ordered General Craig to move us to the Naktong to retake the area. We had to push them back, or they would have captured all of South Korea.[125]

Obong-ni Ridge consists of six adjacent peaks described by Marine

---

[125] Olson correspondence with author, with additional information from Olson interview with Lynnita Brown. Web: Korean War Educator. Used by permission. http://www.koreanwareducator.org/memoirs/olson_richard/#Contents.

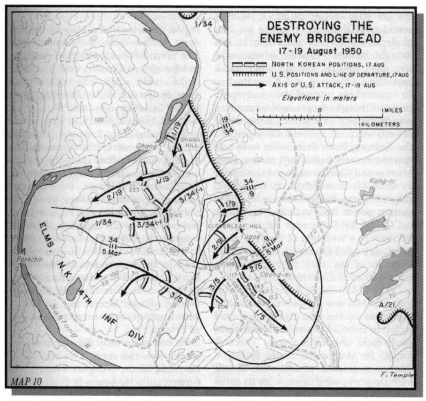

Twedt, Olson, Muetzel and Schryver attacked along the length of Obong-ni Ridge in the Naktong Bulge. (Map Center of Military History)

historian Lynn Montross as sprawling out like "some huge prehistoric reptile."[126] Montross writes:

> The North Korean 4th Army posed the major threat at the so-called Naktong Bulge – a westward loop in the river that forms an area four by five miles (six by eight kilometers), about a third of the way up the perimeter. East of the bulge lay the Miryang railhead, whose capture would cut the main supply route from Pusan to Taegu and force Walker to withdraw his forces into a virtually indefensible slaughter pen. General Church's 24th Infantry Division stood between the North Koreans, who had started crossing the river on August 6, and potential disaster.

[126]Montross, Lynn. *The Pusan Perimeter Part III.* Web: 13 Mar 2011. www.americanmilitaryhistorymsw.com/blog/467507-the-pusan-perimeter-part-iii.

The 2nd Battalion attacked at 8:00 a.m. that morning. To reach the ridge's many spurs and gullies, Dog and Easy Companies first had to negotiate a series of rice paddies – a lethal scenario, because the enemy was heavily entrenched along the high ground on the other side. Richard Olson writes:

> The 2nd Battalion formed a battalion-wide skirmish line and drove the Koreans off the hill, but they were decimated in doing it. It took hours to get the wounded off the hill. The dead were left to lie where they were killed.

Some 60% of the 2nd Battalion's men were casualties by 3:00 p.m., when Able and Baker Companies moved through them to continue the attack. Rain was bringing some relief from the sweltering heat, but it also hampered air support. Olson writes:

> Lt. Col. Newton, the battalion commander, sent Able Company to the high ground on the right (Hills 117 and 143) and Baker to the left (Hills 147 and 153). I remember seeing [Brigadier General Edward Craig] at the side of the hill. I had never seen a Marine General before. He had tears in his eyes and was wishing us luck. Baker Company stepped in it, and they had a terrible firefight.

David Douglas Duncan, a WWII veteran, was traveling with Baker Company as a photographer for *Life* magazine. He wrote that Baker Company edged forward with "every enemy eye in all of Asia peering across rifle sights aimed squarely at their hearts and just waiting for the instant when they stepped into perfect range. Then everything happened at once."[127]

As Able and Baker Companies attacked, enemy fire came from all along the ridge. John Tobin, commanding Baker Company, became a casualty, and his executive officer, Ike Fenton took over. The company lost radio communications that afternoon, but at about 5:00 p.m., they reached the crest of their objective and secured their sector.

On Baker's left flank, Twedt and Olson's Able Company was making repeated attempts to take Hills 117 and 143, but the going was rough, and they were pinned down.

---

[127]Duncan, David Douglas. *This is War*. Unpaginated.

As the battle wore on, Ike Fenton needed reinforcements and ammunition, but both were in short supply and were being diverted to others who were trying to keep his company from being surrounded. Olson recalled an unusual confrontation: "We saw the damnedest sight. Captain Fenton of Baker was chewing out Lt. Col. Newton, and Colonel Newton was merely saying 'Now Ike, you've got to understand.'"

Killing Tanks

By the time the sun went down, Twedt and Olson's company established a toehold and consolidated their positions with Baker to prepare for the inevitable counterattack.

At 7:00 p.m., a column of enemy tanks approached, but a Mosquito spotter plane gave the Marines time to get ready. This was their first encounter with the dreaded Russian T-34s, and they were anxious to see what could be done about them.

The sun had just set when the first tank nosed around a bend – it was still light enough for them to see the dust it raised.

The Americans now had the bigger 3.5 bazookas that had been missing in the early battles. In short order, the first tank was crippled. But it was still able to fire, and they could tell by the wild swinging of the tube that the tanker inside was panicked and firing blindly. The 75-mm recoilless rifles put the tank to sleep.

A second tank tried to skirt the first one and came face to face with a friendly Sherman tank that arrived to block the road and to protect the aid station and command post. The Sherman fired twice. The second shot blew straight through the T-34's turret.

A third T-34 now rounded the bend. Minnesotan Frank Muetzel told author Donald Knox this tank was fired on by "everyone in sight – M26s, 3.5s, 75-mm recoillesses. In a few minutes it was all over. Everyone jumped into the air and cheered as if he was at a football game."[128]

The Enemy's Counterattack

On the Marines' right flank, the Army's 19th, 34th and 9th Regiments had hit North Korea's 16th Regiment with a punishing attack late that afternoon. Unfortunately, the North Koreans captured a field radio that

---

[128]Knox. *The Korean War: An Oral History.* 1985. P 149.

was tuned to the Marines' frequencies, and Colonel Chang Ky Dok now knew where Able and Baker Companies were digging in for the night.

Chang also knew how depleted his own ranks were, so he decided his only hope of holding the ridge was to hit the Marines with an all-out assault under cover of darkness.

At roughly 2:00 a.m., now August 18, Chang's troops attacked the line between Able and Baker Companies, and during the next desperate hours, hand-to-hand combat ensued. Marine historian John Chapin writes:

> With many officers down, and aided by the supporting fire, the noncommissioned officers took the lead in regrouping their units, and so the men of the depleted Companies A and B stood, and fought, and died, and finally held their ground. . . .
>
> Slowly, toward dawn on 18 August, the enemy attacks weakened. But the Marines had paid a fearful price. Company B had begun the night with 190 enlisted men and five officers; the next morning there were only 110 left, with one officer still standing. Company A was in worse shape with just 90 men remaining from the 185 at the start of the night.

It was possibly during the next action that Minnesotan Harold Twedt was killed. Chapin writes:

> Craig ordered a resumption of the attack at 0700 the next morning, 18 August. None of the men on Obong-ni had had any sleep during the night past, but the Corsairs were back on station overhead, the enemy was weakening, and both Companies A and B moved once more into the assault.
>
> Company B worked men to its left to coordinate with Company A's effort to seize Hill 117. Four determined NKPA machine gunners there held up the advance, so the company commander, Captain John R. Stevens, got in touch with Newton to call in an air strike. There was legitimate concern about the fact that his Marines were too close, only 100 yards from the target, but a smoke rocket was fired into the emplacements from the control Corsair, and the next Corsair put a 500-pound bomb right onto the center of the target. The Marines lost one man killed, but the enemy was totally wiped out, and Company A's follow-up rush quickly took control of

the crest.[129]

Twedt was attached to the 24th Division at the time, so he was awarded the Army's Distinguished Service Cross (rather than the Navy Cross).

*The **Distinguished Service Cross** is **(Posthumously)** awarded to Private First Class **Harold Anton Twedt**, U.S. Marine Corps, for extraordinary heroism ... while serving with Company A, First Battalion, Fifth Marines, First Provisional Marine Brigade (Reinforced), in action against enemy aggressor forces in the Republic of Korea on 18 August 1950. In an assault on a strongly defended ridge line, Private First Class Twedt's automatic rifle platoon was pinned down by heavy fire from an enemy machine-gun and was unable to continue its advance. With absolute disregard for his own safety, he exposed himself to intense enemy fire in order to gain a position with a better field of fire for his weapon, and, although mortally wounded in this action, he continued to deliver a heavy volume of accurate fire against the enemy position until it was silenced. The valorous act in which he gallantly gave his life for his country enabled his platoon to continue its advance and to subsequently capture its objective.*

John Chapin's account made note of two other men from the prairies:

> Typical of the unyielding defense were the examples of two platoon leaders, Second Lieutenant Hugh C. Schryver Jr. in Company B and Second Lieutenant Francis W. Muetzel in Company A. Both officers, although severely wounded, continued to lead their men with the "fierce determination" described in their citations for awards of the Silver Star.

Francis Muetzel

Francis Muetzel, leading Able Company's Machine Gun Platoon, grew up in Redwood Falls, Minnesota. His daughter Jeanne writes:

> His background is pretty simple. He was the third of four children. His father was a mechanic who did have a steady job during the Depression. He followed his two older brothers into

---

[129]Chapin, John C. "Fire Brigade: U.S. Marines in the Pusan Perimeter." *U.S. Marines in the Korean War (Chapter 1).* Edited by Charles R. Smith. History Division, USMC. 2007: P 51-52.

service immediately after his high school graduation in 1944 before World War II ended. It was what all young men were expected to do at that time but especially so for those of German descent as my father's family was. His brothers left the service after WWII to return to civilian life. My dad stayed in – it was an opportunity to see the world, and the Corps agreed with my dad. They saw promise in him and sent him to Officers Candidate School in Quantico in the late '40s. He was a 2nd Lieutenant when he went to Korea.

Jeanne said her father rarely spoke of the war when she and her six siblings were young – except when they'd ask about his leg, which he lost in combat roughly a month after the fighting on Obong-ni Ridge.

After the children matured, Muetzel told them more about his experiences, often while spending family vacations at well-known American battlefields.

Jeanne believes her father seldom talked about his war experience, because his memories "were literally the stuff of nightmares – his own nightmares."

He left for Korea with three other house-mates (from Oceanside) in the Marines – Art Oakley, Tom Johnston and Tom Gibson. Oakley died almost immediately after they arrived in Korea, and Johnston died within two weeks. My younger brother, Thomas Oakley Muetzel, was named for them.

Dad was shot three times in roughly 30 days. It was not a question of where you were going to get it, only *How bad would it be?* The situation at Pusan was desperate – a lot of hand to hand fighting and being overrun at night. It was a situation where remnants of platoons were cobbled together to keep fighting. He ended up with command of Johnston's platoon after he was killed.

I understand from those who knew my dad over there, that no one would sleep in a tent with him because of his nightmares.[130]

Muetzel was first wounded August 17, and the experience undoubtedly contributed to his nightmares. It was the 5th Marines' first day on

---

[130]Email exchanges Jeanne Muetzel with author March 2013.

Obong-ni Ridge, and the 2nd Battalion had led the assault that morning. When the 1st Battalion was ordered to move up through their positions that afternoon, Muetzel's machine gun crews (including Harold Twedt) went up in support of Able and Baker Companies.

Muetzel watched their progress from "observation hill" as they ran into the same buzz saw that hit the 2nd Battalion. Muetzel, 1st Lieutenant Fred Eubanks, and an enlisted rifleman moved up into an abandoned machine gun position and started laying down fire along the crest.

Muetzel had with him an excellent sniper rifle, but the targets were too distant to identify. It turned out Eubanks was a sharpshooter, and with Muetzel using his binoculars, the two men began picking off specific targets.

He later said it was a mistake to use the abandoned position, because enemy mortar and artillery had already registered on it. Four mortar rounds landed on them, and as Muetzel flew through the air he saw, "A human body to my left disintegrated."

Badly jarred and unable to hear, Muetzel crawled back to the command post and reported Eubanks' death. But shortly after, Eubanks "stumbled over the ridge." It was the enlisted man who had been killed.

Muetzel was hit again when the enemy struck at 2:00 a.m. The North Koreans' attack, he said, "began with a shower of grenades, followed by infantry armed with burp guns."

The machine gun position he was manning was overrun, and he was hit "by grenade fragments above my right eye and in my scalp, knocking me out cold and shredding my steel helmet."

When he regained consciousness, he had been left for dead, and he was surrounded by North Koreans who also assumed he was dead.

Self-described as impressionable and patriotic, he wondered if anybody would think he was cowardly if he "got the hell out of there."

He waited for a gap between illuminating flares, threw his one and only grenade, and took off down the hill. When he got near his command post, he dived, rolled and landed on his feet before any of them could shoot him.

Lieutenant Thomas Johnston (Muetzel's roommate from Oceanside) was the leader of Baker Company's 2nd Platoon. He was killed in a one-man attack against the enemy the following day.

Muetzel took over Johnston's platoon and was on the hill when he was again wounded. This time he was hit in his right foot, saying the "slug entered my boot, burned my second toe, tore the meat off the third, burned the fourth, and then exited my boot. Two holes." He lost the feeling in his foot, but he could still get by, so he stayed on the hill.

After an air strike that morning, the men took a well-deserved pause. As the "old man" (age 23), Muetzel said he tried to calm his men by pulling off a "John Wayne" stunt. Taking a seat on the ground, he told them to break out their rations while they had the chance:

> I sat on the side of a hole and dangled my feet. On the other side of the hole lay a dead North Korean. He had caught one through the top of the head and looked pretty ugly . . .
>
> When I was halfway through my can of meat and beans, decomposing gases caused the cadaver to belch. Black blood foamed out of its mouth and nose. I promptly lost my entire lunch. By the time the platoon got through laughing, the tension was broken, and they were ready to go back to work.

(Courtesy Muetzel family)

*The **Silver Star (Army Award)** is awarded to Second Lieutenant **Francis W. Muetzel**, U.S. Marine Corps, for conspicuous gallantry and intrepidity while serving as a Machine Gun Platoon Leader, Company A, 1st Battalion, 5th Marines, FIRST Marine Division, in action against enemy aggressor forces on Obongi-ni Ridge, near Yongsan-ni, Korea, on 18 August 1950. Lieutenant Muetzel, after leading a daring assault against a strong enemy hill position, was hit above his eye by a grenade fragment. Regaining consciousness approximately two hours later, he rejoined his company, which had withdrawn for reorganization after a strong enemy counterattack, and, refusing medical attention, he devoted his energies to readying machine gun elements for another impending assault. During these preparations, Lieutenant Muetzel was hit in the right foot by sniper fire. Again refusing medical aid and evacuation, he directed the utilization of machine gun elements in the attack. His aggressiveness in combat and his fierce determination to carry on despite painful battle* *wounds were an inspiration to his comrades and materially aided in the capture of their objective. . . .*

Hugh Schryver, Jr.

The other "fiercely determined" officer mentioned by John Chapin was Hugh "Nick" Schryver Jr., from Laurens, Iowa. He joined the Marines in 1941 and served as an enlisted man before being selected for Officer Candidate School.

Schryver deployed to Korea July 13, just a few days before his second child was born. One reporter later described him as tall and unassuming, but "he looks like a marine and talks the way you like to hear a marine talk." Schryver told the reporter, "It is an all-out war, whether they call it a police action or not. The war was practically lost when we got there. Everything was on paper. We were hanging on by our teeth."

Schryver also told the reporter that when the 5th Marines left for Korea, there was no effort to keep their movements under wraps, saying "every indication that we were coming was given to the enemy." Their departure was even televised.[131]

As the leader of Baker Company's 1st Platoon, Schryver was severely wounded about 90 minutes after the enemy attacked the night of August 17-18. In a 1951 debriefing, Schryver's company commander, Ike Fenton, reported:

> When daylight arrived, I discovered I was the only officer left in the company. The previous afternoon the company counted 190 men and 5 officers. In the morning 88 men were left on the line. The 2nd Platoon, which had borne the brunt of the night attack, had but 11 men left.
>
> First Lieutenant Nick Schryver from the 1st Platoon was reported to have been killed. My gunnery sergeant, Ed Wright, said he'd been hit by a grenade burst. I thought it would be demoralizing to the men to have a dead lieutenant lying around, so even though we were only evacuating the wounded, I told Ed, "Put Schryver on the first available stretcher and take him off the ridge."

---

[131]*Laurens Sun.* 19 April 1951.

But Schryver wasn't dead. He had suffered the same fate as Francis Muetzel; a grenade knocked him out. When he regained consciousness, he dragged himself to an aid station. His head wounds were bandaged to such a degree that he couldn't wear his helmet, but nevertheless he returned to Baker Company – and with his sense of humor intact, according to Ike Fenton:

> He looked like a mummy. I was flabbergasted. I said, "Nick, what are you doing here?" He said, "While I was in the aid station, I got to thinking that very seldom does a Second Lieutenant ever get a chance to command a company, and I thought your luck is running short; you haven't been hit yet. I figured I'd get back and I might get the company."

*The **Silver Star** is awarded to Second Lieutenant **Hugh C. Schryver, Jr.**, U. S. Marine Corps, Platoon Leader, 1ˢᵗ Platoon, Company B, 1ˢᵗ Battalion, 5ᵗʰ Marines. Second Lieutenant Schryver displayed gallantry in action against an armed enemy at Obong-ni Ridge . . . during the period 17 August to 18 August 1950. On 17 August elements of the 1ˢᵗ Battalion, 5ᵗʰ Marines assaulted the heavily defended Ridge at Obong-ni with loss of many casualties. By nightfall the companies succeeded in securing only a small portion of the Ridge. The precarious positions were ordered to be defended while strongly opposed by the enemy 4ᵗʰ Division. Lieutenant Schryver's Platoon played a vital part in the initial assault on the Ridge. At about 0330, 18 August, the enemy counterattacked B Company's zone. During the counterattack Lieutenant Schryver while directing the defense suffered a severe fragment wound on his forehead when a hand grenade exploded near his helmet, knocking him unconscious. He was evacuated to the Battalion aid station. Upon receiving first aid and treatment at the aid station he regained consciousness. Despite protests of Battalion corpsmen, Lieutenant Schryver voluntarily left the aid station and returned to his platoon to reassume command when the platoon situation was critical. His return to duty despite his painful wounds and heavy loss of blood was an inspiration to his Platoon and to the whole Company. Lieutenant Schryver bravely re-assumed command of his platoon, and his outstanding leadership and coolness under fire were highly instrumental in repelling the enemy counterattack and subsequently seizing the vital objective which broke the main defense of the enemy in the area.*

Chapter 27

CONTINUING FATE OF POWS

"I want to thank you, whoever you are, for taking my 5-1/2 EEE boots when I was captured. I didn't like it when you shot me in the leg either . . . At that time I had a severe case of athletes feet, and my boots were all slippery from that. I hope you enjoyed that disease, and I hope you lost a foot because of that. If you are already dead, then disregard this message." (Signed) Shorty the Tiger, to his POW guards

AMERICAN POWS captured at Hadong and elsewhere were fighting a different kind of war at this point.

Because the North Koreans had no POW camps, prisoners moved along with the enemy army – unless they were executed, as was the case of 18 year-old William Brower, of Rock Rapids, Iowa. Brower had been a member of Love Company, 29th RCT, when he was captured at Hadong, and fellow prisoners later reported he was killed by their guards on August 16.

Meanwhile, Jim Yeager (Colorado) and his friend John Toney considered themselves to still be on the job.

"When we were marching, Toney and I gathered intelligence," Yeager said. "Any troop movement that came by us, anything we saw that we felt our side needed to know, we catalogued in our minds. We didn't get demoralized. We were still at work!

"There were things that happened. Some of the prisoners would fall out if they couldn't keep going, and they'd come along and club them to death, beat 'em, and shoot 'em.

"I programmed myself – and I'm still suffering from it – I loved to go to western dances. As we would march, I would program myself that I was in Montrose, Colorado, or some place at a western dance – and now I was walking home. That's how I made it at night. I still have dreams that I'm lost or trying to get home.

"But like I said, Toney and I were still doing our reconnaissance on these marches. We'd see things like they'd run a tank into a house to hide the tank during the day, and they'd run the villagers out. Women and children, they had them out playing around in the yard, or had them doing things, so it looked like a normal situation for aerial observers.

"Another thing they'd do, at dawn they'd take these flatbed trucks they were using – some were 6-x-6s, but the Oriental or Russian style – they would carry 55-gallon barrels of oil in these things. Their men would physically – not only one or two men, I mean a whole group of them – would get out and turn this truck over on its side. Of course, they'd get the barrels off first. And then they would take a barrel and take and put oil around the front of the truck on the road to make it look like they'd been strafed and hit. This oil would show up on the road. At night, when we got ready to move, they'd go and put the truck back up, put the barrels back in the truck, and down the road they'd go," said Yeager.

"These are the things we told them in our debriefing later on – what was transpiring. They'd pull us off the road when these troops were moving south. A lot of times it was hard to see them, and other times it wasn't. But one time we saw a whole platoon of snipers. They all had the old Russian rifle – 7.65 bolt-action rifle. I think we saw these guys before we ever got to Taejon. They were moving them up front to do sniper work.

"We also observed some old bi-wing aircraft and things like that. We tried to keep track of how many people passed us. Not individual count, but like a company has passed us, or a battalion has passed.

"We also observed some cavalry situations, which was really Mickey Mouse. They probably, in this cavalry, had about 30 to 40 horses at the most. This was in the very early days, too. They had a shorter Russian rifle for the cavalry troops."

Because they were moving during daylight hours, the column of prisoners was subjected to constant strafing by American pilots, who were unaware they were prisoners of war. Their guards finally turned them off the main roads.

"One day we started cross-country through some mountains," said Yeager. "Eventually we stopped in a vineyard, way up on a mountain. We all hid under the grape vines as an air strike had started on a town down in a valley below us. We ate as many grapes as we could during

(Courtesy James Yeager)

the strike. After it was over, the guards were upset that we had been eating the grapes and forced us into double-time down the mountain headed for this town.

"Finally we reached the valley floor. We could see that this place had undergone a ferocious battle. They ran us through a bare piece of ground that had been turned into a grave yard. Arms and legs protruded from shallow graves. Some had American uniforms covering parts of the limbs. The air was heavy with putrification.

"After this, they turned us down a street at a somewhat slower pace. We ended up at the police station. As it turned out, this was Taejon."

The Taejon jail cells were filled to capacity with South Korean prisoners, so the Americans were led upstairs to a courtroom. Two desks had rough boards on them for laying out two prisoners who were in very tough shape. One's left arm had been amputated, and the other had lost his right foot and ankle.

"Several other men had head wounds and shrapnel wounds," said Yeager, "but none received medical care. Some of the men had only a G.I. raincoat on and no shoes. Others only had partial clothing on. The place reeked – by this point, just about everyone had diarrhea."

During the next several days, guards took their boots and socks. One man who took Yeager's size-10 boots gave him a pair of size-5 tennis shoes in exchange. Yeager used a C-ration can opener to gash the toes from the shoes so he could wear them. Others ended up with no shoes, and many of these were killed on the march north, because the rocky terrain tore up their feet; when they could not keep up, they were executed.

Yeager's group moved out September 5, this time toward Seoul. After two days, they began marching only at night to avoid American planes.

"This march to Seoul became a nightmare," said Yeager. "We were lucky if we received anything to eat or drink. Usually a rice ball about the size of a golf ball twice a day. They would start us out at dusk and march all night till dawn. There were no rest breaks. The longer we marched the more savage the guards became, clubbing, beating with rifles, kicking – you name it, it happened."

At one point, the men finally had access to fresh water. "Rain was coming off the thatched roofs like a water fall," said Yeager. "I stopped and started to wash myself, as I was filthy dirty. A couple of guards saw me and started beating me with their rifles. Before I could get away from them, they kicked me down, butt-striking me in the head and shoulders. I finally managed to get up and back into the column, but my head, shoulders and chest gave me trouble for quite a while after this."

They finally reached Seoul, where they were held in a girls' school. It was at this point the communists began a determined effort to convince the POWs they were on the wrong side of the political hemisphere. Each man was interrogated about his family and upbringing. The prisoners soon learned they would be better treated if they swore they were from working class families, and soon they all swore they were peasant farmers who did not own automobiles or any other such luxuries of the ruling class.

Their conditions suddenly changed one day. They were allowed to bathe. They had their hair cut and were given shaves. Those without shirts, like Yeager, were given Korean army shirts.

"We couldn't imagine why we were receiving all the attention," said Yeager. "We were all starving to death. Our food consisted of radish green soup with a fish head or two floating around the pot. Then we found out why all the great treatment. We were assembled in the gym behind the school. Sitting on one side was a long row of Korean men and women dressed in fine white clothing. On the table in front of them were vases of flowers and banners attached to the front of the table with Korean writing on them. On the opposite wall, a line of Korean guards with burp guns and rifles were at the ready."

The men sat on the floor while Mr. Kim, their warden, sat on a stage with several Koreans in business suits. News cameras were set up to the side.

"The ceremony started," said Yeager. "Kim gave a rambling speech in both Korean and English. The basic subject was about the capitalist imperial aggression against the peace-loving Korean people, etc."

Captain William Locke, an American pilot, was brought to the stage. "Locke read from some papers the same communist line," Yeager said, "but in closing, good old Captain Locke said, 'You may have us prisoner. But our troops are going to kick the hell out of you.' Mr. Kim and the other communists were visibly shaken."

The prisoners were then formed up in a column and marched three to four miles back to the school. Some were forced to carry propaganda banners, and photographers took photos throughout. One POW died and had to be carried the rest of the way.

Men who failed to cooperate were severely dealt with – especially by a guard they called "Buck" who kept his bayonet fixed on his rifle. (See photo page 258.)

Pat Martin and Carl Anderson

Prisoner Pat Martin (North Dakota) was somewhere on the west coast about this time. He thought he was possibly north of Seoul, but he and his fellow prisoners were never sure where they were.

By now, he had met up with Carl "Andy" Anderson, the tank crewman from Iowa who was also captured at Chinju.

"One day we pulled into a village," Martin told interviewer Elmer Lian. "We had marched all night through the mountains. They never did take us down on a road. We were always on trails some place. And we got in this village, and there was a beach. On the west coast. The Mighty MO (*USS Missouri*) was sitting out there, but we didn't know it. It wasn't daylight. We couldn't see. But it was there, *the Mighty MO*. It was just breaking day, and we had marched all night. It rained all night, and we were soaking wet. That was the first time they ever gave us anything other than the clothes we had on – a blanket to put around us. It was pretty chilly.

"So we were sitting there, and Andy says, 'I wonder what that plane is doing up there? It's unusual.'

"Pretty soon the first round came in. It was high explosive, and boy, thank God it was on the other end of the village – the village was narrow and long, along the coast.

"The minute the shells started hitting, they gathered all their troops up. They took us with them, and we went up into the mountains, [where we] watched the whole thing. This airplane was a spotter. This was our guys out on that ship shelling this village. They didn't know we were there. [. . .] They flattened it. There was nothing left. It looked like a dump truck came in there. They put in one ton of steel, then two high explosives and one white phosphorous.

"My friend Andy, he got hit. One of them big pieces of shrapnel came in and hit him in the fatty part of the leg," said Martin. "He only had two-and-a-half years to go to retire. He was with Patton in WWII, and he always called me *little shit*, because I was just a kid.

"Anyway, the North Koreans just kept moving us every night. We'd watch them early in the morning, after we got to where we'd been moved from. We didn't know where we were going, sometimes we were going north or south, but we thought we were going north. Our own artillery would be going over our head some days, so we knew we were getting close to our own lines.

"There was one night they marched us 30 miles. One night we were sitting there alongside the road, and the Koreans marched eight abreast.

They walk really, really fast – kind of choppy. They were going by us, and apparently Andy was counting them in the rows. He figured there were 10,000 right in that area that night that went by us. We didn't know for sure where they were going.

"In the morning, after we'd get done marching, we'd be sitting around having our – whatever they'd give us. And they'd give themselves a shot of something. I don't know what it was. Then they'd go off to battle. We figured then we weren't too far from the line. I think it was some kind of an upper, dope or drugs, because they just went wild. All of them, they all did it."

"Their clothing was olive green, quilted. They were all real thin but fairly healthy. When they went on patrol, they had two rice balls about [the size of a baseball] tied on their belt, and a little garlic, and that was it. That's why they were so mobile. For G.I.s to go out on patrol, we had a six-by-six following us with groceries and everything else. Not them. The garlic was right on top. They'd eat it and stink! Man-oh-man.

Martin and his fellow prisoners had good guards and bad guards. "What really was scarey was that some of them guards were only nine-years-old, ten-years-old. And boy, you don't know what they're gonna do. We felt better when we had older people . . .

"On our marches, if you got out of line in any shape or form, boy, they'd clobber you. Even their own people. We saw when a young kid – I'm sure he wasn't more than 12 or 13 years old – he was carrying a tripod for a machine gun, and you know they're quite heavy. He dropped it, and this sergeant – apparently he was a sergeant, we were never sure of his rank – he beat this kid senseless. Finally another guy gave the kid a lighter piece, and he took the tripod.

"That scared me. I thought, *What kind of a chance do I have if I fall down?*"

Chapter 28

TESTING THE UNITED NATIONS

The United States has fought nine major wars, four in the twentieth century. Of these conflicts, the war in Korea, 1950-1953, ranks among the most important, yet is the least remembered. Clay Blair, *The Forgotten War*

THE KOREAN WAR marked the first major showdown between the United States and the Soviet Union during the Cold War.

Even though the Soviets still claimed to be uninvolved in Korea, many G.I.s, especially those being held prisoner, had seen countless Soviets in uniform (and civilian dress) in Korea.

The Soviets had developed nuclear weapons by this point, so political dealings between the two superpowers were constantly shrouded by the possibility of doomsday, and the war in Korea set the tone that defined American-Soviet relations for months. And then years. And then decades.

The Korean War was also the first occasion in which members of the newly organized United Nations committed combat troops. On June 28, 1950, Henry Shapiro reported from Moscow that the official Soviet newspaper, *Pravda*, charged the United States with a "direct act of aggression" against North Korea and Communist China. *Pravda* accused the U.S. of violating the United Nations' charter by committing naval and air support to South Korea, as well as to Formosa, the large island off the coast of China to which remnants of Nationalist China had fled during the recent Chinese Civil War.

Pravda reported that by ordering the 7th Fleet to protect Formosa, President Truman was in fact ordering the "occupation of part of China's territory by the American armed forces."

Earlier in the year, the Soviet Union and Communist China signed a 30-year peace treaty that obligated one to go to the aid of the other if attacked by Japan "or any state allied with her." This of course included the United States, which was occupying Japan at that time.

Pravda editorialized, saying "When did the (U.N.) Security Council decide to untie the hands of the U.S. government so as to undertake direct aggression? As is well-known, neither the U.N. nor any other international organization authorized the U.S. government to undertake those actions. [Events in Korea] reveal with all clarity that the imperialist warmongers will not stop half way."[132]

When the U.N. initially decided to aid South Korea, Soviet delegate Jacob Malik was absent from the Security Council. The Soviet Union was boycotting the organization for allowing Nationalist China to be seated at the U.N. while spurning the new nation of Communist China. During the six and one-half weeks the Soviet Union was absent, its veto power could not be invoked – which is why the U.N. Security Council was able to take the most important action in its new existence – to take action against Communist aggression in Korea.

The United States initially went to the aid of South Korea alone, but Great Britain, Australia, Thailand and the Philippines soon committed troops and/or pilots. In mid-August 1950, MacArthur asked other U.N. members to commit ground troops "without delay," at which point offers also came in from Turkey and New Zealand, followed later by Belgium, France, Ethiopia, Columbia, Canada and others.

Standing Room Only

The Soviet Union ended its U.N. boycott on August 1, and a week later, it was their turn to preside over the Council for one month. In New York that day, many thousands of civilians flocked to the U.N. to watch the proceedings. Some 23,000 requests for tickets were turned down for people wanting to view the events in the chamber galleries – or even in conference rooms where the meetings were televised.

Margaret Truman, the President's daughter, squeezed into the press gallery, saying, "History may be made here today."

Malik soon launched into a protracted argument that the situation in Korea had been started by the United States. He called for a peaceful

---

[132] Shapiro, Henry. (UP) *Mason City Globe Gazette*. 28 June 1950. Also this chapter: "The Return." *Time*. 14 August 1950; *Pacific Stars & Stripes*. 13 and 28 Aug 1950; *The Fargo Forum*. 23 Aug 1950.

settlement of the conflict by way of an immediate cease-fire and withdrawal of U.N. troops. As *Time* magazine put it, Malik wanted "the surrender of all Korea to its Communist aggressors."

In what became very familiar rhetoric over the next weeks and months, Malik cried: "American ruling circles . . . endeavor to base their whole policy towards other peoples on a dictatorship of domination and compulsion, which they camouflage with hypocritical references to democracy. . . . By democracy, they mean the natural and unlimited power of domination by a small, cruel and power-loving handful of millionaires. . . . "

Warren Austin, Chief U.S. Delegate to the U.N. Security Council, displays a newly-manufactured Soviet weapon captured in Korea. (DoD)

Time reported, "The U.S.'s veteran Warren Austin made a ripsnorting rebuttal. Shaking his forefinger and waving his arms, he disdained any deal or proposal by the aggressors . . . "

But Malik laid full responsibility for the Korean situation on the South Koreans and their "American masters," stating it was South Korea that invaded North Korea – not the other way around. As proof, he waved a photograph of State Department Adviser John Foster Dulles and other American officials with South Korean soldiers in South Korean trenches.

Speaking for the free world, Britain's Sir Gladwyn Jebb replied, "No amount of photographs of Mr. Dulles in a trench — and I only wish there had been more trenches — no suggestion that he himself first rushed across the frontier, no repetition of arguments which a child could refute . . . can obscure the patent fact that it was the North Korean troops who, in large numbers and heavily armed, crossed the frontier and overran the territory of a government which had been established by the United Nations." Jebb reddened Malik's face by deriding the "queer, upside-down language" used by the Soviet ambassador, saying, "We really do seem to be living in a rather nightmarish Alice-in-Wonderland world."

The Pentagon produced photos of a Russian-made 120-mm mortar shell that had been captured intact in South Korea, but Malik claimed it must have been left behind when the Soviet Union withdrew from North Korea two years earlier. However one spokesman pointed out the high explosive missile "bore numerals in Arabic and letters in Russian" and that it was stamped with the date 1950.

Gallery spectators applauded such challenges toward Malik, and he had electric *Silence!* signs installed soon after.

In related news, an August 23 news story told of two North Korean officers — a captain captured near Chinju and a lieutenant colonel who walked into friendly lines near Taegu and gave himself up. Both identified themselves as having served with the Chinese Communist Army in the recent civil war. The colonel said many men in his regiment wanted to surrender, but they were watched too closely by secret political entities traveling with the troops — such as a Russian advisor with the colonel's own artillery unit.

On August 28, an Associated Press story filed from Berlin reported:

The British said Wednesday night Soviet Russia has stepped up its search for uranium in East Germany to "Frantic," far beyond peaceful needs. A ragged army of 300,000 German men, women and children has been drafted by the Russians and their German Communist front men to dig the ore, basis of atomic weapons, the British said. 'The mines are being worked 24 hours a day.'

An adjoining article titled "New U.S. Weapons do 'Fantastic' Things" described emerging weaponry "capable of overcoming an enemy who has a 20-to-1 numerical superiority."

Baltimore industrialist Glenn L. Martin declared his firm was building four types of homing device missiles, which he compared to bird dogs. "Just give one of those machines the scent, and it will track its game better than an animal."

On September 6, a Soviet bomber was shot down after it attacked a U.N. naval formation "in a hostile manner." Papers that were discovered on a recovered crew member identified him as Lieutenant Mishin Tennadii Vasilebiu of the USSR.

The Korean peninsula had become a global stadium in which the two nuclear superpowers were playing a costly game of "psych." From this point forward, others knew it better as *escalation*.

Chapter 29

2ND DIVISION AND THE NAKTONG BULGE

"We went through men like going after flies with a flyswatter."
John Belgarde, 9th Regiment, 2nd Division

GENERAL PAK KYO SAM, commander of North Korea's 9th Division, anticipated the night of August 31 would be monumental. His men would cross the Naktong River, capture the towns of Miryang and Samnangjin, flank and destroy U.N. forces, and cut their withdrawal routes between Taegu and Pusan.

By the following morning, Pak's troops achieved five major river crossings against the 2nd Division's 9th and 23rd Regiments, as well as a crossing against the 38th Regiment near Hyongpung. In sum total, they punched a hole in the American sector six miles wide and eight miles deep.

This action marked the beginning of the *Second Battle of the Naktong Bulge*. Attesting to the fierceness of the fighting, eight Medals of Honor were awarded to men of the 2nd Division in just four days.

John Belgarde

John Belgarde came into the 9th Regiment as a replacement near the end of August. He grew up in Dunseith, North Dakota, on the Turtle Mountain Reservation. The native population in that region was Metis', a unique culture formed by early French fur traders and Native Americans – particularly Ojibway and Chippewa – along the Canadian border. When Belgarde was growing up, the locals spoke French.

Blessed with an extraordinarily keen memory, Belgarde's account of his stint in Korea allows us to more closely understand the experiences of many young infantrymen who saw combat in Korea.

Belgarde was 17 when he joined the Army in 1948, and he was stationed at Fort Riley, Kansas, when the war broke out.[133]

"When the war started in Korea, I had four months to go to get my discharge. I was of the opinion that I'm so short that by the time they even found me, they'd never send me. Then Truman gave us all another year, and about the second day after he did that, I was on a list. We shipped out immediately.

"I wasn't gung-ho to get into battle. I'd been reading in *Look* magazine and all these other ones, and I could see the area that we were in control of was getting smaller and smaller, despite the fact that we were killing the North Koreans by the thousands. According to what they were saying, there wasn't going to be any North Koreans left, but the area we was holding was getting smaller.

"On my way to the train siding, I stopped and set my duffle bag down. I was thinking about the situation in Korea. It was bad. I said to myself, *John, you're not gonna make it back.* So I came up with some rules I am to follow:

1) *I will do the best I can for as long as I can;*
2) *I will not surrender*; and
3) *I will let no one surrender me.*

"When we got to Pusan, we went to Miryang, which wasn't too far out of Pusan – it wasn't that much of a perimeter anymore. Part of the 2nd Division was there, and I was a first replacement there.

"Most of them were 18, 19, 20 or 21. They could handle the hardship fairly well. Even their mental capacity was more prepared for hardship and so on. You could treat those young guys pretty rough, and they recovered fast. This was something the Army needed.

"That army that went into Korea at the beginning, the majority of those boys were Depression-era boys. Hard times to them wasn't anything new. They were able to withstand the rigors of combat better than any other group I served with. I saw that group first, then I saw the reservists, and then I saw the draftees. And those first young guys were the best of all of them. I attribute that to the life they lived during the Depression.

"We moved by truck over to Yongsan, which was just over the

---

[133]Narrative based on interviews with author, summer 2010, which were compiled into the self-published memoir, *An American Fighting Man*.

mountain from Miryang. We spent the night, we had fried chicken the next day, we went swimming and we thought this wasn't too bad! We all knew about Service Company, so everyone was volunteering for Service Company. Of course Service Company was full. They didn't need any more volunteers. They needed guys in the infantry."

Belgarde became friendly with several other young men during the trip to Korea. One of them was assigned to George Company, 9th Infantry Regiment, so Belgarde and three of his friends volunteered to join the same company. John was the only one assigned to the 1st Platoon.

"When we get down to battalion, we get a pep talk from a field officer. He comes out there, he had his uniform all pressed, and he was telling us about the enemy. He said they were starving. They'd attack, and the only people who had weapons were the first ones – when they get shot, the guys coming from the back would pick up their weapons and continue to fight. Well, that was all bullshit!

"About the 24th or the 25th of August, we went on line and had a big fight – and we kept having fights all along. But in this one particular incident up near Hill 198, after the shooting stopped, I was standing not too far away from the company commander. He said, 'Belgarde, you go and destroy all those weapons,' because we'd killed a bunch of North Koreans there.

"So me and another guy, we go among the dead, and we pick up the burp guns and the automatics with the plates on the top. I'm looking at the receivers of these weapons. They're real nice and blue – they'd been made not too long before. I looked at this one burp gun, and it was made in 1950. Every one of those guys had a weapon, and they all had food – they carried it in something like a roll that they'd put over their shoulder, and it'd come down across their chest.

"But what surprised me, this was a burp gun with a *hammer and sickle* stamped along with the year of manufacture right there on the receiver. It was Russian made, 1950. Now this is just a few days after this major got up and gave us this glorious speech. I thought, *Boy, this is not getting it.* I grew somewhat doubtful about the information that was coming in from the rear, and I grew much more doubtful as time went on."

Belgarde's 9th Regiment was so depleted, it was operating at roughly 25 percent its normal strength, even after receiving the replacements that came in with Belgarde. Yet the regiment was guarding a front 20,000 yards wide – roughly three times the normal infantry assignment, according to infantry doctrine, when operating at full capacity.

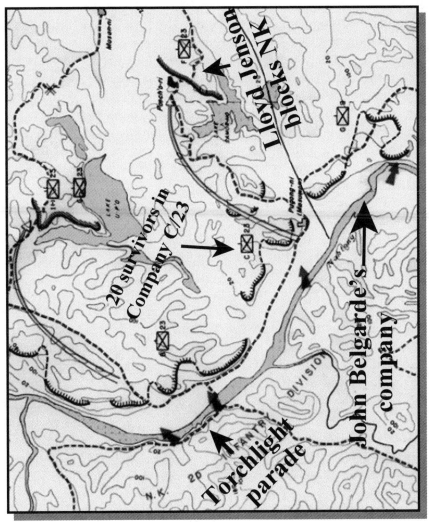

(Map inset courtesy Center of Military History)

"On about the 25th of August," said Belgarde, "George Company moved on line where the 19th Infantry of the 24th Division had been, and we covered 7,000 yards with about 40 or 50 men. The next two guys, if they hollered, you couldn't hear them."

As historian T. R. Fehrenbach wrote, they "were scattered like dust over a few of the higher hills east of the river."[134]

---

[134]Fehrenbach T.R. *This Kind of War*. Brassey's 2001 edition: page 142.

Operation Manchu

Because the Naktong Bulge was bordered by 35-miles of riverbanks, the 2nd Division was, in essence, surrounded on three sides from the very beginning. (This was the same sector in which the 5th Marines had recently fought its bloody battle on Obong-ni Ridge.)

A great deal of enemy movement had been detected in this sector, and the division was planning a river crossing of its own to reconnoiter the situation on the other side. This was called *Operation Manchu*, and it was cut short the night of August 31. John Belgarde's George Company was on the 9th Regiment's right flank overlooking the Naktong River when it happened.

"The North Koreans were fairly well organized; they were fairly well trained," he said. "They knew how to operate and maneuver. They could move their troops wherever they wanted. So, they didn't try to bust the whole line – they had certain spots along the line where they could come across the Naktong River.

"They wanted Yongsan, because just over the mountain from Yongsan they could cut the railroad at Miryang, and they could cut off all our supplies moving north. At night we could hear the enemy's trucks and the tank engines roaring, and we could hear the slap of the wooden boxes where they were storing ammunition and stuff like that. Every night we could hear them. We couldn't hear their voices, but we could hear the other activities going on.

"The 2nd Engineers was gonna come down and put a foot bridge across the Naktong, and Easy Company was gonna go across the river and try to raise hell over there – whatever they could do. We had air strikes going on several times a day west of the river – we were on the east side.

"Battalion brought their personnel down for *Operation Manchu*, not quite to the river's edge, and at the same time, the North Koreans were crossing from the other side. Well, both sides met right there at the east bank. The battalion commander was down there, the assistant battalion commander, and there were some other bigwig personnel – and they had a brush with death right there. I don't know how many times they were shot at before they could get the hell out of the area.

"There was a long firefight. You know, firefights don't last very long, but this one here lasted for maybe two hours. I could hear from where I was, I could hear these young fellas – we're all about 18, 19, 20 – and I could hear those guys, when they'd get hit hard, some of them would go down, and they'd be crying," said Belgarde. "They'd be hollering for their mother. That's the only time I ever heard any of the guys, when they got hit hard, they'd cry for their mom.

"There was too many North Koreans. They overran us and went on. They had a pincer and came up and took Yongsan. So, here we are, George Company, we're surrounded. We're eight miles behind the line. For the rest of the night, we stayed in our positions.

"But the 3rd platoon was gone. They were completely overrun. Two men were out on patrol down by the river. The sergeant was named Flowers, and he had another guy with him. They had a radio, and they'd report any activity down by the river. Well, when the North Koreans came across . . . he tried to call it in, but the radio was dead. So he couldn't notify the 3rd platoon higher up on the ridge. Those two guys survived, and one guy called Big Gibbs, from the 3rd platoon, survived some way. But, all the rest were either killed or captured.

"The enemy was just starting to get into the 2nd platoon area, and one of my buddies, he opened up on them with his BAR (Browning Automatic Rifle) and killed two or three of them. That's as far as they got up the ridge on George Company. They didn't need to come any further, because they were headed for Yongsan."

When the sun rose, survivors began finding each other. Captain Frank Munoz, commanding Belgarde's George Company, consolidated his men and resources with fragments of other units, and by sunset, they were formed up several miles from where the regiment had been hit.

"I looked out across the rice paddy, to my left," John said, "and I could see the North Koreans digging in over there on the hill.

"We didn't wave to each other."

Torchlight River Crossings

The same night that *Operation Manchu* failed, North Korean soldiers had carried out peculiar demonstrations a bit farther upstream, across the Naktong from the 23rd Regiment. The 2nd Division's war diary reads:

> During the afternoon of 31 August, it became apparent that the enemy was building up a considerable force in the 23rd Infantry sector. Many troop movements were observed, and the enemy was seen building rafts, apparently in preparation for an attempt at crossing the Naktong.

Shortly after sundown, the 2nd Platoon of Baker Company was mesmerized by an eerie procession coming out of the hills to the river's west bank.

First Lieutenant William Glasgow Jr. called the battalion command post to report a "large and bizarre torchlight parade" with the torches appearing to form the letters V and O.

A forward artillery observer estimated this parade numbered about 2,000 people, and he wondered if they were refugees being forced forward by the enemy. Colonel Freeman, the regimental commander, was taking no chances. He ordered an artillery strike, but it didn't seem to matter. As torches would disappear, they were picked up and replaced by others in the procession.

Some couple hours later, enemy artillery and mortar fire opened up on the friendly positions, and under cover of this barrage, the torch-bearing troops crossed the river and fanned into the hills. A green flare signaled the North Korean ground assault, and enemy grenades soon rained down on Glasgow's platoon.

By midnight, all elements of the 1st Battalion were under "extremely heavy attack." At 3:00 a.m., only seven men remained in Charlie Company. That number rose to a paltry 20 men three days later (a company generally numbers roughly 200 men).

Later that day, *Pacific Stars and Stripes* reported:

> North Korean Communists broke through American mine fields in their attack Friday by sending waves of infantrymen forward in banzai suicide charges to clear the way . . . Prisoners recently captured in this area indicated that some reinforcements consisted of very recent [draftees] who were apparently destined for a cannon fodder role.

It might be supposed that the "cannon fodder role" included, in part, men in the torchlight parade the night before.

Major Lloyd Jenson

Units from the 23rd Regiment's 2nd Battalion immediately moved up to stop the North Koreans from pressing further into the Bulge, with the war diary reading:

> This force, commanded by Major Lloyd K. Jenson, Executive Officer, 2nd Battalion, 23rd Infantry, established the position which the 23rd Infantry was to occupy through two weeks of the heaviest fighting in its history.

Lloyd Jenson was a middle child among thirteen siblings, the ten oldest being boys. His mother Carla was from North Dakota, where she bore several of her children. After living in Bowbells, the family moved to Sidney, Montana, where Lloyd's father, Jens, ran a meat market. Both his parents were first-generation Norwegian-Americans.

Lloyd was very bright and was reportedly the first male to attend Montana State College, Bozeman, on a scholarship. He became Senior Class President, president of the Lanbda Chi Alpha fraternity, and the business manager for the college's yearbook, *The Montanan*. (Jenson later put his business skills to good use at the Pentagon as Chief of the Financial Management Coordination Group, Office of the Comptroller of the Army, receiving a high commendation for his work in 1957-58.)

Jenson also completed ROTC course work at MSC, becoming a commissioned officer upon graduating in June 1941.

Six of the Jenson brothers served in WWII. Lloyd was wounded in action in 1944, and by the end of the war he had been promoted to Captain, likely leading his own company.[135]

His daughter Susan recalls, "I don't know about my father's wounds, only that he was shot in the legs during WWII and that he had multiple purple hearts. He fought all the way from Northern Africa through Italy and to Germany.

"He never bragged, never complained, and never ever spoke of his own personal valor as a soldier. Scandinavians are pretty closed, and that generation, in particular, did not discuss war time. My dad didn't. Maybe I just never really asked the right questions.

"He was someone who could make the right ethical decision in his sleep. He had that moral radar that was incredibly impressive to grow up around. My mother always said he was a 'soldiers' soldier' whose thoughts were always focused on the welfare of his troops and the best strategy for moving them toward success on the battlefield.

"The fact that he died at Walter Reed Hospital is so my dad. Surrounded by soldiers, my mother, my sister and me. He is buried in Arlington Cemetery at the corner of Patton and Eisenhower Roads."

Jenson was to be decorated several more times before he left Korea, but it was probably more important to him that he was highly respected by the men who served with him. A medical officer named Erik Larsen recalled Jenson "watched after my medics and me like a father to keep

---

[135] *Helena Independent*, 8 June 1941; *(Helena) Independent Record.* 19 Apr *1944; Salt Lake Tribune.* 19 Oct 1945. Author communications with Susan Jenson, 2013.

us out of harm's way."[136]

Major Jenson was the executive officer (second in command) of the 2nd Battalion, 23rd Regiment. From the very beginning, he put himself in the midst of combat, and he justly deserved the awards he earned, beginning with the Distinguished Service Cross the night of August 31, 1950. Although he was a major when he carried out his first decorated action, he was a Lieutenant Colonel by the time his DSC came through.

Colonel Jenson circa 1961
(Courtesy Susan Jenson)

*The President of the United States of America takes pleasure in presenting the **Distinguished Service Cross** to Lieutenant Colonel (then Major) **Lloyd K. Jenson**, United States Army, for extraordinary heroism in connection with military operations against an armed enemy of the United Nations while serving as Executive Officer, 2nd Battalion, 23rd Infantry Regiment, 2nd Infantry Division. Lieutenant Colonel Jenson distinguished himself by extraordinary heroism in action against enemy aggressor forces in the vicinity of Changyong, Korea, on 31 August 1950. Shortly after midnight on that date, Colonel Jenson commanded a task force with the mission of establishing a roadblock to halt an anticipated enemy attack on the regimental flank. Deploying his force with great skill, Colonel Jenson personally inspected the positions held by his men and then spent the remainder of the night reconnoitering every possible avenue of approach available to the enemy. When the advance guard of a large hostile force appeared on the scene the following morning, it was almost completely destroyed by the concentrated firepower of the firmly entrenched tank force. The remainder of the enemy force then launched a fanatical attack, but the friendly troops were prepared and, under the skilled leadership of Colonel Jenson, the assault was repulsed at great cost to the foe. Disregarding their heavy losses, the hostile troops threw themselves*

---

[136] Web: 13 Feb 2014. www.koreanwar-educator.org/memoirs/larsen_erik/index.htm.

against the friendly defensive positions twice more, each time supported by heavy mortar and artillery fire. Exhibiting a matchless fighting spirit, Colonel Jenson, without regard for his personal safety, moved among his men, encouraging them and directing their fire with such skill that the numerically superior enemy force was pushed back repeatedly. When he observed a body of hostile troops moving to envelop the roadblock, he organized a small group of infantrymen and, with one tank, proceeded to an advantageous position from which he directed a deadly fusillade of fire, which ended the threat of encirclement. Through his courageous efforts the positions of the friendly troops remained secure against seemingly overwhelming odds.

Ernest Kouma and Marion Quillen at Agok

On September 1, General Walker's Eighth Army announced three reinforced enemy divisions, with an estimated strength of some 30,000 men, had thrown themselves against the western and southern sectors during the night, "with heaviest pressure at a junction of the Nam and Naktong rivers." This spot was on the 2nd Division's extreme left flank where it adjoined the 25th Division (which was still fighting along the south coast near Masan).

This junction also marks the spot where two Nebraska soldiers and their Spartan crews made one of the most audacious David and Goliath stands in military history. The position overlooked the Kihang Ferry landing at the tiny village of Agok. Had the North Koreans known who they were up against, they may have chosen another spot.[137]

Ernest "Ernie" Kouma and his ten siblings grew up on a farm outside the Czech community of Dwight, Nebraska. Kouma's mother, Mary, was a first-generation American-Czech, and his father, Joseph, was a Czechoslovakian immigrant. Their first language was Bohemian; the children didn't learn English until they started school.

Kouma began hunting when he was nine, and he and his six brothers were well known for their sharpshooting skills. Indeed, a neighbor, Dr. J. J. Srb, complained about the boys ruining the tail of his

---

[137]Kouma sources: *ARMOR*. May-June 1993, p 37; Fehrenbach, *This Kind of War*, p 208; Appleman's *South to the Naktong*; *Pacific Stars and Stripes*. 6 May 1951; *The Independent (Long Beach CA)*. 8 May 1951; *Racine Journal - Times*. 9 May 1951; *Lincoln Star*. 4 Jun 1951; *Omaha World-Herald*. 24 June 1951. Web: 9 Oct 2010, www.globalsecurity.org/military/agency/army/1-72ar.htm;

windmill, saying, "They were good shots, all right; they riddled it." He added, "If this country should ever be invaded, we're going to send out the seven Kouma boys, and the rest of us can stay home and quit worrying."

Srb's assessment proved accurate. Ernie's younger brother Anton was awarded the Navy Cross for actions on Saipan in WWII, and Ernie was about to earn the Medal of Honor this very night.

After graduating from a country school in 8th grade, Kouma rode a horse into Dwight each day to attend Assumption High School, but he dropped out after two years to work full time on the farm. The Koumas didn't own a tractor, so the farmwork was done with horses, oxen and mules. Ernie was rather fond of a particular pair of mules, because he found them challenging.

An expert horseman, Kouma often amused friends and neighbors with trick riding. He dreamed of being a cavalryman, joined the Army and did become a member of a horse cavalry unit in Ft. Riley, Kansas; when that unit became mechanized, he instead ended up riding a tank.

During WWII, Kouma was attached to the 9th Armored Division and took part in the Battle of the Bulge in August 1944. By the time the war ended, he was fighting in his father's homeland of Czechoslovakia.

After the war, Kouma reenlisted and served with the 25th Division, and then went to Korea as a tank commander in Able Company, 72nd Tank Battalion.

He was unprepared for the difficult terrain, saying, "Korea certainly is not a tank country. Tanks are supposed to support the infantry, but you can't spread out in the rice paddies – your tank will sink. We had to stick to the narrow roads cutting through mountains with almost sheer cliffs. Tanks were bunched in threes and fours, and if the head tank was stopped, everything was stopped."

The evening of August 31, 1950, started quietly as Master Sergeant Kouma drove his tank to the front to replace one that was having weaponry problems.

About the time the zombie-like torchbearers were walking through artillery fire a few miles upstream, he and a fellow tanker, Sergeant First Class Oscar Barry, were coordinating positions with two squads of riflemen (15 to 20 men) from Able Company, 9th Regiment. Kouma pulled in beneath a cliff near the house the riflemen were using as a command post near the Kihang Ferry crossing. Along with two anti-aircraft crews, these 30 or so men were the only personnel available to guard this entire sector that night.

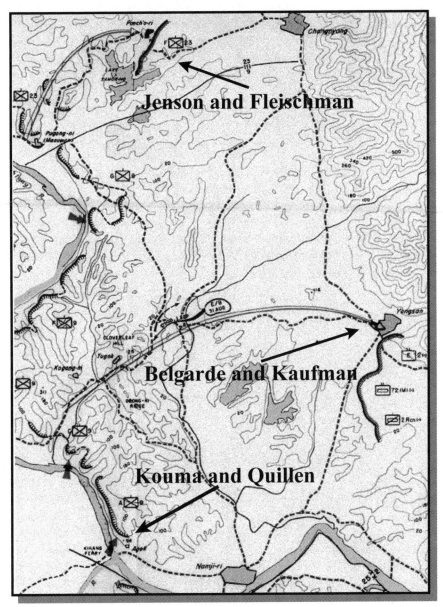

(Map inset courtesy Center of Military History)

By this point, General Walker, because of his shortage of manpower, had developed a tactic of using small units such as this as outposts. Their job wasn't to engage the enemy – they were to assess oncoming enemy troops so that troops in the rear would have the time and means for preparing strong defensive positions.

The two nearby anti-aircraft positions consisted of an M-19 with twin-mounted rifles and an M-16 with quad-mounted rifles from Battery D, 82nd Anti-Aircraft Artillery. Their crews were commanded by Sergeant First Class Marion A. Quillen, the son of Mrs. Vera Pettit of Hastings, Nebraska. Quillen had first enlisted in September 1948 and then reenlisted in February 1950.

After sundown, a fog settled over the river, and at about 8:00 p.m., dogs began barking on the enemy side of the river. About an hour later, mortar shells began falling along the 9th Regiment's 20,000-yard front. About 15 minutes into it, heavy mortar fire landed in their positions.

Some of the men said they were hearing splashing noises, and at about 10:30, when the fog abruptly lifted, Kouma spotted enemy activity in the river. The North Koreans were building a pontoon bridge, which was already two-thirds completed. Kouma got on his tank-mounted machine gun and ordered his crew to fire on the bridge with their 90-mm cannon.

The other tank, as well as Marion Quillen's anti-aircraft weapons joined them until the bridge broke apart and the builders pulled back.

Except for the barking dogs, silence again fell over the sector until 11:00 p.m., when small arms fire started falling on the two rifle squads, who were ordered to fall back to better positions. The armored vehicles remained behind to provide them cover and to also form a roadblock to prevent the enemy from going any farther inland.

Kouma later wrote to Army historian Roy Appleman:[138]

> The infantry outpost had hardly left when I spotted seven men running towards me from the direction of where Able Company's command post formerly was located. I halted them and noticed that they were wearing the (2nd) division patch. One of them spoke excellent English. All seven came next to my tank . . . three of them crawled on the deck of the tank and informed me that a large force had crossed the river farther down approaching my position and that most of Able Company were killed or captured. At the time I had the idea that they were part of the 9th Infantry.
>
> During this time I was on top of the turret checking my 50 cal. machine gun. At a given signal they leaped from the tank and began throwing grenades on the tank, and about the same

---

[138] Appleman. *South to the Naktong*. P 444-5.

time a steady spray of machine gun and rifle fire began hitting the tanks and [antitank] guns from the crest of the high bluff about 150 yards to my right. My gunner at once took them under fire as well as SFC Berry's [sic] tank and the AA guns. I got back in the turret and threw about 7 or 8 grenades over the house as well as inside the house through the door which faced us.

Kouma was wounded twice in this exchange. He and Barry quickly pulled their tanks out from under the cliffs to open ground that offered 200-yard fields of fire in every direction.

Ernest Kouma (Courtesy ARMOR, Ft. Knox)

The Eighth Army Command Report states the enemy hit the 2nd Division in "five places with an estimated 900 to 1,000 men at each point." One of these points was Kouma's position (as well as John Belgarde's position farther north with *Operation Manchu*).

The main attack began at about midnight. At roughly 1:30 a.m., Barry's engine overheated and caught fire, forcing first a withdrawal and then an abandonment of his tank.

Kouma's tank had been pulling two trailers filled with flares, food and equipment. He set these on fire to illuminate the area for the next four hours, but the fight lasted much longer.

By sunrise, after nine hours of battle, Kouma and his crew had fired 15,000 rounds of machine gun ammunition. Withdrawing, they fought their way back through eight miles of terrain that was now in enemy hands. Kouma's intentions were to find more ammunition and go back, but his wounds landed him in a field hospital at Miryang instead.

The President of the United States of America takes pleasure in presenting the **Medal of Honor** *to Master Sergeant* **Ernest Richard Kouma**, *United States Army, for conspicuous gallantry and intrepidity at the risk of his life above and beyond the call of duty while serving with Company A, 72nd Tank Battalion, 2nd Infantry Division, in action against enemy aggressor forces at Agok, Korea, on 31 August and 1 September 1950. Master Sergeant Kouma's unit was engaged in supporting infantry elements on the Naktong River front. Near midnight on 31 August, a hostile force estimated at 500 crossed the river and launched a fierce attack against the infantry positions, inflicting heavy casualties. A withdrawal was ordered and his armored unit was given the mission of covering the movement until a secondary position could be established. The enemy assault overran two tanks, destroyed one and forced another to withdraw. Suddenly Master Sergeant Kouma discovered that his tank was the only obstacle in the path of the hostile onslaught. Holding his ground, he gave fire orders to his crew and remained in position throughout the night, fighting off repeated enemy attacks. During one fierce assault, the enemy surrounded his tank and he leaped from the armored turret, exposing himself to a hail of hostile fire, manned the .50 caliber machine gun mounted on the rear deck, and delivered point blank fire into the fanatical foe. His machine gun emptied, he fired his pistol and threw grenades to keep the enemy from his tank. After more than nine hours of constant combat and close-in fighting, he withdrew his vehicle to friendly lines. During the withdrawal through eight miles of hostile territory, Master Sergeant Kouma continued to inflict casualties upon the enemy and exhausted his ammunition in destroying three hostile machine gun positions. During this action, Master Sergeant Kouma killed an estimated 250 enemy soldiers. His magnificent stand allowed the infantry sufficient time to reestablish defensive positions. Rejoining his company, although suffering intensely from his wounds, he attempted to resupply his tank and return to the battle area. While being evacuated for medical treatment, his courage was again displayed when he requested to return to the front. Master Sergeant Kouma's superb leadership, heroism, and intense devotion to duty reflect the highest credit on himself and uphold the esteemed traditions of the U.S. Army.*

Kouma's fellow Nebraskan, Marion Quillen, was also decorated for his actions that night. Sadly, his award was posthumous; he was severely wounded one week later and died of those wounds September 13, just two weeks shy of his 22nd birthday.

*The **Silver Star** is Awarded **(Posthumously)** to Sergeant First Class **Marion A. Quillen**, U.S. Army, for conspicuous gallantry and intrepidity in action against the enemy while serving with Battery D, 82nd Anti-Aircraft Artillery (Automatic Weapons) Battalion (Self Propelled), 2nd Infantry Division, in action against the enemy in the vicinity of Agok, Korea, on 1 September 1950. On this date, Sergeant First Class Quillen was a Section Leader commanding two anti-aircraft firing vehicles. At about 0300 hours, when the leading elements of the attacking enemy came within range of his gun, Sergeant First Class Quillen gave the order to open fire. The enemy continued to advance, and as the attack developed, enemy fire became devastating. Although units to his right and left started to withdraw, his crews were stimulated by his leadership and indomitable courage and continued to fire smoothly and effectively until forced to withdraw because of ammunition shortage and a defective traversing mechanism. As a result of this tenacity, great damage was inflicted upon the enemy. After withdrawing for a mile, they met a tank crew from whom additional small arms ammunition was obtained. Sergeant Quillen and his crews again engaged the enemy with their individual weapons in his sector until forced to withdraw to avoid certain destruction or capture. Sergeant First Class Quillen's gallantry and indifference to his personal safety were determining factors in causing the enemy's defeat on this occasion and fully upheld the highest traditions of military service, reflecting great credit upon himself, his unit, and the U.S. Army.*

Kouma Learns About His Medal of Honor

Having received multiple wounds at Agok, Kouma was kept in the rear for three days. Five days after he returned to the front lines, his tank hit a land mine, but he amazingly survived. "I flew out through the turret straight up," he said. "I figure I must have gone up 50 feet. When I landed, my knee was injured."

Undeterred, he remained in combat five more months before taking the time to have surgery on his knee.

In May 1951, Kouma learned he was being awarded the Medal of Honor for his actions at Agok, but he wasn't especially happy with the news. It turns out he had always been, according to his mother, "a very bashful boy," and he dreaded the prospects of reporters, ceremonies, or any other situation that would bring him public attention.

Kouma was ordered to return home, and when questioned by reporters in Tokyo, he paid high tribute to his gunner, George C. Brown, saying Brown kept the tank's big gun firing throughout the entire engagement.

Of his other crew members, Kouma said, "The other men were calm during the fight, because they had confidence as a fighting team. We trained together in the States and knew what the other man could do." (George Brown, Corporal Ernest King, and Private First Class John Lacey received Bronze Stars for valor.)

When Kouma landed at the airport in Omaha on May 7, reporters were frustrated by his "yup" and "nope" answers.

"I'd rather not talk about it," he said, as he edged his mother toward the door. What he really wanted to do was to get home to his family and his favorite meal, his mother's dumplings and sauerkraut.

Kouma was decorated by President Truman on May 19, 1951. A few days later, he was whisked to New York to take part in a broadcast for the international radio program *Voice of America*. Aiming his words at Czechoslovakia, the Master Sergeant spoke in Bohemian, urging the Czechs to continue their battle for liberty.

As the only living Medal of Honor recipient of the war (it was not known that General Dean was still alive at this point), the Army hoped to use Kouma as a spokesman and recruiter. But it wasn't in his nature. In fact, when a subsequent ceremony to honor him was planned in Omaha, he asked his priest to pray for rain so it would be canceled.

As for his career, Kouma had previously been offered a battlefield commission to the rank of lieutenant, but he had turned it down, saying he wanted to be where the action was. But when asked about the possibility of now going back to Korea, he said, "I'd do it again, but I'd hate to. I'd know now what I would be in for."

John Belgarde and Loren Kaufman

Another of the 2nd Division's eight Medal of Honor recipients from those four days was Loren Kaufman. He wasn't from the prairies, but North Dakotan John Belgarde was beside him when it happened. Kaufman was his platoon sergeant, and their first encounter wasn't pleasant.

"The sergeants are hollering like mad, cussing and swearing," said Belgarde. "One sergeant is threatening to shoot us. I see this big guy, he's about 6' 1", 210-215 pounds. He's got a full beard, and he's threatening to kick my ass! I'm about 150 pounds, and he's like maybe 215. I'm 5' 8", and he's 6' 1". I think *Who's that ugly sonofabitch!'*

Shortly before dawn on September 4, their company was moving up a hill when they got caught in a firefight. Belgarde recalls: "The enemy was attacking the company. I don't know how many there was, because we couldn't see. Captain Munoz, the company commander, called on the radio. John Murphy, a West Pointer, was the platoon leader, and Munoz got a hold of Murphy and told him to bring the platoon on in, but bring it up the ridge and then over along the ridge line on the top.

"So we move out, and I'm the right-hand scout. It's pretty dark, but I'm not very far away from the main body of the platoon. I'm looking down into this draw and into low ground going back to the valley. I can see movement – but that's where our company was. I thought *The company is pulling back over this way.* They were quite a ways – you couldn't make out anything other than there's movement.

"So we're moving up along this ridge, and this group of soldiers are coming up this draw, and we're gonna meet higher up as we go toward the main ridge line," said Belgarde.

"I'm looking down at them as we're getting closer and closer together. Some of them have Marine ponchos. Well, the Marines had just cut away from us the day before and went to the southwest, and I thought *That's the Marines. They're coming up the draw, and we're coming up the ridge line.*

"Pretty soon, we come together. We're standing in a group. I'm facing to the east, and I could reach out with my right hand, and I could touch a North Korean soldier. I could reach directly to my front, and I could touch one, that's how close we were. There's about 40 of them, and in our platoon there's probably about 33 of us. Sergeant Kaufman is there, and he's supposed to be making the decisions.

"What had taken place, as the North Koreans were coming up, we were on their friendly side. They thought there was another unit coming to join them and help them finish off our company, because we're to their left – and that's their friendly side. Their enemy territory was on their right.

"Now for us, they were on our right, so they were on our friendly side, because the company was over that way. To our left was enemy territory. So that's how we got fooled – both groups got fooled.

"We come up and stop. We're standing there, and two G.I.s come up close behind me. Then Kaufman comes up, and one of these North Koreans – Kaufman can see he has some foliage in his helmet – and he starts beating him on the head and talking to him: *What're you doing with that on your helmet? You know you're not supposed to have that!* He chewed him out. He thought he was one of ours.

"The lieutenant says, '*What* are they, Kaufman?'

"Kaufman stops. He doesn't say a word. He rears back from his hip, hits this guy with his fist, and he knocks him back against his buddies. Now, Kaufman always carried his bayonet on his rifle. He had his rifle in his left hand, and he hit the guy with his right – and he grasped his rifle, and he bayoneted him.

"Now, this is right before my eyes!" said Belgarde. "I'm standing right there. The guy he hit with his fist was probably two-and-a-half feet from me, because I could touch him. I'm looking at him, and he's got a grin on his face. He has nice-looking teeth, I can see.

"When Kaufman bayoneted him – well, we're in for a fight now. I wanted some room, so I

(Courtesy John Belgarde)

stepped over on the other side of Kaufman, and when Kaufman started to withdraw his rifle, he didn't just pull it out, he shot him off. He pulled the trigger and shot him.

"When I stepped on the other side – I'm a right-hand shooter – I pivot to my right, and I can see a little bit of what's going on slightly to my rear – and the whole goddamn platoon is pulling away. There's only four of us standing there.

"The enemy soldiers are lower than us, because they're closer to the draw, and there's a break point where the slope gets steeper. As soon as Kaufman fired, I started to fire, and the other two started to fire. And every time I pulled the trigger, I could see the bodies of those North Korean soldiers – three deep would jerk. My bullets was going through three bodies at a time.

"These North Koreans at the front, they tried to run back, but the ones that we killed, right at their feet, they were being knocked back into them. The guys in the back didn't know what was going on, so they just piled up. We kept shooting, and they just fell out of view.

"I fired my last shot, my eighth round. I couldn't see no more North Koreans. I went down on one knee, I took a grenade, I pulled the pin, and I let the handle flip. That armed it. I waited a couple seconds, and then I just flipped it over the edge. Because I wanted to catch those guys that were closest.

"Normally, when you're using a hand grenade, you pull the pin, and you throw it. As soon as it leaves your hand, that handle will jump free. If you hold it in your hand, and you pull the pin, it won't go off until that handle slides free. So I let the handle flip, and I held it for a couple seconds. Then I flipped it over the edge.

"Then, I took the second grenade, I pulled the pin, I let the handle flip and I tossed it right away, because I wanted it to go a little further down the slope. And then I took the third hand grenade, I pulled the pin, and I threw it. It would go further yet. I'd get some of those guys who were running, if there were any of them left.

"You know, I had just got there. I'm just picking this stuff up. And I'm the type of guy, I'd count all the time. I counted everything. I looked at the ground, and there were nine bodies at our feet. But there was no goddamn way I was gonna stick my head over that edge to count whatever was beyond that. I just wanted to get the hell out of there."

Belgarde did not witness the remainder of Kaufman's action after their platoon rejoined George Company that night. Like Ernest Kouma, Kaufman was, for the moment, a rare living recipient of the Medal of Honor. Unfortunately, he was killed in action five months later, before the award could be bestowed. He was from The Dalles, Oregon.

*The President of the United States of America . . . takes pride in presenting the **Medal of Honor (Posthumously) to Sergeant First Class Loren R. Kaufman**, U.S. Army, for conspicuous gallantry and intrepidity above and beyond the call of duty while serving with Company G, 9th Infantry Regiment, 2nd Infantry Division, in action against enemy aggressor forces at Yongson, Korea, on September 4 & 5, 1950. On the night of 4 September the company was in a defensive position on two adjoining hills. Sergeant First Class Kaufman's platoon was occupying a strong point two miles away protecting the battalion flank. Early on 5 September the company was attacked by an enemy battalion and his platoon was ordered to reinforce the company. As his unit moved along a ridge it encountered a hostile encircling force. Sergeant First Class Kaufman, running forward,* *bayoneted the lead scout and engaged the column in a rifle and grenade assault. His quick vicious attack so surprised the enemy that they retreated in confusion. When his platoon joined the company he discovered that the enemy had taken commanding ground and pinned the company down in a draw. Without hesitation Sergeant First Class Kaufman charged the enemy lines firing his rifle and throwing grenades. During the action, he bayoneted two enemy and seizing an unmanned machinegun, delivered deadly fire on the defenders. Following this encounter the company regrouped and resumed the attack. Leading the assault he reached the ridge, destroyed a hostile machinegun position, and routed the remaining enemy. Pursuing the hostile troops he bayoneted two more and then rushed a mortar position, shooting the gunners. Remnants of the enemy fled to a village and Sergeant First Class Kaufman led a patrol into the town, dispersed them, and burned the buildings. The dauntless courage and resolute intrepid leadership of Sergeant First Class Kaufman were directly responsible for the success of his company in regaining its positions, reflecting distinct credit upon himself and upholding the esteemed traditions of the military service.*

Belgarde on Medics

As in every war, medics carried a heavy responsibility in Korea, where the terrain made their jobs especially difficult.

John Belgarde recalled his platoon medic's struggle with the memory of one man he lost during this time period.

"Some way Doc Strickland took a liking to me, and he used to like to talk to me," said Belgarde. "You know those medics, they ran into some hard moments. He told me about an incident that was very hard for him, and he said this soldier had got shot in the neck and cut one of those big veins in the side of his neck? He had no way of stopping the bleeding. He said he sat there with this guy and talked to him, and they smoked cigarettes. He couldn't help this guy. He was just slowly dying, and that bothered Doc Strickland.

"You know I have no idea why he would tell me that. But evidently that was one thing that was bothering him. I don't know if it helped him to tell me about that or not.

"But I want to say this – all that bullshit about them docs at the hospital level – like M*A*S*H? A lot of that was bullshit. Those weren't the guys who really saved lives. It was the medics that saved the lives. And the medic don't get no credit. We dogfaces, we didn't care much about the doctors, but boy-oh-boy them medics, we wanted them not too far away whenever we were in a hot spot," said Belgarde. "They need to get a helluva lot more recognition than they've gotten so far."

Richard Fleischmann

One such medic grew up in Anaconda, Montana, a small mining and smelting community along the western slope of the Continental Divide.

Richard Fleischmann was active in extracurricular activities and graduated from high school with honors at age 16.

Joe Sheehan, also from Anaconda, said, "Richard was a few years older than I. He was in the same home room as my sister Rita, and they both worked at the Washow Theater. Richard was the doorman and Rita was an usher. He was a little over six feet tall, medium build, a good-looking fellow with a nice smile."[139]

Despite being an honor student, Fleischmann opted to join the military. "Richard wanted to become a doctor," Sheehan said, "and he joined the Army shortly after high school with the hope that it would lead to a college education. He came from a poor family, and they lived on the outskirts of town."

Unfortunately, Fleischmann did not realize his dream. On September 6, he not only performed his duties as a medic, he also took up weapons against the enemy.

Sheehan writes, "I remember when he died, the whole town was very sad when they heard."

*The **Distinguished Service Cross** is (Posthumously) awarded to Private First Class **Richard L. Fleischmann**, U. S. Army, for extraordinary heroism in connection with military operations against an armed enemy of the United Nations while serving as a Medical Aidman with the 23rd Infantry Regiment, 2nd Infantry Division. Private First Class Fleischmann distinguished himself by extraordinary heroism in action against enemy aggressor forces near Changnyong, Korea, on 6 September 1950. On the afternoon of 6*

---

[139]Correspondence with author Sep 2010. Sheehan was drafted in 1952 and served as a combat rifleman with the 223rd Regiment, 40th Infantry Division in Korea.

September 1950, Private First Class Fleischmann was assigned as aid man to the machine-gun platoon of Company H, 23rd Infantry Regiment. One section of the platoon came under extremely heavy machine gun and mortar fire, and the section leader was wounded. In spite of concentrated enemy fire on the immediate area, Private Fleischmann ran forward to the gun position, removed the section leader to safety, and rendered medical treatment. A few moments later, the gunner of this weapon was also wounded, and once again he ran into point-blank machine gun fire and removed this wounded man to safety. Although wounded on the second trip to the machine gun position, he then took over the machine gun and held off the enemy so that the remainder of the section could reorganize and move to a better position. He remained in position firing the machine gun until he was killed.

The Crow Boys

When 18-year-old Dale Crow joined the Army, it was a family affair. Dale and three of his cousins enlisted together on March 23, 1950, and

Dale Crow

all four were deployed to Korea August 5, 1950, arriving 18 days later.

Dale was born on a farm southwest of White Butte, South Dakota, but he grew up in Lemmon, where his cousins David, Richard and Eugene Crow attended high school.

In Korea, Dale and David both ended up in George Company, 38th Regiment, which was on the 2nd Division's right flank, north of the Naktong Bulge.

As the Crow families soon learned, combat would not be kind to their sons. On September 3, Richard was captured, and six days later, Dale and David were both killed in action. (Richard later escaped and made it back to friendly lines a month later, on October 7.)

*The **Distinguished Service Cross** is **(Posthumously)** awarded to Private **Dale Duane Crow**, United States Army, for extraordinary heroism in connection with military operations against an armed enemy of the United Nations while serving with Company G, 2ⁿᵈ Battalion, 38ᵗʰ Infantry Regiment, 2ⁿᵈ Infantry Division. Private Crow distinguished himself by extraordinary heroism in action against enemy aggressor forces in the vicinity of Sibi-ri, Korea, on 9 September 1950. On this date, while participating in an attack against a strongly defended enemy position on Hill 285, Private Crow was seriously wounded. While his wound was being dressed by a comrade, an enemy grenade fell nearby. Without hesitation, and with no concern for his own life, Private Crow threw his body over that of his comrade, thereby receiving the full blast of the grenade, which took his life.*

It wasn't until September 9 that fighting in the Naktong Bulge finally ebbed. By then, only 38 percent of the 23ʳᵈ Regiment was still able to fight; at one point the number of men in reserve – for the entire regiment – was down to just six men.

A captured North Korean medic reported the fighting west of Changnyong (where Richard Fleischmann was killed) had cost the enemy just as dearly. During the first two weeks of September, he told his captors, his own division took 3,800 casualties.[140]

---

[140] *South to the Naktong...* P 468-469.

Chapter 30

HAROLD K. JOHNSON AT TABU-DONG

"Actually I didn't do any more than I should have done under the circumstances, but I'm awfully proud of the fact that my own men thought enough of the action to make the recommendation for the award." Harold K. Johnson, in a letter to his mother

THE 1ˢᵀ CAVALRY DIVISION was deployed to Korea early on, but it arrived piecemeal. The 8ᵗʰ Cavalry's 3ʳᵈ Battalion arrived last, because it was created from scratch in the States. Its commander was from Grafton, North Dakota.

Lieutenant Colonel Harold K. Johnson, 42, was better known as "Keith" to his family, and as "Johnny" among his military peers. He was of true prairie stock in that both of his parents were born in Dakota Territory.

After marrying Edna May Thomson, Johnson's father (also named Harold) managed a lumberyard in Hampden, North Dakota, but when their son was eight-years-old, the family moved to Grafton, where the elder managed another lumberyard.

While in high school, Johnson simultaneously worked three jobs while also participating in sports, drama and the Boy Scouts. He graduated with honors in 1929, and one might suspect he was instrumental in choosing his class motto: *Build for character, not for fame.*

Despite his demanding schedule, Johnson also enlisted in Company C, 164ᵗʰ Infantry, North Dakota National Guard.

Johnson learned about the National Military Academy, West Point, from Alice Holt, a schoolteacher in Grafton. He felt that going to West Point "seemed like an exciting thing to do for a boy from North Dakota who had never been very far from home. Second, it answered the problem of how I could receive a higher education."

Johnson was successful in getting an appointment to the prestigious academy, where he excelled. Although later described as very serious, at the academy he was known for having "a magnificent sense of humor."

(Courtesy U.S. Military Academy)

Johnson graduated from West Point in 1933. The guest speaker that day was Army Chief of Staff Douglas MacArthur, who Johnson would serve under in both WWII and Korea. MacArthur urged them to embrace "tolerance, balance, intelligence, courage – these four will carry you on; for you must go on, or you will go under."[141]

Johnson entered a Depression-era "shoestring" Army, serving four years with the 3rd Infantry at Fort Snelling, Minnesota. During this time, military leaders were brought in to lead projects undertaken under a new program called the Civilian Conservation Corps (CCC), which was designed to put a large number of the unemployed to work.

Johnson was put in charge of a great many Finns (see Clarence Lackner chapter) in the Chippewa National Forest on the Mesabi Iron Range in northern Minnesota. After six months with that group, a new batch of men arrived from the mean streets of Minneapolis, who Johnson described as "very, very smartie."

Because he was in charge of civilians, Johnson needed to learn how to lead without military sanctions. It was likely during this period that he honed one of his most worthy traits: "Personal leadership was the only way that you got things done," he said. "You had to look after these young men, and you had to be sympathetic – not in a maudlin way, not in a weak way, but work with them in order to get their support and to get response from them in their work forces."

Despite all his hard work and efforts, Johnson was not a saint. At

---

[141] Lewis Sorley's 1998 biography, *Honorable Warrior: General Harold K. Johnson and the Ethics of Command,* is highly recommended. Many details within these pages were provided by Sorley's book.

West Point he found ways to ditch chapel services, and while working on the iron range, he said "we were drinking up World War I alcohol in cans, good grain alcohol, and mixing that with some kind of a spirit of the day." He described this period of time as a fine life for a bachelor.

Unlike many of his North Dakota counterparts, Johnson disliked hunting. He was very fond of animals, but while working in the Minnesota woods, he agreed to go hunting with friends. Afterwards he vowed he "would never shoot another bird or animal." Thirty years later he reflected, "I haven't, except for taking aim a couple of times at the two-legged kind."

Johnson at Bataan

When the Japanese attacked Pearl Harbor, Johnson was already in the South Pacific, having deployed to the Philippines in 1940. There, he commanded Company L, 57th Infantry Regiment, otherwise known as the Philippine Scouts.

In the spring of 1941, he was promoted to Regimental S-3 (operations officer) despite his lower rank of Captain. His regimental commander reported Johnson's "energy, initiative and ambition are unlimited," predicting, "He will be at the top in any group."

Theirs was a peacetime regiment, but troops in the Philippines knew war was looming, and they worked hard to prepare.

It happened on December 8, 1941 (December 7, Hawaiian time). With the destruction of the Naval battle fleet at Pearl Harbor, men in the Philippines knew they were in trouble – there would be no means to reinforce or resupply them. In essence, the Philippine islands were cut off and isolated on the very first day of the war.

Johnson's biographer Lewis Sorley wrote that Johnson re-found his religion when bombs began dropping on Manila. However, his Protestant upbringing shifted to Catholicism, simply because he was surrounded by Catholic chaplains and soldiers in the Philippines.

The possibility of a Japanese invasion of the Philippines had been a war-planning consideration for a number of years prior to the war, and the military had decided War Plan Orange No. 3 (WPO-3) was the most prudent option if such an invasion ever took place. The plan was that if the Japanese would land on Luzon, defending forces would try to hold but would also prepare a contingency for a delaying action by withdrawing into the Bataan Peninsula. This plan theorized that by creating inland supply dumps, the defending forces could hold out for six months, long enough for assistance to arrive from the United States.

General Douglas MacArthur took command of American and Filipino forces in July 1941. Against protests from Philippine President Manuel Quezon, MacArthur dismissed WPO-3, stating the troops would defend the island from the beaches, where they would fight to the finish. No supplies were to be stored inland.

Harold Johnson was embarrassed by the resultant public feud that developed between MacArthur and President Quezon, saying, "Neither was going to be able to prove his point in the absence of overt attack."

When the attacks inevitably came, MacArthur's decision proved catastrophic. The Allied forces were swept ten miles inland the first day, and all the supplies and munitions that were ordered forward to the beach were lost to the enemy. Troops ended up having to fall back on WPO-3 – but without much of their food, medicine, supplies and/or ammo.

Johnson's regimental commander, George Clarke, was behaving in a manner suggestive of post-traumatic stress disorder (PTSD), possibly developed in combat during WWI. Because of this, Johnson had been taking on more and more of the command responsibilities for the 57th Regiment, and two weeks into the fight, he was promoted to major.

Two weeks later, they were on half-rations, but as combat progressed, lack of ammunition became more worrisome than hunger. On the evening of January 11, 1942, each of Johnson's artillery batteries had a ration of artillery ammunition estimated to be sufficient for three days, but the following morning they were down to one hour's worth.

Johnson requested more from the corps ordnance officer, but officially, Johnson's men had two more days' worth of ammunition, and his request was denied. Johnson appealed to the corps commander, who also said no, claiming his orders came from above. Johnson refused to give up, as described by biographer Lewis Sorley:

Johnson, undeterred, contacted that next level, back on Corregidor, speaking to Brigadier General Richard K. Sutherland, MacArthur's autocratic chief of staff, and persuading him to break loose the needed ammunition. At this time, Johnson was a major with about three weeks' time in that grade, acting as commander in place of the prostrate Colonel Clarke, and in the midst of a desperate battle with the attacking Japanese.[142]

---

[142]Sorley. *Honorable Warrior.* P 47.

By February, fighting hunger took precedence over fighting the enemy, and cavalry horses and pack mules were sacrificed. On April 1, medical personnel estimated 60 percent of the men on Bataan had malaria and/or dysentery.

Eight days later, Johnson, who briefly commanded of the 57th's 3rd Battalion, learned the Bataan troops had been surrendered. He became a prisoner of war on April 11, and two days later, he became part of the infamous Bataan Death March.

"It wasn't the enemy that licked us," said Johnson. "It was disease and an absence of food."

He survived the death march and 41 months of captivity in the Philippines, then in Japanese "hell ships" and, lastly, in Korea.

When he was released at Inchon, Korea, on September 7, 1945, he weighed only 100 pounds.

Many years later, General "Abe" Abrams, Army Vice Chief of Staff at the Pentagon, described Johnson as, "The toughest man I have ever known." Coming from Patton's iron-willed tank commander during the siege of Bastogne, this was high praise indeed.

A lot had transpired during Johnson's time as a prisoner of war – new weaponry, new tactics, promotions of his peers, new people in command, and a whole new body of military history.

Sadly, Johnson came face-to-face with a new prejudice when he applied for a position at the Infantry School at Fort Benning, Georgia. The policy of the school's commandant, Major General John O'Daniel, was to turn away all officers who had been prisoners of war in the Pacific.

Although officials at a higher level eventually overturned O'Daniel's prejudicial policy, Johnson by that time had found an alternate fit for his personality and skills. He attended the Command & General Staff College at Fort Leavenworth, Kansas.

Johnson Builds a Battalion

After his time at Fort Leavenworth, Johnson was back in the military mainstream, and by the spring of 1950, he was a lieutenant colonel commanding the 3rd Battalion, 7th Division, based in Fort Devens, Massachusetts.

A few weeks into the war, Johnson was summoned by his regimental commander. Although the 7th Division had been stripped of men (needed as individual replacements in Korea), Johnson was ordered to organize a provisional battalion for immediate deployment to Korea. He was to use his existing battalion as the nucleus – and at the moment, that nucleus numbered about 75 riflemen.

One of these riflemen was William "Bill" Richardson, who describes himself as a brash and cocky high school dropout (who later became an Army colonel and a two-time commander in Delta Force in Vietnam). A month earlier, when the Army was downsizing, the Philadelphian had begged to stay in, hoping to be sent back to Europe so he could rejoin a special girl in Austria. The Army kept Richardson in, but his plan backfired.[143]

"I joined the battalion in Fort Devens the same day Colonel Johnson got the order," Richardson said. "About 30 minutes later, we were told to go to this movie theater, and Colonel Johnson let us know we were going to go to Korea. I looked around in this theater, and there were only two rows filled up. I said to myself *There's not enough men here to make a company, let alone a battalion that was going to Korea. This can't be!*

"There was a young sergeant there, Sergeant First Class Roberts, and he said, 'God, I just got married, and I'm on CQ tonight.' He didn't know me – we were just talking, going out of the theater – and I said, 'Hey, I'll take your CQ (in charge of quarters). I don't have anything to do. You go home and be with your wife.'

"Being on CQ means you stay with the company that night. You're in charge, and you make sure nothing happens. So I took the CQ, and I was sitting there daydreaming, when I got a call from the duty officer at battalion who said, 'You're going to get a hundred-some men in tonight. Be sure you're prepared to feed them in the morning and be prepared to bunk them tonight.' Oh geez, my evening of daydreaming went out the window.

"Overnight the company filled up to about 180 men – that was the same with all the companies. So we were brought almost up to strength overnight, mostly with recruits who came from Fort Dix. And then they also grabbed up people from all the units at Fort Devens," Richardson said.

Over the next ten days, Harold Johnson conditioned his men by making them run while carrying out their duties. Equipment was shipped to the West Coast, his troops were processed for overseas duty,

---

[143] Interview with author, Feb 2011; also Richardson's *Valleys of Death, A Memoir of the Korean War*. NY: Berkley Caliber. 2010. Excerpts reprinted by permission. Differentiated by "he said" and "he wrote." No further citations.

and he also carried out as many combat training activities as he could.

When Richardson first saw Johnson that night in the movie theater, he described the colonel as "a slight man with short-cropped gray hair. He wasn't overly impressive but had an air of authority."

Over the next days and weeks, his respect for Johnson grew.

"Colonel Johnson did the best that could ever have been done to get us in condition to leave," Richardson said. "It was almost an impossible task to do everything he did to expose us to simulated enemy fire, and actually it wasn't simulated – he had the heavy mortars fire on a piece of ground right in front of us, and he moved the whole battalion up to within a hundred yards to get people acclimated to that kind of thing. We also threw grenades without using a grenade pit to protect us. We were throwing them right out into the open.

"He did things like that – which ordinarily wouldn't be done – to do as much as he could to get us ready. I would give him top marks. He was a good trainer and then, when we got into combat, a good combat commander. He took care of his troops, and he was great."

Richardson eventually came to know Johnson as "a very religious person who believed in people doing the right things. There was a time, later, when I was brought in from the field in Vietnam to meet with him. He came over there when he was Army Chief of Staff. They brought me in – you know, I was with him before, so they brought me in – but in addition to that, I was a commander in Delta Force, and he had to get briefed on that.

"I heard him say – more than once – 'If you can't be trusted by your wife, you can't be trusted by me.' Whoa! Saying that to Army people was a shock, I can tell you right now! I described it to a group in Saigon – it was all colonels and generals, you know – and they almost dropped their cigars. That's the kind of man he was."

Indeed, two items that Johnson always kept on his desk were his Bible and his Boy Scout manual. General G. Bittman Barth, commander of the 25th Infantry Division, agreed with Richardson, describing Johnson as "very intelligent, very serious"and as a "devoutly religious Catholic" who could pray "without sounding phony."[144]

Despite his religious conversion as a POW in the Philippines, Johnson was still not a puritanical saint. He was reported to smoke four

---

[144]Barth, G. Bittman, Unpublished manuscript, "Tropic Lightning and Taro Leaf in Korea, July 1950-May 1951". As quoted in Clay Blair's *The Forgotten War*, p 255 and 989 (n 49).

cigars and two packs of Winston cigarettes per day. He also enjoyed an occasional drink. But regarding matters on the field of battle, he was very strict, saying, "I want no pickled brains leading my troops."

Johnson was well aware the military had fallen into an almost shameful state of unpreparedness, and he was ruthlessly honest about this when his new unit was deployed to Korea. When an officer from First Army Headquarters arrived to assess the combat readiness of the battalion, Johnson flatly stated their readiness was "zero." He refused to add a silver lining, saying, "This is a thrown-together unit that hasn't done anything together."

Johnson's "1st Provisional Infantry Battalion" headed for San Francisco on August 4. During the journey by rail – and then by sea – Johnson had the men practice disassembling their weapons, and the officers and noncommissioned officers, using chalkboards, continued their training in squad and platoon tactics.

Bill Richardson, who had crossed the ocean before, recalled the trip was hot and unpleasant. "We were stacked four high in the bunks below decks, and the ship didn't have any ventilation. It was taken out of mothballs to get us over there. It was pretty bad. For me, I was used to it, but for most of them it was pretty bad."

Bob Earl, who ended up in the Mortar Platoon of Mike Company, recalls, "Colonel Johnson was against gambling. Well, they had a poker game up on the deck – a bunch of guys were playing poker up there. Johnson came by, and he says, 'Is there any money involved?' And of course the guys playing the game said, 'Oh no, sir!' Johnson says, 'Well, then this box here is of no value,' and he threw it over the side. And that was all their money in that box!"[145]

Richardson recalled, "We were supposed to be going to Japan for 30 days training, but as we neared Yokohama, the ship suddenly made a hard left, went around Japan and went over to Korea. No training. That was it."

It wasn't until they docked at Pusan on August 25 that Johnson learned his men were to become the 3rd Battalion of the 8th Cavalry Regiment.

Because Johnson had seniority among the officers in the regiment, he was offered the job of executive officer (second in command). He

---

[145]Earl interview with author Feb 2011.

turned it down, feeling it was important to stay with his fledgling unit until they were bloodied and ready to stand on their own.

The battalion immediately headed North for Taegu, which was now the temporary capital of South Korea. The weather was still oppressively hot and humid, and the men soon learned about the horrendous fighting at the front. Richardson writes:

> As the trucks rumbled forward, we could see American troops moving south down the road. They looked like ghosts, frail, with torn and dirty uniforms. Their black eyes didn't even register as we passed. They had the infantryman's thousand-yard-stare. They were lost. Gone.

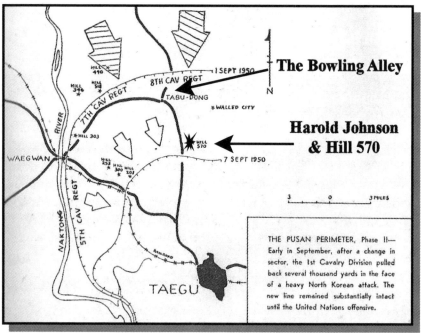

(Map courtesy 1st Cavalry Division)

From Taegu, the battalion quickly moved north to the road earlier dubbed the *Bowling Alley* by Colonel Johnson's fellow North Dakotan, Gilbert Check, and his Wolfhounds.

The North Koreans had again breached the line and were fighting for full possession of Tabu-dong.

When Johnson's untried battalion hit the ground, it was greeted with artillery and machine gun fire – the opening shots of a battle that would continue, for them, around the clock for a week and a half, and then ultimately stretch out to about three weeks.

This wasn't the only bad news that greeted Johnson's men. Even after two months, units at the front were still short of ammunition, equipment and supplies.

More amazingly, their 3rd Battalion was put on half-rations as soon as they arrived. One can only assume the colonel was forced to think of those bleak days prior to the fall of Bataan.

Several historians attribute this state of affairs to General MacArthur diverting supplies for his upcoming amphibious assault at Inchon, up on the west coast.

Whether or not this was true, the treatment of front line infantrymen was nothing short of deplorable in the first months of the war.

A Daring Rescue

Johnson's 3rd Battalion immediately stepped into the fight, and Bill Richardson, now the section leader of a 57 recoilless team in Love Company, moved about five or six miles up the Bowling Alley.

"That night we got hit hard," he said. "The North Koreans went around us and cut us off from the rest of the battalion. We thought we were going to have to come back the best way we could, which was going to be very difficult. We would probably have lost a lot of men.

"There's where Colonel Johnson really comes into the picture for me. The rest of the battalion broke through the North Koreans down in Tabu-dong – to break the road open so we could get through. Then he sent five or six trucks up – and it's pretty difficult to even think about doing this – but he sent them up and, under fire, we got back through the line on those trucks."

In his compelling memoir, *Valleys of Death,* Richardson elaborated on this rescue. Working their way through enemy lines, they searched for a field where the rescue trucks could leave the road to turn around, because they would have to stay rolling or risk being pulverized.

"Move quickly when the trucks get here," Richardson told his men. "I want half of you on each side of the truck ready to fire on my orders, and look for orange panels, because those are friendlies."

Soon, they spotted five trucks barreling up the road. Richardson noted they had machine gun mounts, "but since the Army was short, no machine guns."

The trucks pulled into the selected field, and the soldiers quickly scrambled aboard. "Things were tight," said Richardson, "but in minutes the whole company was crammed into the trucks."

One of his men asked permission to lie on the truck bed and pray for them. "Okay," Richardson told him, "but you better make it a goddamn good prayer."

As they raced back to friendly positions, Richardson saw the truck ahead of them begin to swerve. He swore. If it crashed, the convoy was doomed, because there would be no room to skirt around it. As they neared the orange panels in the distance, North Korean rounds began hitting the trucks, so he ordered his men to keep up steady fire to each side of the road.

"I have no idea if we hit anything," he said, "but I wanted the North Koreans to keep their heads down."

When they finally reached safety, Richardson helped the young prayerful soldier to his feet. "Good work," he said. "He listened."

There was no time to give it any more thought, because they were immediately attacked from the rear.

"It went on every day like that," said Richardson, "You'd be fighting on this hill, and the next thing you knew, you were withdrawing and attacking another hill behind us. That just kept going on all the time."

As days stretched into weeks, this battle became a do-or-die stand. Casualties were high for both the G.I.s and officers, including the loss of Colonel Johnson's peer, Gerald Robbins, commander of the 2nd Battalion. Clerks, cooks, and the division's band members were handed rifles and sent to the front line, and Johnson chose his assault units based on which company could muster half-strength on a given day.

Hill 570

On September 8, Johnson was ordered to seize Hill 570, a difficult, three-pronged peak eight air-miles north of Taegu. From its commanding heights, the enemy was destroying their escape route to Taegu, and Eighth Army Intelligence estimated a thousand enemy soldiers were dug in on its slopes.

Johnson's orders would require him to accomplish a withdrawal and immediately attack in another direction, which he called "a very unusual maneuver."

The North Dakotan assigned each of the hill's three prongs to one of his three half-strength rifle companies. A low cloud ceiling prohibited air support, and while two companies fared well, the company on the highest peak was kicked off. One company commander, an executive officer of another, and several noncommissioned officers were killed in the attempt.

Throughout, Johnson stayed at the front, even moving ahead of the lines to personally call in mortar and air strikes. As he told his officers, "You can't just stand there and yell, 'Hurry it up!' The American soldier has to be led, not pushed."

In an interview for *Time*, one of Johnson's platoon leaders, George Allen, said it was the only time he ever saw the colonel in need of a shave:

> The world was coming apart. Our company commander had been killed. There was heavy firing 100 yards away. Colonel Johnson said we could handle it. He parceled out firepower and called in air strikes. He hadn't slept for three days, but he never used a profane word.[146]

By now, Johnson's green battalion was tenacious. "While we were not successful in taking the whole objective," he later said, "we were successful a couple of days later by going at it from another direction."

"It was like being on a merry-go-round up there," said Bill Richardson. "A couple times I wound up in the same foxhole I'd been in a few days before – lost the position and then went back and regained it again."

With pressure mounting and ammunition in critically short supply, the attack on Hill 570 was finally called off. The battle wasn't over, but Johnson was very proud that his men had "stuck."

That night, the battalion was pulled out for an overnight rest – their first after eleven days of continuous combat. Richardson and his men sprawled in an apple orchard and cracked open some rations. When the inevitable complaints arose about the never-ending need to dig foxholes, Richardson tore the cover off a ration box and wrote to Sears and Roebucks for an automatic foxhole digger.

Colonel Johnson came up with Love Company's commander to ask how they were faring, and Richardson took the opportunity to follow the commander as he was leaving.

"How are we doing?" he asked. "It seems like we never make any headway."

---

[146] Allen, George, LTC. *Time*. 10 Dec 1965, p 33.

Richardson said Johnson stopped and turned back. "Sergeant Richardson," he said, "tell your men they did a great job. Against great odds, we have stopped the North Koreans' main attack."

"Johnson's news had an immediate impact on my section," said Richardson. "We no longer dragged ass. In fact, we were hopeful, even optimistic."

After a major turn of events some weeks later, the cavalry was pursuing the North Koreans up the peninsula. Richardson recalled that when they finally had an opportunity to assemble for a headcount, only 228 of Johnson's original 720 men remained. His biographer writes:

> It is not surprising that he remembered these as "dark, bitter days." The cost had been high, but they had done what was asked of them. "It was," he thought, "a superb effort on the part of a green unit. My pride in that unit has never diminished."

Letcher Gardner, Montgomery, Iowa, mans a lonely position as a member of Dog Company, 8th Cavalry. Battalions should have covered no more than 1,000 yards but instead were covering 8,000 yards while also being under-strength. (U.S. Army)

In a letter to his mother, Johnson wrote:

> During my first week in combat I didn't see any generals unless
> I went to the rear a couple of miles. Our generals weren't any
> cowards, either, but it was really hot. I feel in my own heart that
> the third day we were in [action] my outfit held the Pusan
> perimeter and the main road leading to Taegu. There just wasn't
> anything behind us. We paid dearly but we held pretty well.[147]

Colonel Harold Keith Johnson in Korea. (NARA)

It was for his leadership on that critical "third day" that the future Army
Chief of Staff was awarded a Distinguished Service Cross. But Bill
Richardson says, "It was a continuous thing – to pick out just one day

---

[147]Sorley. *Honorable Warrior.* P 97-98.

for him to be decorated might've been done just because of the paperwork involved."

The **Distinguished Service Cross** *is awarded to* **Harold K. Johnson**, *Lieutenant Colonel (Infantry), U.S. Army, for extraordinary heroism in connection with military operations against an armed enemy of the United Nations while serving as Commanding Officer of the 3rd Battalion, 8th Cavalry Regiment (Infantry), 1st Cavalry Division. Lieutenant Colonel Johnson distinguished himself by extraordinary heroism in action against enemy aggressor forces near Tabu-dong, Korea, on 4 September 1950. When his battalion had been forced to withdraw from their hill position by a series of fierce attacks by an overwhelming number of the enemy, Colonel Johnson immediately directed a counterattack in an attempt to regain the vitally important dominating terrain. Placing himself with the most forward elements in order to more effectively direct and coordinate the attack, Colonel Johnson rallied his men and led them forward. Moving about exposed to the heavy enemy artillery, mortar and small-arms fire, he directed fire, assigned positions and, by personal example, proved the necessary incentive to stimulate and keep the attack moving. When his battalion began to falter due to the devastating enemy fire, Colonel Johnson moved forward to close proximity of the enemy to establish and personally operate a forward observation post. Remaining in this exposed position, he directed effective mortar counter fire against the enemy. When his mortars became inoperable and his casualties very heavy due to the tremendous firepower and numerically superior enemy forces, he realized the necessity for withdrawal. Remaining in the position until the last unit had withdrawn, he directed the salvaging of both weapons and equipment. Reestablishing a new defensive position, he reorganized his battalion and supervised medical attention and evacuation of the wounded. His conspicuous devotion to duty and selfless conduct under enemy fire provided an inspiring example to his men and prevented a serious penetration of friendly lines.*

Chapter: 31

25ᵀᴴ DIVISION ALONG THE SOUTH COAST

"In the first seven days in September, the 25ᵗʰ (Division) buried over 2,000 dead North Koreans behind its lines. This does not include the dead in front of its positions." Uzal Ent, 27ᵗʰ Regiment

THE NIGHT OF AUGUST 31, the same night the enemy had made their major river crossings against the 2ⁿᵈ Division in the Naktong Bulge, the North Korean 6ᵗʰ Division simultaneously hit the 25ᵗʰ Division on the 2ⁿᵈ Division's left/south flank.

Masan was still in friendly hands – but just barely. The Muchon Fork was gone, and so was The Notch and most of the mountain mass between the north and south roads to Chinju. Many lives had been lost in this sector, and the last bit of territory west of Pusan was at this time in grave jeopardy.

General Walker had just diverted the 27ᵗʰ Regiment back to the south coast to relieved the 5ᵗʰ Regimental Combat Team, and for the first time, all three of the 25ᵗʰ Division's regiments (24ᵗʰ,

Col. Check
(U.S. Army Photo)

(Undated news clipping)

27ᵗʰ and 35ᵗʰ) were in the same sector, fighting as a cohesive team.

Reporter Frank Conniff was at Gilbert Check's command post when a small group of G.I.s showed up and asked to speak with the

North Dakotan. Conniff writes:

> The scene has been repeated so frequently in recent weeks that it has become commonplace around the combat areas, but it never fails to stir the emotions of someone seeing it for the first time. It is a rather simple mission. They want to fight. They have left their rear area units, the safe berths far from the shooting, and have hitchhiked to the zone of battle. Riflemen are such a scarce commodity these days and replacements so irregular that combat commanders are always ready to accept volunteers.

Private Joseph Alford, of Akron, Ohio, explained they had been reading about "how tough it is up here, and we want to help." Alford's group included seven men from an engineering unit and two from a railroad unit operating in Pusan. They had spent all night hitching rides to the front lines.

> Colonel Check eyed them quizzically. He's a slight spare man whose voice is seldom raised even in the sweat of combat. His lack of flamboyance has not obscured the fact that he's one of the finest battalion commanders this war has yet produced. And he knows from personal experience the price these men might pay for their gallant decision. His two brothers were killed in the last war, and he's the sole remaining male member of his family.

Check told the volunteers, "I want you all to realize what you're doing. This is a good outfit with a fine record, and anyone who joins it will have to expect a lot of grim, tough fighting. If you can't join us with that understanding, you should pull out now while there's still time." Conniff writes:

> He paused for a moment and looked around the semicircle. Pvt. Kenny Wist, of Cincinnati, shuffled his feet. Pvt. Ennis Sisson, Santa Maria, California, peeped at a nearby hill. But none withdrew. They had made a hard decision and they were going to see it through.

Check said, "All right, then. We're glad to have you with us. I'm going to assign you to Able Company, and you'll get all the action you want. Any questions?"

Conniff writes:

"Sir," said one, "when will I get a chance to pick up my duffle bag?"

The faintest hint of a smile turned the corner of Colonel Check's mouth. It was apparent that the real nature of the life they were beginning had not yet dawned on these eager young men.

"You won't need any duffle bag," Check told them quietly. "All you're going to need is your gun and some ammunition and your blanket and a poncho to keep out of the rain. Forget about your duffle bag. You won't be needing it."[148]

Loss and Recapture of Haman

The plan for the 27th Wolfhounds to hold at Chindong-ni on the south shore changed dramatically afater the North Koreans' massive assault the night of August 31 (the same night the enemy crossed the river into the Naktong Bulge).

North Korea's 6th Division broke through between the 24th and 35th Regiments' lines and left a 3-mile gap as they descended on Haman. On the south side of the breach, Roger Walden, commanding Fox Company, 24th Regiment, held through the night. But communications had broken down, and it wasn't until morning that he was able to warn the 35th Regiment – three-miles distant – that its left flank was now exposed.

Meanwhile, the North Koreans had also broken through other positions, and thousands of North Korean fighters were already in the process of surrounding the 35th.

The enemy was now presented its best opportunity of reaching Pusan, just a handful of miles farther east. The American actions of the following week were among the most important of the entire war, with much of the fighting taking place *in the rear* of the 24th and 35th positions, as explained in the 27th Regiment's war diary:

Between 1-7 September . . . enemy was engaged when and where encountered; battalions operated independently, being attached to other [regiments].

---

[148]Conniff, Frank. *Cedar Rapids Gazette.* 31 Aug 1950.

. . . Based on after action reports, enemy had infiltrated an estimated two regiments through the main battle positions and assembled this force in remote areas. This force then proceeded to harass rear installations, establish road blocks, and attack command posts and artillery positions.

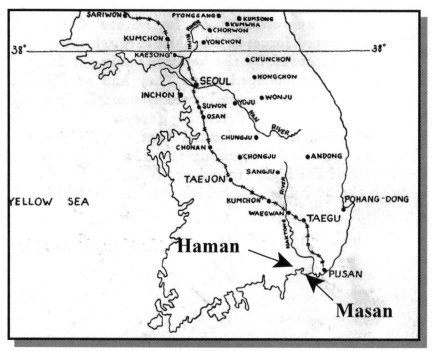

The enemy's attempt to seize Haman, Masan and Pusan was fanatical, with thousands of casualties on all sides.

It was 2:00 a.m. on September 1 when Gilbert Check was ordered to speed northwest up a mountain road to Haman to stop enemy troops pouring in through the gap. As his men prepared for the move, Check went ahead with his staff to confer with Colonel Arthur Champeny, commanding the 24th Regiment. What he found was a state of chaos, and with seemingly nobody in charge, a giant traffic jam delayed Check's attack by some six hours.

Check finally located the 24th Regiment's command post about two miles east of Haman. With mortar fire falling around them, Champeny briefed Check about the situation that had befallen his regiment.

Check received orders for the Wolfhounds to counterattack at 2:45

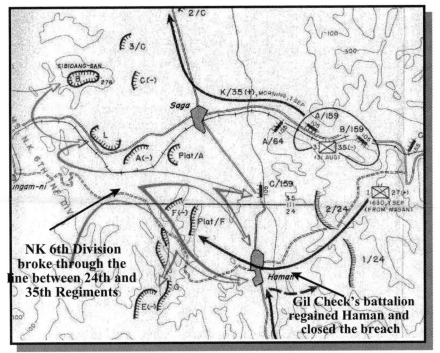

**The enemy's massive offensive broke through lines along
the entire Naktong Perimeter the night of August 31.**
(Map inset courtesy Center of Military History)

that afternoon. After forty-five minutes of preparatory bombing and shelling, Haman was in flames. Check's men seized the town, along with weapons, equipment and vehicles abandoned by the North Koreans.

His next mission was to eliminate enemy troops from a ridge west of Haman. This would be a bloody affair, with the battalion's Report of Operations stating enemy machine gun fire "swept every approach, and the green tracers seemed as thick as the rice in the paddies."

It was here that Able Company, including Gil Check's three new volunteers, took the lead: "Company A stormed its objective, while Companies B and C were held up by fierce enemy resistance 200 yards from the objective."[149]

Check's men sustained heavy casualties, but by 6:25 p.m., they were

---

[149]Ent, Uzal W. (Brig. Gen.). *Fighting on the Brink: Defense of the Pusan Perimeter.* Paducah, KY, Turner Publishing Co. 1996: P 326-327. Ent's detailed research is liberally used in conjunction with the 27th historical accounts for this entire section.

Haman in the foreground on road. After seizing it, Check's battalion attacked (west) into the mountains beyond. (Aerial view, NARA)

in control of the ridge. They dug in at 8:00 p.m. and traded fire with the North Koreans throughout the night.

*The First Oak Leaf Cluster to the **Bronze Star with V Device** is awarded to Lieutenant Colonel **Gilbert J. Check** . . . When assigned the mission of restoring the left flank defense boundary of the regiment near Haman, Korea, on 1 September 1950, Lieutenant Colonel Check immediately went to a forward observation post to reconnoiter the enemy situation and plan his attack. Moving across the line of departure with the leading elements of his battalion, he courageously supervised the progress of the attack, despite the intense hostile small arms, mortar and artillery fire. Shortly thereafter, the former positions were restored and Lieutenant Colonel Check skillfully organized his battalion to retain the position against subsequent counterattacks.*

Check's battalion renewed the attack in the morning, with the tide rising and falling through the night of September 2. The war diary states:

> On the morning of 3 September, 1ˢᵗ Battalion observed hundreds of enemy dead lying in and around position, the results of abortive attacks during the 2-day assault. Captured

enemy stated 1ˢᵗ Battalion inflicted an estimated 1000 casualties on 4 enemy battalions attacking the position.

Gilbert Milburn

Gil Check's men turned the sector back over to the 24ᵗʰ Regiment during the night of September 4-5. During the exchange, Check's Able Company (and its three new volunteers) ran into a buzz saw.

Private First Class Gilbert Milburn, a heavy-machinegunner, provided fire support for them. This 20-year-old soldier grew up in a large family in Manawa Lake, near Council Bluffs, Iowa. Attached to the 1ˢᵗ Battalion's heavy weapons unit, he was killed while almost single-handedly assaulting the enemy before sunrise on September 5. A Medal of Honor may have been appropriate for his level of sacrifice.

(From un-named news clipping of Iowa casualties)

*The **Distinguished Service Cross** is **(Posthumously)** awarded to Private First Class **Gilbert D. Milburn**, U.S. Army, for extraordinary heroism in connection with military operations against an armed enemy of the United Nations while serving with Company D, 1ˢᵗ Battalion, 27ᵗʰ Infantry Regiment, 25ᵗʰ Infantry Division. Private First Class Milburn distinguished himself by extraordinary heroism in action against enemy aggressor forces near Haman, Korea, on 5 September 1950. While attached to Company A, Private Milburn voluntarily remained in position with his section when the company withdrew. Fighting off an enemy assault at about 0430 hours in the morning, Private Milburn used every weapon at his disposal and resisted the overwhelming attack until all ammunition was exhausted and he was forced to withdraw. Upon reaching the next ridge line to the rear, Private Milburn came upon friendly troops of another unit that were completely demoralized and disorganized. Assuming leadership of this group of men, he reorganized them into a cohesive fighting force. He moved out in front of them and led them in an assault on his former position. Advancing about ten yards in front of the troops, he personally destroyed three machine-gun positions. Private Milburn was killed as he reached his objective, the top of the ridge.*

Meanwhile, Gordon Murch moved his 2nd Battalion, 27th Regiment, to the village of Chirwon, where they counterattacked the North Koreans who had worked their way around behind the 35th Regiment's lines.

Fighting in almost every direction, George Company, 35th Regiment, was cut off and surrounded on Hill 179. Over the next several days, Murch's 2nd Battalion fought their way to George Company's positions and soon found themselves equally cut off and isolated.

Between September 3 and 6, lack of ammunition, supplies and food became very serious concerns. In the predawn hours of September 4, Colonel Murch requested an air drop of supplies, and two were successfully carried out later in the day.

Three young men quickly grabbed up the medical supplies, including John Ross, from Boone, Iowa, William Maloney, Ohio, and Sherman R. Thompson, New Jersey, who worked around the clock to save the lives of more than one hundred men. All three were decorated, with Ross's citation reading:

*The **Bronze Star with V Device** is awarded to Private First Class **John M. Ross**, Army Medical Service, Medical Company, 27th Regiment, 25th Infantry Division, U.S. Army. From 3 September to 6 September 1950, Private First Class Ross was a member of a group which operated a temporary medical facility near Chirwon, Korea. Without professional assistance or supervision, he and his comrades provided medical care for the wounded of an isolated battalion of infantry. On the second day, increased enemy action necessitated movement of the aid station to a more secure position. Working tirelessly, he assisted in the movement of all wounded to the new location despite continuing hostile fire. When the critical condition of some of the wounded required immediate professional attention, he and his comrades negotiated an enemy roadblock to take the wounded to a point from which they could be evacuated. Throughout the seventy-two hour period during which the battalion was isolated, a total of 105 casualties were treated with only five fatalities . . .*

Leonard Becicka

"There was no income," said Leonard Becicka of his early years.[150] "No income whatsoever, except what could be derived from a farm. I recall

---

[150]Interview and correspondence with author 2011. Note Becicka went on to a very distinguished career, and he was inducted to the Ft. Benning Hall of Fame in 1995.

one year we had a terrific storm, and it ruined all the crops in the field – oats, wheat and barley. It just beat it to the ground. We had hoped it would be something that would be productive, but . . . It was not an easy life.

"We had cows, sheep and horses, and we had some pigs. I can remember each autumn, we would slaughter a pig, and that provided us some food. But it was mostly living off the land."

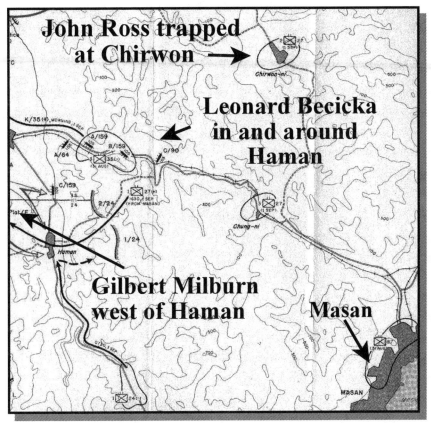

(Map inset courtesy Center of Military History)

Becicka grew up in northern Minnesota, where he attended schools in Goodland, Grand Rapids, and Warba.

"We were raised during the Great Depression," he said, "and living conditions were very difficult. There were ten children in our family. Six sisters and four brothers. I was the second youngest, and I can remember there were very definitely hardship conditions. They'd go deer hunting and use a lot of venison to survive the winter. And there was a lot of fishing up in Minnesota, including ice-fishing in the winter time."

When he was a teenager, Becicka worked on a dairy farm and later at a grocery store. "Working at the dairy farm required awakening at 4:00 a.m. and working until 8:00 p.m., seven days a week, for $30 a month," he said.

He joined the Army three days after his 18th birthday in 1940. "I had not thought too much about it," he said, "but I had three friends – including two brothers, Johnny and Arvid Carlson – who were also joining. We talked, and we joined together. My brother drove us to the recruiting station in Grand Rapids. We caught a train to Duluth and then to Minneapolis, and that's where we were assigned to the 3rd Infantry Regiment.

"The 3rd Infantry Regiment (The Old Guard) is the oldest active infantry regiment in the U.S. Army," he said. "It was created in 1784 to protect our western boundaries. It's older than the Constitution. The regiment represents the Nation to the World as the premier ceremonial unit at the Tomb of the Unknown Soldier and burial ceremonies at Arlington National Cemetery."

About a year after he enlisted, Becicka was promoted to sergeant and was selected to attend Officer Candidate School (OCS) at Ft. Benning, Georgia. He was commissioned as a second lieutenant in March 1943.

Becicka shipped out in May 1944. "We were in a huge convoy when we crossed the Atlantic. I don't know just how many ships, but it was as far as the eye could see – 20 or 30 ships of troops and supplies. While en route, our convoy came under attack, and we could hear the explosions of depth charges that were used to destroy enemy submarines."

Becicka landed on Utah Beach in June 1944 and was assigned to XII Corps, the "spearhead" of General George Patton's Third Army. They spent the next year fighting across Europe and, in May 1945, they reached Czechoslovakia, the homeland of Becicka's father, a Bohemian who emigrated to Minnesota at a young age.

"We were getting ready to establish there," he said, "when a plane flew over and said we were in Russian territory. We had to pull back to Regensberg, Germany, where I stayed until November 1945."

It was during this time that Becicka received a silver star for rescuing trapped civilians from a mine field in France.

After Becicka's discharge, he got a degree from the University of Minnesota, but in 1947, he elected to go back into the Army as a military policeman. He told his young family he would stay in only if he could get a regular army commission, because reservists were vulnerable to cutbacks.

"I went on a competitive tour for two years, and I was approved for a regular army commission. As part of the commission, I had to serve at least one year with a combat unit. That's why I was sent to Okinawa and assigned to the 29th Infantry Regiment. And you know what happened from there," he said, referring to the carnage in late July 1950.

"I was on the range on Okinawa, and we were doing the annual rifle firing for the company. I was the company commander of A Company, and a little plane flew over and dropped us a message. It said *Return to Camp Napungia*. So we closed down the range and promptly returned to camp. We went into a meeting and were told we had a week-to-ten days to get boarded for shipment to Korea.

"At that time, I think I had 90 men and three officers in the company. The strength of the company should have been 212 men and six officers, and within a week's time, they filled us up. They pulled people from everywhere – cooks, mechanics and shipments from the United States. We got aboard this vessel called the *Taka Sagamaru* and sailed to Korea. During that week, we had about two to three hours of sleep each day.

"We were supposed to go to Japan and do some training. Ordinarily, before units go into battle, you'll have squad training, platoon training, company training, battalion, and regimental training. Then you finally get into a divisional type of training, too, demonstrating what would actually be encountered in combat.

"Well, we had people who had never fired their assigned weapons. They didn't know how to fire a recoilless rifle. We didn't know who was capable of doing what, because half of our people were newly assigned to the company. And this was true of the battalion, as well. Men practiced firing weapons off the fantail of the *Taka Sagamaru,* en route to Korea, to give you an idea of how ill-trained and unprepared we were," said Becicka. "Instead of going to Japan for training, we sailed right into Pusan. They put us on a train directly to the front line.

"As I indicated, I was a company commander, and I didn't know my men. Within 24 hours, we were in contact with the enemy. When the North Koreans attacked, we were facing whole battalions and regiments. We were just completely out-manned.

"Unfortunately, as a result of all this, we lost a tremendous number of good men. That was the sorrowful part of it all, and we should never do that again. It was only because of our very vigilant and competent battalion commander, Lieutenant Colonel Wesley Wilson and his Intelligence Officer, Captain Sam Holliday, that our company survived. We fought in the Pusan Perimeter from July until September, and we were nearly pushed into the sea. We were just hanging very tenaciously to a very small enclave of territory surrounding Pusan."

When asked to compare Korea to his experiences in WWII and later in Vietnam, Becicka answered, "The Korean War was the most disastrous, disheartening and physically demanding of them all. In previous wars, there was time to recruit, train, and equip forces for

Leonard Becicka in Korea March 1951
(Courtesy Becicka)

combat. In Korea, we suffered terrible unforgivable losses. Of approximately 1500 men of the two Battalions of the 29th Infantry Regiment that came from Okinawa, some 500 to 600 men were casualties within two weeks.

"The North Korean Army we confronted was highly trained and equipped for combat, and we were not. Furthermore, we did not understand the geography and climate of Korea. The terrain is mountainous, and the climate is hot in the summer, and bitterly cold winters come off the Manchurian waste.

"The Korean peninsula is nearly 600 miles long, which creates logistical and operational support problems. A highly mobile mechanized force was rendered inoperable because of the mountainous terrain and roads that were mostly footpaths.

"They would attack all night, and the following day we would evacuate our wounded and resupply our ammunition and get ready for the next night. That was our schedule for nearly two weeks on the Pusan perimeter. It was terrible."

By September, the 1st Battalion of the 29th RCT had been reduced to paper status. The surviving members became the 35th Regiment's 3rd Battalion, with Becicka now commanding Item Company.

He notes the North Koreans captured more than just acreage when they broke through the lines the night of August 31.

"The North Koreans were using *our* weapons and *our* ammunition to secure their line, and we lost some good men trying to retake those front lines."

The **First Bronze Oak Leaf Cluster to The Silver Star** *is awarded to Captain* **Leonard Becicka**, *Infantry, Company I, 35th Regiment, 25th Infantry Division, [then Company A, 29th Regiment], U.S. Army. Near Oryong, Korea, on 8 September 1950, Captain Becicka's company was mounting a fierce determined assault on enemy positions. Although exposed to a withering concentration of small arms and automatic weapons fire, he calmly supervised effective counterfire. When the enemy attempted a flanking attack, he crawled and ran from man to man, skillfully maneuvered them to meet the hostile threat, delivered devastating fire that inflicted heavy casualties and routed the enemy and secured the position without losses among his men . . .*

The **Silver Star** *is awarded to Captain* **Leonard Becicka**, *Infantry, Company I, 35th Regiment, 25th Infantry Division, U.S. Army. On 14*

September 1950, Captain Becicka led his company in an assault on a key terrain feature near Ungjon, Korea. Although the only route of approach was a steep, open slope and along a barren ridge, he moved out in the face of heavy hostile machine guns and small arms fire to direct the attack. Inspiring his men to great effort and zeal by his personal display of courage and determination, he enabled his unit to seize their objective despite the enemy advantages of numbers and position . . .

*The **First Bronze Oak Leaf Cluster to the Bronze Star with Letter V Device** is awarded to Captain **Leonard Becicka**, Military Police Corps, Company I, 35th Regiment, 25th Infantry Division, U.S. Army. On 17 and 18 September 1950, Captain Becicka led his company in an assault on a barren mountain near Haman, Korea. Although the well-entrenched enemy delivered deadly fire on the tortuous route of advance, he moved the company forward in a series of assaults which culminated in seizure of the key terrain . . .*

Sam Holliday, the intelligence officer of Becicka's battalion, described the Minnesota officer as a "calm, dedicated professional who was highly trusted and respected by not only the men in his company, but anyone who had spent any time with him."[151]

Becicka, himself, was asked the difficult question, *What was it that made you a good leader?* He gave an honest, straightforward answer that might well instruct any prospective combat leader.

"I did all that it was possible to do to care for the men under my command. To survive the hardships, constant danger and suffering in combat, men needed to know and feel that they are being cared for and protected to the maximum extent circumstances allow. Being in a foxhole, especially during the nighttime, is a very lonely and frightening experience – not knowing where or when the enemy will strike. The North Koreans invariably attacked at night.

"Men need to have weapons, ammunition, food and clothing. I remember when we were advancing rapidly, while attacking the North Korean forces, contact with Battalion Headquarters was lost. We were using old World War II radios that were unreliable. Having received no food, the men were hungry. During the nighttime I sent some men to a village which was at the base of a mountain we had occupied for the night. The mission of the men was to have the village people prepare some food for us. The men returned with some chicken and rice. Being

---

[151]Holliday, Sam. *Up and Down.* Unpublished memoir shared with author.

hungry, everyone seemed to enjoy the food – although we did not know until a day later about the unrefined conditions under which the food was prepared.

"Men need to feel secure and confident that under life threatening conditions, the most dangerous any can endure, that if treatment for an injury was needed, someone would be there to assist them. These are all elements of leadership I endeavored to provide, namely always protecting and caring for the men assigned to my command."

George M. Wright

"You just keep chopping them down and down like corn stalks, and all the time there are more of them to bob up behind the fallen, while your guns are getting hotter and hotter," George Wright told a reporter on July 30. "Whole lines waver and fall, and still others push behind them, so you have to allow others to do the mowing-down while you grab fresh ammunition and start again."

War correspondent Charles Rosecrans, Jr., expanded on what Wright referred to as *cornstalkers*, writing:

American doughboys are learning with dread a new phrase – "insan inhae." Translated from Korean it means "human sea wall." The words are used in terror by fleeing South Korean refugees referring to thousands of Korean kids snatched up by advancing Communists and forced into the front ranks. They are the ones in forefronts of massive North Korean frontal assaults. They are the "insan inhae."

George Wright grew up in Mankato, Minnesota, where he went to Loyola High School. He had lost his father when just a toddler, with his younger brother Ron explaining, "Our father died in 1930, thereabouts, from cancer. I wasn't born yet.[152]

"George was good at school," Ron said. "He liked sports, played football and basketball, kind of an all-around guy. He was average height, a well-built kid for his age. He used to box in Golden Gloves.

"He was hoping to go to college on the G.I. Bill, and if you went in the military, you'd get that. I think that's what his plan was. He went in and he went through Officer Candidate School. After he graduated, they

---

[152]Author interview January 29, 2014.

asked him, 'Do you want to go to Germany or Japan?' Unluckily, he said Japan. When the war started, he was with the second division to go to Korea."

Wright was with the 65th Combat Engineers, 25th Division, when he was deployed to Korea. Captain Robert L. Strouse[153] later wrote about the action in which the Mankato man was killed west of Haman on September 14:

> During the Naktong perimeter days, the 65th Engineer Combat Battalion was split among three infantry regiments. Each regiment operated as a separate combat team. Occasionally they used the engineers as infantry – not only in defensive operations, but also in limited objective attacks undertaken as part of the general defense.
>
> Near Chungam-ni, Company E, 35th Infantry, failed to take a hilltop after three successive attacks. The crest was an isolated strong point in the enemy line, and was strongly defended. On 14 September 1950, the regimental commander ordered Company B, 65th Engineer Battalion, to make a supported attack and capture the objective. Only two hours were given the company to prepare for this operation.
>
> In addition to weapons organic to a combat engineer company, Company B's personnel had (two) .30 caliber heavy machine guns and (three) 60-mm mortars. These were a special issue to the engineers in view of their frequent commitment as infantry. Company B did not use its mortars but relied on the infantry for this supporting fire.
>
> The attack lasted only thirty minutes, and the objective was taken. The value of the men can be seen in 2 awards of the Distinguished Service Cross (one posthumous), 3 of the Silver Star, and 10 of the Bronze Star. Casualties were heavy, the company suffering 14 killed and 21 wounded, including an officer killed and another wounded. The 3d Platoon suffered particularly, having its platoon sergeant wounded, 2 squad leaders killed and another wounded, and 3 assistant squad leaders wounded.

---

[153] Strouse, Robert L., Captain 65th Engineer Combat Battalion. "Secondary Mission," *Combat Support in Korea*. Washington DC: CMH Publication 22-1, Facsimile Reprint, 1987, 1990: p 205.

The loss of leaders was particularly felt when the company returned to its primary engineer role. It meant a complete reorganization and training of NCO specialists. The 3d Platoon had only 13 men left after the attack, and could not carry out a platoon task until it received replacements five or six weeks later.

The posthumous Distinguished Service Cross mentioned by Strouse went to officer from Mankato.

(Courtesy Wright family)

*The **Distinguished Service Cross** is (**Posthumously**) awarded to First Lieutenant **George M. Wright**, (Corps of Engineers), U.S. Army, for extraordinary heroism in connection with military operations against an armed enemy of the United Nations while serving as a Platoon Leader with Company B, 65th Engineer Combat Battalion, 25th Infantry Division. First Lieutenant Wright distinguished himself by extraordinary heroism in action against enemy aggressor forces at Taeson-Myon, Korea, on 14 September 1950. Lieutenant Wright was leading his platoon in an attack against a strongly defended enemy position. One platoon had already lost all its noncommissioned officers and officers, either killed or wounded, and Lieutenant Wright assumed leadership over the group and placed them in his platoon. Although seriously wounded in the leg, he continued to lead the men forward in the face of heavy enemy fire, destroying a machine gun position with a grenade and shouting words of encouragement to the men under his control. By his courage and devotion to duty, he so inspired his men that they continued and captured the final objective from the enemy after he himself had been mortally wounded while trying to throw another grenade.*

Chapter 32

MARTIN AND ANDERSON ESCAPE

"We made some soup out of snails. Some of the men caught cats and ate them. I chased a cat for 15 minutes but couldn't catch it." Joe Mistretta, prisoner with Martin and Anderson

NORTH DAKOTA's Pat Martin and his fellow POW, Carl "Andy" Anderson, from Iowa, had now ended up in the main body of prisoners that included Jim Yeager and others captured at Hadong.

But Anderson had a shrapnel wound in his leg, and Martin had malaria, so they were luckily left behind and thus escaped the Sunchon Tunnel Massacre that was to come.

"Man, I was sick," Martin told interviewer Elmer Lian. "I had such a fever my lips were cracked. I just felt awful.

"Well, Andy was a tanker. The Koreans suspected he was a tanker, but they couldn't prove it. Andy and Joe Mistretta were both tankers, they were with about the first three tankers we got in Korea. Then our own bombers knocked out the bridge, they couldn't get the tanks across, and we lost them. They were right there at Chinju at the same time [I was captured].

"Andy was looking at these tanks. They kept taking him out there trying to get him to make them work. What Anderson did, each tank had a solenoid, and they called it the brains of the tank. Like a rifle, if you throw the components away, it won't work. Well, Andy threw the solenoid away. He broke it, and nothing works.

"[The North Koreans] were out there trying to figure out how to make him make these tanks work, and of course he played dumb. While he was out there, he found a G-string in one of these tanks – the piano wire with the handles on the ends? He found one and stuck it in his pocket. Well, I never knew he had it, until this one day Andy says,

'We're gonna leave tonight.'

"I said, 'What the hell are you talking about? If you're gonna go, Andy, you gotta go without me. I'll just hold you back,' I said. 'I can't go.'

"He said, 'You're going with me, you little shit.'

"We're up in the mountains, and our artillery is going over our head all day. You figure from the time you see the flash until you hear the explosion you count *one-thousand-one, one-thousand-two, one-thousand-three* — it'll tell you approximately how many yards you are from that weapon. Andy figured we were about eight miles [from friendly lines], so he says, 'Come on, we're gonna go for it.'

"I said, 'Andy, you gotta go without me.'

"There was one guard," Martin said, "and Andy took care of him [by killing him with that piano string]. He came and got me, and man, I was wiggly, I was so weak. Well, he pulled on me a little bit and got me started down the mountain. It wasn't long before I started to sweat, and it kind of broke the fever. I was weak, but at least that fever was gone.

"We rolled and tumbled and fell down the mountain and down these hills. It was darker than a bugger. It was maybe half an hour after the sun went down. Once we got to the bottom of the mountains . . . the rice paddies there were about two-and-a-half miles across and just like a checkerboard," said Martin.

"We got about a third of the way across when the Koreans spotted us. They opened up on us, but we were out far enough so them burp guns weren't really effective. We went from rice paddy to rice paddy, we'd wait around, and then get up and run like hell again.

"Once we got across the paddies, we found there must have been a hell of a battle there the day before, because there was all kinds of G.I. trucks and tanks and men laying all over. Where Andy had been hit with that shrapnel was bleeding pretty good, so we took some of the first-aid stuff off some of the dead G.I.s and patched his leg up a little bit. Then we spent the night there in back of a six-by-six, hoping nobody would find us.

"Early the next morning, a liaison plane woke us up," said Martin. "He was coming from the direction we were going, so just for curiosity, we grabbed one of the panels off the six-by-six that was knocked out, and we carried it between us. The guy came right over us and flapped his wings and kept right on going. We thought we must be doing the right thing.

"We stayed right on the road, and thank God we did, because

everything on both sides of the road was mined to the hilt. That's the first thing they asked us when we got back, 'How'd you come?' We said, 'Right down the road.' He says, 'Thank God. You'd have never made it.'

"Coming down this road, we ran into a barbed wire entanglement probably 6 feet high. This was for infiltrators or anybody that was coming. They usually hang mines on these wires, and if you go pulling on those, they'd blow up. Andy's leg was giving him trouble, so I told him, 'Andy I'll go over and look it over.' I couldn't see anything, and I looked up and here's a damned rifle. It was a BAR pointed right at us. 'Oh my God, Andy, we're caught again.'

(Courtesy Martin family)

"Well, here comes a helmet up from behind a rock, and I say, 'Don't shoot, we're Americans.' He says, 'What in the hell are you doing out here?' Thank God he wasn't trigger-happy. So we got Andy through the wire. They took us by jeep to an airplane and flew us to Taegu."

Martin and Anderson were in for a surprise when they arrived. "They took us up to General Walker's office, and General Walker says, 'Andy, you S.O.B., what the hell are you doing here?' Because we looked pretty bad – beards and dirtier than hell. But he knew him! And the colonel who picked us up knew him, too.

"Here they were all in the horse cavalry way back. General Walker was the captain, and the colonel was his lieutenant. It was like old-home-week for them. We got treated well. Really well," said Martin.

"General Walker had his maps, and he wanted to know what we'd seen along the road. Well, there was no heavy equipment, it was just manpower, that's all [the North Koreans] had. Because if they got anything out there that moved, we had air force superiority, and we'd blow them off the map. Where they made that big invasion [at Inchon] was right in the area we came out of.

"Old Bulldog Walker, he took Andy and I in there, and he swore us to secrecy. He said, 'What I'm telling you is top secret.' He wouldn't even let news reporters get close to us. He says, 'We're gonna make an invasion, and that's why I gotta know what you've seen.' He told us the day and the time and everything. 'Don't let it get out,' he said. And the way he pointed a finger at you, you didn't ever want to try! He was quite a guy, he really was."[154]

The invasion to which General Walker alluded was to take place at Inchon, roughly 20 miles from Seoul. Historian T. R. Fehrenbach described it well:

> The X U.S. Army Corps, 70,000 men, was at sea. It had been formed from scratch, operating against time, manpower, and every known logistic difficulty, and its very conception embodied the best of American military capability. No other nation in the world had the means and knowledge to put such a force together in so short a time. No other nation would have attempted what MacArthur had planned from the first. Riding into rough seas from a near typhoon off Kyushu, the convoy steamed toward the most brilliant stroke of the Korean War.[155]

---

[154] Martin and Anderson escaped from the POW group that was later massacred at the Sunchon Tunnel. Their friend Joe Mistretta escaped several times but was always recaptured and beaten. Twenty of the 47 men in his group died in the Seoul to Pyongyang death march.

[155] Fehrenbach. *This Kind of War*. P 164.

Part III

✪

THE
TURNABOUT

Chapter 33

FLYING FISH AND SITTING DUCKS

"The landing at Inchon, in a large part, is the story of six brave little ships and a wonderful blunder." Relman Morin, war correspondent

CALLING UPON SOME of his greatest accomplishments in WWII, General Douglas MacArthur had spent a great deal of time and effort planning an amphibious assault to happen behind enemy lines. After much deliberating, he chose a spot that almost every other commander – of any branch – would have rejected: the seaport at Inchon, halfway up Korea's west coast.

The operational plan called for Marines and Army units who – once they were ashore – were to move across the waist of the peninsula to cut off the supply and escape routes of the North Korean troops in the south, essentially trapping them in a giant vice.

It didn't quite play out this way, because MacArthur also wanted to exploit the propaganda potential of regaining Seoul, southeast of Inchon. In the beginning, others at the table appear to have been unaware of the general's political aim.

Many believed Inchon was an unwise choice for carrying out *Operation Chromite*. Amphibious assaults were complex and difficult. Conditions had to be just right, and the harbor at Inchon was subject to some of the widest tide fluctuations in the entire region. In fact, its 30-foot tides turned the harbor from a sea into vast mud flats between sunup and sundown.

MacArthur felt these very tides would lead the enemy to believe Inchon was relatively safe from invasion, providing the Americans with the element of surprise. Despite numerous objections from participating elements, the choice of Inchon was not open for discussion.

This U. S. Navy map depicts Flying Fish Channel when the tide was out.

For optimum conditions, the landing would take place September 15, the high water mark for the month. If the plan didn't come together by then, the operation would have to be postponed one month.

The plan called for the 5th Marines to be pulled out of the Pusan Perimeter, where they were presently heavily engaged. General Walker balked and was finally promised the 17th Infantry Regiment, a fresh unit that would otherwise have participated in the Inchon landing. At midnight on September 5, the 23rd Infantry Regiment relieved the 5th Marines, who walked eight miles to a spot from which they could be transported another 50 miles to Pusan. From there, they reorganized, received replacements, and prepared to move by sea to Inchon.

The landing at Inchon is often spoken of as a complete surprise to the enemy, but China's Mao Tse-tung knew something was afoot. Mao and Chou-en-lai had been studying MacArthur, and knowing the American general's specialty was amphibious assaults, they pinpointed the most likely place, date, and time MacArthur would carry out his plan.

Despite Mao's warning, however, Kim Il Sung was so certain of victory at Pusan that he failed to divert sufficient troops and resources to protect Inchon.

Wolmi-do Island

Before troops could take Inchon, they first had to secure a scenic tourist destination called Wolmi-do – translation *Moon Tip Island*. This island stood like a 350-foot pyramid in front of Inchon with a stone causeway connecting it to Inchon's harbor. Because the island was heavily wooded, it was difficult to discern the type and quantity of enemy fortifications embedded on its slopes.

Air reconnaissance had spotted a cluster of bunkers and trenches on the seaward side of the island, where the first Marines were slated to go ashore. Code named GREEN Beach, a closer look found it to be dotted with additional bunkers and gun emplacements connected by a trench system.

These beach positions would be relatively easy pickings for air and naval crews who were preparing to bomb the island to kingdom come. But it was rightly assumed the island probably had additional big guns beyond the beach, up in the forested areas, and those fortifications needed to be pinpointed. Someone was going to have to force the enemy to reveal their positions.

Harvey Headland & The Sitting Ducks

Six "expendable" destroyers were selected to effectively surround Wolmi-do with the intention of drawing fire. It would be a dangerous job, as they would have to carry out their mission by navigating up Flying Fish Channel alongside the island.

The current in this channel was exceptionally swift, and space was limited. Because it had to be navigated at high tide, the destroyers would have to pull in close to the island in broad daylight. The flagship for the operation was the *USS Mansfield*, followed by the *DeHaven, Lyman K. Swenson, Collett,* and *Henderson.*

The sixth destroyer was the *Gurke*, named for Private First Class Henry Gurke, from Neche, North Dakota. (Gurke was posthumously awarded the Medal of Honor in WWII for sacrificing his life so a Browning Automatic Rifleman beside him could continue to deliver deadly fire on Bougainville, Solomon Islands.)

Together, these six ships became known as the *Sitting Ducks*. As commander of the *Mansfield* and skipper in charge of the operation, Edwin "Harvey" Headland became known by his men as "Papa Duck."

Headland spent his early childhood in Litchville, North Dakota, but after his father lost his banking business in the Great Depression, the family moved to Minot, where Harvey graduated from high school.

With five siblings and the family fallen on hard times, Harvey knew his chances of getting a college education were slim, so he successfully sought a military appointment and was assigned to Annapolis Naval Academy from Fargo.

Slim, fine-featured and classically handsome, Headland didn't exactly sail through his class work but, according to his senior yearbook,[156] he was well liked, with his graduation entry reading:

> From a land where the sea is only a legend comes this aspirant to Annapolis and the Navy. Harvey has experienced several tussles with the Academic Departments, but the end of each term has found him among those present . . . Socially, Harvey is an asset at any gathering, be it a bull session, a dance, a sailing party, or a rumble seat, for he is not only good natured, friendly

---

[156]*Lucky Bag Yearbook.* U.S. Naval Academy, Annapolis, MD. 1935: P 233.

and tactful, but is a true 'bon vivant' of the naval school.

Headland proved himself a very capable seaman, and in WWII he was assigned as skipper of the *USS Pope,* part of the Atlantic Fleet Anti-Submarine Task Group. He received two Legions of Merit with Combat "V" for his leadership. The first was for:

. . . conducting offensive action against an enemy submarine on 9 April 1944. The U.S.S. POPE, screening an aircraft carrier of an Atlantic Fleet anti-submarine task group, made underwater sound contact on an enemy submarine which was in a favorable position to attack the carrier. Taking prompt offensive action, Lieutenant Commander Headland immediately attacked and forced the enemy to break off his projected attack and to attempt escape. Despite the evasive maneuvers of the U-Boat and the difficulties of maintaining contact through the attacking ship's wake and depth charge explosions, the POPE held continuous contact for three and one-half hours and delivered a total of eight additional depth charge attacks.

**Headland at Annapolis in 1935.
(Lucky Bag Yearbook)**

As a result of the skill and persistence of the entire anti-submarine organization of the POPE, the enemy submarine was badly damaged and forced to surface, where it was destroyed by the combined gunfire of the assembled surface ships and aircraft.

Headland's second citation reads, in part:

. . . for offensive action against the enemy on 19 April 1945. The group displayed outstanding teamwork and coordination in carrying out an effective and persistent search that finally located the enemy. Under his continued supervision, ships of the group participated in a series of coordinated attacks which resulted in the destruction of the submarine as

evidenced by a large quantity of oil and debris brought to the surface by
depth charge attack.

Ducks Into Action

It was 7:00 a.m., and the weather was good enough for Headland's
Sitting Ducks to spot a string of mines floating in the water. They fired
at these until they exploded and then focused on the task at hand.
Relman Morin, reporting for *Pacific Stars & Stripes*, writes:[157]

> A destroyer's armor is three-eighths of an inch thick. Practically
> anything stronger than a slingshot will pierce it.
>   On the morning of September 13, "D-day minus two," the
> six brave little ships, moving in column, and slowly, sailed into
> the narrowing channel leading past Wolmi to Inchon.
>   One anchored off of the southern face of the island. Three
> passed through the neck of the channel to the other side. Two
> remained in the channel. None was more than a mile from the
> beaches and some were 1,000 yards – two-thirds of a mile.
>   They were "sitting ducks." That's what they were meant to
> be, juicy targets for concealed guns on the shore . . . The silence
> was like a blanket. . . . Suddenly there was a single white flash.
> Seconds later the muffled crack of the gun came back.

A message came in from Headland that an artillery battery was moving
on the island's east beach. Bystanders watched through binoculars and
held their breaths, but nothing was happening. Morin writes:

> Then the North Koreans made a fateful and wonderful blunder.
> Suddenly a necklace of gun flashes sparkled around the waist of
> the island. The flashes were reddish gold, and they came so fast
> that soon the entire slope was sparkling with pinpoints of fire.
>   The destroyers were quick to answer. Lightning flashes
> leaped from their guns. They hit back, shell for shell, firing
> faster and faster until the whole channel was a tunnel of
> rumbling thunder.
>   The pace increased. On Wolmi, still more gun positions

---

[157] Morin, Relman. "You Can Thank Six Brave Ships for Inchon Win." *Pacific Stars
& Stripes.* 17 Sept 1950.

opened up. The red necklace spread and widened. They were hitting destroyers now. They could hardly miss at that range.

Then a report came down to the bridge, and your blood ran cold. "It looks as though the 783 is dead in the water, Sir." Admiral Struble's answer was quiet, and the words were taut. "Make sure and then see what we have to do to get her out of there."

The big guns dueled for an hour before Headland's "six brave little ships" sailed back out to sea. Three of them had been hit, one seriously, and there were some casualties. But all six were able to move under their own power.

The Ducks repeated their mission against Wolmi-do the following day, allowing air and naval fire to further reduce the threat to the Marines who were to go ashore September 15. When it was over, Headland sent the following message to his ship's crew:

> The MANSFIELD has successfully led the entire invasion force into the INCHON-SEOUL area, after leading two bold raids into the very center of the dangerous enemy harbor on the 13th and 14th. Many treacherous enemy gun positions around the beaches and hill tops were knocked out by our guns. Two or three of our sister ships were hit with casualties to personnel and equipment. Our successful completion of this history-making operation without casualty is due to the maximum efforts of all departments of the ship, plus the favor of Lady Luck. To all hands a VERY WELL DONE and sincere congratulations for your great contribution to the invasion of the INCHON-SEOUL area of Korea. Keep up the good work against the Red enemy who are still active against us until peace is restored on our terms.

*The President of the United States of America takes pleasure in presenting the **Silver Star** to Commander **Edwin Harvey Headland**, United States Navy, for conspicuous gallantry and intrepidity in action in the line of his profession as Commanding Officer of the USS MANSFIELD (DD-728), during the assault on Inchon, Korea, 13-15 September 1950. He navigated his ship through an enemy mine field, engaged enemy shore batteries at close range, and contributed greatly to the successful landings at Inchon.*

Chapter 34

THE INCHON LANDING

"Taplett was to continue the operation until he had sustained eighty-seven percent casualties. Eighty-seven percent was suicide!" John Toland, *In Mortal Combat*

THE TROOPS who were selected to participate in the landing at Inchon were part of *Joint Task Force Seven* (JTF-7), a massive venture as explained by one Marine historian:

> Except for a few gunnery ships held back to protect the flanks of the Pusan Perimeter, JTF-7 – in its other guise, the *Seventh Fleet* – included all the combatant ships in the Far East. Among them were three fast carriers, two escort carriers, and a British light carrier. In the final count, the force numbered some 230 ships, including 34 Japanese vessels, mostly ex-U.S. Navy LSTs (landing ships, tank) with Japanese crews. The French contributed one tropical frigate, *La Grandiere*, which arrived at Sasebo (Japan) with a five-month supply of wine and a pin-up picture of Esther Williams, but no coding machine.[158]

Down on the south coast, the 5th Marines boarded their sailing vessels at about the same time Harvey Headland's *Sitting Ducks* were carrying out their mission in Flying Fish Channel.

Two typhoons had interfered with the operation thus far, but skies were now clearing. After enormous efforts, the 1st and 5th Marine

---

[158]Simmons, Edwin H. "Over the Sea Wall: U.S. Marines at Inchon." *Marines in the Korean War*. USMC: 2007. P 96-97.

Regiments, as well as two regiments of the Army's 7th Infantry Division, were converging off the coast near Inchon on the morning of September 15, soon to be joined by South Korean troops, crucial support units and the Marines' 7th Regiment.

With the primary elements of the fleet in place, the operation was a go, and a South Dakotan prepared to lead the entire ground offensive.

Robert Taplett

One of the Marines' major players in Korea had arrived on the battlefield in early August. He was Lieutenant Colonel Robert "Tapp" Taplett, age 32, and he had since been leading his men through heavy fighting along the Naktong Perimeter.

Taplett was the son of a former semi-pro baseball player who ran a pool hall in Tyndall, South Dakota. Born of French and Czech ancestry, he was tall, dark and handsome, with many comparing him to actor Gregory Peck. His wife disagreed, saying, "I always said he was a cross between Tyrone Power and Robert Taylor."[159]

While attending the University of South Dakota, Vermillion, Taplett completed the university's Army ROTC program and became a commissioned officer. With war looming, the Marines were looking for a few good men, and they discovered Taplett, who had graduated with honors. They convinced him to resign his Army commission and join them, instead.

In early December 1941, Taplett was serving as a Marine gunnery officer aboard the *USS Salt Lake City*, a cruiser escorting the carrier *USS Enterprise* on a mission to deliver aircraft to key islands in the South Pacific. Heading back, they were just six hours out from Pearl Harbor when the Japanese attacked on December 7.

Tapplett's son Bob says they knew war with Japan was imminent. "I have his diary, and they were told to *Look out. We're expecting an attack. We don't know when it will come, or where it will come, but we're on a war footing.*"

After docking in Pearl Harbor the day following the attack, the *Salt Lake City* headed off in pursuit of the Japanese fleet. They stayed in the

---

[159] Sources this section include Taplett's obituary, written by Joe Holley, *The Washington Post,* 8 Jan 2005; interview with Robert Taplett's son, Bob Taplett; and John Toland's *In Mortal Combat.* Toland's accounts are based on direct interviews with Taplett and are thus considered a reliable representation of Taplett's movements and actions.

fight for the three years, participating in battles in the Coral Sea, Aleutian Islands and Guam.

Bob says his father would have preferred to get off the ship and into the infantry. "He asked for a reassignment for Iwo Jima, to be in on the landings. That's what Marines did. They were fighters. If you wanted to be a Marine and progress as a Marine, you're not going to do it by firing guns on a naval vessel. You had to get into battle. You had to lead. But they turned him down, so to my knowledge he never got into combat as an infantry officer in the Second World War."

In Korea, Taplett got as much combat as he could ever have hoped for. As commander of the 5th Marines' 3rd Battalion, he was known as a no-nonsense,

Robert Taplett in Korea. The enemy called Marines "yellow legs" because of their distinctive leggings. (USMC)

outspoken officer with zero tolerance for incompetence. His battalion's surgeon recalled Taplett "seemed hard as nails" and had a commanding presence, saying, "What an enlistment poster he'd have made."

For his performance in Korea, Taplett (along with Colonel Richard Stephens) became one of South Dakota's most decorated infantrymen. It began with his leadership in the months prior to the Inchon landing.

*The **Legion of Merit (Army Award)** is awarded to Lieutenant Colonel **Robert Donald Taplett**, United States Marine Corps, for exceptionally meritorious conduct in the performance of outstanding services to the Government of the United States as Commanding Officer of the Third Battalion, Fifth Marines, FIRST Marine Division (Reinforced), in action against enemy aggressor forces in Korea during the period 7 July to 12 September 1950, in Korea.*

The Landing Commences

Early the morning of September 15, Taplett's men went ashore on GREEN Beach, a popular swimming area on the west side of Wolmi-do Island. His men moved quickly and decisively, and the commander considered it a great stroke of luck that enemy resistance was light, because his orders had been to *discontinue his assault only if he reached 87% casualties*. He likely realized he had fighter bombers, naval gunners and the *Sitting Ducks* to thank when his casualties totaled 17 wounded.

By noon, his men had secured the island, for which he was again decorated.

*The **Silver Star** (Army Award) is awarded to Lieutenant Colonel **Robert Donald Taplett**, U. S. Marine Corps, for gallantry in action while Commanding Third Battalion, Fifth Marines, FIRST Marine Division (Reinforced.), United Nations Command. Lieutenant Colonel Taplett distinguished himself by conspicuous gallantry in action in the amphibious landing resulting in the capture of Wolmi-Do, Korea, on 15 September 1950 in the Inchon-Seoul operation. His actions contributed materially to the success of this operation and were in keeping with the highest traditions of the United States Military Services.*

Taplett would soon demonstrate he had barely scratched the surface of his leadership capabilities.

Edward Boucher

As a member of Battery A, 50th Anti-Aircraft Artillery Battalion, Ed Boucher was one of the first Army men to go into action at Inchon, saying, "They had us tank drivers drive the amphibious ducks unloading the ships."

Boucher grew up on a rented farm near Elk Point, South Dakota, and spent his adult life in Estherville, Iowa. "My dad was crippled when I was five years old," he said, "so me and my mother farmed with horses. She would rather drive a team of horses than do dishes. She was from a big family, and some of the girls did the housework, but she'd rather drive a team of mules.

"Dad was the cook. He could bake the best bread you ever seen, twice a week, without a recipe.

"There were five of us kids, and I never told my dad I was bored, I can tell you that. We played hard, and we worked hard. We made our own toys. Moved bails of hay and made tunnels out of them – 90-

pound bales us kids were moving around, making tunnels through them. I wouldn't trade my childhood for any kid today.

"But I missed 75 days a year in 7ᵗʰ and 8ᵗʰ grade, so I didn't even get out of the 8ᵗʰ grade. It was just work, work, work. And the harder we worked, the poorer we got. So I enlisted in the army. I sent $50 a month home, every month. All told in Korea, I made $1,490. I spent the $90 and sent the rest home, and when I got home, the money was all gone. When I went home on furlough, I went to work at a packing house. A guy in my tank crew said I was the most ambitious sonofabitch he'd ever seen in his life."[160]

Boucher was already a crack shot when he enlisted in 1949. He had also been driving since his feet could reach the pedals, and the Army decided he was a good candidate for operating tanks and armored half-tracks. When the war broke out, he was stationed at Fort Bliss, Texas, and his unit immediately prepared to deploy.

"Our half-tracks was from the Second World War. They were quad-50s, 650 rounds a minute," he said. "We had twin-40s on the tank. We shot the enemy point-blank with them. We had two barrels, and each barrel fired 120 rounds a minute. When a round went into a piece of

M-26 Pershing tanks, new to the Marines, were used during Robert Taplett's seizure of Wolmi-do Island on September 15. (USMC)

---

[160]Author interview, November 2011. (The account of Bouchers heroic rescue of wounded Marines at the Chosin Reservoir may be found in Volume II of this series.)

toilet paper, it would explode. So anytime you hit a guy, it looked like you hit a chicken with a 12-gauge shotgun."

Boucher's unit also got new tanks. "I drove the lead tank," he said. "It was brand-spanking new, and there were only two of us allowed to drive it off the post. We had rubber on them – it's a light tank. We'd go down and get two tanks and bring them up. Go down and get two more tanks and bring them up. We were shipped over to Korea with those tanks. We had to go out and fire ten rounds to get the feel of the gun. Everybody learned.

"We went to Japan, and they gave us some of the stiffest training in the world, getting ready for combat in the Inchon Invasion. They had taken all the weapons off the LSTs and gave them to the Japanese. So to make the Inchon invasion, the Japanese had to float us in. They took our anti-aircraft weapons, our tanks, and half-tracks and put them on the top deck for air support if they needed it. So when we made the Inchon landing, my tank was still aboard ship. They didn't get it off yet.

"The 50th AAA was with the 7th Division, but we was a bastard outfit. We didn't belong to nobody. We had a lot of fire power, so we went with whoever needed us, and most of the time A Battery was with the Marines. I went over the side on one of them rope nets and went in with the first wave of Marines. That was our first combat. Inchon. Once we landed, we never had a (medical) corpsman. We never even seen the battery commander. We were scattered all over hell."

Frank Muetzel & Baldomero Lopez

Minnesotan Frank Muetzel had now recovered from the multiple wounds he sustained on Obong-ni Ridge. But he hadn't yet been able to replace his tattered clothing.

The Marines had always been fond of "borrowing" from the Army, and Muetzel wasn't any different. When he had a brief moment off the line, he paid a visit to an Army quartermaster, where a small group of other Marines was already being turned away by the officer in charge.

Muetzel's steel helmet was pocked from the shrapnel that knocked him unconscious. The elbows of his jacket were worn through, and his knees showed through the holes in his pants. The soles of his boots were worn through, the heels were gone, and a bullet had drilled two holes through the toe on his right boot.

He decided he would not be denied, but the major told him all boots were being held for an airborne unit on its way to Korea.

Muetzel was only a lieutenant, but he followed the major inside. In his arms he cradled a submachine gun, and on his hip he wore his .45 pistol. He faced the "clean, neatly dressed" officer and told him he was a platoon leader, he was just off the line, and he was going right back into combat again. His future didn't look bright, *and he wanted new boots.*

The major looked him over and calmly retrieved a new pair of jump boots for the junior officer. Muetzel said it was the only time he ever talked back to a superior, but by that point, he had nothing to lose.

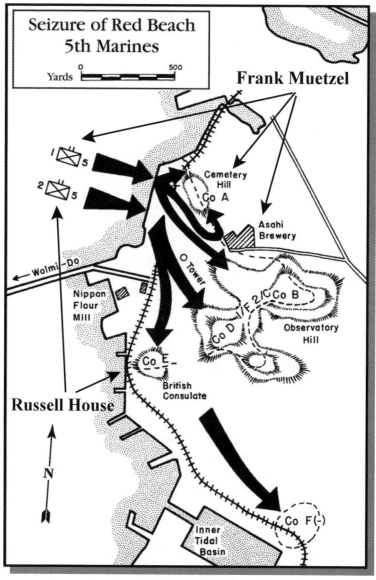

(Courtesy USMC)

After Robert Taplett's Battalion secured Wolmi-do, the next waves of Marines prepared to move in with the next high tide late that afternoon. The 1st and 2nd Battalions of 5th Marines would go ashore on RED Beach, just north of Wolmi-do Island, and the newly arrived 1st Marines, under the leadership of General "Chesty" Puller, would hit BLUE Beach to the south.

When the Marines had first learned their upcoming mission was to carry out an amphibious landing, many of them paled. Bad things had happened earlier during such landings, and although operational plans had improved since then, many WWII veterans were deeply unsettled.

Muetzel figured that with all the newly arriving Marine units, chances were slim that his platoon would have to go in with the first wave. But he was very wrong, saying, "I almost stroked out" when briefed on the schedule of maneuver. Of the thousands and thousand of troops in this gigantic armada, the 5th Marines' 1st and 2nd Battalions would start landing on RED Beach simultaneously. In the 1st Battalion, Muetzel's Able Company would go first, and out of Able Company, Muetzel's 2nd Platoon would lead the way.

Visions of disaster danced in his men's eyes, and he recalled his platoon sergeant, a veteran of a botched landing at Tarawa, "really came unglued."

Their concern was shared by the commanders, including Colonel Harold Roise, who was simultaneously landing his 2nd Battalion on RED Beach:

> Two things scared me to death. One, we were not landing on a beach; we were landing against a seawall. Each [landing craft] had two ladders, which would be used to climb up and over the wall. This was risky . . . Two, the landing was scheduled for 5:30 p.m. This would give us only about two hours of daylight to clear the city and set up for the night.[161]

During the night of September 14, Muetzel and his men used carbon dioxide from a fire extinguisher to chill some beer they had smuggled aboard. They wrote their last letters home, and some attended a church service in the ship's mess hall.

Muetzel joined buddies in a stateroom, where a correspondent from

---

[161] Simmons, Edwin H. (BG, USMC Ret). "Over the Seawall: U.S. Marines at Inchon." *U.S. Marines in the Korean War*. History Division, USMC. 2007. P 103.

Life magazine joined them, and they taught him how to load and unload his pistol while also helping him polish off his fifth of bourbon.

When Muetzel had first learned about the war in Korea several months earlier, he and two other officers had immediately requested combat assignments. One of these was Muetzel's friend, Tom Johnston, who was killed at Obong-ni Ridge while carrying out an action for which he posthumously received a Distinguished Service Cross (it was Johnston's 2nd Platoon that Muetzel took over).

The other officer who requested the combat assignment was Baldomero "Punchy" Lopez, from Florida, now leading Able Company's 3rd Platoon. Lopez dropped by the stateroom that night to offer Muetzel a decent pair of pants. Since this supply item was still unavailable, Muetzel gratefully accepted. "Lopez had a beer with us," he said. "I'll always be glad he did."

First Wave Hits RED Beach

The following morning, the men were as tight as fiddle strings as they drew their allotments of ammunition and grenades. While they were forming into boat teams, word came over the ship's loudspeakers that South Dakota's Robert Taplett and his 3rd Battalion had secured Wolmi-do, and nobody was killed. Muetzel and his men exhaled, and their mood shifted from tense to guardedly excited.

At about 2:30 that afternoon, naval guns began a preparatory bombardment of RED Beach, and Marine air support swooped in so close that hot shell casings landed on men watching from ships.

Muetzel and his men boarded their landing crafts at about 3:00 p.m. In the first boat, he took a reinforced squad of riflemen and a medical corpsman. He placed another squad with a flamethrower and a rocket launcher in a boat to his right, and another squad brought up the rear.

It was now late in the afternoon, and the sky was dark with smoke from fires burning within Inchon. As they neared the shore, they could make out the high stone seawall. The enemy waited on the other side – the big question was how many, and where were they positioned?

As soon as they hit the beach, the second of ten waves was dispatched to follow. Muetzel and his men found a breach in the wall and on the far side they immediately confronted a machine gun crew who froze. They captured these men and quickly moved into the city to their first objective, the Asahi Brewery.

As they prepared to enter the building, they received bad news. Muetzel was to bring his men back to the beach, because the 3rd

Baldomero Lopez scales the seawall on RED Beach moments before his Medal of Honor action. Due to shortage of lightweight aluminum ladders, wooden ones had to be constructed. The high terrain feature in the distance is possibly Cemetery Hill. (Sgt W. W. Frank, USMC)

Platoon, which landed in the second wave, was in trouble. They had just lost Lieutenant Lopez, Muetzel's good friend, and they needed help.

When Lopez had gone over the wall, he landed in an enemy trench and immediately received heavy fire from nearby bunkers. His subsequent Medal of Honor citation reads:

*With his platoon, First Lieutenant **Baldomero Lopez** was engaged in the reduction of immediate enemy beach defenses after landing with the assault waves. Exposing himself to hostile fire, he moved forward alongside a bunker and prepared to throw a hand grenade into the next pillbox whose fire was pinning down that sector of the beach. Taken under fire by an* *enemy automatic weapon, and hit in the right shoulder and chest as he lifted his arm to throw, he fell backward and dropped the deadly missile. After a moment, he turned and dragged his body forward in an effort to retrieve the grenade and throw it. In critical condition from pain and loss of blood, and unable to grasp the hand grenade firmly enough to hurl it, he chose to sacrifice himself rather than endanger the lives of his men and, with a sweeping motion of his wounded right arm, cradled the grenade under him and absorbed the full impact of the explosion.*

As Muetzel and his men circled back to the beach, they went by way of their second objective, Cemetery Hill. This was a high point with sheer rock-face on three sides, somewhat like the Rock of Gibraltar. Upon reaching its base, Muetzel realized they could easily scale it from behind, so he left the captured enemy gun crew in the care of his medical corpsmen and led his men up the hill.

He suspected its defenders would be focused the other way – toward the beach – and he dispersed his men as a skirmish line when they neared the top. He guessed right. They captured this unit of North Koreans, disarmed them, and sent them down the hill to join the other prisoners.

Muetzel radioed his company commander that Cemetery Hill was secured. In turn, he learned Lopez's platoon had regrouped, and it wasn't necessary for him to come back to the beach.

Muetzel suddenly remembered his medical corpsman was the only person guarding the prisoners below, and the corpsman was armed only with a pistol, a weapon he'd never used before. Muetzel raced down to find a "mob of North Koreans squatting on the ground and a white-faced corpsman holding a .45 at arms' length in both hands. It was funny," he said.[162]

It turned out Muetzel's 2nd Platoon was actually fortunate to go in first. Drizzle had now turned to rain, and the gathering darkness, along with billowing smoke, was causing confusion. Some boats were unloading their men in the wrong places, and others had to unload vehicles and equipment onto narrow beaches that quickly became congested and difficult to navigate.

Nevertheless, some 13,000 Marines, along with their equipment, were ashore by 1:30 the following morning.

---

[162] Muetzel quotes are from Donald Knox's *Korean War: An Oral History*.

Muetzel's commanding officer had promised him that he and his men could have all the beer they wanted if they captured the Asahi Brewery intact. They had come close, but the brewery was now in flames, and as they dug in to hold the crest of Cemetery Hill, they could hear barrels of alcohol exploding in the night.

In the following hours, Muetzel received word that two Marines who had crossed in front of Cemetery Hill had been hit by North Koreans from a cave somewhere on the cliff-face below him. He crept forward and was able to see the two Americans lying at the base of the hill calling for help, but he could see no safe way to rescue them, saying "I couldn't order someone to pull them out, and I was afraid to do it myself."

He turned to a South Korean Marine officer for help, and they worked their way "as far forward as I dared." Through his interpreter, Muetzel ordered the enemy soldiers to either come out and surrender, or he would have a tank pull up and blast them out. The enemy chose the first option, but unfortunately, one of the young Marines had died by this time. The other – although rescued – died at the seawall while waiting for the tide to rise enough to take him to a hospital ship.

The rain started letting up as dawn approached. Muetzel made his way to the command post for instructions and found his fellow officers hunched around a wounded North Korean officer he thought he had shot and killed the previous day. He was punchy from exhaustion and emotional strain, saying, "I got so mad I tried to kill him again, this time with my pistol." Muetzel later thanked the men who stopped him – but he refused to let anybody help the prisoner walk back to the seawall, saying, "I just couldn't bring myself to have Marines carry him out."

Two days later, Muetzel was wounded his fourth and final time. While moving toward Seoul, they had just cleared the last hills between Inchon and the Han River when a spray from a Russian-made machine gun tore the calf from his right leg and killed Corporal Tom Callison, one of Muetzel's machine gunners.

Muetzel and Callison were loaded into an ambulance jeep and taken to an aid station, and then to a medical clearing position at the seawall.

There, Muetzel – like the Marine he had tried to save two nights earlier – waited the rest of the day for the tide to rise, so he could receive the serious care he needed.

By the time his casualty boat arrived, Muetzel had lost too much blood to make it all the way to the hospital ship. Instead, he was offloaded onto the "Happy Hank" (USS Henrico), where he received several pints of whole blood. He remembered that as he faded in and out, he gave his pistol and Russian field glasses to two young sailors who had brought him and his men ashore with the first wave – one of them vomited after seeing Muetzel come back on his stretcher.

When he was finally taken aboard the *USS Constellation* late that night, medical personnel found the wounded Marine was still carrying a live grenade and threw it overboard.

As he lost consciousness, Lieutenant Muetzel's last realization was that his fighting days were over. His right leg could not be saved.

His daughter, Jeanne, writes:

> He confided in us about a recurring nightmare he had long after he left the Corps. He would be back at the Inchon Landing as they were about to land, look back to yell final orders, and it would be only Koreans who didn't understand English in the boat.
>
> I do think one of the things that helped him much later was returning to Korea in 1980 for the 30th reunion of the Inchon Landing. He hadn't planned to – didn't think he needed any closure. But General Craig contacted him and asked him to reconsider. General Craig was in his mid-80s at the time and wanted help getting there. Dad couldn't say no to him and went. He told me afterwards he was glad he had gone and not just to help the General.[163]

Russell House

To Muetzel's right, also on RED Beach, 24-year-old Russell House was simultaneously landing with the 2nd Battalion's first wave. From Ames, Iowa, he had joined the military just as soon as he possibly could.

House's brother, Ron – himself a combat veteran – recalled, "He was in school, and WWII was jumping all over the place at that time. At the age of 16, which would've been about 1944, he enlisted in the Merchant Marines. They were on these freight ships that were going from our east coast to England, Belgium and other European places. The German submarines were sinking our freighters faster than we could make them, so it was kind of a scary thing to be in the Merchant Marines going across the north Atlantic.

---

[163] Email exchanges Jeanne Muetzel with author March 2013.

"He spent approximately one year doing that. When he got out sometime in 1945, he decided he wanted to become a Marine. He stayed in the Marine Corps until 1949, when he decided he was done with the military and was going to get out."

Ron described his brother as "big and rugged, an all-man type." Russell's fellow Marines agreed, nicknaming him "Moose."

"He was a boxing champion when he was in the Marine Corps, in both San Diego and the Philippines," said Ron. "Matter of fact, I got a pair of boxing gloves he was awarded."

After returning to Iowa, Russell found civilian life no longer suited him. "It's hard to take the Marine Corps out of a man like that," said Ron. "So, in 1950, he decided to go back in. This was right before the Korean War started. He was with the first group of Marines to go into Korea."

Russell was with the heavy weapons platoon of Easy Company, which had seen heavy fighting down on the Naktong Bulge. Tonight's mission was much different. After scaling the seawall, Easy Company quickly moved off to the right and into the city, and by 6:45 p.m. they controlled the British Consulate and a portion of Observatory Hill.

House's Weapons Platoon, as well as Headquarters and Service Company, was in or near the Nippon Flour Mill when a wild round from a Navy ship killed one and wounded twenty-three others. Further casualties were prevented by the mill's brick walls. Otherwise, the operation went smoothly, and all objectives were taken as planned.

At dawn the following morning, the 5th Marines moved into the vicinity of Ascom City. That morning, 200 North Koreans with six tanks advanced toward them, and in a perfect ambush, the Marines completely destroyed the enemy force while taking only one casualty.

At 9:00 a.m., House's battalion advanced nine miles to Kimpo Airfield, northeast of Inchon. Regaining Kimpo was a key objective – with its 6,000-foot runway, it was one of the largest airstrips in Korea. They came at it from two different directions, overcoming enemy resistance along the way, and by ten o'clock that night, they held the southern end of the airfield.

During the night, North Korean units infiltrated in and around their sector. Some were detected, but others were not, and before dawn on September 18, small arms fire hit Easy Company's positions.

The men first thought they were receiving friendly fire from Dog Company, but soon after, about 200 enemy soldiers attacked Easy's position from the east.

Medical corpsman Herb Pearce later said, "They were all over us. I was sure I was dead. None of us ever expected to live to see the sun come up."

In this melee, Russell House's platoon was pinned down. He rushed forward hurling grenades at an enemy machine gun emplacement while trying to position his 75-mm recoilless rifle. He was yelling for more grenades, when a bullet took his life.

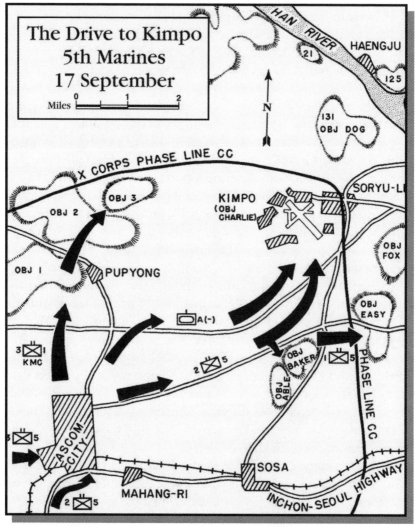

House was killed at Kimpo airfield. Two days later, Bob Taplett led the 5ᵗʰ Marine crossing at Haengju, upper right. (USMC)

*The **Navy Cross** is awarded **(Posthumously)** to Corporal **Russell Junior House**, USMC, for extraordinary heroism in connection with military operations against an armed enemy of the United Nations while serving as a Gunner in a 70-mm Recoilless Rifle Platoon, Company E, 2nd Battalion, 5ʰ Marines, 1ˢᵗ Marine Division (Reinforced), at Kimpo Airfield, Korea, on 18 September 1950. When the rest of his platoon was pinned down by intense small-arms fire from concealed hostile positions, Corporal House moved forward alone in the face of intense enemy fire, throwing a hand grenade and single-handedly killing five of the enemy while bringing his gun into position. Repeatedly exposing himself to enemy fire in order to ready the ammunition for firing, he prepared to engage the hostile troops at point blank range and was sighting in at the target when struck down. As a result of Corporal House's great personal courage, fortitude and fighting spirit, his platoon was inspired to heroic efforts in holding the enemy at bay, and the opposing troops were finally destroyed . . .*

Iowa's Russell House was the first man from the upper prairies to receive the Navy Cross in Korea. (Courtesy House family)

Fifty years later, medical corpsman Herb Pearce wrote to Ron House:

> I was less than 2 feet away from him when he threw the grenade that cost him his life. He was killed instantly and did not suffer even 30 seconds of pain . . .
>
> The most fear of the entire campaign was the night that we were surrounded at Kimpo. Even later, when the Chinese had us cut off at the Chosin Reservoir battle, and I had been wounded, it was not as bad as that night at Kimpo. All that I can say to you is that Russell was a real hero the night that we took Kimpo. He was trying to do something significant to improve our very poor chances of survival that night. Even though it cost him his life, he did make a difference.

House's death left several of his fellow Marines deeply shaken. Corporal Charlie Snow said House "was as rugged as they come, and it was hard to believe that such a big, almost indestructible guy was dead."

Private First Class George Waslinko agreed, saying: "Moose was the classic personification of a Marine. He'd been a bodyguard for the president of the Philippines, and he could pick up a 75-millimeter gun like a loaf of bread. He was the toughest guy I ever met."[164]

---

[164]McBreen, B.B. *2d Battalion, 5th Marines Land at Inchon: a pocket history*. Project Leatherneck: Camp Pendleton CA. 15 Sep 1993; Author interview Ronald House Feb 2011; Letter Herbert Pearce 25 Dec 2000, courtesy Ronald House.

Chapter 35

CAPTURING SEOUL

"I remember vividly my own thoughts, fears and concerns of the time. For example, where the hell was everybody else, and did anybody else really give a damn. This letter is to assure you that there are those who care and care a great deal. You are having to relearn what we learned at Seoul." Frank Muetzel to Sgt. Jim Monroe serving in Vietnam, 1968

THE INCHON LANDING was a triumph that sent hope surging through every United Nations fighter on the peninsula.

As for North Korean leader Kim Il Sung, he quickly realized General MacArthur would now focus on Seoul. In fact, MacArthur had explained his plan to news correspondents before the landing even commenced, and although the operation was top secret, reporters started calling it *Operation Common Knowledge*. By the time Wolmi-do was obliterated, Kim had troops rushing to protect Seoul.[165]

MacArthur had good reasons for wanting to secure Seoul. Most importantly, the city provided North Korea one of its primary gateways for supplying its communist troops down on the Naktong.

Nonetheless, some historians believe the seizure of Seoul was also motivated by politics and glory-seeking and was thus a flaw in the plan to trap the majority of North Korean troops south of the 38th Parallel – a trap that could have decisively ended the war.

In his 1952 book, *Korean Tales*, for which he was later court martialed, Lieutenant Colonel Melvin Voorhees, Eighth Army's chief

---

[165] Handleman, Howard. "MacArthur Briefed Newsman Before the Invasion." *Pacific Stars And Stripes*. 17 Sep 1950.

censor (and previous editor of the *Tacoma Times*) wrote about the deepening gulf between General Walker, Eighth Army, and General MacArthur. MacArthur had just given a great deal of power to General Ned Almond by appointing him commander of the newly introduced X Corps, which included the Marines and the 7th Infantry Division at Seoul. Because Almond's leadership was to become very controversial, especially at the Chosin Reservoir, it's worth having a closer look through Colonel Voorhees' eyes:

> The late General Walker was a proud, aloof, but sensitive man. He fought and finally had won the desperate battle of the Pusan perimeter. It is not surprising, then, that he was hurt and offended, personally and professionally, when a new corps on September 15 was sent into Korea as a separate command in no way answerable to him and not as a part of the Eighth Army team which had borne up under all the war's early bitterness.
>
> He was disappointed when Almond's X Corps, instead of slashing across the peninsula and blocking the retreat of the North Korean Army then in flight before Eighth Army, used the Marines for a frontal assault on Seoul and the 7th Infantry Division in an encircling move around the southern limits and then into that city. As a result of that move, General Almond was dubbed by some reporters "liberator of Seoul," but while it was going on a large part of the North Korean Army, retreating before the onrushing U.S. Eighth, escaped into North Korea by way of the roads east of Seoul.[166]

Either way, Kim Il Sung was determined to delay X Corps in Seoul, and the Americans who were following orders were in for a fierce fight.

Taplett Crosses the Han

For South Dakota's Bob Taplett, the assault on Seoul began the night of September 19-20, when he was tasked with taking the lead as the 5th Marines gathered to cross the Han River.

That night, an advance group from a reconnaissance company was to cross the Han to a small village, Haenju, to determine enemy presence and then signal the rest of their company to come across. After

---

[166]Voorhees, Melvin B. *Korean Tales*. New York: Simon and Schuster. 1952: p 53.

they reconnoitered the high ground on the other side, Taplett's 3rd Battalion was to cross the river and commence an assault on Seoul.[167] Marine historian Joseph Alexander writes:

> Taplett considered the plan too ambitious. The Reconnaissance Company had the heart, he believed, but not the numbers (127 strong) to cover the sprawling high ground along the river. No one knew anything in advance about the possibility of enemy presence in strength along the far bank. Taplett quietly ordered his staff to draw up contingency plans for the crossing.
>
> The North Koreans had not ignored the former ferry site. Aware that the Marines would likely cross the Han soon, the NKPA deployed an infantry battalion in the underbrush along Hill 125. Their camouflage discipline proved excellent. The Marines did not detect their presence throughout the afternoon and evening of the 19th. (See map page 352.)

The advance reconnaissance unit silently swam the 400-yard river to the far shore, arriving 55 minutes later. After checking the surrounding terrain, they signaled the remainder of their company to cross over in AmTracs (amphibious tractors that moved on tracks, like tanks). The North Koreans hit the tractors midstream with mortar, and the mission was soon aborted.

Taplett later explained his "contingency plans" to historian John Toland. Taplett's initial orders had been to make an administrative crossing – rather than going over as an assault unit, this was to be more of a relocation of the 5th Marines to the north side of the Han River. But with nobody on the other shore to cover his men, he knew he had to get his orders changed.

Taplett headed for the regimental command post at Kimpo Airfield to discuss the plan with his commander, Colonel Raymond Murray, but Murray was asleep. The operations officer refused to wake him but did tell Taplett they were changing his orders. They didn't think there was enough room on the far shore to land Taplett's AmTracs abreast, so they wanted him cross over in a single file column.

"I think it's suicide to go across single file," Taplett told him.

---

[167]Toland, John. *In Mortal Combat*. P 204-213; Alexander, Col Joseph H. USMC (Ret). *Battle of the Barricades: U.S. Marines in the Recapture of Seoul*. Monograph. Marine Corps Historical Center. Washington, DC: 2000.

"They'll just pick off one tractor after another."

Still unable to speak with Murray, Taplett left the command post and made a fateful decision. Back at the river, he had his men convert the AmTracs into assault vehicles manned by combat teams.

Taplett then motored back to the command post to confer with Murray, but again he was told the colonel was sleeping. Refusing to back down, Taplett told the major in charge, "I'm going to go across in waves of tractors and land my companies in columns. But I'm going to land in waves of tractors – four or five in each wave."

Taplett went back to the Han knowing he could be court-martialed, but Colonel Murray soon radioed him to say he agreed with Taplett's assault plan. Murray postponed Taplett's launch two hours and arranged for artillery and air support to cover the crossing.

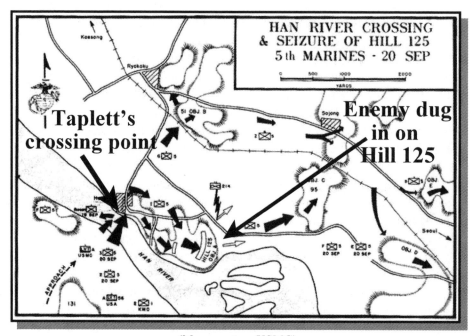

(Map courtesy USMC)

As the sun rose, Taplett's concerns had turned out to be well founded. His AmTracs had come under heavy fire as soon as they hit the water. Item Company landed first, moved right and immediately engaged the battalion of North Koreans on Hill 125. Theirs was a violent fight, including hand-to-hand combat, but they made it possible for the remainder of the 5th Marines to cross almost without incident.

Eight miles away lay the heart of Seoul. As the other elements of X Corps moved forward, General MacArthur arrived at Taplett's crossing point. All seemed under control, and the general assured Colonel Murray the enemy would "all evaporate very shortly."

Marine historian Joseph Alexander writes MacArthur's prediction "proved famously false" for the 5th Marines. "The regiment would suffer a casualty rate more reflective of its recent history at Peleliu and Okinawa than the Korean peninsula." Between the regiment and the city of Seoul, he wrote, the Marines would be dealing with "convoluted terrain, a sprawling series of hill masses, ridges, and draws . . . "

Marine historian Robert Heinl Jr. agreed, writing: "As an exercise in map reading, this ground is confusing and deceptive; for the tactician, it is a nightmare."

Besides the terrain, the operation would also include street fighting and door-to-door searches for snipers. The dominant feature was Hill 296 and a series of extending hills that soon became known as Smith's Ridge. For the North Korean defenders, it was ideal terrain that had long been used by the Japanese for tactical training of its troops. Indeed, some 10,000 enemy soldiers were waiting on that ridge when the Americans moved against it, and by September 23, the 1st Marine Division would report 1,158 casualties since landing at Inchon.

Bob Taplett & Joe Trompeter

Bob Taplett and Joseph Trompeter got to know each other in the late 1930s, when they were running backs for the University of South Dakota Coyotes in Vermillion. Tackle Joe Foss, Sioux Falls, played on the same team for a time, and all three became highly decorated Marines.

Foss became legendary as a fighter pilot in WWII, becoming an ace in just one week over Guadalcanal in 1942 and going on to earn the Medal of Honor. After serving again during the Korean War, he was twice elected South Dakota's governor. He returned to his favorite sport when he became the first Commissioner of the American Football League, and he is credited as being one of the primary initiators of America's favorite football game, the Superbowl.[168]

Taplett was a gifted athlete like his father, becoming a record-setting track star in high school and later playing baseball, basketball, and three

---

[168] Web: 28 Feb 2014. http://www.joefossinstitute.org/about-jfi/joe-foss-the-man/

MEET IN MARIANAS

Tragedy brought together for the first time in four years two former star football players at the University of South Dakota—Marine Major R. D. Taplett, of Tyndall (left), and Marine Captain Joseph D. Trompeter, of Rapid City. This picture was taken aboard a ship which rescued survivors of the carrier Princeton, sunk in the Second Battle of the Philippines' Sea. Captain Trompeter was in command of the Marine detachment aboard the Princeton, and in charge of all survivors arriving in the Mariannas. Taplett and Trompeter were halfbacks on USD football teams of 1938-39. Both played three years of varsity football. Taplett also starred in basketball, baseball and track, graduating in 1940, a year ahead of Trompeter. (U. S. Marine Corps photo)

Taplett and Trompeter were reunited in October 1944.
(News clipping courtesy Taplett family)

years of varsity football at Vermillion.

While Taplett ended up in USD's Athletic Hall of Fame, it was Joe Trompeter, one year behind him, who grabbed the attention of reporters, who variously referred to the Rapid City veterinarian's son as *Slippery Joe Trompeter, Rapid City Speed Boy, "Jumpin' Joe" Trompeter*, and the *Coyotes' stop-and-go artist*.

In the fall of 1938, however, coach Harry Gamage wasn't happy with Taplett or Trompeter, telling reporters, "Before the season started, I thought our first team would be as good as last year's. But it certainly hasn't been. I'm afraid we won't even be able to gain against a good team. My backs won't run tough. They sneak and look for daylight. They don't drive. They're trying hard enough, but they just don't realize what's wrong . . . If Joe Trompeter and Bob Taplett have one of their sneaking fumbling days, we could lose to Omaha without any trouble at all. If the backs don't start driving, running tough, we could lose a lot of ball games."[169]

It appears it wasn't until the following season that the Coyotes rose to Gamage's expectations. But when the 1939 season was over, UND, Grand Forks, had stolen the North Central Conference Championship from them.

It's unknown whether Taplett and Trompeter found each other again in Korea, but they were both decorated for actions on the same day during the fight for Seoul. Unfortunately, details of their actions are lacking other than what can be found in their citations.

Taplett circa 1938/39

*A **Gold Star in lieu of a Second Award of the Silver Star** is awarded to Lt. Col. **Robert Donald Taplett**, USMC, for conspicuous gallantry and intrepidity . . . in action against enemy aggressor forces in Korea, on 21 September 1950. Assigned the mission of seizing and occupying two hills*

---

[169] *Evening Huronite*. 13 Oct 1938.

overlooking the regimental objective, Lt. Col. Taplett skillfully carried out this hazardous task and, upon its completion, coolly remained in an exposed area to personally direct the placing of supporting fire on strong enemy positions which were bringing intense small-arms, machine-gun, mortar and artillery fire to bear on the entire battalion front and causing many casualties . . . in the face of heavy enemy fire . . .

Trompeter circa 1941

*Major **Joseph D. Trompeter**, U.S. Marine Corps, is awarded the **Silver Star** for conspicuous gallantry and intrepidity as S-3, Third Battalion, First Marines, First Marine Division (Reinforced), in action against enemy aggressor forces in Korea on 21 September 1950. Assuming command of the battalion when its commander was wounded and its executive officer stationed with the reserve element, Major Trompeter fearlessly established his observation post on the highest terrain in the area in order to gain complete control and conduct the attack more effectively. Remaining in this position despite intense hostile fire, he successfully maneuvered the assault companies into strategic locations from which they could overrun the enemy-held ridge line and, after gaining the line, directed the assault companies to continue the attack. Repeatedly reestablishing and manning his observation posts in positions from which he could best control and direct the assault despite hostile fire, he succeeded in keeping the enemy moving rapidly, thereby permitting them no opportunity to employ an effective delaying action. His strategic ability, skilled leadership and indomitable courage were contributing factors in the success of the assigned mission and reflect great credit upon Major Trompeter and the U. S. Naval Service.*

Chapter 36

HEROISM IN THE AIR

Naval and Marine air, flying more than three hundred sorties from the carriers, were successful in cauterizing the infested area, and the enemy, seemingly stunned by the magnitude and speed of the operation, made no attempt to get reinforcements into (Inchon). Andrew Geer, *The New Breed*

BECAUSE OF TELEVISION'S M*A*S*H series, helicopters seem central to all aspects of the Korean War. But in the beginning, the military was just beginning to learn how to best utilize this aircraft. These early "whirlybirds" were very basic. Missions flown at night, for example, required pilots to use flashlights to read their instrument panels and to illuminate their landing positions.

It didn't take long, however, to realize that in the harsh terrain of Korea, helicopters were well suited for search and rescue, transport into and out of combat zones, evacuating wounded, and conducting reconnaissance.

Arthur Bancroft

Arthur Bancroft was one of eight Marine officers deployed from Quantico, Virginia, to fly helicopters in Korea when the war broke out. Born in 1920, Bancroft grew up in Hillsboro, Iowa, where he enlisted in the Marines in 1941. Bancroft's air group, Observation Squadron Six (VMO-6), was the Marines' first helicopter unit to be used in combat.

Jim Westendorf served with Bancroft both in the States and in Korea: "Lt. Bancroft was an outstanding marine officer and a very good helicopter pilot. I had the occasion to fly with him, both back home in HMX-1 and a time or two in Korea. I, as a helicopter mechanic, and Lt.

Bancroft, as a helicopter pilot, were in the Marine Corps' very first (experimental) Helicopter Squadron. Just after the outbreak of the Korean War, some twenty-five of us helicopter types, i.e. officer pilots and mechanics, joined VMO-6 at Camp Pendleton, Calif, and sailed off to Korea."[170]

Arthur Bancroft (right) with his crew chief Jim Bailey circa August 1950. (Courtesy Jim Westendorf)

During the Inchon landing, VMO-6 pilots were scouting key terrain for suitable areas for the Marines to cross the Han River and to locate optimum assault routes for the assault on Seoul. At 8:15 a.m. September 17, Ensign R.R. Sanders' F4U Corsair was shot down over enemy territory, but he managed to make a belly-landing on a gravel road about two miles west of Seoul. Two other Navy pilots spotted him and reported his coordinates to an aircraft carrier.

Newspapers[171] reported Bancroft volunteered to rescue Sanders, and

---

[170] Westendorf email correspondence with author 2011.

[171] *Cedar Rapids Gazette.* 18 Sept 1950; *Dunkirk Evening Observer* (NY). 18 Sept 1950; *The Mt. Pleasant News* (IA). 2 October 1950.

escorted by two fighter planes, he flew through heavy anti-aircraft fire until locating the downed airman in a rice paddy. Over the next hour, the two fighter planes "worked over the enemy ack-ack batteries that tried to down [Bancroft's] helicopter."

Sanders' plane was less than 300 yards from the anti-aircraft position, but Bancroft eventually managed to set down behind a small hill that protected him from the enemy guns. Bancroft told a reporter, "They kept me circling . . . while they tried to knock out the North Korean battery, but I don't think they got it, for the ack-ack started to walk right up to the plane. However, it eventually stopped for some unaccountable reason, and I was able to drop over Sanders without further trouble."

Another story reported, "Sanders fired a flare to help Bancroft locate him and, once on the helicopter, pounded and slapped his Marine rescuer on the back so enthusiastically that the latter had trouble getting back off the ground."

*The **Silver Star** is awarded to First Lieutenant **Arthur Richard Bancroft**, U.S. Marine Corps, for gallantry in action while serving as a helicopter pilot in Marine Observation Squadron SIX (VMO-6), by successfully rescuing a carrier based pilot who had been shot down by the enemy. On 17 September 1950, Lieutenant Bancroft received information that a carrier based pilot had been shot down approximately three miles south and east of Seoul, Korea. Without thought of the personal danger involved in landing his helicopter deep in enemy territory, Lieutenant Bancroft immediately volunteered to attempt a rescue. While en route to the scene of the crash, he was provided an escort of two fighter planes. Nearing his destination he was forced to circle while his escort destroyed a gun position and distracted enemy troops which were near the crashed aircraft. During the action Lieutenant Bancroft continued on with his mission, landed near the location of the enemy troops, and effected a successful rescue. Due to his actions, the downed pilot was saved from certain capture by the enemy . . .*

Four days later, on September 21, Bancroft and his crew chief were assigned another rescue mission. This time, the downed pilot was trapped inside his cockpit. Because they were flying into a hot zone, they were again escorted by a combat air patrol.

After locating the downed plane, Bancroft set his HO3S down and stayed at the controls. His crew chief was unable to free the pilot alone, so Bancroft left the chopper to assist him. The helicopter was idling, with the rotors still slowly turning, and the "collective friction device worked loose," causing the craft to tip on its side. The beating rotors destroyed the aircraft.

With the pilot now free of his cockpit, a fellow pilot flew in and picked up all three men. Their combined weight staggered the second chopper, but they successfully reached friendly lines. Despite this trauma, Bancroft secured another helicopter and rescued a second Navy pilot later that same day.

On September 29, a VMO-6 craft was shot down about five miles north of Seoul. The aerial observer was killed, but the pilot was able get free of the crash. Both Bancroft and a fellow pilot, Lloyd Engelhardt, volunteered for the mission. Their air officer learned the pilot went down near Uijongbu, where there were heavy concentrations of enemy troops, as well as plentiful anti-aircraft weaponry, so Bancroft and Engelhardt flipped a coin. Bancroft won the toss and became the lead helicopter, while Engelhardt trailed about a mile back. Bancroft located the crash site, but as he was setting down, he was hit by enemy fire.

Due to his fateful coin toss, he entered into history as the first Marine helicopter pilot to be killed in combat.[172]

*The **Navy Cross** is awarded **(Posthumously)** to **Arthur Richard Bancroft**, First Lieutenant, U.S. Marine Corps, for extraordinary heroism in connection with military operations against an armed enemy of the United Nations while serving as Pilot of a helicopter in Marine Observation Squadron SIX (VMO-6) during operations against enemy aggressor forces in the Republic of Korea on 29 September 1950. Receiving information that a friendly observation plane was overdue from its mission and presumed downed behind enemy lines, First Lieutenant Bancroft voluntarily took his unarmed helicopter over enemy-infested territory to search for the missing aircraft. In the face of intense hostile small-arms and anti-aircraft fire, he deliberately flew at a low searching altitude and apparently sighted the downed plane just before hostile fire found its target and sent his helicopter crashing to the ground. By his daring initiative, outstanding courage and selfless devotion to duty, First Lieutenant Bancroft upheld the highest traditions of the United States Naval Service.*

"We all were devastated upon his loss, particularly as he was our very first helicopter pilot loss," said Jim Westendorf. "There was no

---

[172] Brown, LTC Ronald J. U.S.MCR (Ret). "Whirlybirds, U.S. Marine Helicopters in Korea." *U.S. Marines in the Korean War.* Charles R. Smith editor. History Division U.S.MC. 2007: p 673, 688, 690.

recovery, and his status and whereabouts at the time were unknown. Even today, I do not know the truth of the matter."

John Beebe & Karl Kludt

John Beebe, from White Bear Lake, Minnesota, first gained widespread attention February 4, 1943, in WWII. The Japanese were losing the battle on Guadalcanal, and fleets of enemy vessels were speeding to the island to evacuate their men. When 20 Japanese destroyers were spotted sailing toward Guadalcanal near New Georgia, American torpedo and bomber planes swooped down, and three dive bombers, including Beebe, scored three direct hits on one destroyer, sinking it in three minutes.[173]

Beebe was now a "Tiger" in the Marines' All Weather Squadron 542 (VMF(N)-542). After Russell House and his fellow Marines secured Kimpo Airfield, this squadron immediately started using the airstrip. Flying new, twin-engine, radar-upgraded F7F-3N *Tigercats*, the squadron carried out both day and night missions.

On September 24, troops on the ground were now fighting within the sprawling city of Seoul, and close air support was essential.

During day missions, Beebe flew by himself, but night runs required a second crewman to handle radar. Beebe's crew-mate for the night run of September 25-26 was Technical Sergeant Karl Kludt.

Born in 1916, Kludt was the 10th of 12 children in his family. They lived in McClusky, North Dakota, before moving to McLaughlin, South Dakota. After high school, he moved back to North Dakota to get a teaching degree at Mayville State Teachers College. He was artistic, well liked and worked as a school teacher until he joined the Marines (or Navy) in the summer of 1940.

Kludt saw a great deal of action at sea during WWII and was seriously wounded during the Battle

Karl Kludt

---

[173] *The Bismarck Tribune.* 12 Feb 1943.

of Tassafaronga in November 1942. The gun turret he was manning was hit by enemy fire, and he fell into burning oil. He was evacuated to the States and spent the rest of the war recovering. He later attended Naval Flight School and received radar training.[174]

Beebe and Kludt's mission over Seoul was extremely difficult, and withering crossfire coming at them through thick clouds of smoke proved fatal. After being hit, their plane crashed into the Han River near a power plant. Both men were reportedly killed, although the remains of neither were recovered.

John Beebe

*Major **John Ward Beebe**, U. S. Marine Corps, is awarded the **Silver Star (Posthumously)** for conspicuous gallantry and intrepidity as Senior Pilot of a flight of aircraft, while attached to Marine Night Fighter Squadron Five Hundred Forty-two (VMF(N) 542) "Tigers" in action against enemy aggressor forces in Korea, on 24 September 1950. Engaged in close support of ground forces, Major Beebe led his flight in attacks against a hostile position which was inflicting heavy casualties on friendly forces. Although the target was obscured by dense smoke and haze, which made its location from the air extremely difficult, he repeatedly descended to perilously low altitudes through intense enemy anti-aircraft fire in order to neutralize the assigned target. Pressing home his final attack with determination in defiance of all personal danger, Major Beebe lost his life when his plane was struck by enemy fire and crashed. His cool courage, skilled airmanship and devotion to duty reflect the highest credit upon Major Beebe and the U.S. Naval Service. He gallantly gave his life for his country.*

---

[174]http://koreanwarmemorial.sd.gov/SearchEngineForm/profiles/160.htm. Jan 2013.

Max Volcansek, Jr.

The commander of Beebe's squadron was Lieutenant Colonel Max Volcansek, from Eveleth, Minnesota, who often said playing basketball had greatly influenced his skills as a fighter pilot. His 1987 induction tribute into Macalester College's Athletics Hall of Fame reads:

A junior college transfer, Max J. Volcansek had an enormous impact on the success of the entire athletic program in his two years at Macalester.

Volcansek came to Macalester from Eveleth Junior College in the fall of 1934. Despite the fact that the Scots had nine lettermen returning in basketball, he immediately cracked the team's starting five and helped lead the club to a second-place finish in the final conference team standings. He was named to the all-conference squad the next year when the Scots missed the league title by just a few percentage points.

Despite weighing only 135 pounds, Volcansek started as a blocker for the Scots football team as a senior in 1935, before a knee injury sent him to the sidelines. In the spring of 1935 and 1936, the gifted athlete lettered on the Scots tennis team. The 1935 squad captured the state conference title.

"Max was an inspirational player who possessed, besides great athletic ability, the leadership qualities which fired up the team when it appeared that the breaks weren't going their way," said Harlan "Sempty" Westrell '36.

In addition to his intercollegiate success, Volcansek won the handball singles championship and was high point man in track in intramural competition in 1936.

Volcansek was shot down the day after Beebe and Kludt crashed.

*Lieutenant Colonel **Max J. Volcansek Jr.**, U.S. Marine Corps, is awarded the **Silver Star** for conspicuous gallantry and intrepidity as a Pilot and Commanding Officer of Marine All Weather Fighter Squadron Five Hundred Forty-two (VMF (AW) 542) during operations against enemy aggressor forces in Korea on 25 September 1950. Assigned the mission of reducing an enemy strong point opposing friendly ground forces in the center of Seoul, Lieutenant Colonel Volcansek led his four-plane flight in a determined attack against the objective through heavy smoke in the face of intense hostile anti-aircraft fire. Although his aircraft was damaged on the first run, which later necessitated his abandoning it by parachute, and* *despite shrapnel wounds in his leg, he steadfastly refused to discontinue his attacks until his ammunition was expended and the target was destroyed.*

Max Volcansek, Jr.

Naval Aviation News provided an entertaining backstory about this:

> [Volcansek] owes his life today to a lusty kick on his stick and a quick-opening parachute. He tried to drop his right empty wing tank, but it jammed between the right engine and the fuselage. Airspeed and control of the plane were lost.
>
> After fighting vainly to control the plane, he decided at 1,000 feet to jump. He pushed back the hatch cover and attempted to crawl out, but the slipstream of the plunging plane was too strong. He put his foot on the stick and gave a desperate kick. The plane nose-dived and he plummeted out of the cockpit pulling his ripcord at 500 feet. The chute opened just seconds before he hit the ground. The *Tigercat* crashed 75 feet away. A rescue helicopter soon picked him up and took him back to Kimpo Airfield. . . .
>
> The sequel to this story came a few days later when Volcansek went back to the village to thank personally old Ujong Chi, a South Koran peasant, and give him a present of two boxes of rations. Curious men of the village swarmed around to watch the ceremony. They and others had helped

carry wrecked parts of his F7F up to the village's democratic center, Ujong being the first to greet Volcansek after he landed in his chute.

The Marine flier wanted his ripcord ring, so half a dozen children went with him to hunt for it, even though they didn't know what they were looking for till Volcansek drew them a picture of it. One then dashed off and ran back with the souvenir. As he left the hamlet, Volcansek was presented with a dozen eggs carefully wrapped in rice straw.[175]

Edward Hammerbeck & John LaMontia

Another notable airman during this time was Edward Hammerbeck, from Duluth, Minnesota. He was a graduate of St. Olaf College, Northfield, receiving an economics degree in 1942.

Hammerbeck and Major Vincent Gottschalk, pilot, were flying an unarmed aerial observer known as a *Grasshopper* near Seoul. Their only weapons were the pistols on their hips, and although Hammerbeck didn't fire his weapon, he did put his bullets to good use.

*Captain **Edward E. Hammerbeck**, U.S. Marine Corps, is awarded the **Silver Star** for conspicuous gallantry and intrepidity as an Aerial Observer attached to Headquarters Company, Headquarters Battalion, 1ˢᵗ Marine Division (Reinforced), in action against enemy aggressor forces in Korea on 26 September 1950. Flying on a reconnaissance mission ahead of advancing infantrymen, Captain Hammerbeck observed a large, well-concealed group of enemy troops in position to ambush the friendly forces. Realizing that radio communications with leading elements of the ground troops were not available, and that his supply of message-drop containers was exhausted, he dropped a message wrapped in his handkerchief and weighted with bullets, warning friendly troops of the impending danger. Although the vulnerable aircraft was severely damaged by intense enemy anti-aircraft fire during the initial low dive over the hostile concentration, the pilot carried out a second low run in the face of the heavy fire and, Captain Hammerbeck determining further details, dropped another message to the friendly troops. After quickly summoning fighter aircraft to the scene, he remained over the area in the badly damaged plane, until the enemy troops had been dispersed with heavy casualties.*

---

[175] Web:9 Feb 2012. http://athletics.macalester.edu/hof.aspx?hof=85&path=&kiosk=. "Navy Air Power in Korea." *Naval Aviation News*. December 1950. P 8-9.

Captain Gus Lancaster shot this photo of Chief Davis, Captain Ed Hammerbeck and Lieutenant Pete Braun in 1950.

Naval Aviation News (December 1950) reported Hammerbeck took off his shoe and used his sock, weighted with another couple bullets, for dropping the second message. When they returned to base, he and Gottschalk found eight bullet holes in the tail of their plane. One was a fraction of an inch from a main control cable.

Meanwhile, another pilot, John Lamontia from Omaha, was decorated for his Mosquito mission in support of Army units breaking out from the Naktong Perimeter.

*The **Distinguished Flying Cross (1st Bronze Oak Leaf Cluster)** for heroism while participating in aerial flight against the enemy in Korea is awarded to First Lieutenant **John A. Lamontia**, Infantry, U.S. Army. A member of Headquarters, 6th Medium Tank Battalion, 24th Infantry Division, Lieutenant LaMontia distinguished himself by extraordinary heroism during an aerial flight over Kumchon, Korea, on 25 September 1950. While engaged in an aerial flight observing enemy positions and directing the movement of ground troops, his plane was damaged by enemy anti-aircraft* *fire and disabled to the extent that all controls, other than rudders, failed to function. Ordering his observer to bail out, Lieutenant LaMontia was forced to keep his plane in the air when he noticed that his companion had become entangled in the many radio wires. Only after the observer had managed to free himself and clear the plane did Lieutenant LaMontia leave the controls and abandon his aircraft. His courage and coolness when his own life was endangered and unhesitant consideration for the safety of his endangered comrade reflect the greatest credit upon himself and the U.S. Infantry.*

Chapter 37

BREAKOUT FROM THE NAKTONG

"... we boarded an old Japanese cargo ship for an overnight trip to Pusan, South Korea. I remember a grizzled old sergeant telling us most of us would be dead in 48 hours ... I'll never forget then boarding a troop train for a brief trip to the front – and seeing cattle cars on the tracks alongside us filled with wounded and dead G.I.s." Pat Murphy, war correspondent

DOWN ON THE NAKTONG PERIMETER, spirits rose when men learned they were to break out and head north to link up with troops of the 7th Infantry Division moving down from Seoul.

General Walton Walker's breakout plan was influenced by his experience as a cavalryman in Patton's Third Army in Europe in WWII. He gained permission from General MacArthur to wait to launch his attacks until the day after the landing at Inchon, so the North Koreans along the perimeter would be distracted and thrown off balance.

On September 16, four South Korean divisions would attack up the center and east side of the peninsula, while the four American divisions would head toward the west coast and pivot north, trapping the enemy between their fronts. Author Clay Blair described it colorfully:

> Armored task forces would crash out of the perimeter everywhere at once, on available roads, to be followed by infantry. The tanks would stun and awe and overrun the NKPA in a single, overpowering blow; the infantry would come along to mop up. It was reminiscent of old cavalry tactics in which (as the joke had it) "the soldiers went out and charged in all directions at the same time, with a pistol in each hand and a saber in the other."

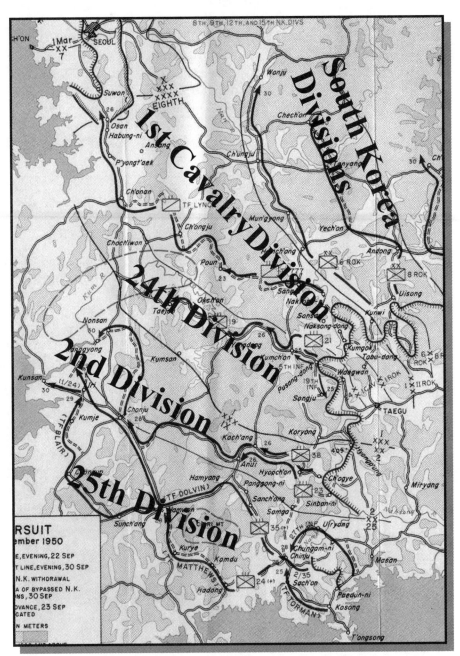

The 25th Division cleared the lowest tier, and the 2nd Division cleared the next tier north. The 24th attacked toward Taejon, while the Cavalry headed for Seoul. (Inset courtesy Center of Military History)

Frank Milburn

To help with the command load, two Army Corps were activated in the States and provided to Walker's Eighth Army in Korea. Two highly experienced commanders were selected to head up I and IX Corps, one of whom was Major General Frank "Shrimp" Milburn. Although he grew up in Jasper, Illinois, he called Missoula, Montana, his home.

Milburn was a 1914 graduate of West Point where – despite being short and wiry – he was a standout athlete. After WWI, one of his assignments allowed him to coach football while also heading up the ROTC department at Montana State University. (After he retired in 1952, Milburn went back to Montana, where he coached at Rocky Mount College.)

Milburn in 1945. (Signal Corps)

In WWII, Milburn commanded XXI Corps within Seventh Army, and at the time Korea flared up, he was Deputy Commander of American Army forces in Europe.

Upon activating IX Corps at Fort Sheridan, Illinois, Army Chief of Staff J. Lawton Collins chose Milburn to take it to Korea. Milburn asked his previous chief of staff, Rinaldo Van Brunt, if he would go to Korea with him, and Van Brunt agreed.

In a 1984 interview with historian Clay Blair, Van Brunt, who had also served with Milburn in combat, described his boss as "a wonderful soldier but a very quiet type. He'd never talk in meetings."

Milburn and Van Brunt filled out their staff with a cadre of about

30 officers and then flew to Tokyo to confer with General MacArthur.

"I had served under MacArthur in Manila in the late 1930s," said Van Brunt, "but Milburn had never met him. We had a hard time getting by Ned Almond. He kept us sitting outside MacArthur's office that day from 8:00 a.m. to late afternoon. Almond made us mad; we came to detest him."

From Tokyo, they flew to Taegu, which did nothing to brighten Milburn's introduction to Korea, as he hated flying. But Milburn received a warm reception from General Walker, with Blair writing, "Walker was apparently pleased to discover that Milburn shared his detestation of Ned Almond."

Meanwhile, General John Coulter had been getting I Corps up and running. Walker decided I Corps would lead the break out, but he wasn't sure Coulter was aggressive enough for the job. He lamented the loss of the first commander to serve under him in Korea, confiding to fellow officer Gene Landrum, "I wish I had Bill Dean here now. I would put him in command of I Corps and know that he would crack through the Red line, open a gap and push everything through that I could give him."

After much deliberation, Walker decided to switch the commanders so that Frank Milburn would lead I Corps – a decision that riled more than a few. As Clay Blair put it, "That Coulter was a 'MacArthur-Almond man,' as opposed to Milburn, who as a 'Collins-Walker man,' may have influenced Walker's decision not a little."

Big Six to Lead the Breakout

Lieutenant Harry Maihafer recalled the speech given by South Dakota's "Big Six" to his 21st Infantry Regiment on September 16:

> Colonel Stephens, looking tough, stood on top of a truck and began to speak. He had big news. Americans had pulled an end run, an amphibious landing at Inchon, far up on Korea's west coast. Stephens told what he knew of the landing, then said our own part in the counteroffensive was about to begin.
>
> "We're breaking out of the Naktong Perimeter, and **the 21st is going to spearhead it.** I want you to be aggressive, bold, and to move fast! If anyone delays you, move around them. We have the numbers now to overflow 'em, so don't worry about leaving any enemy bypassed; there'll be lots of people behind you to mop up."

Big Six was a leader. I for one felt charged up and inspired.
His was an emotional talk of a coach at halftime: hard hitting,
go-get-'em words that aroused.[176]

Colonel Stephens addresses his men September 16. (Courtesy Stephens family)

Private First Class Leonard Korgie felt the same way. He had been with
the 34th Regiment until it was reduced to paper status and then was
transferred into George Company, 21st Regiment. Korgie recalled his
commander's speech a bit more colorfully:

> "OK, men, we're done farting around . . . we've had enough of
> their shit. In the next couple of days we're going to rack their
> asses. You guys are *infantry*! The infantry closes with and
> destroys the enemy. We're going across that river, bust through
> the resistance and go north. If they try to stop us, we're gonna
> bayonet the sumbitches in their holes."

[176]Maihafer, Harry J. *From the Hudson to the Yalu.* . P 90.

... I noticed everyone moved with some vigor and spirit. It
was a far cry from those days when we dragged ourselves like
whipped pups down the long road from Taejon . . .[177]

*The Bronze Oak Leaf Cluster to the Silver Star is awarded to Colonel
Richard Warburton Stephens, Infantry, U. S. Army, for gallantry in action
against the enemy as Commanding Officer, 21st Infantry Regiment, 24th
Infantry Division, in action near Waegwan, Korea, on 18 and 19 September
1950. When instructions were received for his regiment to cross the
Naktong River and break through the Pusan perimeter, Colonel Stephens
personally led the reconnaissance party to the vicinity of the proposed river
crossing site. Continuously exposed to concentrated enemy fire and
observation, he voluntarily went forward alone to a vantage point from
which he could better observe the proposed river crossing area. From his
visual observation the attack was planned and launched during the early
morning hours. Again with complete disregard for his own safety he
established his command post at the river crossing. Although under heavy
enemy artillery, machine gun and small arms fire, he moved among his men
giving last minute instructions and encouragement where necessary. His
courage and superior leadership influenced materially the success of the
river crossing by his command. His gallant actions and unhesitant devotion
to duty reflect the greatest credit upon himself and the U.S. Infantry.*

Lloyd Jenson, Alfred Kaufman & Robert Cooper

As Eighth Army's pincer movements began to squeeze, Kim Il Sung's
troops, he spurred them to fight to the death. United Nations troops
were meeting rigid defiance as they pushed out of the shell-cratered
perimeter – but they were making progress.

The first obstacle for the 2nd Division was to successfully cross the
Naktong, and hurdles included negotiating roads badly damaged by
artillery, heavy rains and ever-increasing vehicle traffic.

Engineers cleared mines and built pontoon bridges for tanks,
equipment and supplies to be taken across the river.

Elements of the division first needed to seize several critical hills
overlooking the river, and by September 19, the 23rd and 9th Regiments
captured two of these – Hill 201 and Hill 174 – thus providing an
opening for crossing the Naktong.

---

[177]Knox, Donald. *The Korean War: Pusan to Chosin.* P 355-356.

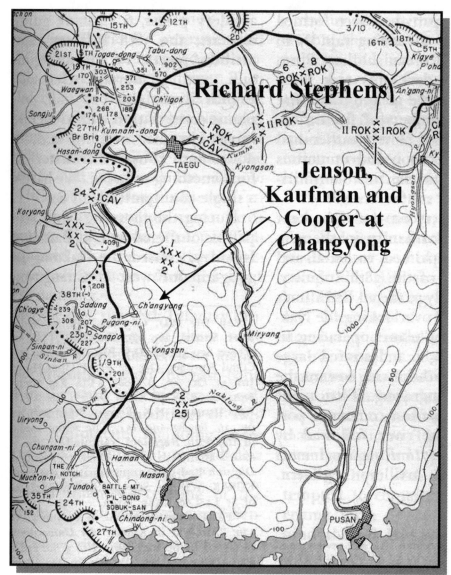

Richard Stephens

Jenson,
Kaufman and
Cooper at
Changyong

(Map inset courtesy Center of Military History)

During the fight for Hill 174, Montanan Lloyd Jenson (who had already earned the Distinguished Service Cross August 31) again rallied men of the 23rd Regiment's 2nd Battalion.

The first **Bronze Oakleaf Cluster to the Silver Star** *is awarded to Major* **Lloyd K. Jenson** *. . . who displayed gallantry in action against an armed enemy on 18 September 1950 in the vicinity of Changnyong, Korea. On that* *date he voluntarily led a task force composed of infantry, tanks and antiaircraft firing vehicles, with the mission of driving the enemy from Hill 174. Approximately 400 yards from the objective, the task force encountered an enemy outpost and, under Major Jenson's direction, inflicted heavy casualties upon the enemy and forced them to withdraw. He realized, at this time, that it would be impossible to take the objective and decided to hold a ridge nearby to be used as a line of departure for a larger force. As a result of his initiative and complete disregard for his personal safety, the task force insured the success of the attack launched on the following day and enabled the assault elements to complete the mission with a minimum of casualties . . .*

Among those who participated in the assault the following day was Alfred "LeRoy" Kaufman. He was born in Wisconsin, but after age seven, he lived with his uncle and aunt, John and Kate Kaufman, on their farm in Yankton County, South Dakota. LeRoy attended a country school, then graduated from Gayville High School, and worked as a farm hand before joining the Army from Sioux Falls in 1948.[178]

Alfred Kaufman

In Korea, Kaufman was attached to George Company, part of Major Jenson's 2nd Battalion. Under normal circumstances, his assignment as a cook would have kept him relatively safe, but the fierce fighting and heavy casualties in the Naktong Bulge not only put him in harm's way, it also brought forth his heroism.

*The **Silver Star** is awarded **Posthumously** to Corporal **Alfred Leroy Kaufman**, Infantry, U.S. Army, a member of Company G, 23rd Infantry Regiment, 2nd Infantry Division, who displayed gallantry in action against an armed enemy on 19 September 1950 in the vicinity of Changyong, Korea. On that date, his company had launched an attack against high ground defended by well entrenched enemy forces. In the initial stages of*

---

[178] http://koreanwarmemorial.sd.gov/SearchEngineForm/profiles/166.htm. 12 Dec 2013.

the advance, the company sustained severe casualties. Corporal Kaufman, who was a cook, realizing that riflemen were urgently needed, left his safe position in the rear and joined the depleted ranks of his company. Without hesitation and with complete disregard for his personal safety, he joined his comrades in a charge up the fire-swept slope. During the assault he killed four enemy soldiers at close quarters and was greatly instrumental to the success of his unit in overrunning the enemy positions. While engaged in the mopping-up operations which followed, he was killed by hostile artillery fire . . .

Robert Cooper was the fourth of fourteen children born to Walter Cooper, a miner, and his wife Audrey, from Deer Lodge, Montana. He joined the Army four days after his 17th birthday and was now a member of Love Company, 23rd Regiment.

Before dawn the morning of September 19, Cooper's 3rd Battalion slipped unopposed across the Naktong, and their element of surprise was so successful they caught a high-level North Korean officer and his staff sleeping. They also captured an enemy map that revealed the locations of North Korea's 2nd, 4th and 9th Divisions, and by noon, the battalion seized Hill 227, the dominant terrain near their river-crossing point.

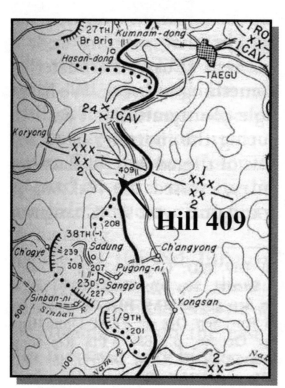

Hill 409 was surrounded on three sides by the river – and the enemy.
(Inset courtesy Center of Military History)

Cooper and his fellow soldiers dug in on the hill, and during the night a rain storm covered the movement of a company of enemy soldiers who infiltrated to the back side of the crest. The following morning, they charged Cooper's company while they were eating breakfast, taking back the position while inflicting 26 casualties. But the American boys counterattacked and regained the position by noon.

Their next objective was the region's dominant terrain feature, Hill 409. North Dakota's John Belgarde and his 9th Regiment had moved simultaneously with the 23rd during this phase, and he remembered this hill, saying, "You have to understand the vertical height is 409 meters above sea level, and we're right next to the Naktong River, which is pretty much at sea level. So Hill 409 is totally sticking up out of the ground vertical – you're up there."

It is unclear whether the hill was captured, or whether the men were in the process of taking it, but Cooper was manning a machine gun when the enemy counterattacked into his company's positions. The 18-year-old resisted with lionhearted grit for which a Medal of Honor may have been appropriate.

*The **Distinguished Service Cross** is **(Posthumously)** awarded to **Robert Cooper**, Corporal, U.S. Army, for extraordinary heroism in connection with military operations against an armed enemy of the United Nations while serving with Company L, 3rd Battalion, 23rd Infantry Regiment, 2nd Infantry Division. Corporal Cooper distinguished himself by extraordinary heroism in action against enemy aggressor forces at Changnyong, Korea, on 21 September 1950. Corporal Cooper's platoon was holding a position on Hill 409 when it was attacked by greatly superior numbers. He remained in position with his machine-gun for a period of four hours under constant artillery and mortar fire. Finally, despite an enemy banzai charge up the hill, he left the comparative safety of his foxhole and moved his weapon over an open route to an exposed position far down the hill in order to occupy a more favorable firing position. When his machine-gun was destroyed and he was wounded by enemy grenades, he continued to fight off the enemy with his pistol until his ammunition was exhausted. He then took his assistant's rifle and, ordering his helpers to the rear, held off his foes with rifle fire until he was killed by the enemy.*

George Hannan

"Although with his unit in Korea only a very short period before his untimely death, George made an indelible impression upon both the officers and enlisted personnel of his company by his remarkable ability to understand the situation and solve the problem at hand," reads a memorial to George Hannan, who graduated from West Point in June 1950. "On one occasion, he led a convoy of trucks almost one hundred miles over unchartered roads, with the constant threat of the enemy to his flank . . . "

Hannan was born in Mobridge, South Dakota, but he also lived in Aberdeen and Rapid City before graduating from Pierre High School in 1945. His father, Colonel William Hannan, had commanded a prisoner of war camp in Wyoming during WWII, and George followed in his footsteps by joining the Army on his 18th birthday. He received an appointment to the United States Military Academy from South Dakota Senator Harlan Bushfield while training at Fort Snelling, Minnesota. Hannan spent the following year at the Academy's Prep School at Amherst before enrolling at West Point.

As described on his memorial page,[179] Hannan appears to have been very creative, as well as musical:

> His first year was not the easiest plebe year ever spent at the Academy, and he seemed to appreciate his upper class years more than did most cadets. Always a studious person, George managed to survive, and his graduation in the middle of his class was a major victory. During his four years as a cadet, he participated in many extra-curricular activities, including work with the *Howitzer*, the Camera Club, the Concert Orchestra, and the Record Lending Library. He was a co-founder of the Record Library, and in his first class year served as president of the organization. Athletically inclined, his forte was handball, at which sport he easily held his own against all comers.

Hannan married Georgia Banks the day after he graduated, and a few weeks later, the newlyweds learned he was headed for Korea. He reported to the 205th Signal Repair Company in Fort Lewis, Washington, on July 26, 1950, and landed at Pusan, Korea, on September 16.

On October 2, Hannan's signal repair detachment was supporting South Korea's 6th Division in a very fluid situation near Wonju (see map page 387).

Unbeknownst to the Allied troops, in the quickness of their drive north, an entire North Korean regiment was bypassed and had

---

[179]Hannan, Georgia Banks (Hannan's wife) and classmate Harold G. Nabham. Web. http://www.usma1950.com/1950/memorials/HannanGE.htm

remained undetected in the mountains surrounding Wonju.

When South Korea's 8th Division moved up from a different direction, these trapped enemy troops made a desperate effort to escape, and unfortunately, Hannan and his crew of 19 were right in their path. At 1:00 a.m., approximately 2,400 enemy troops descended on Hannan's detachment inside a walled compound. That any of his crew survived is largely due to Hannan's sacrifice.

*The President of the United States takes pride in presenting the **Distinguished Service Cross (Posthumously)** to **George Ervin Hannan**, Second Lieutenant (Signal Corps), for extraordinary heroism in connection with military operations against an armed enemy of the United Nations while serving with Detachment E, 205th Signal Repair Company, attached to the 6th Republic of Korea Division, II Corps. Second Lieutenant Hannan distinguished himself by extraordinary heroism in action against enemy aggressor forces near Wonju, Korea, on 2 October 1950. Lieutenant Hannan was second in command of Detachment E, which consisted of two officers and seventeen enlisted men. While bivouacked in a compound on the outskirts of Wonju near the division command post, the detachment was attacked at 0100 by a banzai charge of approximately 2,400 enemy troops who had apparently been bypassed in the surrounding hills. The position of the detachment within the compound was discovered by the enemy. After subjecting the small force to heavy small-arms, mortar and automatic weapons fire, the enemy charged the compound in a frontal assault. The detachment commander ordered his troops to get out over the rear wall of the compound while he covered their withdrawal. With total disregard for his own safety, Lieutenant Hannan voluntarily took up an exposed position near the front entrance and distracted the enemy with his harassing fire to enable the unit to withdraw. Lieutenant Hannan maintained his position, although wounded several times, until all the enlisted men had cleared the area. When the enemy stormed into the compound, by sheer weight of numbers, Lieutenant Hannan was overwhelmed.*

Chapter 38

TASK FORCE LYNCH

"[This has been] the most rapid advance ever made in the history of American arms – you have added a new and glorious chapter to our national military history." General Hobart Gay to the 1st Cavalry Division

THE 1ST CAVALRY DIVISION'S breakout began at 5:00 p.m. on September 21 near Tabu-dong. The plan was for elements of the 7th Cavalry to first link up with the 8th Cavalry, after which a powerful assault team led by Lieutenant Colonel James Lynch, commander of the 7th Cavalry's 3rd Battalion, would push north. Beside him was his Operations Officer (S-3), James Webel, Duluth, Minnesota.

Task Force Lynch[180] first needed to fight its way through 25 miles of scorched and cratered enemy territory just to reach the Naktong. Then, after crossing the river, they would shove north to Osan, where the 24th Division had made its first stand against the Communists on July 5.

If the plan worked, the cavalrymen would meet up with the 7th Infantry Division, which was simultaneously heading south from Seoul. When the road from Seoul to Pusan was back in friendly hands, thousands of North Koreans would theoretically be trapped in the southwestern quadrant of the peninsula.

The area in and around Tabu-dong, Taegu, and the Bowling Alley had been the scene of intense combat for many weeks – including the magnificent showing of North Dakota's Harold K. Johnson and his 3rd Battalion, 8th Cavalry. North Korea's 1st and 3rd Divisions had since taken a tremendous beating here, and Colonel Lynch was counting on

---

[180] Alternately referred to as *Task Force Penetration*, *Task Force Lynch* and/or Task Force 777. To avoid confusion, *Task Force Lynch* will be used for this chapter.

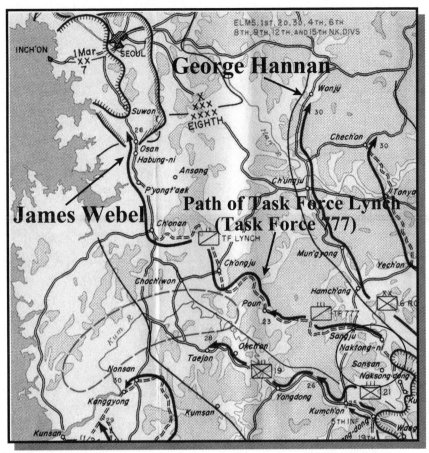

Task Force Lynch was headed straight for Seoul. Note Sonsan and Naktong-ni, lower right. (Inset courtesy Center of Military History)

them being near the point of collapse.

Step one of the mission was accomplished by 7:00 p.m., September 21, when the 7th "Custer" Cavalry seized Tabu-dong and joined forces with the 8th Cavalry. Lynch had his men form a perimeter defense for the night, and the officers worked on their battle plan for the following day until 3:30 a.m.

Lynch called for the men to reconvene at dawn, writing:

> But around 4 a.m., some 2,000 North Koreans let loose. They had been trapped between the 7th and 8th Cavalry Regiments and now tried to break through and get away to the north. Their supposed escape route included our battalion perimeter and the area just to the east of it. For the next two hours we were busy.

But repeated banzai attacks into the command post and the area around it were all repelled. . . .[181]

The task force jumped off again at 8:00 a.m., moving up the main highway without incident. About five miles out, the "two-hour-long column" came under sporadic small-arms fire, and the cavalrymen dispersed off the road to return fire. Lynch soon went forward and instructed everyone to return to their vehicles and keep driving; they should ignore "anything except determined resistance."

Meanwhile, Lynch's spotter planes informed him of a fleeing enemy column about five to ten miles ahead and that air attacks were being carried out. Soon after, Lynch's lead tank was hit, but the enemy's antitank weapons were eliminated, and the friendly troops kept moving toward the town of Sonsan, their next objective.

It was about this time that Lynch received an airdropped message that he was to change his objective to a ferry-crossing at Naktong-ni. While the message appeared to be from division headquarters, it was "unsigned and unauthenticated," and General Hobart "Hap" Gay, the division's commander, was actually with Lynch at this time. Gay knew nothing about this change in plans, so they decided to stick with the original order until the change could be verified.

After more enemy encounters, the column finally came within sight of Sonsan and the Naktong River. It was now the middle of the afternoon, and they still hadn't received confirmation on whether their mission was changed.

Meanwhile, a reconnaissance scout informed Lynch that a mass of enemy soldiers was seen crossing the river. Lynch deployed his men forward, but they came up empty. It was now about 4:00 p.m., and they were 25 miles into enemy territory. Still unable to verify his mission, General Gay instructed Lynch to dig in for the night.

Pulling such an enormous column into a perimeter was not a quick or easy task. Two hours later, just when this was accomplished, the orders were confirmed – they needed to immediately head north ten miles to Naktong-ni and make their crossing. Their time had not been wasted, however, as they had flushed some 50 North Koreans from the surrounding hills and paddies.

---

[181] This section based on: Lynch, James H. "Task Force Penetration." *United States Army Combat Forces Journal*, Vol. 1, January 1951. Copyright 2014 by the Association of the U.S. Army and reprinted by permission of *ARMY* Magazine.

The column led out again at about 7:00 p.m. They traveled in blackout conditions, but Mother Nature helped out with a bright three-quarter moon. Progress was smooth and steady until they were about halfway to their new objective, when they began passing burning buildings.

The column soon ran into the rear of a retreating North Korean column, but instead of engaging them, Lynch writes, "We followed a novel procedure." The task force disarmed the enemy soldiers and started them to the rear of the column with their hands on their heads.

After almost five miles of this, the column stopped again. Lynch went forward and found his lead elements perched on a bluff overlooking the river-crossing site. Just as he arrived, one of his tanks opened fire and scored a direct hit on an enemy ammunition truck laden with "heavy stuff, and it began to blow up a part at a time."

By the light thrown off by the explosions, they could see a column of 400 enemy infantrymen crossing the river by way of a sunken bridge below the bluff to their left. There were some problems with communications, but within a few minutes, friendly tanks and infantrymen all opened fire, with Lynch writing "the resulting slaughter in the river was terrific."

Meanwhile, "shells, grenades and small-arms ammunition were bursting and popping and whizzing all over the place," wrote Lynch. One shell hit the forward command post and wounded a tanker, so he ordered the column to back off a hundred yards. A reconnaissance of the forward area showed they had captured many heavy weapons, trucks and tanks, all abandoned.

It was now an hour before midnight, and Lynch still needed to secure the opposite riverbank. Getting his men across was going to be tricky, because they had no way of knowing how many North Koreans were waiting on the other side, and captured enemy soldiers indicated at least a battalion was scattered in the hills beyond the river.

The road they were using was so narrow and jammed that the column's assault boats couldn't be brought forward, and in front of them, six burning vehicles blocked the road.

Another factor now occurred to the command group. What if more enemy troops were moving up from behind to use this same escape route? It was possible they were completely surrounded at this point.

The combat engineers' lone bulldozer had earlier been lost when it broke through a bridge, but working with tanks, the engineers went to work clearing the road block before the fires could spread any further. Lynch later wrote that during the next several hours, there were "many individual acts of genuine heroism, when you consider the explosive situation and the intense heat."

Two reconnaissance parties crossed the river to size up the enemy threat and to figure out how to best get the friendly troops across the river. At about 3:00 a.m., they reported the foot soldiers could use the underwater bridge, but the water was waist high, the current was swift, and the footing was slippery. They still hadn't secured information about the roads on the far side, so Lynch assigned objectives based on best guesses.

Item Company took the lead at 4:30 a.m. The going was difficult, and men who slipped off the underwater bridge had to be rescued. When they finally made it to the other side, they were greeted by another surprise – a large pile of ammunition began to burn and explode at their exit point.

Whatever element of secrecy the Americans had was gone. Their main goal was now to just get across and avoid being hit by exploding ammunition on the far riverbank.

When the sun rose at 5:30, two full companies had made it across and were now moving toward their objectives. Since jumping off less than 24 hours earlier, *Task Force Lynch* had penetrated 36 miles into enemy territory, captured large amounts of equipment and vehicles, secured the division's bridgehead on the Naktong River and had killed or captured more than 500 enemy soldiers.

After successfully crossing the Naktong, the 7th Cavalry's 1st and 3rd Battalions leapfrogged north against minor opposition, and by the morning of September 26, Lynch's men were only 55 (air) miles from Osan. They now traveled many miles unopposed, and large groups of liberated South Koreans came out to cheer them as they went. The turnabout was invigorating.

The column halted at 5:30 p.m., when the six tanks up front ran out of gas. It turned out the column was missing its refuel truck, so the men collected gas cans from the column's trucks. This only gave them enough gas to fill up three of the tanks, but right then, a three-truck North Korean maintenance convoy happened by. They surrendered, and the tanks gained enough gas to get moving again.

At sundown, Lieutenant Colonel William A. Harris, commanding the 7th Cavalry Regiment, decided on a bold plan. He authorized the column to use headlights, and Lynch also ordered his lead tanks to pick up the pace. If, when they reached Osan, the 7th Infantry Division had not yet arrived from Seoul, they would go straight on through to Suwon.

To his rear, Lynch writes, "were miles of lights winding through enemy-held territory." They started spotting small North Korean units in each village, with both sides equally surprised to see the other.

Lynch writes, "The next vehicle behind me was some distance back, so I decided that discretion was in order, rather than valor, and held fire."

Most of the North Koreans surrendered, but one truckload refused, and a firefight erupted. Lynch joked that a "quick mental review of Field Manual (FM) 7-20 revealed no situation in which the battalion command group is supposed to act as point for a column in enemy territory." So the officers pulled over and let a platoon of infantry take the point with a 3.5 rocket launcher and a .50-caliber machine gun.

They were now only 10 miles from Osan. Tracers from small arms fire appeared in the distance, punctuated by the booming of artillery and tanks. Lynch decided "the parade was over." He ordered the trucks to turn off their lights. The fight was on.

James Webel

James Webel was a boy-wonder who also happened to be a high school dropout. Many years later, after a standout military career, he would hold several Master's degrees, including one from Harvard. He would also be a key player in creating "open office" space, more commonly known as cubicles, while working as the vice president and general manager for Owens-Corning's Architectural Products Division.

Webel was on the B Honor Roll when he dropped out of Duluth Central High. He joined the Minnesota National Guard in February 1941, and by the time war in the Pacific broke out ten months later, he was a corporal in the 125th Field Artillery.

It didn't take long for the Army to notice the 16-year-old's potential, and about the time his Duluth classmates were finishing high school, Webel was setting a record for being the youngest graduate of the Army's Officer Candidate School. He also became the Army's youngest officer to tackle the rigorous demands of Command and General Staff School. He finished with a "superior" academic rating and, at 19, became the Army's youngest captain.

It wasn't until 1946, after WWII, that Webel – now 22 – finally found time to get his high school diploma. By this point, he had also married his highschool sweetheart, Ramona, also from Duluth.

By the following year, Captain Webel was the acting chief of intelligence for the 24th Infantry Division, a post normally held by a

Lieutenant Colonel, and when the assignment became official in April 1949, he broke another record of being the youngest division-level intelligence chief in Japan.[182]

When fighting flared up in Korea, Webel ended up being transferred from the 24th Division into the 7th Cavalry to serve as that regiment's Operations Officer (S-3). As such, he was a central player in *Task Force Lynch.*

Webel's actions were poetic, in a way, as his personal fight took place near Osan, where his (previous) 24th Division's *Task Force Smith* had first met the enemy in ground action. Now, ten weeks later, Webel would avenge those men who died on July 5, including a fellow soldier from Duluth, Paul Larson. As with that earlier fight at Osan, Webel's action would be man-against-tank.

(Courtesy Webel family)

The actual clash on the night of September 26-27 took place just south of Osan at Hambung-ni. The column bypassed a bridge, and as they were rolling through, they noticed an enemy tank to their right. It was about 20 yards off the road, and its cannon was aimed at them. At first they thought it was a casualty of the Air Force. Lynch writes:

> Just as we passed the tank, the solemn voice of CPT Johnston, commanding the regimental mortar company, came over the radio: "Don't look now, but to our right is a T34." Almost at that very moment, the tank opened up with machine-gun and cannon fire.

The command group pulled over, and the entire column soon dispersed into the ditches as numerous enemy tanks marched their fire up and

---

[182] *Oakland Tribune.* 3 June 1973; "Captain adds post of G-2 to 'Records'." *Pacific Star & Stripes.* 14 April 1949.

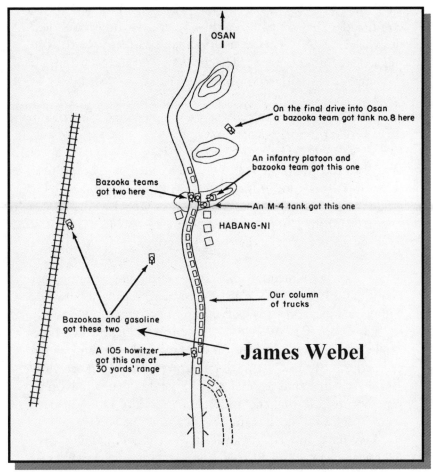

OSAN

On the final drive into Osan
a bazooka team got tank no.8 here

An infantry platoon and
bazooka team got this one

Bazooka teams
got two here

An M-4 tank got this one

HABANG-NI

Our column
of trucks

Bazookas and gasoline
got these two

A 105 howitzer
got this one at
30 yards' range

James Webel

(From *Army* magazine, January 1951. Reprinted by permission)

down the road.

An officer rushed forward to pull back the men who had already passed through, including the infantry platoon with the precious 3.5-inch rocket-launcher. Another officer tried in vain to contact the regimental commander, while another led a bazooka team and a platoon of riflemen in an attack on two of the tanks. One of these tanks was disabled, but the other moved out and started crunching straight into the column, running over several vehicles before reaching a better position in a nearby field. Lynch writes:

> A 75-mm recoilless rifle returned the enemy fire, and this halted
> the tank but didn't stop its fire. But now a bazooka team with

CPT James Webel, regimental S-3, and LT Woodside, commander of Company L, closed with the other tank and destroyed it. CPT Webel administered the *coup de grâce* with a can of gasoline into the engine. The gas exploded and blew him off the tank, but he suffered only minor burns.

Actually, Webel also had cracked ribs, but he shook it off and continued his crusade against the T34s.

Corporal Pat Murphy was a newly arrived information specialist traveling with the task force at that time. Decades later, he wrote about his 13-month reporting stint: "Heroes were everywhere. One I remember more than others was Major James Webel, of the 7th Cavalry Regiment." Murphy's first-person account was published by *Stars & Stripes* about a week after Webel's heroic actions:

Three North Korean tanks met a flaming death near Hambung-ni when a 1st Cavalry Division officer angrily attacked with a bazooka and a five-gallon can of gasoline.

Capt. James B. Webel . . . emerged from the two-hour single-handed battle burned on the face and arms and with a cracked rib. The 27 year old infantry officer's spectacular assault, which stands as one of the most daring of the Korean war, occurred during the 180-mile 1st Cavalry Division dash from Taegu to Osan, a scant 35 miles south of Seoul . . .

The tank moved forward and began crunching over American jeeps and light trucks and firing into the masses of troops hiding in ditches.

While Webel moved closer to the action to see how the tank could be stopped, another tank approached dangerously close.

Thinking the second tank was American, he leaped up in its path and yelled, "Watch the hell where you're going, Mac!"

After the tank raked his position with machinegun bursts, the tall American officer knew it wasn't American.

Captain Webel climbed up the tank from behind and tried to drop hand grenades into an air vent. But the tank swung about sharply and threw him to the ground.

Three rounds from a 75-mm recoilless rifle, fired by a convoy gun crew, proved to be ineffective against the thick-shelled tank. Several grenades lobbed by another convoy crewman plunked through an air vent and exploded. For a few minutes the tank sat idle.

"But darned if that thing didn't start up again," Webel said. "It swung its turret around, fired at the convoy some more and began driving right over our jeeps again – smashing them flatter than pancakes."

He climbed atop the tank and poured five gallons of gasoline into the white-hot engine pit.

"As near as I can remember," he said, "the tank blew up immediately. I was thrown about 35 feet into a rice paddy. I just rolled around for a few minutes, trying to get back on my feet. I was pretty dazed, and the burns began to pain me all over."

As he sat in the paddy, several more enemy tanks rounded a bend in the road to take up where the first tank was stopped. At less than 25 yards, Webel fired three bazooka rounds into the tank's guts.

"The damn thing was blown to hell. And the crew didn't get out either," he said.

While another bazooka crew distracted the other tanks, Webel reloaded his rocket launcher and crept toward another target.

"The third tank was like a sitting duck," he said. "That is, it was like a sitting duck until it turned in my direction and began bearing down. I fired four bazooka rounds into it from about 40 yards. That did it. Nothing left but a smoking hunk of metal."[183]

*The President of the United States of America takes pleasure in presenting the **Distinguished Service Cross** to Captain (Infantry) **James B. Webel**, United States Army, for extraordinary heroism in connection with military operations against an armed enemy of the United Nations while serving as Operations Officer of the 7th Cavalry Regiment (Task Force 777), 1st Cavalry Division. Captain Webel distinguished himself by extraordinary heroism in action against enemy aggressor forces at Hambung-ni, Korea, on the night of 26 - 27 September 1950. As the leading elements of the task force entered the sleeping village of Hambung-ni, ninety-eight miles behind enemy lines, they were suddenly ambushed by a force of ten hostile T-34 tanks supported by foot troops. When the rapidly firing enemy tanks smashed the column, the outnumbered and outgunned men withdrew to the*

---

[183] Murphy, Corporal Pat (1st Cavalry Division). "Angry Cav Officer Destroys 3 Tanks." *Pacific Stars And Stripes*. 7 Oct 1950.

flanks to make their stand. As the ensuing battle raged fiercely in and near the village, Captain Webel, realizing that drastic action would be necessary to save the column, stepped out to destroy the leading tank. Suddenly swerving and almost overrunning its daring adversary, the enemy tank averted Captain Webel's attempt to climb aboard to drop grenades through an open periscope slot. Continuing to smash through the column, the tank swung off the road and into a rice field, gaining a more advantageous firing position. In the meantime, Captain Webel moved swiftly to a point opposite the tank's new location. Seeing the ineffectiveness of a group of men attempting to put the tank completely out of action by throwing grenades into an open hatch, he seized a five-gallon can of gasoline from the nearest vehicle, ran to the side of the tank, and after a comrade had failed to set fire to it by dashing gasoline on its sides, he climbed aboard. Knowing full well that an explosion might cost him his life, Captain Webel poured the gasoline through the ventilator over the hot engine, whereupon, in a burst of flame, he was blown approximately thirty feet through the air by the resultant blast. The lull provided by the spectacular destruction of the lead tank enabled the task force to reorganize. Disregarding shock, two broken ribs, and second-degree burns on his face and hands and, notwithstanding concentrated enemy fire that continuously swept the narrow streets, Captain Webel refused medical attention as he established cohesive defensive positions. Then, with a loaded bazooka, he proceeded to a point on the edge of the city where, from a range of approximately twenty-five yards, he fired alternately into two assaulting enemy tanks until they were destroyed. As enemy troops started withdrawing, Captain Webel dropped the bazooka and, from an exposed position on the road, opened fire with his submachine-gun. Then he again refused medical attention until all other wounded persons were treated.

Chapter 39

ATROCITIES

"It was beyond my comprehension that any human beings could treat other human beings as badly as our men were treated by the North Koreans. I could hardly believe that a human being could be so bestial as these people were." General Frank Allen, *Hearings on Korean War Atrocities, 1953*

THE HONOR OF RECAPTURING TAEJON rightly went to the 24th Division, which had lost a tragic number of men there in July. For the men of the 19th Regiment, it was perhaps their most satisfying action in the Korean War, as they had been utterly green when they were committed to the battle on the Kum River some nine weeks earlier.

Taejon had since become a major assembly point for the North Korean Army, with elements of seven enemy divisions located in and around the city.

On September 27, the 19th Regiment, assisted by the Air Force, pummeled the city. The following morning, the 2nd Battalion reached the city limits only to discover the enemy had withdrawn during the night. Heavy concentrations of enemy were spotted fleeing north by road and rail, and the Air Force made quick work of them.

Meanwhile, friendly scouts moved into Taejon, and by late afternoon, the 24th fulfilled its mission of reclaiming the city.

But the division's satisfaction was soon muted by gruesome evidence of mass murders of soldiers, prisoners, and civilian men, women and children in and around Taejon. Other mass graves were soon discovered at Sachon, Anui, Mokpo, Kongju, Hamyang and Chonju. No exact count could be made, but an estimated 5000 to 7000 were killed in Taejon, alone. Veteran war correspondent Bem Price writes:

The pall of death hangs heavily over this town of rubbled tile and tin. Already the bodies of 1,100 massacred Korean civilians have been found. Nearly 700 were in and around a Franciscan monastery.

Some authorities say 5,000 to 6,000 persons may have been killed by North Korean security police Wednesday and Thursday.... There were 3 known survivors of the slaughter – two Americans and one South Korean. One of the Americans died since.

Lt. Robert W. Shultice, Norfolk Va., said both Americans and the South Korean were buried alive but only lightly. They were discovered as they struggled through the dirt for air . . . The Americans were tied by their wrists to dead men. All of the slain were bound arm to arm.

Seeing this stung the imagination. It was no mad orgy. There was no wild machine-gunning, it was a coldly calculated massacre; each man had been shot individually. Many apparently were clubbed to make sure they were dead. One man had a hatchet sticking from his skull. . . .

The story of these atrocities began unfolding 5 days ago. A few minutes after the victorious U. S. 24th division recaptured Taejon, excited South Koreans began telling of mass murder.

First, the trench containing the G.I.s was found in the rear of the west Taejon police station. Later that night, a patrol entered the Taejon prison and found 400 civilians posed in death in every imaginable position of agony.

Now this. A former French Canadian monastery is a temple of death – a huge grave surmounted by a desecrated cross. How many South Koreans are sprawled in the basement of the cathedral, no one knows . . . I could not force myself into the basement, past the tangle of arms and legs and the smell of the dead.[184]

Rescue at Namwon

Rodger Jones and other wounded POWs from the 29th RCT held back at Hadong had spent about a month in a filthy bus station before the breakout forced their captors to start marching Jones' group north.

---

[184]Price, Bem. "Find 1,100 Korean Civilians Massacred in Taejon Sector." *Mason City Globe Gazette*. 2 October 1950.

"Lieutenant [Kenneth] Reid said they were gonna take us north, and we started marching. And they said no, you can't take these guys – the eleven who weren't ambulatory. 'Leave them here, we'll care for them,' they said. But we thought they'd kill them, right? But they didn't. They started carrying them.

"We were on the road, and boy, the natives was running us off the road. One time, *Oh my God, what's the matter?* Here comes a cavalry unit! I never saw a horse cavalry unit in my life. They were going hell bent for leather – North Korean, huh? Oh! If somebody would've had a log and threw it in there, they would've been a mess. Boy, were they traveling!

"We did about ten miles that night. They put us in a barn, and they gave us a bowl of . . . like, soup, you know? It looked like a little piece of meat with hair, but I ate it. The bowl was made out of a coconut shell, you know? So they left us in there, and they gave us water, let us sleep all day. And that night they put us on the road again," said Jones.

"But the next place we got to, they weren't so nice about everything. They put us in a jail cell, but before we went in I got a rifle butt right down the middle of my back, because I guess I wasn't moving fast enough for this jerk, huh? They put 21 out of us 23 in one small cell. Sam and the Lieutenant were behind us, so they put them in another room by themselves, right?

"Of course we said, *Jeez, this is awful. We can't even rest*, you know? So what we did was just lay down on top of everybody, okay? And that was a no-no, which they never told us. There was no laying down. We had to sit all day long. The only time you moved was you put your hand up to go to the bathroom, huh? That's the only time you could move. And when it got dark, we didn't think we were going anywhere, so we laid down again. And we got beat up again.

"The next night was a tough one, because that's a long one, and we went up over this mountain, Cheonwangbong (also called Chiri Mountain). I looked it up. It's the second highest mountain in Korea, the highest one being in North Korea. When we came down off that mountain, that's the first time we were still on the road at daylight. We were in this town, Namwon, and did it stink! They had a big military hospital there, and you could smell that before you even got near it – even though we smelled pretty ripe ourselves.

"There was a railroad train in the tunnel," said Jones. "He was playing footsy with the American planes. He comes *shoock, shoock, shoock*, out that tunnel, and a plane would come down strafing, and he'd go *shoock, shoock, shoock, shoock* back into that tunnel. Out again, back in. Out again, back in. I think they finally got him, though."

Jones' group of 23 was combined with another group of POWs in an abandoned building. They had no way of knowing, but American forces were hot on their trail. On September 27, the 25th Reconnaissance Company, along with Company A, 79th Tank Battalion, led the advance of *Task Force Torman* to Hadong, capturing North Koreans as they went. The prisoners, as well as local civilians, told them American prisoners had just passed through.

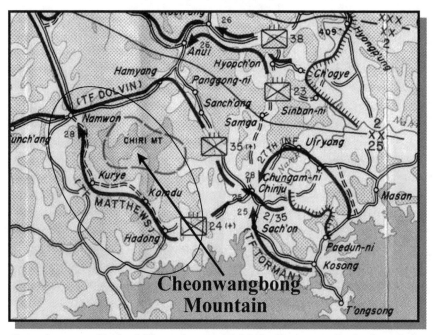

Jones' group climbed Korea's second-highest mountain during their march from Hadong to Namwon. (Inset Center of Military History)

Bright moonlight allowed the task force to turn north in hot pursuit that night, and ten miles north of Hadong they rescued the eleven wounded men Jones' party had been forced to leave behind.

The following day, the task force became stalled when several vehicles got stuck while crossing the river below the town of Namwon. Sergeant Raymond Reifers, Mississippi, was with the lead tank of the 25th Reconnaissance Company. They had already made the river crossing, so he and his crew continued on alone.

Entering the streets of Namwon, Reifers found the town crawling with enemy soldiers who were distracted by strafing and rocketing from two F-84 jets. Apparently unaware American ground forces were so nearby, the enemy soldiers fled in panic when they suddenly noticed Reifer's tank approaching. Army historian Roy Appleman writes:

> Reifers said later that the scene would have appeared ludicrous if his own plight had not been so precarious. Suddenly he heard American voices calling out, "Don't shoot! Americans! G.I.s here!" A second later, a gateway leading into a large courtyard burst open and the prisoners – shouting, laughing, and crying – poured out into the street.
>
> Back at the head of the stuck column, 1st Lt. Robert K. Sawyer over his tank radio heard Reifer's voice calling out, "Somebody get up here! I'm all alone in this town! It is full of enemy soldiers and there are American prisoners here." Some of the tanks and vehicles now pushed ahead across the stream. When Sawyer's tank turned into the main street he saw ahead of him, gathered about vehicles, "a large group of bearded, haggard Americans. Most were bare-footed and in tatters, and all were obviously half starved. We had caught up with the American prisoners," he said, "there were eighty-six of them."[185]

Several liberated prisoners told reporters their guards had been tying them up in preparation for executing them. When the F-84 jets swooped in, the guards scattered, and before they could return, the men were rescued by the tank. Several prisoners asked to immediately go back into combat to seek revenge; they were, of course, turned down.

"We were quite fortunate," said Rodger Jones. "It was cold, and we didn't have any clothes. I lost my jacket somewhere, and I was really cold. The men that were really sick and wounded – real, real, real bad – they put them on ambulances right away. But us guys had to wait for a 2½-ton truck. Then I bummed a sweater off the driver, huh? I didn't steal anything off a tank or anything like that.

"But I didn't eat anything like some of them did. They got so sick it wasn't even funny. I ate some crackers, and I had some coffee. These other guys were eating out of #10 cans we called 'em, right? Spaghetti and meatballs and things like that. It was too much for their system.

---

[185] Appleman. *South to the Naktong.* P 576-577. The valiant Sgt. Reifers was last seen alive November 27, 1950, when the Chinese attacked near Kunu-ri. He remains missing in action.

"We got deloused and we got new fatigues, put on a plane and flown to Japan. Deloused again, given new fatigues. Then we moved to Tokyo General, and from Tokyo General they moved us all over to different places. Moved us down to a field hospital outside Yokohama, which was really nice and peaceful and comfortable there. I was getting ready to leave there, and the doctor says, 'Okay, let me look at your record.'

"He looks at my x-rays, and he says, *Hey*. I says, *What?* He says, *You got a foreign body in you*. I said, *Who is he??*

"There was a hunk of shrapnel up there, about three months, in my right shoulder.

"Later, after I got rescued, I was back in the States. I went down to personnel, and he says, 'You're on the levee.' I said, 'Where?' He said, 'Korea.' I said, 'Like hell I am, chief, I've been there.' 'Well,' he said, 'you're going.' I said, 'No I'm not.' He said, 'Yes you are.' I said, 'Were you there yet, chief?' He said, 'No.' I said, 'Why don't you go, then?'

"I was really angry. He didn't know it was Army regulations, see? I'm not being a wise guy, don't get me wrong. But I had looked it up already. You can't send a man back to a war zone where he was a prisoner."[186]

John M. Hanley, Jr.

Colonel John Hanley Jr. obtained his law degree from the University of Chicago in 1931. He then returned to his hometown of Mandan, North Dakota, where his father, John Hanley Sr., was a prominent lawyer, politician, and a high-ranking officer in the National Guard.

The apple didn't fall far from the tree. When WWII came along, the younger Hanley was serving as Assistant State Attorney General and was a high-ranking officer in the North Dakota National Guard.

Hanley was called up to serve in Europe, where – as a lieutenant colonel – he commanded the 2nd Battalion of the famed "Go for

[186] Casualty reports for men of the 29th Regiment were severely compromised due to their immediate decimation at Hadong and Anui and the chaos over the following weeks. At the time of their liberation at Namwon, the 29th Regiment had been dissolved to paper status, and record-keeping seems to have become non-existent. Therefore, it is impossible to recreate a roster of the 86 prisoners liberated at Namwon. Rodger Jones, for example, isn't listed as being returned to military control until October 20, 1950, the date the other Hadong prisoners were massacred at the Sunchon railroad tunnel.

Broke" 442nd Regimental Combat Team. The 442nd was made up of Japanese Americans, and during the course of this assignment, Hanley was awarded the Combat Infantryman's Badge, Legion of Merit, Bronze Star, French Croix de Guerre and the Italian Cross of Valor.

After the war, Hanley pursued a military law career and received a Regular Army commission. He was serving in the Office of the Judge Advocate General in Washington when the Korea War broke out. Lessons about prosecuting war crimes had been learned from WWI and WWII – primarily that it was a mistake to wait until a war's conclusion before investigating crimes. Thus, when atrocities came to light almost immediately in Korea, plans were quickly set in motion for officially investigating them as war crimes.[187]

It was likely his background in both combat and law that led to Hanley being chosen the first Chief of the War Crimes Division in Korea. He and his team carried out thousands of investigations into the mounting atrocities.

On December 4, 1953, Colonel Hanley appeared at a congressional hearing before the Subcommittee on Korean War Atrocities. Because the fates of political prisoners in North Korea remain relatively unchanged since that time, Hanley's testimony is as important now as it was then:

> Colonel HANLEY. They were killed by the tens of thousands.
> Senator POTTER. The South Korean civilians?
> Colonel HANLEY. Yes, sir; they certainly were. And we found and have in the files of the War Crimes Section pictures of the South Korean civilians lying in windrows on hillsides by the hundreds, tied together and consisting of men, women and children . . .
>
> Most of the atrocities against the civilians, the vast bulk of them in number, took place in the latter part of September of 1950, and were part of the program that the Communists had of getting out of South Korea in order to prevent them being bottled up between the landing at Inchon and the Pusan perimeter. They determined quite readily that they couldn't take the prisoners with them, of course, which wasn't practical under the circumstances – they had no transportation – most of those

---

[187] Borch, Fred L. "Investigating War Crimes. The Experiences of Colonel James M. Hanley During the Korean War." *The Army Lawyer*. Sep 2012. P 1-2.

North Koreans marched out of South Korea through the mountains, and taking the prisoners with them [wasn't] possible.

The other alternative of leaving them where they were, or turning them loose, was never even discussed, at least in any of the records that we have of these meetings that they had before they actually disposed of the prisoners. The only question at issue in any case that I know anything about was the question of how to dispose of the prisoners, where to get the ammunition, whether they had ammunition enough, where to get trucks if they intended to take them out to the mountains, and possibly where to get the rope or wire to bind their hands with an order to take them out.

Senator POTTER. But there is no question as to the ultimate fate?

Colonel HANLEY. There was no question about the fate. In some cases they threw them down mine shafts alive. In other cases they buried them alive in big pits. In some cases they set fire to the jails, with the jails locked and the cell doors locked, burned them up that way, and in other cases they went through the jail spraying the inside of the jail with burp gun fire, the inside of the cells, and in other cases took them out in the mountains in groups, truckloads, and shot them down, always on telling the prisoners they were taking them north, they were going north quite a distance. They would be taken from the truck off to the side of the road and lined up and shot down. There were a surprisingly large number of survivors from those incidents. We found not only the bodies but have stories of the survivors.

Senator POTTER. You were chief of the War Crimes Commission at the time of the Taejon massacre, is that correct? ...Did you secure evidence of the fact that on the vast majority of the [prisoner death] marches the same pattern held true, that the weak who were unable to keep up with the march were slaughtered as they fell back?

Colonel HANLEY. If there were any marches in which that did not happen, it has not come to my attention.

Mr. O'DONNELL. Colonel, at Taejon, when our boys were massacred as well as the South Korean troops, were any civilians killed?

Colonel HANLEY. Yes, sir.

Mr. O'DONNELL. Could you give us an approximate number of civilians killed at that time?

Colonel HANLEY. It would be very difficult to arrive at that. Our investigators got on the scene, investigating and looking into the matter of the civilians, 3 or 4 days after the Communists killed them. In the meantime, the relatives of these deceased had come into the various areas where they were buried, had taken away many bodies for their own burial, funeral, and so it is impossible to know how many. Nobody will ever know. Nobody has ever counted them. . . . I would like to note, a great deal has been made in the past, particularly 2 years ago, about the number of Americans and number of South Koreans who were victims of these atrocities. I don't think that numbers are too important. When you are talking about 30,000, 40,000, 50,000 victims, numbers cease to have any real significance. The fact that the Communists committed atrocities, and many of them, is established beyond any shadow of a doubt. Whether this particular man or that particular man was a victim of an atrocity doesn't seem to me to be the important thing. The numbers are not the important thing.

Senator POTTER. The fact that it took place is the important thing?

Colonel HANLEY. It took place, and it took place beyond any peradventure of doubt. The story is far too well documented for any dispute on the question of the commission of the atrocities. . . . I think it might be noted, and I think it should be noted particularly that the evidence in the War Crimes files is a result of affidavits, pictures, eyewitness accounts, participants, and perpetrators. It is not a compilation of rumors and hearsay evidence that some people seem to think it was. I think that point is very important.

Senator POTTER. In other words, it is composed of documented cases which were gathered to hold up in a court of law?

Colonel HANLEY. Yes, sir. And any particular individual may look at any particular case, any particular affidavit, any particular circumstance, and possibly raise a question about it. But he cannot raise a question about the pattern and about the existence of the atrocities. That he cannot do.

Hanley's investigative findings were never used for prosecuting Korean

War criminals. There were two reasons given for this:

1. The United States is technically still at war with North Korea and China; and

2. The United States turned the matter over to the United Nations, and the matter of who should conduct the trials was never determined.

One can speculate a third possibility exists: the South Koreans were guilty of large-scale atrocities toward communist political prisoners, often with full knowledge of American servicemen.

To prosecute one side of this travesty would open an ugly can of worms for the other.

Chapter 40

FALLING DOWN UMBRELLA MEN

"Our basic load [was] ammunition, 3 days assault rations, canteen of water, pack, rifle, extra ammo, grenades, our pistol and ammo, and anything else we could carry that we figured we would need. Had a hard time walking after we chuted up and had to be helped into the plane." Don Martin, 187th Airborne

AS OCTOBER ARRIVED, the United Nations pondered the future as MacArthur unsuccessfully called upon North Korea to surrender. South Korean troops were massing at the border waiting to take the fight into North Korea, where large numbers of enemy soldiers were escaping the trap that had been sprung at Inchon.

There was frustration within General Walker's Eighth Army, because the men and supplies he needed for continuing his mission were tied up at Inchon, as well as Kimpo airfield, both of which were congested and clogged for two reasons:

1. Generals MacArthur and Almond (X Corps) were pulling the Marines out of combat to send them by sea to the opposite side of the peninsula, where they were to make another amphibious landing.

2. MacArthur was keeping the newly arrived 187th Airborne Regiment, along with hundreds of planes, at Kimpo Airfield until the moment was right for his next big move.

Thus, supplies for Walker's troops weren't getting through, and the Marines and paratroopers – manpower he badly needed – were not only out of reach, they would remain that way for weeks. Meanwhile, the enemy continued to escape north.

U.N. troops were soon given the okay to cross the 38th Parallel into North Korea, but MacArthur waited three more weeks before he finally gave the 187th Airborne a mission worthy of their skills and specialized training. The regiment's three battalions – along with all vehicles, heavy weapons, equipment and supplies – were to be airdropped into two zones above the North Korean capital of Pyongyang on October 20.

The 187th (commonly called the 187th RCT) was the only airborne unit to fight in Korea. They called themselves the Rakkasans, a term the

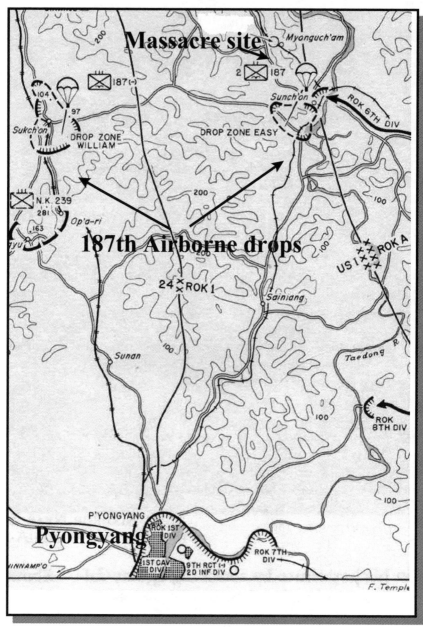

(Inset courtesy Center of Military History)

Japanese used for them in WWII. Translated, rakkasans means *falling down umbrellas.*

The drop was postponed several times due to weather and other circumstances, so it wasn't until the afternoon of October 20 that the regiment finally jumped near the towns of Sukchon and Sunchon.

Their mission, as the men understood it, was to cut off North Korean officials escaping from Pyongyang and to also intercept a train carrying American POWs. Although their jump was brilliantly executed, they were unfortunately too late to carry out either mission, as explained by Army historian Roy Appleman:

> The airborne troops had not cut off any sizable part of the North Korean forces. The main body of the enemy had already withdrawn north of Sukchon . . . No important North Korean Army or government officials were cut off and killed or captured. Civilians in Pyongyang said that the principal North Korean government officials had left Pyongyang on 12 October [and] most of the American and South Korean prisoners had been successfully removed into the remote part of North Korea.[188]

Nonetheless, the 187th did engage the enemy's rear guard units over the next several days and ended up capturing 3,818 North Koreans.

Ken Levasseur, Frank Bowen & Bruce Iverson

Kenneth "Frenchy" Levasseur was among the paratroopers who completed the jump at Sukchon. He was born in Minneapolis, but two years later, his mother died after the birth of her eighth child. His dad, a Greyhound bus driver, did his best to hold the family together, but a few years later, the beleaguered father had to appeal to his parish for help. Four of his children, including Ken, were consequently raised in an orphanage in St. Cloud.

After high school, Levasseur decided to join the military. He was interested in electronics, and his dad suggested he could receive training if he joined the Navy. He agreed and went to Alexandria to sign up.

"When I got into the bus depot, there were like seven of my high school buddies there sitting in a couple booths. They said, 'Frenchy,

---

[188] *South to the Yalu. . .* P 658.

what are you doing here?' I said I came down to the join the Navy. '*Navy??*' They'd all joined the Army. They said, 'We're all going Airborne.' I said, 'Why Airborne?' They said, 'Because you get fifty bucks more than anybody else.'

"Hey, I'll go for that! I'd do damn near anything for an extra fifty bucks. If you're a private first class and getting jump pay, you're getting as much as a staff sergeant in the regular army. I was 18. That was a good deal! So all seven of us volunteered for Army Airborne, but only two of us actually made it through jump school."

Levasseur was a member of Baker Company, and his 1st Battalion (as well as the 3rd Battalion) jumped over Sukchon.

"Man, that was one of the worst jumps I ever made," he said. "I was the last guy on the stick, and the lieutenant came up to me and handed me a walkie-talkie. He said, 'Levasseur, you take this down.' I said, 'I never operated one of these.' He said, 'Just get it down there.'

"When I went out the door I tossed it. I needed my right hand to pull the rip cord. Well, we jumped so low I never had a chance to pull the rip cord anyway. I came down through some power lines and got really mangled – just really beat up. My chute collapsed as I fell through the wires, and I fell the rest of the way without a chute. So that wasn't fun at all. There was no time to correct anything.

"In a combat jump at that time, 700 feet is about as high as they'd go – sometimes even lower. The reason was because the longer you were in the air, the more chance you had of getting shot. On that jump, one guy did get killed, but that's amazing, because over in Europe when they were jumping, a lot of people got killed. That's why they were choosing to jump lower. Better to be injured than shot."

Among their veteran members, the 187th Rakkasans count such notable commanders as Generals William Westmoreland, David Patreus, and Normand Schwarzkopf, Jr. Although he was still a colonel at the time, Frank Bowen, Jr. was on a par with these commanders, and indeed was promoted to Brigadier General the day after the jump.

His father, Frank Bowen Sr., was a career army officer serving in the Philippines when Frank Jr. was born there in 1902. Over the years, the younger Bowen lived many places, but he entered West Point from Nebraska, and in 1944, the *Abilene Reporter News* reported his hometown was Cedar Rapids, Iowa.

Bowen is among the most decorated soldiers in United States history. During WWII, he fought in New Guinea and the Philippines, receiving a Distinguished Service Cross, Distinguished Service Medal, three Silver Stars, the Legion of Merit, and three Bronze Stars. His actions in Korea and the Cold War added another Distinguished Service Cross, a fourth Silver Star, two Distinguished Service Medals, and many other honors.

When the airdrop took place, the 48-year-old officer made the jump with his men over Sukchon.

Brigadier General Bowen after receiving his first star in Korea.

*The **Bronze Oak Leaf Cluster in lieu of a Second Award of the Distinguished Service Cross** is awarded to Brigadier General [then Colonel] **Frank Sayles Bowen, Jr.**, U.S. Army, for extraordinary heroism in connection with military operations against an armed enemy of the United Nations while serving as Commanding Officer of the 187th Airborne Regimental Combat Team, 11th Airborne Division. Brigadier General Bowen distinguished himself by extraordinary heroism in action against enemy aggressor forces in [North] Korea on 20 October 1950. General Bowen, gallantly risking his life, personally conducted the daring* *maneuvers of more than four thousand paratroopers approximately thirty-five miles behind the enemy front lines. After six hours' delay caused by extremely adverse weather conditions, the perfectly coordinated airdrop was accomplished with an absolute minimum loss of personnel and equipment. General Bowen parachuted with his men to pre-designated drop zones in the Sukchon-Sunchon area known to contain enemy ground forces and anti-aircraft batteries, concentrating his forces in a strategic move to block the enemy's main escape, communications and transportation lines, including the two road and rail lines leading north out of Pyongyang. As a result of General Bowen's dauntless and inspirational leadership, this operation was highly successful and effected the immediate seizure of initial objectives. General Bowen's heroic and exemplary action in constantly exposing himself to danger while personally leading his units reflects great credit on himself and the military service.*

Bowen later told reporters the jumps caught the enemy by complete surprise and that both Sukchon and Sunchon held stockpiles of ammunition, weapons and supplies held in garrisons guarded by small detachments of North Korean soldiers.

Upon further investigation, Bowen's men also discovered the hills were honeycombed with defensive positions linked by underground communications. Bowen theorized the North Koreans had been planning on falling back to these positions if the capital city of Pyongyang was lost – which had indeed happened.

An unexpected problem soon presented itself to Bowen's men, as reported by war correspondent Joe Quinn[189] several days later:

Paratroopers of the 187th Regimental Combat Team, which jumped on Sunchon and Sukchon five days ago, disarmed the 14 and 15-year-olds and told them to go home, but they still wound up with 3,000 prisoners who seemed to be happy to be in American hands. The return of paratroopers to the regrouping area was delayed by the big haul of prisoners. G.I.s beefed, because the Reds seemed hopelessly beaten but had no one to tell them to surrender.

Regarding the handling of prisoners, an unusual event put a Mosquito pilot in the spotlight around this time. Bruce Iverson grew up in South Minneapolis, the son of Emil and Maurine Iverson. He first joined the

---

[189] Quinn, Joe. "3000 prisoners big headache." *Pacific Stars & Stripes*. 26 Oct. 1950.

Navy, and he used his diving skills for disarming underwater bombs and/or mines in Korea. But his father flew in WWI, and he also had a cousin who flew, so Bruce also endeavored to become a pilot.

"He was always an adventurer and thrill seeker," his daughter Katie explains. "I believe he was about 14 or 15 when he was in college, as he skipped a few grades. He was an only child and had very few cousins, so his childhood was spent mostly with adults. Because he was in college at such an early age, it was detrimental to him socially, and most of his stories he told of his childhood were about being with adults, having money, and being on his own a lot.

(Courtesy Iverson family)

"I could go on and on about his stories and the things he taught me. He was smart, funny, witty, strong, loving and a great teacher of life. I hung on his every word, and I thought he hung the moon.

"He also had his downfalls and demons to deal with. It would be easy to say that the war changed him, and it did, as it brought on a whole new set of issues he had to deal with. Many night terrors my father had. So many memories and guilt of what he was part of. However he was the best of the best as far as pilots go."[190]

Bruce often recounted to his family a story of scouting with his Mosquito when one of his comrades – an Iowa farm boy – noticed, "There are too many bales for this size field." They called in some firepower, and sure enough, the enemy was found hiding inside the hay.

War correspondent Leif Erickson described the event that put Iverson in the news the day after the 187th jumped at Sukchon:

It happened shortly after noon on a road between Anju and Sukchon where American paratroopers were dropped north of Pyongyang Friday.

When fighter-bombers hit a 10-truck convoy just south of

---

[190] Communications with author March 2014.

Anju, two trucks survived. The Fifth Air Force voice plane – a C-47 with a loudspeaker – then flew over broadcasting instructions to the North Koreans to turn their trucks around and drive south. The shaken Communists complied.

On the way south, Mosquito T-6 pilot Lt. Bruce T. Iverson of Minneapolis and observer Lt. Thomas L. Lewis spotted 300 soldiers with two more camouflaged trucks.

The voice plane broadcast orders for them to turn around and head south. The voice in Korean mentioned an "or else." Fighter-bombers were circling above waiting for the Mosquito to call them in on targets.

The 300 troops with their two trucks turned south. Iverson and Lewis criss-crossed over the highway, herding them. They delivered them as prisoners to United Nations troops outside Sukchon.[191]

William Gore, Special Ops

"When I jumped, my parachute failed to open," William Gore wrote to his parents in Lewistown, Montana. "As I fell through space I suddenly went through the top of a captain's parachute. His parachute then collapsed and we both headed for the ground."[192]

Gore's parachute finally opened just above the ground, slowing them both enough to land unhurt in a rice paddy, which absorbed much of the impact.

Gore was a seasoned combat veteran, having fought in the Pacific during WWII, and he had gained his officer's stripes the hard away – being offered a battlefield commission, which he accepted at age 22.

Gore had always seemed destined for the soldier's life, as described by his son, Dennis:[193]

Dad was born in 1921 on a dryland farm around Beckett, Montana, which was homesteaded by his maternal grandparents Dennis and Emma Monger. Dennis was 46 when he homesteaded. This was pretty old for such an adventure. Dennis

---

[191] *Pacific Stars And Stripes.* 23 Oct 1950.

[192] *Ogden Standard Examiner.* 12 Nov 1950.

[193] Dennis Gore email communications, March 2014. Reprinted by permission.

was known for a keen eye for horses, raising and racing them in the county fairs. He was also known for his foot speed and was the winner of local races for money. The Mongers had one daughter, Bernice. They also had a hired hand, John Jordan Gore who had come to Montana from Tennessee when he was 16, and they married. John always went by Jordan (pronounced Jerdan) and his father and Al Gore's grandfather were brothers. When my Dad's sister was married in Washington, D.C., the senior Al Gore, senator from Tennessee, was the one who gave the bride away.

Dad's parents eventually tried their hand at farming, but the Depression ended that. Moving to Lewistown, Jordan took a job in law enforcement being both a policeman and probation officer. Dad stayed on the farm with his grandparents for a while, not wanting the city life. He was raised on horseback riding to and from school daily. At 13 he was a jockey at the county fair, but by the following year he was too big. He was saving his money to buy a bike, but when he went to the store he wound up buying a single shot .22 rifle instead. He always said they couldn't afford shotguns, so when pheasant hunting they would just shoot them through the head.

Eventually, his parents made him move into town, and in high school he played football and ran track. His real love, however, was boxing. Each town had their own team and the sport was covered in the local paper routinely. He had a fair amount of success.

When Dad was a senior in high school, he and a friend took the bus to the Canadian border with the intent of enlisting in the Canadian cavalry, since they were already at war (in WWII). His Dad somehow found out where they were going and called the border and had both boys thrown in jail. When he went up to get them, the first thing he asked them was did they need a smoke? Apparently Dad had been smoking since he was 12. They wouldn't have been able cross the border anyway, since that required $20 that they didn't have. The offshoot of this was that his parents allowed him to enlist in the National Guard at 17.

The point of all this, I think, is that Dad was raised to be a warrior. Not by intent but by his environment and his love of outdoor and physical activities. When the Korean War broke out, he was in Alaska in the Artic survival school and assigned to the 11th Airborne. He was immediately recalled and sent to Korea with the 187th RCT. Sometime in the 1990s he was actually installed as a DMOR (Distinguished Member of the Regiment) for the 187th in ceremonies at Ft. Campbell, Kentucky.

Two days after the jump at Sukchon, William Gore was highly decorated despite disobeying orders to surrender. Because the 187th was behind enemy lines, the Montana officer's 3rd battalion was set up to defend itself from all directions. Gore was the leader of the Pioneer and Ammunition Platoon, and the night of October 21-22, he was in charge of security and defense of the perimeter.

As the sun rose, they were approached in the same manner as so many units had experienced in the opening months – through the early morning fog. Gore was with the command group when word came in that "Orientals" were in front of their position. His commander believed them to be South Koreans who had arrived in this sector before the jump every took place. By the time they realized they were face to face with North Koreans instead, the commander, who Gore admitted was physically and emotionally exhausted, realized they were vastly outnumbered and likely surrounded. He thought it was too late to put up a fight, and they would have to surrender. As a result of a 1993 interview with Gore, Lieutenant Colonel Thomas Greco writes:

> Gore, standing next to the commander, heard this order in disbelief. . . . seeing absolutely no advantage in surrendering, and realizing the North Koreans would not take any prisoners, Gore told the S2, a captain, not to put [the order to surrender] out on the radio. He then directed the S3, a major, to take charge of the CP while he went forward to direct the fight and to "Do as I tell you."
>
> LT Gore moved forward about 100 yards and came within 50 yards of the North Korean commander. The North Korean officer told him to surrender and lay down his weapon. Gore responded, "No we won't. You should surrender to me." The North Korean raised his rifle to kill Gore, but Gore raised his carbine quicker and killed the officer.[194]

In the six-hour fight that developed, Gore literally took charge of the battle and did all he could to help overcome the confusion and

---

[194] Greco, G. Thomas, LTC. *Values: Lest we Forget.* USAWC Military Studies Program Paper. U.S. Army War College: Carlisle Barracks, PA. 1993.

disorientation the rifle companies were experiencing. There were times he called in artillery strikes within 40 yards of his own position, staying in a spot where two men had just been killed and two others were wounded.

"The enemy was firing right at me," he told Greco, "but it seemed like their bullets would stop short of me and then go in another direction."

The **Distinguished Service Cross** is awarded to First Lieutenant (Infantry) **William E. Gore**, U.S. Army, for extraordinary heroism in connection with military operations against an armed enemy of the United Nations while serving with Headquarters Company, 3rd Battalion, 187th Airborne Regimental Combat Team, 11th Airborne Division. First Lieutenant Gore distinguished himself by extraordinary heroism in action against enemy aggressor forces near Sukchon, Korea, on 22 October 1950. On that date, Lieutenant Gore was in command of troops defending the perimeter when the enemy attacked in strength of approximately one battalion. Due to poor visibility in the early morning light, the enemy was able to advance to within forty yards of the perimeter before being observed. Lieutenant Gore, being the first to recognize the enemy, ordered his men to open fire causing the enemy to immediately deploy to the left and right of his position. The enemy attempted a ruse at this time by calling out "ROK" giving the impression that they were friendly troops and causing most of the men to cease firing. Lieutenant Gore, recognizing the trick, ordered his men to continue firing. Exposing himself to intense and accurate small arms fire, he went from one position to another around the perimeter directing fire and designating targets. The enemy began to close in on the position, and Lieutenant Gore, realizing the situation was becoming desperate, completely exposed himself to the enemy fire by dashing up a hill to the rear where a radio was located and called for artillery fire. Standing in an exposed position where two men had just been killed and two wounded, he personally directed the artillery fire, which *caused the enemy to become disorganized and halt their encirclement of the defending positions. The fight continued for approximately six hours, but the enemy was unable to advance. During the battle Lieutenant Gore made at least ten inspections of the perimeter, distributing ammunition and boosting morale of his troops by his presence. His heroic actions and leadership were inspiring to his men, who rallied and held the perimeter inflicting heavy casualties on the enemy.*

Afterward, Lieutenant Gore had to own up to his "disobedience of orders and insubordination to two senior officers," but to his great relief, his commander told him, "You did the right thing. Thanks."

Gore's initiative earned him more than the DSC. Three months later, when he was about to go on R & R in Japan, he learned a special Ranger Company was going to be formed, and he volunteered. When he got back from Japan, the decision had been made that not only was he accepted – he would lead it. Gore later described *Task Force Red Wing* to interviewer Jack Swantsrom:

. . . in January of 1951, I was assigned to organize, train and command a special Ranger company for operation behind enemy lines. The regular ranger companies that went over were disbanded by then. Colonel [John] McGee at that time had a mission of organizing a unit to go behind enemy lines for the purpose of [gathering] intelligence and – at the proper times – for sabotage and guerilla warfare. I felt highly honored to be selected out of the Far East Command to command this unit.

My particular unit was hand picked South Korean Marines. They would be more likely to survive in North Korea than would Americans. As a Caucasian in Korea, you don't need a trained military advisor to tell you you don't belong there, where the others did – although we wore uniforms all the time, with the exception of a few agents we had; they wore civilian clothes.

The Korean Marines at that time actually did get the pick of the troops. This was no joke. They actually did. So Eighth Army, the high command in Korea, made an agreement with the Korean Marines that this particular unit would be picked by them and commanded and trained by an American officer for hazardous duty. The Korean general of the Korean Marine Corps hand-picked these men. There were a hundred men, and they were absolutely outstanding. And believe me, if you're an up front Ranger trainer, and you have to stay ahead of these guys, it's an awful tough job. We never lost a single man in training, not one.

The unit was top secret all the time, even during training. Don't ask me why. Our most sophisticated equipment was a machine gun. The boats we had, we had to capture from the enemy. So I don't really see anything all that secret, but it was several years before I could say anything about it.

We didn't have much to scrounge from, and I would not allow them to use an air drop – I don't think you had to be a military genius to see that when you saw a parachute coming down, somebody's going to be underneath it. The only time we ever had a parachute drop was – the Air Force, and it's the only time in my career this happened, they mistakenly strafed us. They didn't hit anybody in the Ranger company, but they killed a whole bunch of civilians, and I authorized them to use an awful lot of our medical supplies. So I authorized an air drop the next day to give us some medical supplies, but we left two days later. Otherwise, we were supplied by boat.[195]

When 6' 2" Gore was given this special ops unit, he was told he could choose any man from the 3rd Battalion to be his second in command. More than a few were surprised when he chose 5' 7" Hubert Frost – a mess sergeant from Tennessee. But Gore knew Frost had turned out to be a fighter after seeing him in action during their 6-hour battle on October 22.

Gore was inducted into the Army Ranger Hall of Fame 1994, and Frost, a three-war veteran, was inducted two years later. Their induction entries provide vivid accounts of their mission(s) with *Task Force Red Wing,* as well as a description of the day Gore suddenly found himself unable to move his arms or legs.

. . . placed under the operational control of the 8086th Army Unit, Lieutenant Colonel Gore and his Korean Rangers conducted a series of successful reconnaissance, raid, and ambush operations on the west coast of Korea. Task Force Red Wing remained on the move, conducting their operations behind enemy lines for five months while successfully avoiding a pursuing enemy force. He lost only three men during his time in action behind enemy lines and caused the North Korean and Chinese Armies to

---

[195] Swanstrom, Jack, *Interview with LTC William E. Gore,* Special Operations History Foundation. www.specialoperationshistory.com/items/show/705. Web: 3/20/2014.

commit large numbers of troops to his pursuit that could have been used to fight against the United Nations forces. His actions have been chronicled in books and articles. He has been cited as an example of the value of courage. Lieutenant Colonel Gore was an outstanding combat Ranger and his actions and deeds set the example for all future Rangers to follow.

*Sergeant Major **Hubert H. Frost** is inducted into the Army Ranger Hall of Fame for his outstanding service as a Ranger in airborne and infantry assignments. During his service in Korea, then First Sergeant Frost deployed with the 187th RCT to Korea and led his unit in the combat jump into the Sukchon area in October 1950. When the Headquarters, 3d Battalion, 187th RCT came under attack from a superior force, First Sergeant Frost rallied all Headquarters personnel and fought along with Lieutenant William Gore for over six hours to defeat a North Korean battalion. Because of his demonstrated courage and tactical acumen, First Sergeant Frost was selected by Lieutenant Gore to accompany him and a handpicked force of South Korean raiders to be amphibiously inserted behind North Korean lines to raid, ambush, and gather intelligence. His tactical advice, resupply coordination, and courageous presence during long range reconnaissance patrols and agent insertions contributed largely to the success of this mission. Both Lieutenant Gore and First Sergeant Frost were known by name, rank, and service number to the North Koreans and were pursued but never captured as they raided and gathered intelligence behind enemy lines. After several months, newly promoted **Captain Gore was stricken with polio**. First Sergeant Frost rowed out into the Yellow Sea in a rubber boat until he flagged down a British destroyer to get medical assistance for his crippled friend. When the British diagnosis revealed that Captain Gore required immediate evacuation, First Sergeant Frost successfully coordinated and controlled an aerial medical evacuation by a small fixed-wing aircraft. First Sergeant Frost remained behind as the lone American with this reconnaissance force. Throughout his entire career, this Ranger has always "Led the Way" by his physical presence and personal example.* [196]

Dennis Gore remembers his dad and Frost became friends for life:

Besides achieving the rank of Command Sergeant Major, Frost also climbed the Matterhorn. Not bad for a kid from Tennessee who I believe only had an 8th grade education. When Frost was rotated out of the Ranger unit shortly after Dad was evacuated

---

[196] www.benning.army.mil/infantry/rtb/rhof/RHOF.xml Web: 20 March 2014.

with polio, he went to visit my Dad. The problem was that he was on a hospital ship moored at the dock somewhere along the Korean coast. The gangplank was up, so Frost shinnied up the mooring ropes, past the rat catchers, and reported to the radio room, asking to see the ship's captain. The captain initially refused to let him visit my dad due to quarantine issues, but eventually allowed him a 10 minute visit, as Frost said he wasn't leaving until he saw Gore. The captain agreed to lowering the gangplank when Frost left.

Gore, Frost and several members of
***Task Force Red Wing* in 1951.** (Courtesy Gore family)

Chapter 41

THE SUNCHON TUNNEL MASSACRE

"Between the crosses, row on row, that mark our place; and in the sky the larks, still bravely singing, fly scarce heard amid the guns below. We are the Dead. Short days ago we lived, felt dawn, saw sunset glow, loved and were loved . . ." Canadian WWI medic John McRae, *In Flanders Fields*

THE LARGER GROUP of the Hadong-Taejon POWs had been consolidated with other prisoners in the Moo Hak girls' school in Seoul, where crammed to capacity, they slept on floors, body against body. Men sick with dysentery and diarrhea were unable to contain their bowels, and the prisoners were overwhelmed by stench, misery, frustration and rage.

James Yeager, Colorado, recalled they started hearing thumping sounds one day and thought the guards were playing basketball in the school gym. But they soon realized they were hearing artillery fire.

Soon after, new prisoners arrived – Marines – and they learned of the amphibious assault at Inchon. When the fall of Seoul became imminent, their enemy captors started burning their paperwork. Seriously ill POWs were taken out and executed, and at least one was buried while still alive.

On September 23, the survivors were again formed up to move out, but before they left, they wrote their last names on the chalk boards in hopes American soldiers would discover they were still alive.

A 14-year-old prisoner known to Yeager as "Kid" had obviously lied about his age to get into the Army. "He was always taunting Mr. Kim, and Mr. Kim hated him. Well, Kid discovered a door ajar on the ground floor, and inside the room he found bags of rice crackers and cigarettes. He filled up his pockets, and he stuffed his shirt into his pants and filled it up also. Kid returned to the room and passed out smokes and crackers till his supply was used up. Later, he did it again a couple more times.

"Toney and I had planned on escaping the next night shortly after dark. As the day wore on, the more excited we became. To our dismay, about an hour before dark, the guards had us fall out and form up in the school yard. Then Mr. Kim and a couple of guards, with Kid stripped to the waist, marched up in front of the formation. Two large rocks were placed in Kid's outstretched hands, and Mr. Kim delivered a raging, raving speech about stealing from the Korean People's Republic. Every time Kid moved his arm or hand, the guards would hit him in the face with a rifle barrel.

"Mr. Kim ordered our guards to move us out, and we marched to the road. The last time I saw Kid, he was still standing there, and they were beating him.

"After turning onto the road, I noticed a railroad paralleling the road about 10 to 20 feet away," Yeager said. "A short time later, we heard a steam engine, and then three flat cars appeared, being pushed by the engine.

"The flat cars were loaded with men in blue quilted-uniforms. This puzzled us, because they didn't look like Koreans. From this point on, the march turned more brutal by the day."

Seoul to Pyongyang Death March

Dodging active combat sectors, this column of some 400 prisoners was hustled on foot for a day and a half without letup. Soon, Mr. Kim announced there would be no more rice for the prisoners.

The group's heroic senior officer, Major William McDaniel, finally talked Mr. Kim into letting them march in daylight instead of at night. This allowed two things: American planes could possibly keep track of them, and the men could better cope with the increasingly cold nights.

"It was a forced march to keep us ahead of our own troops," wrote Burdett Eggen. "They fed us things like dog biscuits. We didn't have much water, but the biscuits had to be soaked before you could eat them. But pretty soon, even the biscuits ran out, and we had nothing to eat except what we could steal along the way."

"None of it was very pleasant," said J.T. Monscvitz, "but it was more comfortable during the day. It was more beneficial for us, because boy, one of the worst experiences we had there, one of our Corsairs jumped over a mountain and started shooting. The plan was you hold fast, and they'll recognize something is wrong. And sure enough, they quit shooting. But I can still feel them flying at me!

"So they had us moving in the day, and we ended up in some little village after several days. And the Americans made a bombing run on us, and I thought *Sure as hell, my own people are gonna kill me*. My ears still ring from that. Boy, stone and glass – it was really a mess."

"The first several days was really hair raising," Yeager said. "The old 'Hung-Go' call would ring out, but we didn't break stride but kept marching and waving our rice rags. A jet would come roaring over the column, and after he passed to the front, he would go into a steep climb and execute several rolls and go out of sight. At that point all eyes were fixed on him, but all of a sudden three more jets in succession would buzz us, firing their guns and hitting the road or anything that looked like a target ahead of us. The three planes would peel off to the right and left and center and execute the same routine that the leader had executed. Then the leader would do another run, and then they would leave. It finally dawned on us that they must be keeping track of us and maybe taking pictures also."

Yeager and Toney were in "A-Group" and experienced both the best and the worst of the guards. "We were the lead group, and there was a tall Korean that we called John," Yeager said. "Now, there's some controversy about John, but to my knowledge, I never saw him after we got to Pyongyang. He disappeared there. The reason, I think, for his disappearance was that John, in the dark of the moon a couple times, helped Toney and me carry some people that weren't able to make it.

"John would point out places where we could steal along the road, because they had their red peppers drying out on rice mats. One day Toney would steal out of the gardens and off the mats. I would pick up cigarette butts and field strip them and put them in a Pall Mall package that I had run across, and that was my tobacco pouch. Then we would trade off. The next day I would steal out of the gardens. And this damn Buck, in the second group, would shoot at us. He was one who would beat, and club, and bayonet people who were falling out."

"We lost a lot of men in the march," said Minnesotan Bill Henninger. "When we crossed the 38th parallel, a big stream there, the fishermen were waiting to get across and sell their wares. And I thought *I'm gonna see if I can get a couple of fish*. They were all dried, packed in their ox-carts, and I got about four or five and stuck them inside my jacket. Then a couple of the others, they seen it, and they grabbed some. Later, we got

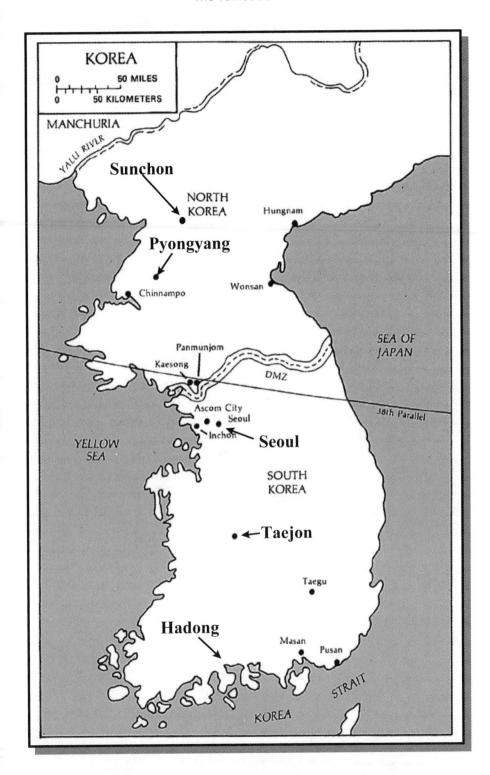

KOREA

0   50 MILES
0   50 KILOMETERS

MANCHURIA

YALU RIVER

Sunchon

NORTH KOREA

Hungnam

Pyongyang

Chinnampo

Wonsan

SEA OF JAPAN

Panmunjom

Kaesong

DMZ

38th Parallel

Ascom City

Seoul

Inchon

Seoul

YELLOW SEA

SOUTH KOREA

Taejon

Taegu

Hadong

Masan

Pusan

STRAIT

KOREA

a chance to eat them. They were full of maggots, but we cleaned them off, and we had some good fish. But it didn't last long."

Few ex-POWs care to describe what they were willing to eat, but bugs, live frogs, and undigested food in feces were all fair game. Some men would catch rodents and cats. Others purposely ate maggots, because the medics told them they were a good source of protein.

This march ended October 10 in the North Korean capital of Pyongyang. Men who were captured at Taejon had covered more than 400 miles, as the crow flies. "The government says we must have hiked about 600 miles," said Bill Henninger. The men from Hadong had covered a far greater distance. Either way, the price was very high.

"Out of approximately 400, only about 275 men made it from Seoul to Pyongyang," said Jim Yeager.

Once again, they were quartered in a schoolhouse. "The next day we just laid around in the rooms trying to recover from the march. That evening we received a piece of rice cake for supper. This was passed out after dark. The only lights were candles, and some of the men did not get a piece . . . The pieces were about the size of a fig newton. We had not had anything to eat for 36 hours or more."

"When we finally got to Pyongyang," said J.T. Monscvitz, "we were interrogated by real Russians. We were surprised about all the Caucasians around. Most of them were Russian soldiers. Before that, everybody in North Korea interrogated you. Every damn soldier they had thought he was an interrogator. They asked the same stupid questions, and whatever they want to hear you tell them.

"We didn't know what the hell was going on with the war. I sure didn't. I was two months away from the front lines, two months away from my own people. No way I knew what was going on. You just tell them whatever they want to hear.

"I think a lot of the patriotic ideas – when you're back in an office, nice and warm, comfortable, and you're fat and sassy, you can come up with all these great ideas. 'I'll be a great hero.' Well, by this point, you're kind of out of your mind. You don't know what the enemy is doing, and you don't know what your people are doing. You can tell 'em whatever you want. You can tell 'em you're a general, you're a private, whatever you want. Whatever they want to hear. I even told them about water supply, and it was really interesting, because they didn't understand one bit of what I was saying. You can tell them all the chemistry you want. It's all the same stupid questions – you give them the same stupid answers.

"But, the Russians were more savvy to that. They knew what they were doing. Those people there were true interrogators. It was great. *We'll give you an opportunity to go to Siberia.*" Monscvitz laughed. "As an 18-year-old, my idea of Siberia was a big iceberg, so I wasn't turned on by that idea. But they offered all kinds of great opportunities there. *You want to get into communism. It could really be a great opportunity*! 'I just want to go back to the United States.' *No, you don't want to do that.* Their interrogators were truly people who knew what they were doing."

During their week in the North Korean capital, the men continued hearing distant artillery, and they could see muzzle flashes from big weapons at night. One morning at about 2:00 a.m., the men were herded out of the school and formed up into columns.

Lloyd Krieder, a medic from Pennsylvania, later testified: "They moved us out again the same as they did in Seoul – in a hurry. I would say one-third of the men couldn't possibly stand up, they were so weak. So some of them came out, we carried them out, and some we couldn't even get off the floor. The North Korean guards went in there and said, 'Let them go,' and they hit them over the head with butts of rifles and they were possibly killed. They couldn't make the march, and they didn't want them liberated. Probably they didn't want them to speak the truth when they came back to the States and that is why they killed them, so they would be better dead than to come back and tell the truth. . . . They kicked them and spit on them and hit them over the head, like animals."[197]

The guards told Burdett Eggen they were being taken to salt mines in Manchuria. They learned the next part of their journey would be by rail, and it was at the Pyongyang rail yard that Bill Henninger's good friend, George Kitchens, died.

"We were forced to climb into dirty open steel coal cars," said Jim Yeager. "During this event, the guards were especially brutal, beating and clubbing us. It was bitter cold, and the steel walls of the cars intensified it. We all huddled together trying to keep warm, to no avail. The car jerked, slamming us against the walls as it pulled out.

"For the next three days, the train moved slowly towards the northeast. It moved only at night. During the day, the guards took us off the train in groups of 30. They led us out into the fields and let us find our own chow. We scrounged up red peppers, grass roots and anything that was edible. When near a stream, we would catch snails and

---

[197] *Hearing before the subcommittee on Korean War Atrocities, Part I.* 3 Dec 1953. P 50.

eat them raw, we were that hungry."

Like so many other POWs in Korea, they were given almost no fresh water, leading to continued dysentery and internal parasites. "We would lap it up like dogs out of puddles in fields or rice paddies that had been fertilized with human waste," Yeager said. "No man in his right mind would have dared drink that stuff, but we were so crazed with thirst we didn't care about the after effects.

"About once a day the guards passed out to us a handful of grainy substance, which was millet. It was hard and gritty, like sand, and tasted like bird seed. We ate it for a while but then gave it up. It not only ruined our teeth but made our tongues swell and our throats raw. It only added to our terrible thirst. We lost 30 men during that five-day ride. Some succumbed during the freezing nights, and others just keeled over dead while in the fields hunting for food. Most of the time the guards made us bury these poor souls. We had no tools to do this. We had to use our bare hands."

GI MISSING — Mr. and Mrs. John H. Wood of Iowa Falls received word that their son, Cpl. Lyle Wood (above), 22, is missing in action in Korea since Aug. 18. He served 22 months in the navy before enlisting in the army Sept. 30, 1948. He left for overseas in June, 1949, and was stationed in Japan before going to Korea. He was serving with a mechanized cavalry unit. He is the 1st Iowa Falls serviceman reported missing in Korean action.

Among those who died during this phase was Sergeant Lyle E. Wood, from Iowa Falls. He was a squad leader with Company G, 5th Cavalry Regiment, 1st Cavalry Division, when he was captured in very heavy fighting on Hill 303 near Taegu on August 16, his 22nd birthday. He had just written his mother to say there was a

(*Mason City Globe Gazette* Sept. 1, 1950)

rumor his unit was going to be pulled back for a rest, and he hoped it was true, because they were all very tired.

A few days later, the family received the news that he was missing, and on October 1, they were notified a North Korean radio broadcast reported he had been captured.

Lyle's brother, Arnold "Buck" Wood, had been serving in the Navy in Korea when he learned Lyle was missing. He later reenlisted in the Army and volunteered for Korea in hopes of finding his brother.

Buck's daughter, Carol Wood, writes, "Til the day my father died he talked of his love for his brother Lyle and how he wished he could one day bring his remains home and lay them to rest."[198]

At the time of this writing, the family's wish is unfulfilled.

Rescue Attempts and Escapes

"*FOOD*" was spelled out on the ground, said a spokesman for the 5th Air Force on October 9. The story appeared in two conflicting reports in *Pacific Stars & Stripes*. The first article reported pilots had spotted a group of about 1,500 POWs on the ground, but a second report put the number at approximately 150. This group had been spotted the previous day behind enemy lines, about 50 miles north of Kaesong, "in a flat space near the foot of a mountain."

The word "food" had been formed from mounds of dirt, and the observation pilot who spotted the men thought they were Americans. That evening, planes flew from Kimpo Airfield to drop food and supplies to these men.

The Air Force planned a rescue effort for the following day, but by then they could no longer find these men. The spokesman surmised they may have been POWs who had escaped from their captors. "Indications point to the fact that the food supplies and other equipment had been sufficient for them to scatter and start moving south individually or in small groups."[199]

Leonard Warren had escaped three times since his capture at Hadong. He was always recaptured, but the Alabaman finally succeeded the night of October 17, when the train stopped because of damaged tracks.

"This time the guards fell asleep, and I got off the train," Warren said. "There was three other guys got away with me. There was four of

---

[198] www.koreanwar.org/html/korean_war_project_remembrance_2011.html?casualty _id=20638

[199] *Pacific Stars & Stripes.* 9 Oct 1950.

us together total. It worked out just right," he said. "Clouds came over the moon, and it got dark. I was the first one off. Another guy was supposed to go with me, because he and I planned it.

"I got off the train and got down between the couplers and looked to see if there was any guards walking up and down the railroad tracks. Then I went back and told him there was a tree about three or four miles away. You could see it up on the hillside – there was a silhouette – so I told him I'd meet him up there. So that's where I went. Pretty soon these other three guys, one at a time, showed up. My buddy sent word with the last guy that he couldn't come, because he was too sick. We were about the same age, and he and I were gonna go back to North Carolina and raise tobacco after we got out," Warren said. [200]

The men who escaped with Warren were Joseph Cerino of Bangor, Pennsylvania, Raymond Hamilton of Branson, Michigan, and Robert Morris of Chester, Pennsylvania. They were rescued by North Korean farmers who took them in and protected them.

In a subsequent newspaper interview, Robert Morris said, "They gave us four hard-boiled eggs. They were the first fresh eggs I'd had in Korea. We had corn on the cob and even a small jar of honey. They gave us cigarettes and blankets. They were wonderful."

These four men made contact with the air force through a South Korean unit. "Me and the other three showed them on a map where the train was before we got away from them," said Warren. "They said they were gonna drop the 187th Airborne on them the next morning. But it was too foggy, so they couldn't do that. They had to wait until the next day to do it. If they could've dropped in, they could've saved more of them. But they didn't get to do that. They got there one day late."

Ray Rindels, Frank Torigian & Barney Ruffato

Several months earlier, Raymond Rindels, from Shell Rock, Iowa, had been a 19th Regiment military policeman guarding prisoners at Sugamo Prison in Tokyo. Two weeks into the war, the strapping MP found himself fighting as a rifleman on the front lines. He was well built, 6' 3" and 235 pounds, with a good-natured smile.

Rindels was the oldest of five children. His younger sister Myrna described him as "intelligent, thoughtful, artistic and creative, and he had a great sense of humor."

---

[200] Author interview Leonard Warren 2008. *Chester Times.* 21 Oct 1951.

Ray and his brother Vern left school after 8th grade to work on farms near Allison, Shell Rock and Tripoli. Myrna writes:

> Ray had a difficult childhood and adolescence, as our father was physically abusive to him, Vern, and to my mother. In 1948, my mother divorced my father. We moved into town (Shell Rock) and Ray had a horse he trained and tended to. Both boys were "scrappers" and loved to engage in fights with peers. In 1949, both enlisted in the service. Ray became an MP and was assigned to Japan. Vern enlisted in the Navy and did not see combat.

Ray and Vern Rindels, 1949. (Courtesy Myrna Rindels)

> When we were notified that Ray was a POW, the town of Shell Rock was very supportive. I remember the congregation praying for him each Sunday. His status of "missing" was very difficult for our mother. We would go to area movie theaters after the regular features had shown to watch Korean War news reels hoping to see him.[201]

---

[201] Author interview with Myrna Rindels Taylor, 2013. Rindel's quotes are from interview with the *Waterloo Daily Courier*. 13 Dec 1950. No further citations.

Rindels had survived the battle of Taejon, but on July 29, he got separated from his unit. The following morning, he came over a hill and spotted American trucks and equipment in a village. Relieved, he ran down the hill and walked straight into the hands of the North Koreans.

They tied his hands behind his back and left him with a guard who offered to get Rindels some tomatoes. When the guard was out of sight, Rindels ran around a corner to escape but found himself in an open square. His guard spotted him and shot him in the arm with his burp gun, telling him he was very lucky an officer had not seen the escape attempt – but gave him the tomatoes anyway.

Rindels was marched to Chinju, and like the men caught at Hadong, he had walked from the southern tip of the peninsula to Pyongyang since his capture.

The group of POWs he joined – the men captured at Hadong – had been stripped of their belongings and any clothing items the enemy wanted for themselves. For Rindels, this also meant the loss of his glasses and dentures. He could eat the meager rice balls he received twice a day, but the rock-hard crackers the guards gave them were out of the question. Like the others, Rindels suffered from dysentery and internal parasites. Rampant body lice now plagued them, as well.

Rindels was subjected to the Red propaganda efforts during their stay at the girls' schoolhouse in Seoul, but he was more disturbed by the fact that Seoul City Sue announced his death over the radio. She knew their names "from the dog tags they took from us," he said.

He remembered standing fast and waving, describing for a reporter the morning after their march to Pyongyang began, when four P-51 fighters flew over, circled for 20 minutes and dipped their wings. "The jets suddenly pulled up in recognition. They waggled their wings and strafed the area around us for 200 feet. From that time on, we always expected a rescue."

By the time they reached Pyongyang 18 days later, the tall MP had lost almost half his body weight, dropping from 235 pounds to 120.

Frank Torigian, Aberdeen, South Dakota, was another who was listed as missing in action after the fall of Taejon. Frank was one of nine children, and while his oldest brother received a hardship exemption so he could help run the family business, Frank and his three other brothers all served during WWII.

Torigian ended up with the 24th Division in the South Pacific and received a Bronze Star for valor for his actions at Mindanao in the Philippines. Frank wasn't assigned to a combat role, but his duties as a wire man put him on (or in front of) the front lines. It was while carrying out his duties in communications that he and several others spotted a unit of Japanese soldiers preparing an ambush by laying land mines on an American-held road. The wire men took the unit under fire, killing four and driving the remaining members into the jungle.

After the war, Frank returned to Aberdeen, got married and worked as a line man for Northwestern Bell Telephone Company. In the fall of 1948, he reenlisted and was deployed to Japan, where he rejoined the 24th Division as a member of Mike Company, the heavy weapons company for the 19th Regiment's 3rd Battalion.

When American soldiers discovered the Moo Hak girls' school in Seoul, they found Torigian's name among the other names the POWs left on the chalkboards, mistakenly recording his name as "Toriglan."

Master Sergeant Barney Ruffatto, from Lead, South Dakota, had seen a lot of life before going to Korea. Born in 1906, he was already an "old man" when fighting in North Africa and the Pacific during WWII.

Other than a 49-year-old prisoner who died of starvation, Ruffatto was the oldest member of this POW group. As a member of the 34th Regiment, he was captured at Taejon and imprisoned in what he called a "madhouse," telling a reporter, "It was something that should have been used for the insane. One man in our group was wounded in the leg. The sore was open from his knee to his hip, and it was covered with maggots. But they never gave him much medical attention.

"Each night the Red guard would change, and each night they woke us up and threatened to kill us. They would wake us just for the [hell] of it. And they stole our shoes and our belts."

By the time they reached Pyongyang, the tall South Dakotan was down to 130 pounds, and conditions weren't going to improve.

The Massacre

There was nothing about October 20 that suggested a significant shift in their situation. Their train was in a railway tunnel near Sunchon avoiding detection by U.S. bombers. Seven skeletal men laid dead or dying near the north end of the tunnel, but this, too, was now commonplace.

"The men on the water and burial details got off the train and headed back toward a village," said Jim Yeager. "I never saw any of those men again after they left that morning."

In 1953, Lloyd Krieder testified: "We made an SOS with our bodies lined up on the ground a few times. Our planes, a few times, dropped supplies to some of the men, C-rations. I believe the Red Cross dropped, too, but I'm not sure. But the North Koreans took the supplies and kept them. We saw a lot of planes going over that day, and we figured they were planes going to send food, but it was one of the 187th Airborne drops at Sunchon."

As the sun began to set, the guards started taking the men out of the tunnel in groups of about 30, supposedly to be fed. The men did not question where they were going, because this was routine.

"Toney and I were talking about the only thing we ever discussed – food – when we heard the shots," Yeager said. "There was just the sound of a burp gun and a few scattered rifle shots. The whole thing didn't last over five or six seconds. 'I guess some poor devil tried to get away,' I said. Toney agreed."

The guards came back for the second group about 20-30 minutes later. Besides Toney and Yeager, this group also included Minnesotan Bill Henninger, Iowan Ray Rindels and South Dakotan Barney Ruffatto. In a subsequent memoir, Yeager wrote:

> The guards were nervous and hurried. It was the first time I had seen them like this. They were usually cocky and arrogant, but now they were quiet and sullen. I didn't like it at all. Something was up, and it didn't look good.
>
> We were marched outside and down the tracks for 200 yards and then guided into a field. We went through a plowed rice paddy down into a dry creek bed, and then the guards ordered us to halt. I glanced nervously out of the corner of my eye and saw one of the guards standing about five yards away on top of a little ridge facing us. A burp gun was cradled in his arm. I recognized him from Pyongyang. He was a South Korean who had turned communist.
>
> The guards ordered us to sit down. Toney and I, luckily, were in the third rank, the farthest away from the guard on the ridge. We were sitting there, not saying a word, when all of a sudden the guard turned to his right. The burp gun came out of the cradle position in his arms and stiffened, like a snake that was about to strike. Then all hell broke loose. With his gun held waist-high, the Commie slowly moved his body in an arc to the left and began firing.
>
> The men in the front row just slumped over, not uttering a sound. But the others in the second and third rows, hit by the

burp slugs, screamed and yelled in agony. When he reached the end of the first row, the guard retraced his fatal arc spraying further death among the group. Eight slugs ripped through the chest of the man in front of me, and he died instantly. I pitched forward the moment he was hit and managed to crouch my head under part of his body. The blood from his wounds covered my head. It was hot and sticky as it ran down my face, and I gritted my teeth to keep from vomiting.

Ray Rindels spotted Korean civilians burying bodies and later theorized they were burying the prisoners murdered in the first group.

When the firing started, he took six bullets in his right shoulder and fell over. Another prisoner fell on top of him, but he took six more slugs in his left arm. The guards walked up and down finishing up with a 50-caliber weapon that "practically tore the head off a man," he said. "One boy lying next to me was hit bad in the legs. He kept wanting them to end it."

When the guards finished off this boy, his flesh covered Rindels' face, which he believed saved his life. He played dead while the guards searched for anybody still alive. He was certain he was the only survivor, but after about an hour and a half, he heard another man quietly call, "Is anyone else still alive?" It was Jim Yeager.

After the initial burp gun sweeps, a guard had approached the spot where Yeager and Toney were feigning death.

"I was breathing so hard I was gasping," said Yeager. "The body on top of me had all but shut off the air, and I was having a difficult time trying to breathe. I prayed, oh God, how I prayed. I guess I had so much blood on me the guard thought I couldn't possibly be alive."

Someone moaned, and when the guard moved off to finish him, Yeager whispered to Toney, asking him if he was alive. Toney told him to stay quiet; he was hit in both thighs, but he was alive. It was starting to get dark. "I lay there for what seemed like an eternity, not daring to move so much as a finger," he said. "Finally, Toney whispered, 'I think they're gone.'" Carefully, they disentangled themselves from the dead and Yeager raised his head. "God, it was a horrible sight. The men in the front row had literally been cut in half by burp guns. The heads of some of them just hung by small pieces of ragged skin."

Fifty yards away, a guard was turned away smoking a cigarette. Worried he might come back for one final pass at them, Yeager and Toney decided to make a run for a shock of millet 100 yards behind them. Toney went first – although his leg wounds were bad, he could still crawl. Yeager followed, keeping a close eye on the guard. They crawled over Bill Henninger, who had not been hit, and the Minnesotan crawled out after them.

They inched away 25 yards when the guard suddenly looked around. They froze until he flicked his cigarette and walked back to the tunnel.

"It was colder than hell, but the sweat was dripping off my forehead," said Yeager. "My heart was pounding so fast I thought he would hear it."

Barney Ruffatto's gaunt "thousand-yard stare" could be seen on the faces of other survivors, as well. (Uncited news clipping)

South Dakotan Barney Ruffatto told reporters, "They didn't give us any reason for shooting us. They just told us to sit down and then opened up with burp guns and rifles. Most of the men were shot in the belly. The wounded were groaning, and when they groaned, the Reds shot them. Then the guards left and we laid there until it was dark. I kept praying that the men would cough quietly, so they wouldn't attract attention again."

"I realized we were fairly safe, so some of us took the clothes from the dead to keep warm. I figured we should take everything we could use. With two other men, I walked down a cornfield.

"One of the men was wounded, so we got into a corn shock to stay warm. I could hardly walk, but one of my buddies helped me. He was Private First Class Lloyd Krieder from West Willow, Pennsylvania. That little guy doesn't weigh more than 140 pounds, but he picked me up and pulled me through the ditches when I couldn't make it myself. We were cold and dead on our feet."[202]

After some time, the survivors heard the train leave the tunnel. "After they left, Yeager and I tried to help those who were still alive, but there wasn't much we could do for most of them," said Henninger. Ray Rindels was one of three men they found alive. The other two were Max Reid, of Winnsboro, Texas, and Roy Sutterfield, of Cameron, West Virginia. All were in bad shape.

"Early the next morning I got up and saw a North Korean boy, about 10-years-old, walking by," said Lloyd Krieder, "and I yelled to him in Japanese that we wanted some food, but he didn't understand. They could speak Japanese from about 14-years-old up in that country, as they were under the Japanese before. I don't believe he understood Japanese, but he brought his dad out, an old man with a beard, and he came out and took us down to the house and gave us food and then he took us to Sunchon and turned us over to South Korean forces, and the South Koreans turned us over to the 187th [Airborne], and the 187th to the 1st Cavalry."

From his vantage point, Coloradan Jim Yeager could see a nearby village when the sun came up. "I went down to figure out what was happening, and I met this old papa-san and a man in his forties. I asked them for tobacco. My hair was curly and blond, and they thought I was Russian. I told them, *No, I'm no goddamned Russian!*

"I saw they were cooking rice, and I tried to get them to give me some. But they wouldn't do that. They would only give me some water. As I took it back up the hill, the younger man followed me with something under his shirt – a brass bowl full of rice."

Yeager took the rice and water up to Toney and the others. Then, they spotted a different Korean man walking toward them, and they prepared for the worst.

Prior to reaching the Sunchon tunnel, the train had to stop a number of times while damaged railroad tracks were repaired. On one of these occasions, Douglas Blaylock, George Snodgrass and Victor Stevens held onto each other and stumbled off into some weeds.

---

[202] *Sheboygan Press-Telegram.* 23 Oct 1950; *Austin Daily Herald (MN).* 24 Oct 1950.

Snodgrass later said, "It was a pitch-black night. We couldn't see anything, and then a couple of us realized the guards couldn't see anything either. I've never since seen anything as black as that night."[203]

After three harrowing days behind enemy lines, these three men eventually reached an advancing column of trucks from the 1st Cavalry Division. It was October 21, the day after the massacre. The commanding officer in this column was Brigadier General Frank Allen. He was part of *Task Force Rodgers,* made up of elements from the 8th Cavalry Regiment and support units advancing north to link up with the 187th Airborne. Lieutenant Blaylock told General Allen about the train, and a civilian soon reported the executions at the tunnel.

General Allen later testified: "I was of the opinion that if they were that anxious to get rid of our people, that they must have been in a very great hurry and unquestionably some of [the POWs] must have remained alive."[204]

Allen decided to check it out himself and drove into enemy territory with his aide, two South Korean officers and two newspaper reporters. War correspondent Don Whitehead's subsequent report provides an invaluable account of what they found. The first soldiers they discovered were the seven who starved to death near the mouth of the tunnel:

The flesh had wasted from their bodies. The skin was drawn tight on their arms, legs and over their ribs. Their faces were bony masks . . . All we found in their pockets was a handful of hard, dry crackers. Two of the youths were huddled as though for warmth. One had his arms protectively about the other. Beards were heavy on their faces. Four of them were barefoot. One still had his G.I. shoes, but the soles were worn through. One wore tennis shoes – the same kind worn by North Koreans.

At first, General Allen and his companions believed these were the only victims. But, the realization of what happened filtered in when they spotted piles of dead soldiers.

The general later testified: ". . . we came across the most gruesome sight I have ever witnessed. That was in sort of a sunken road, a pile of

---

[203] Avery and Faulkner. *Sunchon Tunnel Massacre Survivors.* P 127.

[204] *Hearing before the subcommittee on Korean War Atrocities, Part I.* 2 Dec 1953. P 57. Further quotes from General Allen: *Mason City Globe-Gazette.* 23 Oct 1950.

Americans dead. . . . In the pile were men who were not dead, who were wounded. With the aid of one or two of the North Koreans in that area, we removed the dead from above the bodies of the wounded and brought them out. We [also] found a very shallow grave, it must have contained at least 60 bodies, the other side of the road down maybe 50 yards from that place. We unearthed some of the bodies but apparently there were no live soldiers in that group."

Whitehead wrote it was "equal to anything I saw in 1945 at Buchenwald, the infamous Nazi concentration camp."

They continued along the tracks and found a "gaunt, trembling figure whose face was filled with fear." This was Valdor John from Milwaukee, who threw his arms around Whitehead and sobbed "Thank God!" The young private apologized for trembling, saying he was very cold. General Allen whisked off his coat and, gently joking he was promoting John to brigadier general, he draped it around the skeletal boy's shoulders. John resisted, saying he was too dirty, and he had lice. "Don't you worry about that," the General told him.

Private John directed them to 17 bodies in a death pit he survived the night before. "On top of the pile – as though trying to claw his way to freedom – lay the body of a big Negro boy," Whitehead wrote.

He realized a set of eyes were peering at him from this pile. They belonged to Corporal Dale Blake, of Hutchinson, Minnesota. "Oh God, so glad you came," he said through tears. "I didn't think anybody would ever find us." The reporters gave Blake a cigarette and assured him he was now safe.

In a dry cornfield stained with blood, Whitehead spotted fifteen others who had been sitting in a semicircle when they were executed.

From a ridge, General Allen yelled he had found more survivors. As the reporters started climbing up, they found three others: John Martin, Eugene Jones, and Melvin Rookstool. Whitehead writes:

Martin and Rookstool were helping Jones, who was the weakest. They stumbled across the plowed fields. Like scarecrows, their clothing hung to their thin frames. Jones saw us and cried: "Look, Americans! They're Americans!" Then he fell to the ground.

General Allen wept as he sat with six other survivors. "It's a great day, boys," he kept repeating. "I just wish we could have been here soon enough to save the others." The men he had found were Jim Yeager, John Toney, Bill Henninger, Ray Rindels, Max Reid and Roy Sutterfield. Their war was finally over, although their experiences would never fade.

Men from the 187ᵗʰ Airborne gave Jim Yeager and Bill Henninger clean
Korean jackets, hot coffee, and C-rations prior to evacuation.
The plane's pilot turned out to be from Yeager's home town in Colorado.
He sent news of the rescue to Yeager's parents, who were
in church when the news reached them. (Courtesy James Yeager)

Burdett Eggen and J. T. Monscvitz didn't make the papers until
October 25. When members of the 187ᵗʰ Airborne joined the hunt for
survivors on the 21ˢᵗ, Eggen, Monscvitz, and four others heard voices
calling for them to come out and be saved. But they thought it was a
trick and stayed hidden.

These men had been in the third group to be "fed." When the guards
opened up on them, Eggen was hit in his right leg, while the men on
either side of him were killed. The guards left and then returned.

"Some of our guys were coughing up blood, and I moved my head
so it wouldn't go down my neck," said Eggen.[205] "One of these Koreans

205 All Eggen quotes this section are from his account in *North Hollywood Valley
Times*. 20 Jan 1951. Newspapers identified the survivors in Eggen-Monscvitz group
as SGT Robbie O. Bomberry, Long Beach, CA; CPL Leo C. Ross, Springfield, MO;
PFC Robert P. Ross, Oakhill, WV; and Andrew Henderson, Jacksonville, FL.

saw me move. He was about 12 feet away, and he aimed his rifle right at my head and fired. The bullet went down the back of my head. It took off a big patch of hair and some scalp. I guess he thought I was really dead."

Like the men from the second group, everybody laid still until they thought it was safe to move. It was dark when Eggen heard Sergeant Robbie Bomberry softly call out that he was alive. *Was anyone else?*

"Another guy, a Corporal Ross, sounded off. He had eight or ten slugs in him. His left side and his hip were all shot away. Altogether there were six out of these 30 who were still alive. I carried Ross, and another kid who wasn't wounded at all carried Bomberry, who had been hit in the foot and the shoulder. We struggled into the hills and hid in a ravine.

"Ross and Bomberry were very weak by the next day. About 4 p.m., up on the ridge over our ravine, we saw two guys dressed like American airborne troops and two South Koreans. They called down to us: 'If you wanna go home, come on out. You can go back to San Francisco and Los Angeles.' But we didn't believe they were Americans," said Eggen. "A lot of those gooks can speak English pretty well. So we stayed in the ravine for three more nights and four days."

"When you're starving to death, your mind doesn't work as well," Joe Monscvitz said years later. "But one of the things that always has bothered me over the years is that day, October 20th, when the 187th Airborne made the jump up there? Myself and another character were burying a guy on the hillside, and you could see what was happening. You could see their parachutes. And the guard then ran us back into the tunnel. So now, in my own mind, I knew the Americans were that close. Yet never did it occur to me. My mind just didn't work the way it ought to have.

"When they took us out that evening – and boy, it's fortunate it was at sunset, and it got dark – the thing that I learned early on was to stay the hell inside of the ranks, because I got beat up in one of the communities coming north. I was sitting on the outside, and some damn Korean comes along – I assume it's a South Korean, too – and he beats the hell out of me. After that, I always tried to stay inside the ranks, and boy, when they started shooting I got into the ground right now.

"Some kid that's standing next to me took bullets that I probably would've gotten, and he fell on top of me. Now I was scared. I laid there not breathing – I had to be breathing, or I wouldn't be alive – but not breathing and feeling warm blood running on you, and you think,

Who the hell is it? Is it him, or is it me? Because you're so damn . . .

"But the adrenalin worked. When they left, we got up and ran for a hedge row and over a small little hill or mountain, and we just collapsed after that. Boy, I did it all on adrenalin, because I sure didn't have any body fat to use. But oh, it's nice to be free. No matter how complicated it is, you feel better when you're free. You don't have somebody with a gun in your eyeballs.

"We went across a couple fields – they couldn't have been too high, but they still were quite high. We ended up in a valley, and of course with people shot up – and I think the one kid, it was clear, was in really serious shape. So we couldn't move from there.

"But we were very fortunate. Several hundred feet away from us were the railroad tracks that we were going up when the train was there. But we were far back in the woods, so you couldn't see us. And across the railroad tracks was a garden with radishes and what have you, and a water supply – a little mountain stream. I think it was Bomberry who had survived with a small metal container [mess kit]. So we were able to get water that way, and some of the vegetables from the garden. So now we were living better than we ever had while we were prisoners.

"But coming back one evening, I ran into a South Korean patrol who were checking the railroad tracks. As soon as they saw who I was, they were gonna pick me up and carry me back. And I said *Wait!* It took me a little while to persuade them – *Wait a minute, I've got some other comrades here.*"

Burdett Eggen spoke about this: "On the fourth day . . . one of my buddies went down to see if he could steal some food. He came back with the whole South Korean Army, it seemed like. They marched us back to the tunnel, to an officer, who said our G.I.s were very close. He wanted us to go up with his troops and help them fight, but we were too weak.

"So he took us across the fields about a half a mile to a highway where G.I. trucks were going by. We got a ride with one from the 62nd Gun Battalion, and they took us about 30 miles north to their camp. I got my first decent American food off of the truck engine. They kept some hamburgers warm, so we had a hamburger. Best hamburger I ever ate!"

Cecil "Buddy" Hardaway was one of the medics with the 187th Airborne who jumped at Sunchon. He later worked on missile sites in North Dakota, saying "I didn't last long. I couldn't take the cold."

Hardaway was only 17, but he had already gone through basic

training, jump school, medical training, and ranger training. As a medic, he was on hand when the survivors of the massacre began trickling into the 187th's perimeter.

"I took care of some of those POWs they found," he told the author. "It kind of tore me up to see some of those guys, how they was treated. Deep down, it hurt me to think somebody would treat people like that. You don't get used to seeing stuff like that, but you have to go ahead and do your job when you're a medic. But you never forget it."

Several days later, Tom Lambert wrote, "[Ray] Rindels gulped and spoke with great difficulty from his cot in an Army hospital."

Rindels with his mother and younger siblings in 1950.
(Courtesy Myrna Rindels, lower right)

The tall young Iowan told Lambert about Yeager and Henninger saving his life, saying "Yeager was a little guy but a real man." Rindels' sister Myrna relates:

> Ray never regained his health after he returned. Farm life didn't suit him, and he was deemed disabled by the VA. He was unable to do any physical labor, and he had difficulty with his left arm. He couldn't bend it, because several bullets remained embedded. He also suffered from malaria, and he was always quite thin.
>
> But he was always creative and artistic and was excellent at drawing. After he returned from the war, he built extraordinary bird cages and was always involved in trying new ideas or inventions.
>
> He was the kind of man who would give you his last dollar. He doted on our mother and made sure she was remembered with gifts. In my last conversation with him before he died in 1997, he made me promise to always take care of her.

"Everybody but me was wounded," said J.T. Monscvitz years later. "I live a charmed life, but one of the Rosses was in really serious trouble, you know? They took us and dropped us off at a MASH unit of some sort, and they took them right in and operated on them, because they were in serious trouble. The guys who were ambulatory, and I was one of them, they threw us in an ambulance and took us back to Pyongyang to an evacuation hospital. I can still remember that. A nurse comes in and takes me to the bathroom, strips me down, burns my clothes, and sprays me down with DDT. She gave me a robe, and I felt better.

"When we got back to Japan, they gave me a little goody-bag that had a razor and stuff in it, and I went into the bathroom to take a shave. I looked in the mirror, and I looked around to see who the guy was in the mirror. I didn't recognize him – because I'm 5'10", and I'm down to 116 pounds. There wasn't much left of me. My hair and beard had quit growing – your body doesn't do it if it doesn't have to.

"From the beginning, my first thought was 'If they don't kill me, I'll get out alive.' Whatever you had to do to come out alive, that was the important thing.

"Philosophically, as I look back on it, it's just man's inhumanity to mankind. It's just all the same. We're still doing it today. It doesn't ever change."

Aberdeen's Frank Torigian didn't survive the executions. He and more than seventy others (including those who died inside the tunnel) were temporarily buried along the tracks after their discovery. They were exhumed ten days later and moved to Pyongyang, where Torigian was buried in plot 1, row 8, grave number 108. But what happened to his remains beyond that point is a mystery. For many years, and for unknown reasons, he and 18 others were listed as killed in action on the dates they were captured.[206]

(Courtesy Torigian family)

Robert Hofland, Frank's brother-in-law and a Korean War veteran himself, recalls that after Frank was reported missing, the youngest of the five Torigian brothers volunteered for Korea so he could search for Frank – but he ended up being deployed to Germany instead.

As for the 150 to 175 prisoners who were still aboard the train when it pulled out that night, they had no idea what had happened to their fellow POWs at the tunnel.

Several nights later, when the train could go no farther, some 30 more of them were shot, bayoneted and/or burned alive four miles north of Kujang-dong. Three survivors said the last remaining prisoners were marched away on foot that night, and their fates are unknown.

Many surmise that when all was said and done, the Hadong-Taejon prisoners may have suffered a fatality rate that surpassed anything ever endured by American prisoners in any war. Indeed, it is widely accepted among researchers that only two POW groups in modern history are

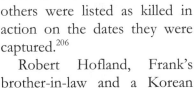

[206] http://koreanwarmemorial.sd.gov/SearchEngineForm/profiles/242.htm; Author interview with Torigian's brother-in-law, Robert Hofland, 13 Mar 2014; *U.S. Dead in North Korea*, Graves registration Pyongyang, undated; *Identified Atrocity Victims*, group #76, undated, courtesy John Zimmerlee, Coalition of Korean & Cold War POW/MIA Network.

known to have suffered higher death rates than Americans did in Korea: Germans held by Russians, and Russians held by Germans, both during WWII. One group that wasn't able to be counted, however, were South Koreans captured by North Koreans. This author suspects they ranked very high in the "worst" category.

North Dakota's James Hanley Jr. didn't believe the barbaric massacres at Sunchon and Kujang-dong were isolated incidents. In 1953, Hanley's War Crimes Division published the following:

One thousand two hundred and fifty (1,250) American prisoners were slaughtered in cold blood by their communist captors, if the confession of a North Korean prisoner is true. Unfortunately, that is all the evidence contained in the file. However, after several days of questioning, during which the suspect gave very detailed information, it was the belief of the interrogators that the facts contained therein were well founded and reliable.

This North Korean stated that in his assignment as a truck driver, on 10 September 1950, he was driving from Namchon to Pyongyang and passed a group of 24 warehouses surrounded by barbed wire and noticed that many American prisoners were confined therein. Five days later, his unit was ordered to prepare for a long trip. He added that about 30 Russian made trucks were in his battalion, and that they loaded approximately 650 prisoners on them and commenced their journey about midnight. At their first stop, they were joined by an additional 24 trucks loaded to capacity with U.S. prisoners of war.

During the next stop, which was for a meal and rest for the cargo, he noticed that 50 trucks were in the convoy. At the final halt, the men were unloaded and led into a mountain valley where they were fed rice and wine, but, upon a blue flare signal, the guards and drivers began firing into the group and continued for about 40 minutes, completing the slaughter of the estimated 1250 prisoners. They then uncovered three large pits which had been excavated earlier, but found them insufficient to hold all the bodies, and so were required to dig another.

Following this macabre execution, the trucks returned and later transported all the remaining prisoners from the warehouses to a new camp further north. The confessor was unable to explain why the one convoy load was murdered but the others spared. To the extent that it has been possible to check, such as locations and units, this confession appears accurate. Every effort should be expended to discover corroborating evidence for this reported atrocity. (Interim Historical Report, War Crimes Division, Cumulative to 30 June 1953. P 26-27.)

Chapter 42

THE END IS NEAR?

"It looks like we closed the trap. Closing that trap should be the end of all organized resistance. The war is very definitely coming to an end today." General Douglas MacArthur, October 20, 1950

AS OCTOBER DREW to a close, MacArthur's gamble at Inchon, as well as the surprise achieved by the paratroopers north of Pyongyang, appeared successful. The Marines were now back at sea, skirting down around the peninsula to land on the east coast, where they were to move inland to meet up with Army troops moving across the peninsula from the west.

In news of the day, the United States and five other nations called on the United Nations to declare aggression "the gravest of all crimes against peace and security through the world" – this being a direct response to a Soviet peace plan that called for arms reductions and also for branding the United States a war criminal for being the first government to use the atom bomb.

Meanwhile, the U.S. Navy announced a "piston-jet AJ-I attack bomber" was now aboard an aircraft carrier off the coast of Norfolk, Virginia, explaining this type of plane was now capable of carrying atomic bombs from flattops to "anywhere in the world."

From newly captured Hungnam, on the northeast coast of Korea, came a highly detailed account by William Chapman regarding "a heavily guarded concrete structure full of fantastic electrical equipment" with labels and signs written in Korean and Russian. Local civilians believed it was a massive Soviet complex for carrying out atomic research, but the machines inside, which were "screened from the eyes of North Koreans, defied the limited technical knowledge of the intelligence officers."

Foreboding news also came in from Vietnam, with Robert Branson reporting:

> Viet Minh forces attacked the isolated French fortress of Laokay
> Wednesday night in what appeared to be the start of a major
> battle ... Earlier, it was learned that French war planes carried out
> a large-scale evacuation of civilians from Laokay, and informed
> sources said it might be a prelude to a general French withdrawal
> to new defense lines far to the south.

Back in the States, General Dwight Eisenhower disclosed he was
heading for Washington for conferences "which may result in a military
future for himself." Reporters speculated the general would be named
commanding general of the Allied armies in Europe, but others pressed
him with the frequently asked question of whether he was a Republican?
And did he intend to run for president in 1952? He declined to answer,
saying, "I am a soldier, and I am not certain my active days are over."

Also on October 26, another report out of Washington indicated
investigations were underway after two U.S. planes were shot down
over North Korea by gunfire originating from within Communist
China.

Of even more importance was news buried in an article about South
Korean soldiers now being "within guns' range" of the Chinese border
and pledging to "wash our swords in the Yalu river." It reads:

> A captured Chinese Communist soldier claimed that Chinese
> Communists 20,000-strong already had come to the defense of
> Korean Reds, but American intelligence officers gave little
> credence to the report.
>
> At Eighth Army headquarters, the intelligence officers told
> United Press correspondent Jack James that they had put the
> report in a classification that indicated "neither the reliability of
> the source nor his information can be judged."

Officials gave five reasons for more or less dismissing this Chinese
threat:

> 1) It is late in the war for the Chinese Reds to be coming to the
> aid of their Communist neighbor;
> 2) Soldiers trained in Red China are not new in the North Korean
> army;
> 3) There is a large Korean population in Manchuria;

4) There have been no recent air or intelligence reports of large-scale movements southward across the border; and

5) Other Communist prisoners have not given the same story.[207]

At that very time, however, at least one American knew the Chinese threat was very real. Lieutenant Colonel Cameron, a West Pointer from Brookhaven, Mississippi, knew first-hand China was entering the war.

*The **Silver Star** is awarded to Lieutenant Colonel **Robert Carroll Cameron**, United States Army, for gallantry in action against the enemy in the vicinity of Taepyong, Korea, between 25 and 27 October 1950. On 25 October 1950, the 10th Republic of Korea Regiment was given the mission of relieving a friendly unit that had been cut off by a large Chinese Communist force. Colonel Cameron, Senior U.S. Advisor to the regiment, moved out with the leading elements of the unit and for the next two days repeatedly exposed himself to intense enemy fire to direct air strikes and artillery fire against hostile positions. At 0100 hours on 27 October, the enemy launched a massive enveloping attack against the regiment and succeeded in overrunning friendly rear area security troops. Although the regiment suffered tremendous casualties, Colonel Cameron aggressively moved among the remaining troops, encouraging them and directing the establishment of a defensive perimeter which the regiment held throughout the night. At daylight he led a counterattack which enabled the regiment to halt the enemy advance and reestablish the friendly lines.*

Just one week later, North Dakota's Harold K. Johnson was going to experience the excruciating loss of his beloved cavalry battalion in a massive Chinese ambush.

But it would take even bigger and more devastating losses before General MacArthur and his staff finally acknowledged the Chinese threat was real – and then declaring it "a whole new war."

---

[207] News quotes this section: *Pacific Stars & Stripes*. 26 October 1950.

Appendix

Additional Citations

Following are additional known citations found for July–October 1950, presented in chronological order.[208]

SFC HARRIS J. OUTZEN, Army, Company D, 21ˢᵗ IR, 24ᵗʰ ID, is awarded the Bronze Star with V Device for heroic achievement on 9 July 1950 at Chonan, Korea. SFC Outzen's platoon was attached to Company A which was occupying a defensive position on a hill when the enemy attacked in great strength. SFC Outzen moved about the position directing the fires of both crew-served weapons and riflemen. At the same time, he was exposing himself continually to enemy fire. He was twice wounded by shrapnel. When the position was ordered evacuated, SFC Outzen remained behind with his machineguns and covered the withdrawal of Company A before he led his own platoon to safety . . . Home of record: Davenport, IA. (Outzen was a POW who survived the Bataan Death March after the fall of Corregidor in WWII.)

1LT GUY E. MITCHELL JR., Army, HQ Company, 21ˢᵗ IR, 24ᵗʰ ID, is awarded the Silver Star (posthumously) for gallantry. He distinguished himself by courageous action near Chonui, Korea, on 10 July 1950. Voluntarily joining two rifle companies in their attack against an enemy force estimated at regimental strength, he moved forward, through intense artillery, mortar and small arms fire, in order to maintain vital communications. His actions, without regard for his own safety, on a mission of his own choice, was an inspiration to those who fought about him and aided materially in the success of the attack . . . Home of record: Madison, SD. (Lieutenant Mitchell survived this action. This award was posthumous, because he was killed in action on September 19, during the breakout from the Naktong perimeter.)

CPL ORVILLE W. WILLIAMS, Army, Company D, 19ᵗʰ IR, 24ᵗʰ ID, is awarded the Bronze Star with V Device for heroic action near Taejon (Kum River), Korea, on 16 July 1950. During a withdrawal movement north of the city, the convoy in which he was driving was fired upon from a strong enemy roadblock. Intense fire raked the road, disabling several vehicles and pinning down a squad of soldiers of another Company. Observing an unmanned machine gun on one of the disabled vehicles, he exposed himself to the full fury of the enemy's fire and manned the gun. Firing with great

---

[208] Many more such citations exist but are difficult to locate. The following abbreviations are used: FAB (Field Artillery BTN); IR (Infantry Regiment); ID (Infantry Division); HQ (Headquarters); BTN (Battalion); Company (Company); USMC (U.S. Marine Corps); AAAW (Antiaircraft Artillery Automatic Weapons).

volume and accuracy, he so engaged the enemy that the squad of vehicles was permitted to continue their movement to new defensive positions . . . Home of record: Broken Bow, NE.

SFC JAMES D. ANDREWS, Army, BTY B, 13th FAB, 24th ID, is awarded the Bronze Star with V Device for heroic achievement at Taejon, Korea. During the morning of 19 July 1950, SFC Andrews' BTY was under intense counter-BTY fire from the enemy. The BTY continued to fire under these hazardous conditions when a shell burst about 20 yards from SFC Andrews, wounding the assistant gunner. SFC Andrews crawled to the BTY executive officer's position and reported that the wounded man needed immediate medical attention. At this time the enemy fire was so intense that everyone had to remain under cover. SFC Andrews then volunteered to get the wounded man out. In spite of the heavy enemy fire, SFC Andrews succeeded in reaching the wounded man, administered first aid, and brought him back to a place of safety. SFC Andrews then returned to his gun position . . . Home of record: Minneapolis.

1LT ELLSWORTH "DUTCH" NELSEN, Army, BTY B, 13th FAB, 24th ID, is awarded the Bronze Star with V Device for heroic achievement on 20 July 1950, near Taejon, Korea. When a heavy concentration of enemy infantry and tanks threatened the withdrawal of his BTY and elements of the 34th Infantry and the 19th Infantry from the airstrip north of Taejon, LT Nelsen deployed two of his BTY's 105mm howitzers as anti-tank weapons. Wounded by the enemy's intensive artillery and mortar fire, LT Nelsen refused evacuation, but instead remained to direct the fire of his howitzers. Through his actions, the friendly infantry and artillery units withdrew with a minimum loss of equipment and personnel . . . Entered service: Grand Island, NE.

2LT RONALD NORBY, Army, Heavy Mortar Company, 27th IR, 25th ID is awarded the Silver Star for gallantry in action. In the early morning of 24 July 1950 near Yongdong, Korea, an enemy force of infantry and tanks penetrated the 1st BTN where LT Norby was acting as Liaison officer. He quickly and accurately brought mortar fire on the hostile infantry. Since he could not observe the tank positions, he rushed across an area swept by machine guns to a vantage point on a hill from which, despite the direct fire from the tanks and sporadic mortar fire, he directed the mortars until the attack was successfully repulsed . . . Entered service: Fargo, ND. Home of record SD.

The Silver Star is awarded (posthumously) to PVT STANLEY DUMPMAN, Army, Company A, 8th Cavalry Regiment, 1st Cavalry Division, who displayed heroism in action against the enemy at Yongdong, Korea, 24 July 1950. The enemy, superior in numbers, launched a strong attack against the COM's position at daybreak. PVT Dumpman, assigned to the outermost flank of his Company, immediately commenced a devastating fire upon the advancing enemy. He succeeded in inflicting heavy casualties upon the enemy and delayed the advance temporarily. Remaining in his position he continued to deliver effective fire upon the enemy force until his position was finally overrun. When last seen, he was engaged in hand to hand combat with the enemy . . . Entered service from the area of Stillwater, MN.

The Silver Star is awarded (posthumously) to PFC MICHAEL A. DWORSHAK, Army, Company B, 5th Cavalry Regiment, 1st Cavalry Division, for conspicuous gallantry and intrepidity in action against the enemy on 24 July 1950 near Yongdong, Korea. PFC

Dworshak was one of a group of men riding on tanks which were going forward into intense enemy mortar and small arms fire to break up a roadblock. Seeing an enemy machine gun nest to the rear, PFC Dworshak, displaying great presence of mind, swung his automatic rifle around and, at the same time, shoved one man off the tank to keep him from getting hit by the machine gun's fire. With utter disregard for his life, PFC Dworshak stood fully exposed and exchanged fire with the enemy machine gun until he killed every enemy crewman manning the machine gun. PVT Dworshak's gallantry saved the lives of his comrades riding on top of the tanks and reflected great credit upon himself and the military service. Home of record: Flasher, ND. (PFC Dworshak was killed in action the following day.)

The Bronze Star with V Device is awarded to CPL JAMES E. GARMAN, Army, Company F, 27th IR, 25th ID, for heroic achievement on 25 July 1950 near Yongdong, Korea. CPL Garman was in charge of a squad whose mission was protection of the observation post. When the enemy subjected the observation post to intense automatic weapons and small arms fire, CPL Garman refused to withdraw and by skillful deployment of his squad repelled the enemy attack and enabled the forward observer to continue his fire mission . . . Entered service: IA.

The Bronze Star with V Device is awarded to SFC FRANCIS V. NYDLE, Army, Company G, 27th IR, Army. On 26 July 1950 near Yongdong, Korea, Company G, which was serving as rear guard for the withdrawal of the entire 27th Regimental Combat Team, was subjected to a heavy barrage of artillery and mortar fire and direct tank and automatic weapons fire. By his skillful maneuvering of his platoon and by his gallant leadership, SFC Nydle effectively delayed the numerically superior enemy force so that the Regimental Combat Team could complete an orderly withdrawal. Entered service: Wapello, IA.

The Bronze Star with V Device is awarded to SGT (then CPL) WALTER M. BRITT, Army, HQ and HQ Company, 1st BTN, 27th IR, Army. On 28 July 1950 when the BTN was ordered to displace to a better position near Hwanggan, Korea, SGT Britt volunteered to remain with the rifle companies in order to assist in the evacuation of casualties. Braving intense enemy artillery, machine gun and small arms fire concentrated in the area, he made repeated trips throughout the positions to recover wounded personnel and assist them to the aid station, thereby saving numerous lives . . . Entered service: NE.

CPT ERNEST D. MCDONALD, Army, HQ Company, 3rd BTN, 34th IR, 24th ID, is awarded the Bronze Star with V Device for heroic achievement on 30 July 1950 near Kwonbin-ni, Korea. The 3rd BTN was withdrawing in the face of heavy enemy frontal attack and encirclement. CPT McDonald assisted in salvaging of weapons and ammunition which were in the immediate vicinity of the Command Post. At that time the Command Post was under heavy enemy mortar and automatic weapons fire. He also assisted many of the wounded who were being brought back from the front lines to places of safety . . . Entered service: Vermillion, SD.

The Bronze Star with V Device for heroic action is awarded to 1LT RALPH LONGBOTHAM, Army, HQ and HQ Company, 1st BTN, 27th IR, 25th ID. On 2 August 1950, LT Longbotham, BTN S-2, accompanied his unit on a penetration 20 miles into enemy territory near Chonson-ri, Korea. Organizing a small group of men, he led attacks in by-passed positions, eliminating the enemy and obtaining documents and weapons of great intelligence value. Heedless of constant harassing fire and the danger of attacking the fanatic emplacements with his small group, he continued his mission and secured invaluable information and materiel . . . Entered service: MN.

PFC DELBERT D. KINGERY, Army, Company D, 19th IR, 24th ID, is awarded the Bronze Star with V Device for heroic achievement in action against the enemy in the vicinity of the Naktong River on 5 August 1950. During an attack on well fortified enemy hilltop emplacements, his unit was erroneously attacked by friendly aircraft supporting the infantry. Realizing the seriousness of the situation and the possibilities of needless casualties, PVT Kingery left his position of relative safety and although exposed to both the strafing and enemy fire, secured an air identification panel, dashed to the top of the hill and displayed it in such a manner that the air attack was discontinued. Through his courage and fearless devotion to duty, many casualties were prevented, and the attack was successfully completed . . . Entered from Knoxville, IA.

PFC JACK W. CHRISTENSEN, Army, is awarded the Silver Star (posthumously) for conspicuous gallantry and intrepidity in action against the enemy on 5 August 1950 while serving with Company F, 35th IR, 25th ID, near Chungam-ni, Korea. "PFC Christensen's Company was overrun by the enemy, and Christensen's position was isolated. He remained in his foxhole directing fire and throwing hand grenades at the numerically superior forces. Although wounded and finally surrounded by the enemy, he continued the fight until he was killed. His gallant and heroic action inspired his fellow soldiers to greater effort." (*Pacific Stars & Stripes*. 12 Sep 1950.) Home of record: Sidney, MT.

1LT JAMES W. STOLL, Army, is (posthumously) awarded the Silver Star for conspicuous gallantry and intrepidity in action against the enemy on 8 August 1950, while serving with BTY B, 555th FAB, 25th ID, in Korea. 1LT Stoll was subjected to intense counter BTY and mortar fire to his outfit's position, but steadfastly maintained his position and directed fire from an exposed point until mortally wounded by a direct hit from a mortar shell. (Synopsis based on newspaper accounts.) Home of record: Lincoln, NE.

CPL LEONARD E. TALPT, Army, Company F, 19th IR, 24th ID, is awarded the Bronze Star with V Device for heroic achievement near Ohang Hill, Korea, on 8 August 1950. After an assault upon enemy positions, his Company was subjected to intense automatic fire and suffered casualties. A member of the lead platoon fell in a position being swept by fire. Attempts to reach the wounded man were unsuccessful. With utter disregard for his own safety, CPL Talpt moved forward into the face of the withering fire, reached the wounded man's side and carried him to the comparative safety of friendly lines. Returning to the fight, he sought enemy positions he had observed while rescuing his comrade and by his effective fire destroyed the positions . . . Entered service: Sioux City, IA.

CPL CLARENCE A. COOK, Army, Medical Company, 19th IR, 24th ID, then a member of Medical Company, 34th IR, 24th ID, is awarded the Bronze Star with V Device for heroic achievement on 8 August 1950 at Yongsan, Korea. Without regard for his own safety, CPL Cook entered the area of Company G, 19th IR, which was then under heavy enemy fire, and administered aid to the wounded. He remained in the open and refused to leave until all the wounded were attended. His actions were an inspiration to the troops in the area . . . Entered service: Marquette, IA.

CPL DICK MOORE, USMC, Reconnaissance Detachment, 1st Provisional Marine Brigade, 1st Marine Division (Reinforced), is awarded the Silver Star for conspicuous gallantry and intrepidity in action against enemy aggressor forces near Kosong, Korea, on 10 August 1950. When an estimated enemy Company ambushed his platoon, CPL Moore, with complete disregard for his personal safety, attacked and destroyed two heavily supported machine gun emplacements. His daring actions completely demoralized the enemy troops and enabled his platoon to rout them from the area. Home of record: NE.

The First Bronze Oak Leaf Cluster to the Bronze Star with V Device is awarded to 1LT GARNARD E. HARBECK, Army, HQ and HQ Company, 5th RCT. On 10 August 1950 in the vicinity of Pongam-ni, Korea, the assault BTN advanced so rapidly in an attack that all means of communication were disrupted by the distance and hostile action. When a message vital to the success of the operation was received and could not be transmitted by mechanical means, LT Harbeck drove a vehicle through three miles of enemy infested territory to deliver the important document. LT Harbeck's courageous action materially assisted in the success of the attack . . . Home of record: IA.

The Silver Star is awarded to 1LT ROBERT M. CARROLL, Army, Company H, 7th Cavalry Regiment, 1st Cavalry Division, who displayed gallantry in action against the enemy at Yongpo, Korea, on 12 August 1950. Company H was attacking a numerically superior enemy force. Because of wounds sustained just prior to the attack, LT Carroll had been told to stay at the Command Post and take charge of communications. Finding that the right flank had become pinned down by sniper fire, LT Carroll, although wounded, rushed up the hill and directed fire upon the sniper thus enabling the right flank to move forward. He then assisted in a bayonet charge which drove the enemy from their positions. During this charge LT Carroll was again wounded by enemy hand grenades. His superior leadership so inspired his men that they continued the attack and forced the enemy to retreat . . . Entered service: Mason City, IA.

The Silver Star is awarded to PFC MYRON STUFFELBEAM, Army, Company B, 5th RCT. During an intense hostile attack on the Company position near Taejon(?), Korea, on 13 August(?) 1950, PFC Stuffelbeam was seriously wounded in the face. Despite his painful wound, he continued to fire his rifle on the fanatic attackers until he was wounded in both hands and unable to hold his weapon. By his selfless devotion to duty, he assisted materially in repelling the hostile forces and contributed greatly to the esprit of his unit... Entered service: Waterloo, IA.

CPL LUMIR J. DRASKY, Army, Medical Company, 19th IR, 24th ID, is awarded the Bronze Star with V Device for heroic achievement near the Naktong River, Korea, on 13 August 1950. His litter squad, carrying a wounded soldier, was subjected to direct fire from an enemy tank. With utter disregard for his own safety, he directed his men to positions offering the best cover and shielded the wounded man from enemy fire with his own body until the tank withdrew . . . Entered service: Linwood, NE.

PFC DANIEL W. SHEEHAN, Army, Company A, 34th IR, 24th ID, is awarded the Bronze Star with V Device for heroism on 15 August 1950 along the Naktong River in Korea. During an attack by Company A on a heavily defended ridge, PVT Sheehan, although exposed to enemy fire, placed his squad in an advantageous firing position. When his platoon was forced to withdraw, he again exposed himself to enemy fire in evacuating the wounded to a place of safety. He proceeded to the Company rear and guided stretcher bearers to the wounded . . . Entered service: Madrid, IA.

PVT JOHN DEAN BENDIX, Army, Company G, 2nd BTN, 5th Cavalry Regiment, 1st Cavalry Division, is awarded the Silver Star (posthumously) for gallantry in action on 16 August 1950, near Waegwan, Korea. While his Company was participating in a combined tank-infantry attack on a strong enemy position, two friendly tanks were made inoperable by enemy action. Realizing that in order to escape, the crews of the disabled tanks would need strong covering fire, PVT Bendix, with complete disregard for his own personal safety, mounted the open decks of another tank and opened fire on the enemy with a .50 caliber machine gun. Remaining in his exposed and vulnerable position until he was certain that all the tank crew had withdrawn, PVT Bendix continued to man his machine gun until he was mortally wounded. His courageous aggressiveness, at the sacrifice of his own life, was directly responsible for the safe withdrawal of two tank crews . . . Home of record: Minneapolis.

2LT (then MSGT) PATRICK J. STOWELL, Army, Company B, 19th IR, 24th ID, is awarded the Silver Star for gallantry in action against the enemy near Chon-do, Korea, on 17 August 1950. During an advance by his Company on enemy hillside positions, his platoon was held up by intense mortar and machine gun fire. Seeing that this fire threatened to disorganize the Company's advance he determined to attack. Organizing the platoon, he led the assault, and the men, inspired by his example, overran the position. When strengthened enemy forces counter-attacked, LT Stowell led the defense of the position and through his effective us of hand grenades, the enemy was repulsed with heavy losses . . . Entered service: Stanley, ND.

CPT (then 1LT) ADOLPH "CAC" FOSSUM, Army, HQ Company, 1st BTN, 19th IR, 24th ID, is awarded the Silver Star for gallantry in action against the enemy in the vicinity of the Naktong River, Korea, on 18 August 1950. Serving as S-3 when his BTN was engaged in clearing the enemy from the Naktong River bulge, he distinguished himself by courageous actions. Preparatory to an attack, he moved under intense enemy machine gun and rifle fire into the Company area to issue the operational plan. During the attack itself, he established an observation post far forward of the leading elements. Although his post was promptly observed by the enemy and subjected to an intensive artillery and mortar barrage, he remained in his exposed position. With utter disregard for his own safety, he continued to observe and control the area. In this gallant action CPT Fossum was wounded. . . Entered service: Stillwater, MN.

The Bronze Star with V Device is awarded to PFC GASPER J. MINOR, Heavy Mortar Company, 35th IR, 25th ID, Army. On the night of 18 August 1950, while shelling Chungam-ni, Korea, PFC Minor's Company was attacked by infiltrating enemy troops. Despite an intense concentration of hostile fire, he immediately took his place on the line and delivered effective counterfire. Although wounded early in the action, he remained in his exposed position and continued firing until the attack was repulsed . . . Entered service: IA.

The Bronze Star with V Device is awarded to SFC JOSEPH E. RUARK, Army Medical Service, Medical Company, 29th IR, Army. On 19 August 1950 during a concerted enemy attack on the regimental reserve unit in the vicinity of Taegu, Korea, SFC Ruark braved the intense hailed hostile mortar and artillery fire to make his way to a severely wounded soldier, rendered first aid, stayed with them and until medical equipment arrived, and assisted in evacuating the soldier from the danger zone. Returning to the battle area, he continued to assist in the evacuation of casualties until all wounded were cared for . . . Entered service: IA.

2LT RALPH H. QUEEN, Army, was awarded the Silver Star (posthumously) for conspicuous gallantry and intrepidity in action against the enemy while serving with Company D, 1st BTN, 35th Regimental Combat Team, 25th ID, in action on 19 August 1950 near Sansi-ri, Korea. LT Queen was in charge of a 75-mm recoilless rifle crew. He was fatally wounded by enemy fire after he assisted two wounded crewmen to safety and was attempting to service the rifle. (Synopsis) Home of record: Billings, MT.

1LT (then 2LT) FRANCIS B. WILSON, Army, Company M, 7th Cavalry Regiment, 1st Cavalry Division is awarded the Silver Star for gallantry in action against the enemy on 21 August 1950 near Taegu, Korea. While his recoilless rifle platoon was firing to break up an enemy attack supported by heavy artillery concentrations, LT Wilson and several comrades were seriously wounded by an enemy tree burst. Disregarding the intense pain of a leg wound, LT Wilson refused to be evacuated, but crawled courageously through the enemy barrage to a friendly platoon near his position to get aid for his wounded men. After directing the evacuation of his comrades, LT Wilson attempted to return to his position but collapsed from loss of blood and was evacuated while unconscious. His selfless behavior and devotion to duty saved the lives of several men and possible capture of a friendly mortar platoon. . . Home of record: MN

The First Bronze Oak Leaf Cluster to the Bronze Star with V Device is awarded to 2LT CHARLES JONES, BTY A, 8th FAB, Army. On 21 August 1950 near Taegu, Korea, 2LT Jones' BTY was subjected to intense counter-BTY fire which inflicted numerous casualties among the gun crews. Moving from gun to gun despite the hail of enemy artillery on the position, 2LT Jones rendered emergency first aid to the wounded and moved them to places of safety, thus saving the lives of many of his comrades . . . Entered service: IA.

The Silver Star is awarded to PFC GERALD L. PEARSON, Artillery, Army, a member of BTY B, 37th FAB, 2nd ID, who displayed gallantry in action against an armed enemy on 22 August 1950 in the vicinity of Taegu, Korea. On that date, PVT Pearson's BTY was subjected to an intense enemy artillery and mortar barrage which prevented the artillerymen from servicing their howitzers and inflicted severe casualties upon them. Orders were received to vacate the position immediately, leaving the guns and equipment in the area. Later that day, volunteers were called for to reenter the vacated position in an attempt to secure a howitzer and take it to the new BTY position. PVT Pearson volunteered for this hazardous mission and, with two comrades, entered the area which still was under observation by the enemy and still under heavy concentrations of artillery and mortar fire. With complete disregard for personal safety and indifference to the hostile fire, he moved calmly through the area and, added by his comrades, succeeded in placing the piece in traveling position, hooked it to a truck and moved it to the new position. The timely arrival of this desperately needed howitzer allowed the BTY to furnish support to the hard pressed infantry, and the fire delivered by the gun succeeded in breaking up an enemy attack. . . . Entered service: MN.

The Bronze Star with V Device is awarded to CPL CLAUDE BOSLEM, Army, Company A, 35th IR, 25th ID, Army. On the morning of 22 August 1950 at about 0400 hours, a large enemy force drove CPL Boslem's platoon from its position near Haman, Korea. Joining a group of seven men, CPL Boslem participated in a bold counter-attack in the face of overwhelmingly superior numbers of enemy and regained the position. Although grenades and ammunition were nearly gone, they held and inflicted severe casualties on the hostile force until withdrawal to better positions was necessary. By his courageous devotion to duty and will to fight, CPL Boslem enabled his unit to reorganize and finally repel the enemy . . . Entered service: Appanoose, IA.

PFC BERNARD E. ROHDE, Army, Company A, 5th RCT, is awarded the Silver Star for gallantry in action. At about 0400 hours, 27 August 1950, the enemy launched a vigorous attack on the Company which was defending the high ground near Sobuk San, Korea. Although weak from wounds, PFC Rohde crawled forward to advise the unit of the flank threat. On reaching an advance post and finding a machine gunner dead, he manned the gun, although he had never fired one before, and delivered effective fire on the enemy. By his exceptional courage and bold initiative, PFC Rohde enabled the hard pressed platoon to dig in and hold . . . Entered service: MN.

The Silver Star is awarded to PFC DEAN O. CLARK, Company D, 35th Regiment, 25th ID, Army. During the early morning hours of 30 August 1950 near Masan-ni, Korea, a large hostile force advanced under cover of darkness to within twenty yards of an infantry company's position. When the position became untenable and withdrawal was ordered, PFC Clark remained to provide covering fire with a machine gun. After displacement had been effected, he carried a wounded man to safety and removed his machine gun to the new position. He then joined his Company in a counterattack, which regained the former position and inflicted severe casualties on the enemy . . . Entered service: IA.

The Silver Star is awarded to PFC (then PVT) ELVIN W. HAASE, Company L, 35th IR, 25th ID, Army. On the night of 31 August 1950 near Saga, Korea, a strong column of enemy including mechanized elements attacked the Company positions. In the heavy barrage of small arms, mortar and artillery fire, PFC Haase moved about with his 3.5 inch rocket launcher to obtain most advantageous fields of fire. Frequently exposing himself boldly to the intense hostile fire, he succeeded in destroying a 76mm self-propelled gun and three antitank guns, and in damaging an artillery piece. His skillful and courageous actions were of vital importance in disrupting the hostile assault . . . Entered service: Todd, MN. (Haase moved up quickly in rank; he was a SGT when he was captured November 26, 1950. He was not returned in the prisoner exchanges at war's end and was declared dead.)

457

The Bronze Star with V Device is awarded to CPL WILLIAM L. HAASE, Army, a member of Company A, 72nd Tank BTN, 2nd ID, who distinguished himself by heroic achievement on 31 August 1950 in the vicinity of Chakkyaz, Korea. On that date he was a crewman in a tank platoon attached to a rifle Company in a defensive position. The enemy had penetrated the line forcing the rifle Company back, thus leaving the tanks without infantry support. It was imperative that this line be reformed at once or not only would the tanks be lost, but the whole, but the whole line of defense would be endangered. Knowing this, CPL Haase volunteered as a member of a patrol whose mission was to contact and rally the outnumbered rifle Company. Supported by two tanks the patrol made its way through intense enemy artillery and small arms fire, and succeeded in reforming the line of defense and recovering the ground that had been lost . . . Home of record: MT.

CPL HAROLD MERVIN OLSON is awarded the Silver Star for conspicuous gallantry and intrepidity in action against the enemy while serving with BTY B, 82nd Anti-Aircraft Artillery (Automatic Weapons) BTN (Self Propelled), 2nd ID, in action against the enemy in the vicinity of Changn-yong, Korea, on 1 September 1950. On this date, CPL Olson was a Squad Leader of an anti-aircraft firing vehicle attached to an infantry battalion which had been surrounded and was desperately defending its perimeter. At dark the enemy overran and captured a hill overlooking the battalion positions. From this point the enemy delivered devastating mortar and small-arms fire on the Battalion Command Post, the Battalion Aid Station, and the motor vehicles in the area. Ordered to place fire on the enemy position, CPL Olson and his squad covered the positions with such intensity and accuracy that the enemy fire was silenced and thirty enemy soldiers killed, and this without regard for the fact that in order to do so they must expose themselves to the intense enemy fire. The hill was retaken a few minutes later by the infantry . . . Home of record: Willmar, MN.

The Bronze Star with V Device is awarded to PFC HAROLD O. TAYLOR, Artillery, BTY C, 159th FAB, Army. Early in the morning of 1 September 1950 PFC Taylor's artillery BTY near Haman, Korea, was subjected to intense small arms and automatic weapons fire by a determined enemy from a position commanding the only route of withdrawal. Remaining with his crew, PFC Taylor delivered direct fire into the enemy to cover the withdrawal of the remaining sections. Despite the increased small arms fire concentrated on his position, he did not withdraw until his howitzer was march-ordered and withdrawn . . . Entered service: NE.

The Bronze Star with V Device is awarded to CPL CHARLES A. CORTEZ, Company C, 35th Regiment, 25th ID, Army. On 1 September 1950 near Uiryong, Korea, CPL Cortez's Company was attacked by a strong enemy force. When the enemy concentrated for mass assault, he subjected them to accurate machine gun fire. Although exposed to small arms and automatic weapons fire, he maintained his position, inflicted heavy casualties and drove the enemy to flight . . . Entered service: IA.

The Bronze Star with V Device for heroic achievement is awarded to CPT LEROY R. ANDERSON, Artillery, HQ and HQ BTY, 64th FAB, 25th ID, Army. CPT Anderson distinguished himself on 2-3 September 1950, when his artillery BTY was attacked by a strong infiltrating force in the vicinity of Haman, Korea. Despite an intense concentration of machine gun and mortar fire, CPT Anderson moved about the area to set up a strong defense perimeter. Although the enemy barrage increased in intensity, he conducted a spirited defense which repulsed every enemy thrust. [CPT Anderson also received a Silver Star in March 1951.] Home of record: Mason City, IA. (*Mason City Globe-Gazette*. 11 July 1951.)

The Silver Star is (posthumously) awarded to PFC LESTER BASON, Infantry, Company L, 5th RCT, Army. During the night of 2-3 September 1950, when numerically superior hostile forces launched an attack on the Company positions in the vicinity of Chinmock, Korea, PFC Bason remained in his position despite the huge volume of enemy machine gun and rifle fire concentrated in the area. He courageously held his position and directed withering fire at the attackers until he was mortally wounded. By his indomitable courage, soldierly ability and outstanding devotion to duty, PFC Bason contributed materially to the successful defense of the position . . . Entered service: MN.

The Silver Star is awarded to CPL ADLORE L. GIRARD, Army Medical Service, Medical Company, 35th IR, Army. On 3 September 1950 in the vicinity of Chuam, Korea, the Company to which CPL Girard was attached as medical aid man was attacked repeatedly by numerically superior enemy forces, and numerous casualties were sustained. Despite the heavy barrage of enemy machine gun and mortar fire, CPL Girard crawled about the position to administer first aid to the wounded personnel, and evacuating the seriously wounded casualties from the area. By his professional skill and courageous devotion to duty, he was instrumental in saving numerous lives and assisted greatly to inspire the platoon to repel the enemy attack. . . . Entered service: Des Moines.

The Bronze Star with V Device is awarded to CPL DONALD G. ROTHLAUF, Company K, 35th IR, Army. On 3 September 1950 near Chuam, Korea when his Company was attacked several times by an overwhelming number of enemy forces, CPL Rothlauf repeatedly braved the intense enemy small arms and automatic weapons fire to distribute ammunition. Moving from foxhole to foxhole under the constant enemy barrage, he redistributed the dwindling supply of ammunition. When the supply of rifle ammunition was exhausted, he removed the cartridges from machine gun belts and loaded rifle clips to supply the riflemen. Entered service: Des Moines. (CPL Rothlauf was captured 29 November 1950 and is missing in action.)

The First Bronze Oak Leaf Cluster to the Bronze Star with V Device is awarded to Master SGT HERBERT B. RAWLINGS, Company E, 35th Infantry, 25th ID, Army. On 3 September 1950, near Haman, Korea, when he was cut off from his unit by the enemy forces, Master SGT Rawlings contacted a patrol from his Company which was operating in the area and joined in an attack to break through the enemy lines. When ammunition became dangerously low, he stormed through hostile positions, secured a resupply of ammunition at his unit, and returned to the patrol through a gauntlet of enemy fire. The patrol attacked the enemy with renewed vigor, and having repulsed them rejoined the unit . . . Entered service: NE.

The Bronze Oak Leaf Cluster in lieu of a Second Award of the Silver Star is awarded to CPT (then 1LT) DOUGLAS W. SYVERSON, Army, for gallantry in action while serving as Commanding Officer, Company G, 21st IR, 24th ID, near Angang-ni, Korea, on 4 September 1950. His Company was attacked by an enemy force estimated at over 400 troops. One of his platoons had been subjected to a particularly fierce assault and was being disorganized by the fury of the fire sweeping its positions. One of three tanks supporting the platoon was disabled in this action. Utterly disregarding the enemy's intense fire, CPT Syverson moved among the men encouraging them on to greater efforts and placing them in defensive positions. Dispatching a small group of his men to the rear with instructions for setting up a defense of the town, he remained in his exposed position. He personally placed explosive charges to destroy the disabled tank and directed the evacuation of the wounded on the remaining tanks. After the disabled tank had been destroyed and he was assured of the safe removal of the wounded, CPT Syverson led the platoon through the encircling enemy to the company's position in the town. Here he quickly organized an effective defense, and in spite of overwhelming odds the enemy was repulsed withy heavy losses . . . Home of record: Webster, SD.

The Silver Star is awarded to SGT JAMES L. WINNER (then PFC), Medical Company, 8th Cavalry Regiment, 1st Cavalry Division, who displayed gallantry in action against an armed enemy near Kasan, Korea, during the period of 3 September to 5 September 1950. During a withdrawal SGT Winner, who was assisting two wounded men up a hill, left them temporarily in the custody of others to administer aid to men wounded in the withdrawal. Completing this, SGT Winner returned to evacuate his previous patients, saving the life of one who requested to be left behind. On 5 September, while serving as the only aid man left in two companies in the Walled City engagement, SGT Winner moved back and forth between the companies' areas, 300 yards of territory actually occupied by the enemy and under heavy fire. With complete disregard for his own safety and often fighting his way to various positions, SGT Winner made possible the first aid treatment and safe evacuation of many of the wounded . . . Entered service: Davenport, IA.

PFC GEORGE H. OLSON, Infantry, HQ and HQ Company, 19th IR, 24th ID, Army, is awarded the Silver Star (posthumous) for gallantry in action against the enemy near Yongsan, Korea, on 4 September 1950. The motorized patrol of which he was a member was ambushed by an enemy force and pinned down by intense mortar and automatic weapons fire. With complete disregard for his own safety he exposed himself to the withering fire and poured such a volume of accurate fire into the enemy that the remainder of the patrol was able to extricate itself from its untenable position. He continued firing until his ammunition was exhausted. When the enemy subsequently overran his position PVT Olson was killed . . . Entered service: Bigfork, MN.

The First Oak Leaf Cluster to the Silver Star is awarded to CPT RICHARD I. GREEN (then 1LT), Army, Company A, 8th Engineer Combat BTN, 1st Cavalry Division, for gallantry in action. . .on 4 September 1950 at Kanp-Yong, Korea. Company A was assigned the mission of securing the center of a ridge overlooking the main supply route leading into Taegu. When the left flank of the ridge was attacked by a numerically superior enemy force and the infantry defenders were forced to withdraw, the flank became exposed and gave the enemy direct fire into the friendly units in the valley below. The North Koreans immediately began to drop mortars on the infantry command post and on friendly mortar positions. CPT Green quickly deployed his platoon to protect the exposed flank. Courageously leading a squad of men across the open ridge, he directed a counterattack in the face of heavy automatic weapons and small arms fire. Although it was impossible to retake the lost ground, CPT Green led a counterattack time after time with different groups of men, thereby forcing the enemy to cease fire on the friendly forces below. By this insistent attacking, the infantry troops in the valley were able to withdraw with a minimum of casualties . . . Home: Steamboat Rock, IA.

The Silver Star is awarded to SGT ALBERT W. YEAKEY, Medical Company, 35th IR, 25th ID, Army, for gallantry in action on 5 and 6 September 1950 near Haman, Korea. The unit which SGT Yeakey served as aid man was subjected to repeated fanatic hostile attacks which cut off supply routes. Having set up an emergency aid station within the perimeter, he moved about the area, heedless of the intense hostile action, to render first aid and remove wounded to the aid station. By his expert care and bold courage, he saved numerous lives . . . Entered service: IA.

The Bronze Star with V Device for heroic achievement is awarded to 1LT RONALD J. NORBY, Heavy Mortar Company, 27th IR, 25th ID, Army. On 5 September 1950 when a large group of enemy had infiltrated the regimental perimeter and were attacking the rear installations in the vicinity of Chirwon, Korea, LT Norby braved the heavy barrage of hostile fire to direct the fire of his mortars on the onrushing enemy. The accurate and timely barrage laid down by his mortar platoon resulted in the annihilation of over one hundred enemy and was instrumental in repelling the concerted enemy attack . . . Entered service: Fargo, ND.

The Silver Star for gallantry in action is awarded to CPT (then 1LT) RALPH M. LONGBOTHAM, Company D, 27th Regiment, 25th ID, Army. On 6 September 1950 during an attack by an estimated 300 enemy on the BTN assembly area in the vicinity of Chirwon, Korea, CPT Longbotham ran through the heavy volume of small arms and automatic weapons fire to the 75mm recoilless rifle position and from an exposed position personally directed the fire of the guns. Later, while bringing up vitally needed ammunition, he was painfully wounded but refused medical aid, continuing, despite the severe action to direct the fire of the guns until the enemy attack was repulsed . . . Home of record: Minneapolis.

The Bronze Star with V Device is awarded to PFC DUANE C. MCCUNE, Infantry, Company D, 27th Regiment, 25th ID, Army. When his Company was attacked on 6 September 1950 by a strong enemy force near Chirwon-ni, Korea, PFC McCune dismounted a .50 caliber machine gun from a vehicle and placed it into position on the ground. Despite the intense fire and nearness of the enemy, he stayed with the weapons inflicting numerous casualties on the foe and repulsing the frontal attack. Later, he moved the gun forward fifty yards to an exposed position and with accurate fire helped drive the hostile force from the area . . . Entered service: SD.

The Bronze Star with V Device is awarded to SFC (then SGT) NORMAN R. MASON, Corps of Engineers, Company A, 65th Engineer Combat BTN, Army, for heroic achievement on 7 September 1950 near Haman, Korea. When his squad was pinned down by intense hostile machine gun fire, SFC Mason remained in his exposed position to deliver devastating fire at the enemy to cover the displacement of his squad. . . Entered service: MN.

The Bronze Star with V Device is awarded to CPL VERNON A. EGGENBURG, Army, Company G, 23rd Regiment, 2nd ID, who distinguished himself for heroic achievement on 9 September 1950 near Poncho, Korea. On this date, while his Company was under attack by a large enemy force and while he was moving his mortar squad to a better firing position, an enemy artillery burst wounded him and another member of his squad. Ignoring his wound, he administered first aid to his comrade and sent him back to the aid station. With no thought of his personal welfare, CPL Eggenburg continued his mission, first placing his mortar in a new firing positions, and then taking an exposed position from which to direct its fire. This action resulted in the destruction of two enemy machine gun emplacements. He remained in his dangerous position giving support to the Company until he was evacuated to the aid station . . . Home of record: IA City. (CPL Eggenburg was killed in action March 9, 1951.)

The Silver Star is awarded to Major JOHN C. BARRETT, JR., (then 1LT), Army, who distinguished himself by gallantry in action on 12 September 1950. As a Platoon Leader, Company K, 5th Cavalry Regiment, 1st Cavalry Division in Korea, Major Barrett's courageous conduct in battle during a critical period of highly concentrated enemy action was thoroughly manifested by his outstanding bravery, selfless devotion to troop welfare and superior leadership. Leading a platoon in an aggressive assault on an enemy-held position north of Taegu, Major Barrett's bold and skillful actions were conspicuously evidenced. Despite the fact that he was wounded, he never stopped fighting and valiantly led his men in the face of heavy mortar, small arms and automatic weapons fire from a fanatically determined and numerically superior enemy. His singular efforts were instrumental in successfully capturing the strategic hill and in holding it against the enemy until reinforcements moved up and organized the position . . . Home of record: Omaha. (Major Barrett was decorated again at Chip-yong-ni in the spring of 1951.)

The Silver Star is awarded to Technical SGT HOWARD W. SOLHEIM, USMC, for conspicuous gallantry and intrepidity while serving as a Platoon SGT in Company E, 2nd BTN, 5th Marines, 1st Marine Division (Reinforced), in action against enemy aggressor forces in Korea on 15 September 1950. Unaware that the boat with his platoon leader and one squad aboard had crashed and had not come ashore as scheduled during the initial Inchon landing, Technical SGT Solheim quickly organized the rest of the platoon and commenced to carry out the platoon's assigned mission. Directing the capture and evacuation to the rear of approximately fifty prisoners taken by his platoon, he then skillfully directed a flanking assault upon his platoon's objective which was secured with no casualties among his own men and approximately twenty of the enemy destroyed. . . . Home: Fessenden, ND.

SFC GORDON L. WALLIN, Company I, 23rd IR, 2nd ID, Army, is awarded the Silver Star for gallantry in action against an armed enemy on 16 September 1950 in the vicinity of Changnyong, Korea. On that date, he was leading his squad in an attack against strongly defended enemy positions. During the assault on a hill he was severely wounded and was hurled half way down the slope by the force of an exploding shell. Realizing the importance of retaining control of his men, he made his way forward to his squad and continued to lead them in the attack. With complete disregard for his personal safety he advanced under the intense hostile fire until he was once more wounded and was ordered to be evacuated. His intrepid leadership inspired his squad to such an extent that they closed with the enemy, overrunning and seizing the hostile positions . . . Home of record: Newfolden, MN.

SFC EDWARD J. CHMELKA, Company E, 23rd IR, 2nd ID, is awarded (posthumously) the Bronze Star with V device for heroic achievement on 19 September 1950 in the vicinity of Sanden-ri, Korea. On that date SGT Chmelka was leading his rifle squad in an attack upon enemy-held ground. During the advance the squad was subjected to such intense enemy mortar fire that it was pinned down and was unable to continue the assault. Disregarding the heavy mortar fire falling all about him, SGT Chmelka left his covered position and skillfully maneuvered his squad to safety. He then established contact with his platoon and, having done so, continued to lead his squad forward. Following his courageous leadership his men moved forward and, in a final rush, overran the enemy positions and secured their objective . . . Home of record: Saunders County, NE. (SGT Chmelka, 34, was killed in action 27 September. He is buried at the National Bohemian Cemetery at Touhy, where his gravestone indicates he received a Silver Star, possibly an upgrade.)

The Silver Star is awarded (posthumously) to CPL WALTER J. LANKEN, Army, for gallantry in action against the enemy as a member of the Medical Detachment, 70th Tank BTN (Heavy), attached to the 1st Cavalry Division, on 19 September 1950 near Singdong, Korea. CPL Lanken, a Medical Aidman, was attached to Company A, 70th Tank BTN which was supporting an infantry attack on Hill 202. When several friendly tanks in a river bed for repairs came under heavy enemy mortar and artillery fire, seven of the tank crewmen were wounded. CPL Lanken, disregarding his own safety, moved from man to man in the impact area rendering first aid to the wounded. While engaged in this selfless consideration and treatment of others, CPL Lanken lost his life when he was struck by a shell fragment. His voluntary and extreme devotion to duty on this occasion was an inspiring example and was responsible for saving the lives of many of the wounded men . . . Home of record: Webster City, IA.

1LT ELLSWORTH NELSEN, Army, a member of BTY B, 13th FAB, 24th ID, is awarded the First Bronze Oak Leaf Cluster to the Bronze Star with V Device for heroic achievement near Waegwan, Korea, on 19 September 1950. Company E, 19th IR, to which he was attached as a forward observer, assembled in a forward area preparing for an assault crossing of the Naktong River, was subjected to intense enemy artillery and mortar fire, and suffered many casualties. With utter disregard for his own safety, he unhesitatingly left his position of relative security and went to the aid of the wounded. He coolly and efficiently rendered first aid while the intense shelling continued, and subsequently assisted in their evacuation . . . Entered service: Grand Island, NE.

The Silver Star is awarded to CPT ALMOND H. SOLLOM, USMC, for conspicuous gallantry and intrepidity as Executive Officer of Weapons Company, 1st BTN, 5th Marines, 1st Marine Division (Reinforced), in action against enemy aggressor forces in

Korea on 19 September 1950. When a group of by-passed hostile troops opened fire on him while he was reconnoitering for advance mortar positions, CPT Sollom, together with the Company gunnery SGT, immediately engaged the enemy soldiers, killing four and capturing twelve and, despite hostile mortar and small arms fire, delivered the prisoners to the Company area. Later, he organized and led a patrol back to the scene of action to engage the remainder of the enemy force, thereby materially aiding his Company in successfully displacing forward and supporting the continuation of the attack . . . Birthplace: Thief River Falls, MN. Home of record: Bagley, MN.

CPL DAVID A. HAITH, Army, a member of Company A, 21st IR, 24th ID, is awarded the Bronze Star with V Device for heroic action near Waegwan, Korea, on 19 September 1950. After the successful assault crossing of the Naktong River, his platoon was pinned down on a narrow strip of beach by accurate enemy fire. In the ensuing exchange of fire, the limited supply of ammunition initially carried across the river was expended. Answering a call for volunteers, CPL Haith and three other soldiers left their positions of relative safety, exposed themselves to the withering fire, crossed the river to the ammunition supply point and then, with their vitally needed supplies, re-crossed to their platoon's exposed position . . . Entered service: Auburn, NE.

The Silver Star is awarded to LT JOHN YORDE, Army, for courageous action in Korea on 19 September 1950. The citation states, in part, LT Yorde was leading troops across the Naktong River: "With utter disregard for his own safety, Yorde moved through a hail of withering fire, rallying his men and assisting in the launching operations. Completely unmindful of the intense fire, he repeatedly exposed himself in order to better direct his platoon in their most vital operations. His continued presence on the fire-swept beach served well to inspire his men . . . Home of record: Inverness, MT. (Helena *Independent Record*, 7 Jan 1951)

The Bronze Star with V Device is awarded to PFC DALE F. SILL, JR, Medical Company, 27th IR, 25th ID, Army. On 20 September 1950, PFC Sill was serving as a member of a four-man litter team attached to a rifle Company which was attacking in the vicinity of Chingdong-ni, Korea. When the attack was temporarily halted by intense hostile mortar, small arms and automatic weapons fire, the team rolled through the concerted fire to the forward positions to evacuate the wounded. Making repeated trips to the forward areas, they evacuated all casualties, then carried them five miles over precipitous mountain trails to safety . . . Entered service: IA.

The Silver Star is awarded to 1LT DONALD F. DARNELL, Company C, 27th IR, 25th ID, Army. On 20 September 1950, during an attack on enemy positions located on a hill near Chingdong-ni, Korea, LT Darnell courageously braved the constant hostile barrage of grenades, small arms, and mortar fire to lead his Company. Although wounded in the arm by grenade fragments, he remained with the forward elements of his Company to encourage his men and control the fire of his unit until the objective was taken . . . Entered service: NE.

The Silver Star is awarded to CPT ROBERT A. MAHOWALD, HQ and HQ Company, 1st BTN, 35th IR, 25th ID, Army. On 20 September 1950, a heavy barrage of artillery delayed one Company in a BTN attack toward Chungam-ni, Korea. To prevent further delay and possible disastrous losses, CPT Mahowald moved forward 1,000 yards through the intense hostile fire, contacted the Company commander and assisted in an alternate attack. As enemy resistance increased, a mine sweeping detail was pinned down, thereby delaying movement of supporting tanks. Again CPT Mahowald braved severe enemy action to reach the lead tank, reorganized the mine sweeping detail which, inspired by his example of determination and courage, moved out so that the attack could be pursued to successful conclusion . . . Entered service: MN.

The Gold Star in lieu of a Second Award of the Distinguished Flying Cross is awarded to 1LT THOMAS R. BRAUN, USMC, for heroism while participating in aerial flights over enemy territory from 5 August to 20 September 1950. 1LT Braun successfully completed his first through thirty-fifth combat missions against the enemy over Korea where enemy fire was either received or expected. His actions throughout were in keeping with the highest traditions of the United States Naval Service. Birthplace: Glen Ulin, ND. Home of record: Fromberg, MT.

PFC JACK HOWARD SHRAMEK, USMC, is awarded the Silver Star (posthumously) for conspicuous gallantry and intrepidity as an Automatic Rifleman in Company G, 3rd BTN, 1st Marines, 1st Marine Division (Reinforced), in action against enemy aggressor forces in Korea on 21 September 1950. While his platoon was attacking a strong enemy position, PFC Shramek moved forward in the face of intense hostile fire in order to gain a more favorable firing position. Boldly subjecting himself to the barrage of enemy fire, he accurately directed his fire against hostile positions, destroying several automatic weapons and annihilating many enemy troops before he received a fatal wound. By his courageous actions, he materially aided his platoon in successfully completing its assigned mission . . . Home of record: Omaha.

The Silver Star is awarded to CPL THEODORE R. WILDER, HQ and HQ Company, 27th IR, 25th ID, Army. On 21 September 1950, CPL Wilder accompanied the Intelligence and Reconnaissance platoon on a mission near Chindong-ni Korea. As the platoon advanced up a hill the enemy opened fire from well concealed positions. Although carrying a radio set and wounded in one foot at the start of the action, CPL Wilder refused to withdraw, but continued to operate his radio to keep contact with supporting weapons. Only after he had been painfully wounded in the other foot and when the entire platoon displaced, did he return to his vehicle with his equipment . . . Entered service: IA.

The Bronze Star with Combat "V" is awarded to 1LT RICHARD CARLSON, HQ, Second BTN, 32nd IR, 7th ID, Army, for gallantry in action against an armed enemy on 21 September 1950, near Kuroil-li, Korea. On this date, Company G had suffered heavy casualties and had the route of communication to the rear cut by the enemy. Without regard for his personal safety, LT Carlson voluntarily guided litter jeeps to and from the Company, laterally across the front lines. Despite constant enemy observation and frequent automatic weapons and mortar fire, LT Carlson assisted in loading and evacuated the wounded men. This action was instrumental in saving the lives of four men . . . Home of record: MN.

MSGT LESTER W. OLSEN, Company F, 32nd IR, 7th ID Army, is awarded the Bronze Star with V Device for heroic action near Tok-San-ni, Korea, on 22 September 1950. On this date, MSGT Olsen was a member of a patrol of sixty men who were clearing a small village near Tok-San-ni, when it was fired upon by a strongly entrenched enemy force of approximately one hundred fifty men. Heavy enemy automatic weapons and rifle fire scattered the patrol and pinned it down in rice paddies and ditches over an area of approximately two hundred by five hundred yards. MSGT Olsen, with complete disregard for his own personal safety, and while exposed to heavy enemy fire, moved from one group to another and directed fire on the enemy positions. His actions were responsible for the patrol's effective return of fire and contributed immeasurably to the success of the mission. Several times MSGT Olsen purposely exposed himself to draw fire from the enemy in order that his men could locate the enemy position . . . Entered service: MN.

PFC ROBERT C. JENKINS, USMC, is awarded the Silver Star for conspicuous gallantry and intrepidity while serving as a Rifleman in Company I, 3rd BTN, 5th Marines, 1st Marine Division (Reinforced), in action against enemy aggressor forces in Korea on 23 September 1950. Forced to seek cover when his patrol was subjected to intense hostile fire while moving through an enemy-held village, PFC Jenkins immediately left his protected position when he observed three wounded Marines in an open area. Despite the heavy enemy fire, he made three separate trips across a fire-swept area to move the casualties to a position affording cover. By his heroic actions, he materially aided the wounded in receiving prompt medical treatment and a hasty evacuation. . . Birthplace: York, NE. Home of record: Stromsburg, NE.

The Silver Star is awarded to CPL ROBERT D. DEEDS, USMC, for conspicuous gallantry and intrepidity in action while serving as a Fire Team Leader in Company G, 3rd BTN, 5th Marines, 1st Marine Division (Reinforced), during operations against enemy aggressor forces in Seoul, Korea, on 23 September 1950. When the right flank position was pinned down by intense enemy small-arms and machine-gun fire while his Company was advancing in the attack on Seoul, CPL Deeds voluntarily moved forward alone and, with his rifle fire and hand grenades, personally destroyed two hostile emplacements, thus enabling his fire team to advance and destroy the remaining enemy right flank positions with well-directed fire and grenades. By his exceptional courage, initiative and fighting spirit, CPL Deeds was instrumental in regaining his platoon's fire superiority to continue the attack . . . Home of record: Isle, NE.

PFC THOMAS M. BURKE, USMC, is awarded the Silver Star for conspicuous gallantry and intrepidity in action while serving as a Squad Leader of Company E, 2nd BTN, 5th Marines, 1st Marine Division (Reinforced), during operations against enemy aggressor forces near Seoul, Korea, on 24 September 1950. Observing an enemy machine gun nest on the right flank of his platoon during the assault on a heavily fortified position, PFC Burke fearlessly exposed himself to intense hostile fire to attack the position single-handedly, killing two of the enemy, wounding another and destroying the machine gun. By his courageous initiative and fighting spirit, PFC Burke aided materially in furthering the advance of his platoon . . . Birthplace: Helena, MT. Home of record: Great Falls, MT.

PFC BERNARD E. GALVIN, Company L, 5th RCT, 24th ID, Army, is awarded the Bronze Star with V Device for heroic achievement near Kumchon, Korea, on 24 September 1950. During an attack his Company was pinned down by concentrated enemy tank and machine gun fire resulting in numerous casualties. Realizing that only one aid man was available to tend the many wounded, PVT Galvin left his position of relative safety and although continuously exposed to the heavy enemy fire, assisted in rendering life saving medical aid. Through his courage and unhesitant devotion to duty the many who died were materially comforted . . . Entered service: Askov, MN.

1LT KEITH W. WHITHAM, Army, a member of Tank Company, 5th RCT, 24th ID, is awarded the Bronze Star with V Device for heroic achievement near Kumchon, Korea, on 24 September 1950. During an attack in which his tank platoon was supporting the infantry, the enemy retaliated with intensive small arms, mortar and artillery fire. With complete disregard for his own safety, he dismounted from his tank and personally deployed his tanks to positions from which closer support could be furnished the attacking troops. Although exposed to withering fire he subsequently manned the .50 caliber machine gun atop his tank and inflicted many casualties among the enemy force . . . Entered service: Spring Creek, NE.

1LT KEITH W. WHITHAM, Army, a member of Tank Company, 5th RCT, 24th ID, is awarded the 1st Oak Leaf Cluster in lieu of a Second Silver Star for courageous action near Kumchon, Korea on 22 (believed to be a typo - more likely 24) September 1950. He was in command of the leading element during the BTN's advance. Completely disregarding his own safety he led his men again and again in their successful assault against strong enemy defenses. Constantly exposed to heavy enemy fire, he continued to press the attack. So swift was his advance that his small force liberated 45 allied prisoners of war whose captors were routed before the onslaught of his attack. In the course of this gallant action many casualties were inflicted among the enemy and over 100 of his troops captured . . . Entered service: Spring Creek, NE.

The Bronze Star with V Device for heroic achievement is awarded to 1LT GEORGE H. SCHAPPAUGH, Army, a member of Company A, 72nd Tank BTN, 2nd ID, distinguished himself by heroic achievement on 24 September 1950 at Mullim-ni, Korea. On that date the enemy had halted the advance of a rifle Company by heavy machine gun and small arms fire. After the attack was delayed for four hours, LT Schappaugh came forward and organized a platoon of tanks to counterattack. Approaching the tanks by crossing a rice paddy under intense enemy fire he succeeded in getting the attack underway. Because of radio failure, orders had to be relayed verbally. Ignoring the enemy fire, he moved along the tank column urging the crews forward until the attack succeeded in reaching its objective, the Hwang River. By his complete disregard for personal safety and exposing himself repeatedly to enemy fire, LT Schappaugh enabled our troops to accomplish their mission . . . Entered service: NE.

CPL JAKE NEIL VOERMANS, USMC, is awarded the Silver Star (posthumously) for conspicuous gallantry and intrepidity while serving as a Fire Team Leader in Company D, 2nd BTN, 5th Marines, 1st Marine Division (Reinforced), in action against enemy aggressor forces in Korea on 24 September 1950. Observing a member of his fire team wounded and lying in an open fire-swept area, CPL Voermans unhesitatingly left the protection of his own position and ran to the aid of the wounded Marine. While attempting to bring the casualty to a position of cover, CPL Voermans was himself fatally wounded . . . Birthplace: Whitefish, MT. Home of record: Helena, MT.

PFC GENE HENRY LEASE, USMC (Reserve), is awarded the Silver Star (posthumously) for conspicuous gallantry and intrepidity while serving as a Rifleman of Company D, 2nd BTN, 7th Marines, 1st Marine Division (Reinforced), in action against enemy aggressor forces in Korea on 26 September 1950. When his platoon commander was wounded by intense hostile fire as the unit proceeded through Seoul, PFC Lease unhesitatingly ran forward to the officer's completely exposed position and, lifting him up, carried him toward the shelter of a nearby building. By his prompt and heroic action, he was responsible for saving the life of the wounded man although he himself fell, mortally wounded, after covering all but the last few steps to safety . . . Home of record: Fairfield, MT.

The Bronze Star with V Device is awarded to SFC WILLIAM H. FISHER, BTY B, 15th AAAW BTN, Army, who distinguished himself by heroic action against an armed enemy near Suwon, Korea, on 26 September 1950. On this date, SGT Fisher, while in command of an automatic weapons section acting in support of the 31st IR, 7th ID, discovered a camouflaged enemy tank. Realizing that a friendly tank located near him had not seen the enemy tank, SGT Fisher voluntarily and without regard for his personal safety, left his position of safety and exposed himself to heavy enemy fire as he made his way on foot to warn the crew of the friendly tank of the danger. He continued to expose himself to enemy fire while he directed friendly fire on the enemy tank until it was destroyed. This courageous action on the part of SGT Fisher resulted in the destruction of the enemy tank and contributed immeasurably to the success of the mission of his unit . . . Entered service: IA.

Major RICHARD D. GILLIS, HQ, 2nd BTN, 32nd IR, 7th ID Army, is awarded the Silver Star for gallantry in action against an armed enemy on 26 September 1950. On the above date at 0530 hours Company F, 32nd IR, 7th ID, was located on South Mountain near Seoul, Korea, when an estimated 500 enemy infantrymen supported by artillery and mortars attacked, forcing F Company's right flank to withdraw to the topographical crest of the hill. At 0630 hours Company F reported that the situation was critical; the enemy still had the initiative, and the company's ammunition was almost exhausted. Under intense enemy automatic weapons and mortar fire, Major Gillis, the BTN Executive Officer, quickly organized a carrying party and moved over exposed terrain to the BTN ammunition dump. He then led the party to within 50 yards of the enemy's attacking elements and, while continually under fire, supervised the distribution of the ammunition. Major Gillis led the carrying party back to a secured position and then returned to Company F to assist in the reorganization of the Company. With complete disregard for his own safety, Major Gillis moved about the Company pointing out targets and directing fire on the enemy. The action of Major Gillis inspired the men and greatly expedited the successful attack the Company F . . . Home of record: Shellsburg, IA.

The Bronze Star with Combat "V" is awarded to CPT JOHN H. BURKE, Company H, 32nd IR, 7th ID Army, for heroic achievement in connection with military operations against an armed enemy on 26 September 1950 near Seoul, Korea. CPT Burke, acting as observer in a forward point on Hill 262 for the mortar platoon of his Company, directed approximately five hundred rounds of mortar fire upon an enemy force advancing toward our front lines. CPT Burke, constantly exposing himself to heavy small arms fire, voluntarily remained at his position and directed mortar fire to within twenty-five yards of his observation point. His courageous act materially aided in forcing the enemy to withdraw . . . Home of record: MT.

SGT RICHARD L. VAN NICE, USMC, is awarded the Silver Star for conspicuous gallantry and intrepidity while serving as a Section Leader of Company H, 1st BTN, 5th Marines, 1st Marine Division (Reinforced), in action against enemy aggressor forces in Korea on 27 September 1950. When his platoon became pinned down by intense hostile machine gun and small arms fire while advancing toward its objective, SGT Van Nice skillfully maneuvered his machine gun section into position where his men could bring fire to bear upon the enemy despite a lack of covered positions. To adjust the fire of his section more effectively upon well-entrenched and camouflaged enemy positions, he repeatedly exposed himself to intense hostile fire. Although wounded in the wrist while observing his section's fire, he steadfastly continued to direct the fire attack against enemy positions until he was wounded a second time in the chin and shoulder and allowed himself to be evacuated. By his courageous actions, he contributed materially to the subsequent capture of the hostile positions . . . Birthplace: Des Moines, IA. Home of record: Mankato, MN.

CPL GEORGE O. JETTE, Company F, 32nd IR, 7th ID Army, is awarded the Bronze Star with V Device for heroic action near Seoul, Korea, on 28 September 1950. On this date, Company F was assigned the mission of holding Hill 262, when their position was attacked by numerically superior enemy forces. Pinned down by intense automatic weapons fire, and with the right flank of his squad overrun by the attackers, CPL Jette displayed daring leadership and courage by exposing himself to enemy grenades and rifle fire in order to keep his squad in position and prevent a wider penetration of the Company perimeter. . . . Entered service: Polson, MT. (Salish tribe, Flathead Nation)

SGT DONALD CLARENCE LINDQUIST, Army, is awarded the Silver Star (posthumously) for conspicuous gallantry and intrepidity in action against the enemy while serving with BTY D, 82nd Anti-Aircraft Artillery (Automatic Weapons) BTN (Self Propelled), 2nd ID, in action against the enemy on 28 September 1950 in Korea. On that date, SGT Lindquist voluntarily joined a section of his BTY, composed of two anti-aircraft firing vehicles, which was supporting a rifle Company in a patrol along a mountain road. While moving forward on vehicles the entire column was ambushed by the enemy who was located on high ground along the road. From this position the enemy was able to drop grenades into the vehicles and spray the personnel with automatic weapons and small arms fire, at point-blank range. The riflemen on the vehicles had deployed to the sides of the road upon initial contact with the enemy. SGT Lindquist immediately realized that the entire patrol would be annihilated unless reinforcements could be contacted. He remained exposed in the vehicle, manning his radio, and attempted to contact friendly forces. Finally the anti-aircraft gunners had to abandon the vehicles when their guns were neutralized by the severe enemy fire. Still, SGT Lindquist refused to abandon his post and, displaying complete indifference for his personal safety, remained at his radio until he successfully contacted a nearby rifle

Company who by proper maneuver forced the enemy to withdraw. When the enemy had been driven off SGT Lindquist's body was found near the vehicle. His unselfish sacrifice saved the entire patrol from annihilation and allowed several severely wounded men to be evacuated . . . Home of record: Dalton, MN.

CPL GORDON W. JENSEN, Company F, 17th IR, 7th ID, Army, is awarded (posthumously) the Bronze Star with V Device for heroic action near Kumgong-ni, Korea, on 29 September 1950. On this date, CPL Jensen's platoon was engaged in attacking a high hill to the left of the BTN front across an area consisting of approximately four hundred yards of rice paddy, when it was pinned down by enemy fire. Without regard for his personal safety, CPL Jensen, accompanied by five other members of the platoon, went forward in the face of intense automatic weapons fire and occupied the platoon objective on top of the hill, forcing the enemy to withdraw with many casualties. During this action, CPL Jensen was mortally wounded . . . Entered service: MN.

The Bronze Star with V Device is awarded to SFC JOHN ROSENWALD, Armor, Company A, 89th Medium Tank BTN, Army. During the period 3 August to 1 October 1950 in the initial phase of the Korean conflict SFC Rosenwald rendered outstanding service as a member of a tank maintenance section. Repairing tanks and vehicles under intense artillery, mortar, and small arms fire in the front line unit areas, SFC Rosenwald was instrumental in maintaining a maximum number of vehicles available for operations during this critical period . . . Entered service: MN.

The Bronze Star for Merit is awarded to CPL ELDON R. WAETCHER, Heavy Mortar Company, 27th IR, 25th ID, Army. As Ammunition CPL of the heavy mortar Company from 11 July to 6 October 1950 in Korea, CPL Waetcher rendered outstanding services. Leading his ammunition vehicles through intense enemy mortar and small arms fire, he was instrumental in alleviating many critical situations by his timely delivery of ammunition to the platoons actively engaged in combat. It was often necessary to run the gauntlet of enemy road blocks and snipers in order to procure ammunition from supply installations in the rear . . . Entered service: IA.

The Bronze Star Medal is awarded to CPL JOHN L. FISH, 25th Counter-Intelligence Corps Detachment, Army. During the period 10 July to 10 October 1950, CPL Fish was responsible for the automotive maintenance of all vehicles of the 25th Counter-Intelligence Corps Detachment. The task was rendered particularly difficult due to the rugged terrain over which the vehicles traveled, necessitating constant maintenance. He was further handicapped by a shortage of replacement parts. He exhibited unusual ingenuity and resourcefulness in maintaining all vehicles in operating condition, frequently working long hours to accomplish his mission. When members of the unit were on field trips, CPL Fish assisted with the administrative work on numerous occasions, displaying notable versatility. CPL Fish's technical ability, determination and devotion to duty are in keeping with the highest traditions of the U.S. Army and reflect the highest credit on himself and the Counter Intelligence Corps. Entered service: SD.

PFC ROBERT R. GOMEZ, a Rifleman in an Infantry Company of the 1st BTN, 7th Marines, 1st Marine Division (Reinforced), USMC, is awarded the Silver Star for conspicuous gallantry and intrepidity in action against enemy aggressor forces in Korea on 2 October 1950. Painfully wounded during a vicious hostile counterattack near the crest of a hill, PFC Gomez steadfastly refused evacuation, courageously remaining to drag other wounded men to positions of cover and to encourage the platoon to continue in its assault. Although wounded a second time, he still refused to leave, remaining until the platoon had taken its objective and the enemy had been driven back . . . Home of record: Omaha.

The Distinguished Flying Cross is awarded to LT [then LT, Junior Grade] NORWALD R. QUIEL, U.S. Navy, for heroism and extraordinary achievement while participating in aerial flight as Pilot of a Fighter Aircraft and as Division Leader in Fighter Squadron ONE HUNDRED THIRTEEN (VF-113), attached to the *U.S.S. PHILIPPINE SEA* (CV-47), during operations against enemy aggressor forces in Korea from 5 August to 19 October 1950. Completing thirty-five missions during this period, LT Quiel led his division in close air support flights and bombing attacks against enemy airfield installations, lines of communication, transport facilities, bridges, gun positions, shipping and large troop concentrations. By his courage, skilled airmanship and devotion to duty in the face of hostile anti-aircraft fire, LT Quiel materially aided in inflicting extensive damage upon the enemy. . . Born: Grand Marais, MN.

CPL DONALD D. CALDWELL, 8th Cavalry Regiment, 1st Cavalry Division, Army, is awarded the Silver Star (posthumously) for gallantry in action against the enemy on 9 October 1950, near Kaesong, Korea. The Company with which CPL Caldwell was serving was assigned a mission of forcing a crossing of the 38th parallel. A hail of automatic weapons and small arms fire pinned down the attacking unit. CPL Caldwell quickly evaluating the situation, inched his way forward under blazing small arms fire to search for an advantageous firing position for his automatic riflemen. Their fire was critically need at the time. Heedless of the heavy fire striking the ground around him, CPL Caldwell located a desirable firing position and signaled his automatic riflemen. At the same time he was shot and killed instantly. As a result of his intrepid devotion to duty and supreme sacrifice, effective automatic fire was delivered from the position and forced the enemy to withdraw. CPL Caldwell's extreme gallantry denoted the highest credit to himself and the military service. Entered service: Independence, IA. (Non-official wording. *Waterloo Daily Courier*. 24 June 1951)

The Bronze Star with V Device is awarded to PFC BILL G. CORNELL, HQ and HQ Company, 3rd BTN, 35th Regiment, 25th ID, Army. On 24 October 1950 a road repair detail from the Pioneer and Ammunition Platoon, while enroute to repair a break in a road vital to combat operations in the vicinity of Chung Bolgok, Korea, was ambushed by a large hostile group armed with automatic weapons and hand grenades. PFC Cornell quickly dismounted from the truck and despite the intense fire, took up an exposed position from which he directed devastating fire on the enemy until the other members of the detail deployed to covered positions and joined in the fight. PFC Cornell's courageous and aggressive action was responsible for a minimum of casualties among the repair detail . . . Joined service: IA.

The Bronze Star with V Device is awarded to PFC RONALD V. HANSON, HQ and HQ Company, 3rd BTN, 35th Regiment, 25th ID, Army. On 24 October 1950 near Chung Bolgok, Korea, PFC Hanson's convoy was attacked by a strong enemy force.

Dismounting from his vehicle, he immediately delivered effective counter-fire. Despite an intense concentration of small arms fire and hand grenades, he remained in position, covered the displacement of his comrades and withdrew only after their evacuation had been completed . . . Joined service: MN.

The Second Bronze Oak Leaf Cluster in lieu of a third award of the Silver Star is awarded to CPT (Infantry) DOUGLAS W. SYVERSON, Army, for gallantry in action while serving as Commanding Officer, Company G, 21st IR, 24th ID, in action near Kwaksen, Korea, on 31 October 1950. When his Company was spearheading the regiment's drive toward the Yalu River, its advance was temporarily halted when it encountered severe fire from seven enemy tanks and an estimated BTN of enemy troops. When the enemy opened fire on his company's lead platoon, CPT Syverson, displaying outstanding leadership ability, courage and devotion to duty, moved forward into the severe enemy mortar, automatic weapons and small arms fire to his lead platoon's position where, with utter disregard for personal safety, he personally directed establishment of a base of fire by the platoon. Then, although under intense enemy fire, he moved to the rear and in the extreme darkness, contacted his support platoon. CPT Syverson, again displaying utter disregard for personal safety led his support platoon back into the face of the enemy fire to a position from where it placed heavy fire on the enemy position and neutralized the enemy fire . . . Home of record: Webster, SD.

Selected Bibliography

Appleman, Roy E. *South to the Naktong, North to the Yalu (June-November 1950).* Washington DC: Center of Military History, U.S. Army, 1961, reprinted 1992.

Balchen, Bernt (Colonel), Major Corey Ford & Major Oliver LaFarge. *War Below Zero: The Battle for Greenland.* Boston: Houghton Mifflin, 1944.

Belgarde, John with Merry Helm. *An American Fighting Man.* Fargo, ND: Caesar's Coin Publishing. 2010.

Biderman, Albert D. *March to Calumny: The Truth About American POWs in Korea.* NY: The Macmillan Co., 1963.

Blair, Clay. *The Forgotten War.* NY: Doubleday, 1989.

Cagle, Malcolm, Frank A. Manson et el. *The Sea Services in the Korean War: 1950-1953.* Naval Institute Press, 2000.

Chinnery, Philip D. *Korean Atrocity: Forgotten War Crimes 1950-1953.* Naval Institute Press. 2000.

Cohen, Eliot a & John Gooch. *Military Misfortunes: the Anatomy of Failure in War.* Simon and Schuster, 2005.

Collins, J. Lawton (General U.S. Army Ret.). *War in Peacetime: The History and Lessons of Korea.* Boston: Houghton Mifflin Company, 1969.

David, Allan A., ed. *Battleground Korea, The Story of the 25th Infantry Division.* Tokyo: Kyoya Co., 1951.

Deanne, Philip. *I was a Captive in Korea.* NY: WW Norton & Co, 1953.

Duncan, David Douglas. *This is War! A photo-narrative in three parts.* NY: Harper & Brothers, 1951.

Ent, Uzal W. *Fighting on the Brink: Defense of the Pusan Perimeter.* Paducah, KY: Turner Publishing, 1996.

Fehrenbach, T.R. *This Kind of War.* NY: Macmillan Company, 1961.

Galdorisi, George & Thomas Phillips. *Leave No Man Behind: The Saga of Combat Search and Rescue.* Google eBook, 2009.

Gamble, Harold L. *Korea, I was There.* Chapel Hill: Professional Press, 2001.

Goncharov, Sergie, John W. Lewis and Xue Litai. *Uncertain Partners: Stalin, Mao and the Korea War.* Stanford University Press, 1993.

Goulden, Joseph C. *Korea: The Untold Story of the War.* NY: Times Books, 1982.

Hockley, Ralph M. *Freedom is not Free.* Houston: Brockton Publishing, 2000.

Knox, Donald and Alfred Coppel. *The Korean War: Uncertain Victory.* NY: Harcourt Brace Jovanovich, 1988.

Maihafer, Harry J. *From the Hudson to the Yalu: West Point '49 in the Korean War.* Texas A&M Press, 1993.

Murphy, Edward F. *Korean War Heroes.* Presidio, 1992.

Polk, David. *Korean War Ex-Prisoners of War.* (Korean War Ex-POW Association.) Paducah KY: Turner Publishing Co, 1993.

Province, Charles. *General Walton H. Walker: Forgotten Hero of the Forgotten War.* Create Space, 2008.

Richardson, William Col (Ret). *Valleys of Death, A Memoir of the Korean War.* NY: Berkley Caliber, 2010.

Schnabel, James. *The United States Army in Korea: Policy and Direction.* Washington DC: Center of Military History, 1992.

Sloan, Bill. *The Darkest Summer: Pusan and Inchon 1950.* NY: Simon & Schuster, 2009.

Smith, Charles R. (Editor). *U.S. Marines in the Korean War.* Washington, DC: History Division USMC, 2007.

Sorley, Lewis. *Honorable Warrior: General Harold K. Johnson and the Ethics of Command.* University of Kansas, 1998.

Strait, Sandy. *What happened to American prisoners of war in Korea.* NY: Royal Fireworks Press, 1997.

Thornton, John W. *Believed to be Alive.* Annapolis Institute Press: Bluejacket Books, 1981.

Toland, John. *In Mortal Combat: Korea, 1950-1953.* NY: William Morrow, 1991.

Tomedi, Rudy. *No Bugles, No Drums: an Oral History of the Korean War.* NY: John Wiley & Sons, 1993.

Valley, David J. *Gaijin Shogun.* San Diego: The Sektor Company. 2000.

Valley, David. *Bright Life, Framing Japan's Constitution.* Sektor Publishing. 2009.

Voorhees, Melvin B. *Korean Tales.* NY: Simon and Schuster, 1953.

Other publications (partial listing):

Stewart, Richard W. *Korea, The Chinese Intervention: 3 November 1950-24 January 1951.* Center for Military History, publication 19-8. (No date)

Robertson, Dr. William G. *Counterattacks on the Naktong, 1950.* Combat Studies Institute, U.S. Army Command and General Staff College. Ft. Leavenworth, KS. December 1985.

Perret, Geoffrey. "Warrior Mao." *MHQ: Quarterly Journal of Military History* (Spring 2007): 6–15.

1950: The Year in Review. Time Capsule: Time Magazine. Time Inc: 1950 and 1999.

Sambito, William J., Major, USMC. *A History of Marine Fighter Attack Squadron 312,* Washington, DC: History and Museums Division Headquarters, U.S. Marine Corps. 1978.

Argosy: The Complete Man's Magazine. November 1950.

Index

group 259; fatality rates 446; held by North Korea 256; Mr. Kim 260; North Korean handling of 201; Seoul to Pyongyang death march 327; the capture experience 175; used for propaganda 260)

Puller, Chesty 345

Pusan 12, 17, 25, 26, 60, 139, 158-161, 177, 185, 199, 201, 207, 234, 241, 246, 268-269, 299, 318, 333, 374, 386

Pusan Perimeter (see also Naktong Perimeter) 146, 219, 305, 318

Pyongtaek 46, 53, 72

Pyongyang 14, 70, 409, 412-413, 424, 426, 432-434, 444-447

Quantico (Virginia) 251

Queen, Ralph H. 456

Quezon, Manuel 295

Quiel, Norwald R. 471

Quillen, Marion A. 5, 277, 280, 283

Quinn, Joe 412

Raibl, Tony J. 165, 166

Rainville, Leon 65

Rakkasans (see also 187th Airborne) 408-409

Red Cross 88

Reid, 2LT Kenneth 399

Reid, Kenneth R. 184

Reid, Max 437

Reifers, Raymond N. 400

Reinholte (Norwegian freighter) 12

Repko, Louis 122-125

Reserve Officer Training Corp (ROTC) 62, 77, 140, 142, 275, 339, 376

Rhee, Syngman 3, 4

Rhineland Campaign 150

Richardson, William "Bill" 297-299, 301-303, 305 (*Valleys of Death* 301)

Ridgway, Matthew 156

Rindels, Myrna 444

Rindels, Raymond 430, 432, 434-435, 437, 439, 443-444

Robbins, Gerald 302

Roberts, Gordon 297

Rocky Mount College 376

Roelofs, Thomas 225

Roise, Harold 345

Rookstool, Melvin 439

Roosevelt, Franklin 2

Rosecrans, Charles Jr. 321

Ross, John M. 314

Ross, Leo C. 440

Ross, Robert P 440

ROTC (Reserve Officer Training Corps) 62, 77, 140, 142, 275, 339, 376

Roy, Robert 22

Ruffatto, Barney 433, 434, 436

Russian/Soviet personnel in Korea 3, 426

Russian/Soviet T-34 tanks 3

Sachon 228, 397

Saga 458

Saipan 278

Saint Olaf College (Northfield, MN) 371

Samgyo-ri 85

Samnangjin 268

Sanden-ri 463

Sanders, Ensign R.R. 364

Sangju 134, 241

Sangyong-ni 146

Sansi-ri 456

Sawyer, Robert K. 401

Sayre, Darrell 12

Schappaugh, George H. 468

Schlinghoff, Leonard 98

Schofield Barracks, Oahu 22

Schryver Jr., Hugh "Nick" 228-229, 245, 250-251, 254-255

Schultz, Melvin F. 153

Schwarzkopf, Jr., Norman 410

---

[209]The following abbreviations are used: Field Artillery Battalion (FAB); Regimental Combat Team (RCT); Antiaircraft Artillery Automatic Weapons (AAAW); Battalion (Btn).

About the Author

Merry Helm is an award-winning writer and documentary film-maker with extensive background in creating history-based radio stories for Prairie Public Radio and also worked as a screenwriter in the movie industry from 1994 to 2008. She serves as the historian for the 24th Infantry Division Association, which bestowed on her an honorary lifetime membership in 2009. She lives with her husband Roger Gress in Fargo, North Dakota.

She continues to work on the Prairie Boy Books, with the next volumes covering the Chinese intervention, the Chinese Spring Offensives of 1951, the Allied offensives in the fall of 1951, and the emergence of jet warfare over MiG Alley. She will also cover the deadly outpost/trench wars of 1952-1953, which have never before been fully presented.